HISTORY OF
BALLET
AND
MODERN DANCE

JUDITH STEEH

HISTORY OF
BALLET
AND
MODERN DANCE

JUDITH STEEH

MAGNA BOOKS

A Bison Book

Published by Magna Books
Magna Road
Wigston
Leicester, LE8 2XH

Produced by Bison Books Ltd.
176 Old Brompton Road
London, SW 5
England

ISBN 094 850955 4

Printed in Hong Kong

Reprinted 1987

*Page 1: The Royal Ballet production of George
Balanchine's* Serenade. *One of his most successful
works it has found a home with many companies.*

Page 2–3: The greatest of all classic ballets, Swan
Lake. *This is Act II of the Festival Ballet production
with Irina Borowska and Oleg Briansky.*

*Page 4–5: A spectacular 'Tree of Hands' effect from
members of the French, Ballet Theater Contemporain
in their ballet* Hopop.

CONTENTS

INTRODU

UCTION

Human beings, like other animals, instinctively express themselves through movement; we draw near those we love, pull back from those we fear or dislike, and so on. But man is the only animal that dances – that consciously devises series of connected, nonutilitarian movements so that they are pleasant or meaningful to watch.

Dance can tell a story, depict an emotion, or just present a shifting pattern of precise, expressive movement. What it does and how it does it depend on the choreographer – the person who selects the various movements and combines them in the series. Though dance forms vary tremendously throughout the world, a surprisingly large number of gestures (like those for stop, come, go, peace) are common to virtually all people.

Dance is one of the oldest arts, which developed in prehistoric times as a natural expression of feeling and action. Primitive man imitated animals and various natural phenomena, hoping in this way to appease the powerful, mysterious forces of nature; most dances were rituals concerning fertility (of the land or its people), war or exorcism.

As time went on every great civilization developed its own dances. The Bible mentions dance many times. The ancient Greeks saw dance as the expression of mind and body in perfect harmony, and dancing was an essential part of weddings, funerals, religious festivals and even military exercises. In this way, dance also became important as a means of establishing a certain measure of unity within the community.

For the most part, dance has lost its magical or religious connotations and has become a recreational activity. It also functions as an aid to courtship and as a means of physical conditioning. Captain Cook, for example, ordered his sailors and marines to dance the hornpipe whenever possible on long voyages, as a way to fight disease and keep the men healthy. Carlo Blasis, one of ballet's greatest theoreticians, tells us that 'dancing is very useful to women, whose delicate constitutions require them to be strengthened by frequent exercise'; certainly the history of both ballet and modern dance is studded with the names of dancers who were active even in their seventies.

Today dance can be divided into two

Previous page: Cell, a modern work by choreographer Robert Cohan for the London Contemporary Dance Theatre, with William Louther.

basic kinds: that which is designed as a social activity, mainly for the benefit of the dancers themselves, and that devised as a form of entertainment. Both the forms current in the West today (folk or ballroom dancing and theatrical dancing) have their origins in the lively peasant dances and stately court dances of the Renaissance. Though this book traces the history of ballet and modern dance from the fifteenth and sixteenth centuries, it still covers only a small portion of the long history of dance in general, and discusses just two of the many different kinds of dance popular in our time.

Classical ballet is a formal technique that smoothly combines strict rules for body placement into harmonious, controlled movement; the *danse d'école* – the motions, postures and steps that make up the dancer's vocabulary – stems from more than 400 years of work by dancers, choreographers and teachers. Like the actor's vocabulary of words, the dancer's language is always changing and developing. But it remains, always, a part of its long history.

Modern dance, on the other hand, is a much newer art form which, in the absence of ballet's tradition, looks within the individual; its movements and techniques are determined only by the needs of the dancer or choreographer. Personal style, then, takes precedence over an established form; though it only has been in existence for less than a century, modern dance has already changed radically – and will continue to do so.

This is not to imply, however, that ballet is static or cold. It has been estimated that the total number of ballet positions, in their various combinations, is 39,850, and when movement is added the number of possibilities passes $1\frac{1}{2}$ billion. Advances in costuming and theatrical technology have changed the look of ballet, as has improved physical conditioning; 150 years ago the great Marie Taglioni extended her leg at a 90-degree angle to her body in her arabesques, but today even most intermediate students can raise their legs above their waists. Just as the modern dancer must impose some form upon the expression of emotion in order to avoid chaos, so the classic dancer who is also an artist will inject feeling into ballet's form, to lift it above the level of a gymnastic exercise. Both kinds of dance produce visual dramas from combinations of various elements (dance, music, the plastic arts), through a collaboration between many different

people (dancer, choreographer, designer, composer). Both must have balance, style, rhythm and symbolic meaning if they are to fulfill their ultimate function.

The word 'ballet' itself comes from the Italian (*ballare*, to dance; *ballo*, a dance; *balleto*, a little dance), while most of its terminology is French. This reflects its historical development; ballet began in the courts of the great Italian princes, but much of its early development took place in France.

During the fourteenth and fifteenth centuries there were three very popular forms of entertainment at court functions. Interludes were short entertainments provided by singers and dancers between the courses of the banquet. Masquerades were parades of gaily decorated carts filled with actors; each would stop in front of the guest of honor, while members of the company delivered a poem or recitation. Mummers were masked dancers who would burst into the assembly and perform for the crowd.

During the great flowering of the Renaissance in Italy in the fifteenth and sixteenth centuries, these forms were gradually merged into lavish spectacles that combined singing, dancing and recitations. Princes vied with each other to put on the most extravagant shows, as concrete reflections of their wealth, power and taste. The fashion moved to France early in the sixteenth century when Catherine de Medici – who not only appreciated its artistic merit, but fully realized its political value as well – married Henry II.

While these court entertainments were soon popular all over Europe, they reached their height in France during the seventeenth century. The *ballet à entrée*, as it was called, was a series of scenes, loosely connected by a common theme. The dancing was a stylized version of the court dances popular at the time; even today many of the poses and mannerisms in ballet can be traced directly to the dances and manners popular in Louis XIV's court. Since the performance took place in the ballroom, with the audience on three sides, patterns and various formations were more important than individual dancers. The performers themselves were all men, and also were all amateurs; the only professional at court was the ballet master who organized the productions. In addition to their fantastic costumes, the dancers always wore masks, which were sometimes made of a very fine gold mesh.

Two legendary ballet stars, Tamara Karsavina and Vaslav Nijinsky, in the Diaghilev production of Le Spectre de la Rose *to Weber's music.*

Louis XIV, who ruled France from 1643 to 1715, was an enthusiastic and accomplished dancer. Many changes occurred in ballet during his reign, but perhaps the most important was the shift in venue from the ballroom to the Italian-type proscenium arch stage. Instead of surrounding the dancers and looking down on them, the audience was out in front, looking up at the raised stage. This change in perspective had an immediate and drastic effect on choreography; the elaborate geometric formations, which could no longer be appreciated, gave way to a focus on individual dancers. Techniques were adapted to better display the

dancer's skill, and as dancing became more difficult, the number of professionals increased. In 1681 the first professional female dancers appeared on a French stage.

It had taken women over a hundred years to become part of ballet – and it was only a first, small step. The eighteenth century was the era of the great male dancers, like Gaetano and Auguste Vestris, who achieved what was virtually 'superstar' status. Much of their domin-

ance was the result of the costumes of the day. Women, weighted down as they were by their heavy, awkward skirts and towering wigs, could do little more than glide elegantly around the stage and strike graceful poses. Men, though their costumes certainly were not designed for complete freedom of movement, at least had their legs free for impressive leaps and complicated steps.

Ballet became really established as an art form during the eighteenth century – but in the process it became extraordinarily formal and stuffy. Before it could suffocate itself, however, a new wave of reformers arose. The two foremost female dancers of the time, Marie Camargo and Marie Sallé, pushed for costume reforms that would give them some of the advantages men enjoyed, while dancers like Jean Noverre, Franz Hilferding and their disciples worked toward developing a new kind of ballet altogether – *ballet d'action*.

If ballet itself was stuffy, the dancers of the eighteenth century were anything but. Both actors and dancers were bitterly condemned by the Church, which would neither marry nor bury them unless they gave up their livelihoods and publicly 'recognized through divine mercy that the art of representation in the theater is contrary to the profession of Christianity.' Many dancers, then, simply lived in sin – it was the only way they could be together and still keep their jobs. Female dancers were expected to have one or more wealthy lovers; by the time they reached retirement age they would hopefully have saved enough money to repent in comfort. The Paris Opéra was a world unto itself, and until 1775 it was an unwritten rule that dancers and singers there could not be controlled by their parents, spouses or even the police. No self-respecting courtier was without his string of lovers from the Opéra, though few approached the Prince de Conti's record. He was said to have had 60 recognized mistresses, in addition to innumerable occasional affairs.

By around 1750 *ballet d'action* was well on its way to acceptance. Its main achievement was to tell a coherent story without words, which meant that ballet no longer had to share the stage with singing and drama. It emphasized dramatic unity in place of variety and dramatic action instead of display.

By the time of the French Revolution comic ballets and stories of ordinary people had begun to replace the plots

Natalia Bessmertnova and Mikhail Lavrovsky in the Bolshoi production of the best known of all ballets, Swan Lake.

taken from the classical mythology, as audiences came to be drawn from a wider base than just the aristocracy. This trend continued during the Republic, and so did costume reform. In fact, costumes became so abbreviated that dancers began wearing tights to avoid outright indecency.

Toward the end of the eighteenth century overwhelming political and economic events – like the French Revolution, the Napoleonic Wars and the Industrial Revolution – helped set the stage for a revolution in arts and letters. The great Romantic movement began in Germany where writers like Tieck and Hoffman wrote fairy stories which transported their readers into magical, make-believe worlds. As Romanticism spread to England and especially France, this passive escapism became more militant; in Paris 'ferocious Romantics' like Gautier, Hugo and Sand gleefully battled the 'academic blockheads.'

Overall, the Romantic movement had as much influence on society as had the Renaissance 300 years before. Ballet and the other performing arts – by this time dependant on support from the public at large (especially the new middle class) rather than on royal patronage – responded quickly.

Four choreographers form a bridge between the *danse noble* of the eighteenth century and the Romantic ballets of the nineteenth. Carlo Blasis was one of the most influential figures in the whole history of ballet; his emphasis on *ballon* (lightness), for example, was one of the first steps toward ballet as we know it today. Charles Didelot was a master of stagecraft, and also produced the first adagio on record (in 1796, in *Zephyre et Flore*). Jean Dauberval, one of Noverre's students, spread the concepts of *ballet d'action* throughat Europe. Salvatore Viganó perfected the 'heroic ballet.' All four emphasized dramatic expressiveness and unity of plot, music and choreography.

The Romantic period in ballet began about 1830 and was effectively ended by the Franco-Prussian War in 1870, but in that 40-year period ballet completely changed. For example, the *pas de deux*, now an indispensible part of any classic ballet, began its development in the Romantic era. *Pointe* dancing became popular – though without blocked shoes, dancers could do little more than strike graceful poses *en pointe*. New technologies like gas lighting made many more stage effects possible (and also tremendously increased the risk of fire). Marie Taglioni's costume in *La Sylphide* (1832), with its tight bodice and white, billowing skirt, set a fashion which is still followed in ballet circles today.

The Romantic period saw the meteoric rise of the ballerina and the corresponding decline of male dancers in public favor. Everywhere but in Russia and Denmark men were suddenly expected to become inconspicuous, mobile, supporting machines rather than real dancers. Sometimes they were replaced altogether by female dancers 'en travesti.' The notion that ballet was a feminine art form was not challenged until Michel Fokine began to provide substantial roles for men in 1909, but it had become so deeply rooted that traces of it remain today. Despite examples like Rudolf Nureyev and Mikhail Baryshnikov, most American fathers would still rather see their sons become professional football players than dancers – even though many athletes study ballet themselves in order to improve their balance and coordination.

Romantic ballets were concerned with emotion and the supernatural rather than with reason; stories about exotic, faraway places were also popular. Ballerinas like Marie Taglioni portrayed ethereal, spiritual, other-worldly creations; others were flashing, seductive virtuosos like Fanny Elssler. Most of them hardly resembled a modern dancer, however; the fashion of the day favored substantial, well-endowed women, with strong stocky legs and ample curves. Gautier once wrote a description of Elssler's physical deficiencies that probably would be considered complimentary today: 'Her hips are but little developed, her breast is not more rounded out than that of an antique hermaphrodite; but just as she is a very charming woman, so might she also be the handsomest young man in the world.'

The history of any art is a story of peaks and valleys. Ballet flourished in the court of Louis XIV, but gradually became stultified until it was empty posturing, devoid of any meaning. It was rescued first by the proponents of *ballet d'action* and then by the advent of the Romantic movement, which raised it to even greater heights. But inevitably, another period of decline set in. The star system became so entrenched that there were not enough good companies left to support the stars. Male dancers, with a few exceptions, were in danger of disappearing altogether. Once again ballet became one dimen-

sional. The French and the Danes stolidly carried on as before; the English flocked from ballet to hear the singer Jenny Lind; in Germany and Austria public support for ballet began to melt away; Italy still was producing great dancers at La Scala, but choreography was in a dismal state.

Only in Russia did ballet remain a vital, exciting art. There the best element of French, Italian and Danish ballet were being combined with something uniquely Russian to produce the strong, buoyant, impeccable technique we now call the 'Russian school.' The moving force behind Russian ballet during the second half of the nineteenth century was Marius Petipa, who devised and perfected the form that represents the classical style today.

This form, best demonstrated in works like *Sleeping Beauty* or *The Nutcracker*, calls for lavish, five- or six-act productions, with a distinct division between pantomime sequences and 'real' dancing. Petipa was the choreographer who brought the *pas de deux* to its peak and established it in its present form: the romantic adagio, variations for the male and female leads, and the final coda.

Russia kept ballet alive through the late 1800s and when, around the turn of the century, Petipa's classical formula had become stale through overuse, another Russian was ready to step into the breach. Serge Diaghilev, the first and still the greatest impresario in the history of ballet, gathered the cream of young Russian talent for his company, Ballets Russes. Their premiere in Paris in 1909 rocketed ballet back into favor in Europe; their revolt against tradition and their devoted adherance to new, dynamic choreography and design once again brought new life to a dying art.

At about the same time that Diaghilev and the companies that succeeded Ballets Russes were revitalizing ballet, a number of dancers in America and Europe were struggling to create a dance form that reflected inner feelings rather than technique. They faced a formidable task: with no royal patrons, no avant-garde workshops at universities or 'little theaters,' they had to forge their own place in the entertainment marketplace, outside both the ballet and show dancing traditions. This was why the earliest rebels, like Duncan, St Denis, and Fuller, often used seductive costumes or advanced stagecraft – to attract their audiences away from the competition.

World War I upset far more than the political boundaries of Europe; almost

overnight the whole structure of society was torn apart and all over the world people groped for ways to come to terms with their strange, new environment. Dancers like Mary Wigman in Germany and Martha Graham and Doris Humphrey in the United States rejected both the harmony and lightness of ballet and the theatricality of the earliest modern dancers. Their art was spartan, sturdy, angular and earthy rather than glamorous. Even their sets and costumes were sharp and severe.

The cause of modern dance in America was aided in 1927 when John Martin was appointed dance critic at *The New York Times* and Mary Watkins to a similar post at *The New York Herald-Tribune*. This meant that the first generation of modern dancers finally began to get some measure of respect and recognition. At this time, too, Americans were in the grip of an intense nationalism as a result of the Depression; they were inclined to reject 'European imports' like ballet. During the 1930s the first dance departments opened at American colleges and universities – which have remained centers of dance ever since.

After the struggles of the 1920s and 1930s and the great cataclysm of World War II, a new breed of modern dancers arose in America. This younger generation did not have to face the same battle for recognition that had occupied their elders, and thus could afford to cast a tolerant or even friendly eye toward former rivals like ballet or show dancing. By the early 1950s the number of dance departments at colleges and universities had mushroomed; modern dancers had virtually taken over choreography on Broadway, greatly improving the quality of dance seen there; and others were striking out into entirely new directions. In Europe, once more torn apart by war, modern dancers filled the gaps in many ballet companies, especially in countries without a strong popular ballet tradition like Holland and Germany.

Modern dance, by definition, must continue to change and develop in defiance of, rather than within, tradition. Fashions in design, costumes and music come and go as a matter of course. One of the most fertile areas of exploration in recent years has been in the kind of space dancers use; today we accept dance productions in parks, churches, museums and even in the streets almost as easily as in traditional theaters. But perhaps the greatest controversy has been over movement itself. Some modern choreographers are questioning whether any kind of training is necessary – in other words, whether one can philosophically maintain that any one kind of movement is more acceptable than any other kind.

Both ballet and modern dance recently have adopted a less suspicious attitude toward one another, and have demonstrated an awareness that each has something valuable to offer the other. In 1959, for example, Graham and Balanchine collaborated on *Episodes* – now one of the latter's most famous ballets. In 1966 Merce Cunningham choreographed a ballet version of *Summerspace* for the New York City Ballet which worked well, despite the dancers' initial difficulty with movements that went beyond their traditional training. In 1975 Margot Fonteyn and Rudolf Nureyev appeared in Graham's *Lucifer*, then in Jose Limon's *The Moor's Pavane*. In Europe companies like Ballet Rambert and The Netherlands Dance Theater have been working for years in the half-world between classic and modern dance.

With many dancers now familiar with both styles, there has been some interaction between techniques as well. A half-turnout (about 90 degrees) is fairly common among modern dancers; for its part, ballet is beginning to forego its emphasis on a rigid torso in favor of modern dance's more supple spine, with its possibilities for more expressive dancing. Though there is no reason to think that ballet and modern dance will ever merge completely into one new dance form, it is certainly reasonable to assume that each will continue to adapt elements from the other, while still remaining true to its own traditions and philosophy.

Today's dancers live in a far different world from their counterparts of 200 years ago; they are respected members of society, not moral outcasts. Women are no longer expected to collect wealthy lovers as their major means of support. Male dancers, unfortunately, are still viewed with a certain amount of suspicion – but thanks to the pioneering work of modern dancers like Ted Shawn and Charles Weidman, and the entirely masculine image of classical dancers like Nureyev and Baryshnikov, men no longer need put up with overt hostility from their audiences.

Dance lovers have the opportunity to see an unparalleled number of different kinds of dance. There is traditional ballet – like the classic Russian productions, the impeccable performances of England's Royal Ballet, the bouncy Bournonville revivals of the Royal Danish Ballet or Balanchine's neoclassical works. There is modern ballet, which often makes good use of nontraditional techniques. Black dance has made tremendous strides since the 1930s and 1940s when choreographers like Asdota Dafora Horton, Katherine Dunham and Pearl Primus began working it into a recognized art; later choreographers like Alvin Ailey, Talley Beatty and Donald MacKayle have continued to develop this exciting, energetic dance form from elements of jazz, modern dance, ballet and the dance traditions of the American South, Africa and the Caribbean. Modern dance, of course, covers a tremendous range of styles and philosophies, limited only by the number of individuals under consideration.

Both ballet and modern dance exist today because of their adaptability, which allows them to change in response to changing artistic tastes and social/political/economic pressures. No one can predict what dance will be like 10 or 100 years from now. But hopefully the words and pictures in this volume will help both dancers and those who love watching dance gain some feeling for the traditions and the many years of work by hundreds of dancers, choreographers and teachers that have gone into producing the art we see today on the stage.

Mikhail Baryshnikov the Russian prodigy who followed in Nureyev's footsteps and defected to the West seen here in the Kirov's Stone Flower.

The corps de ballet of the Vienna Staatsoper Ballet line up in a hall of the magnificent Vienna Opera House.

BALLET

ITALY

Liliana Cosi prima ballerina of La Scala, Milan, partnered by Peter Breuer in the Festival Ballet's production of Giselle.

Ballet was born in Italy, child of the great political, commercial and cultural upheaval of the fifteenth and sixteenth centuries that we call the Renaissance – a period that marks the transition from medieval to modern times.

Italy of the *quatrocento* was an exciting place. The rigidity and desolation of the Middle Ages were being swept aside by a surge of new political and commercial changes, as new technological advances sent merchants and explorers out into the world. On their return they brought back not only profits, but also ideas from far-away lands.

The resulting improvement in the quality of life was matched by a more stable political situation, as independent city-states arose, based on the burgeoning economy. Most of these states were ruled by powerful princes who maintained, through diplomatic relations, a situation much like today's delicate balance between national governments.

As life on this earth became more appealing, there seemed less need to concentrate all one's energies and hopes on the hereafter and the result was a new preoccupation with man and his potential. It was a time of tremendous intellectual excitement and great advances in science, literature and the arts.

Not surprisingly, the upper class – the group with the education to appreciate the arts and the leisure and money to indulge them – was in the forefront of all this activity. The great ruling families of Italy – the Sforzas of Milan, the Medici of Florence, the Estes of Ferrara and Modena, the Gonzagas of Mantua, the Montefeltros of Urbino – were all notable patrons of scientists, writers and artists of all kinds. They were also subtle, astute politicians who soon discovered that great art enhances the reputation of the state that produces it, in both the eyes of its citizens and the world at large – a fact that future leaders would rediscover many times in succeeding centuries.

Within a very short time the ruling houses of Italy were vying with one another to develop the most civilized, glittering court, to collect the most brilliant minds, to produce the most grandiose spectacles. These last were the beginnings of ballet.

Every prince worthy of the name in fifteenth and sixteenth century Italy hired a resident dancing master; the ability to participate in the graceful, intricate court dances of the day was a social necessity for everyone with any

Buontalenti's design for a lavish costume in a Florentine court dance of 1589, obviously meant for spectacle rather than ease of movement.

pretentions to noble birth. In addition to instructing the courtiers, the dancing master was also responsible for staging the elaborate entertainments that were part and parcel of the court atmosphere.

These *balli* bore little resemblance to a classical ballet like *The Nutcracker*. In fact, they were more closely akin to a floorshow at the Folies Bergères or a Las Vegas nightclub, consisting of a series of scenes that combined music, dancing, song and poetry, all staged with elaborate costumes, scenery, lighting and stage effects. The scenes were usually rather loosely connected by a theme such as the attributes of an honoured guest, or (for a wedding celebration) love and marriage. Often they took the form of 'dinner ballets': interludes (or 'entries') with themes that complemented the food being served. It is hard to imagine a custom that offered wider opportunities for a prince to impress his peers and it is little wonder that by the end of the sixteenth century Italian dancing masters were in demand at courts all over Europe – an export trade in virtuosity that Italy maintains to this day.

One of the most famous of the early dancing masters was Pompeo Diobono,

who taught at the court of the Sforzas in Milan before moving to Paris. In 1462 Domenico di Piacenza published the earliest known book on dancing, *De Arte Saltande et Choreas Dudende* (On the Art of Dancing and Conducting Dances). In the manuscript (which was written by hand, before the invention of printing, and is now kept in the National Library of Paris), he makes the distinction between a *danza* (a dance with a regular rhythm throughout) and a *ballo* (a dance production with varied patterns and rhythms). It was an important distinction because at the time there was little difference between ballet steps and those of the usual court dances, except that the former were a little more polished.

Di Piacenza's followers, Antonio Cornazano and Guglielmo Ebreo di Pesaro (more commonly known as William the Jew), soon produced books of their own. In 1489 Bergonzio de Botta staged a magnificent dinner ballet at Tortona to help celebrate the marriage of Galleazzo Visconti, Duke of Milan, to Isabella of Aragon. Each course in the great feast was presented with an appropriate interlude, all loosely connected by a theme based on the story of Jason and the Argonauts. The production was so impressive that accounts of it circulated throughout the courts of Europe – almost a century before Catherine de Medici sparked the beginnings of ballet in France with the *Ballet Comique de la Reine* in 1581.

The Italian Wars (1494–1559), in which France, Spain and other European powers battled for supremacy in Italy, proved ruinous to the country for centuries to come. However, they did spread Italian cultural influence in Europe and, despite political weakness and economic decline, Italians continued to lead the way in the development of music and the dramatic arts. Opera had its beginnings in Florence around 1600, while the *commedia dell'arte*, which was to have such a decisive effect on Western drama, was already well developed. Stagecraft too was advancing. The famous Teatro d'Olympico, built in Vicenza in 1580–84, featured a proscenium arch (an elevated stage within a 'picture frame'), as did Parma's Teatro Farnese, built in 1618. Perspective scenery had been in use since the second quarter of the sixteenth century.

On the ballet front, Cesare Negri (c.1536 – after 1604) was working in Milan where, in addition to staging elaborate extravaganzas, he trained many students. At one point some 40 of his former pupils were working for various European princes. In 1604 he published *Nuove Inventioni di Balli*. Another dancing master, Fabrizio Caroso, had written *Il Ballarino* in 1581. Though both works were basically concerned with court dancing, they did address more complex rhythms and techniques as well.

Through the seventeenth century and a good part of the eighteenth most ballet activity was centered in France, while in Italy opera was king. At the Teatro San Carlo in Naples (opened in 1737), ballets were offered only as divertissements between acts and after operas. Toward the end of the 1700s, however, things began to look better. Jean Noverre composed many of his *ballets d'action* in Milan and his methods spread from La Scala (opened in 1778) to other towns and companies in the country. Gasparo Angiolini, Noverre's greatest rival – and strongest ally in the promotion of the art of ballet – was also

Salvatore Viganó's dramatic choreography in his 'heroic' ballets, brought about the flowering of Italian ballet as never before or since.

active in Italy. The first mention of ballet in Rome is made in 1783, with the appearance of Vicenzo Trente, Onorato and Salvatore Viganó.

In 1812 Salvatore Viganó arrived in Milan. The master of heroic ballet, Viganó and his wife, the beautiful Spanish dancer Marie Medina, had long since conquered Europe. It was at La Scala that he produced his masterworks: ballets like *Prometeo* (1813). *Dedalo* (1813), *La Vestale* (1818) and *Otello* (1818). His productions were big, elaborate and exciting, and were very popular with Italian audiences. More than this, Vigano expanded on Noverre's concept of a unified dramatic theme and also did much to achieve a variety of streamlined pantomime, somewhere between normal gesture and traditional dance movements – a sort of mime-dance, which allowed him to advance the plot more easily and offer almost continuous dramatic action. Two other important choreographers in Milan at about the same time were Noverre's pupil Francesco Clerico (c.1755–1833) and the prolific Gaetano Gioia (1768–1826), whose most famous ballet, *Cesare in Egitto*, was first produced at La Scala in 1815. Both Viganó and Gioia composed leading roles for Antonia Pellerini (1790–1870), a ballerina who was hailed not only as the *prima ballerina seria assoluta*, but also as *la piu gloriosa delle attrice italiane d'ogni genera* (the most glorious Italian actress of all time).

Gioia was also the dominant figure on the ballet scene in Naples, where he created no less than 44 ballets. Dance there had progressed to such an extent that a school was opened at Teatro San

Carlo in 1812, a year before La Scala's famous academy was established. (Though it had an excellent reputation, it was to close in 1841.)

During the Romantic era, ballet in Italy and elsewhere in Europe flourished as never before. Rome, where ballet has always had a precarious existence, was excited over visits from the great ballerinas of the day: Fanny Cerrito (1833), Carlotta Grisi (1834), Fanny Elssler (1845) and Marie Taglioni and Lucile Grahn (1846). The Teatro San Carlo – Naples's social center and its pride and joy – was another regular stop on the circuit. Though the Neapolitans still preferred opera, they were a knowledgeable and critical ballet audience. If they were not quite as rowdy as London audiences, the noise and confusion during a poor performance was still more suited to a street fight than to one of the most beautiful opera houses in the world.

Milan was still the most important ballet center in Italy, however. Luigi (Louis) Henry had left the Paris Opéra and was experimenting with new styles. His ballet *Dircea* featured some of the first dancing on *pointe*, by Amalia Brugnoli, and his *La Silfide* (1828) was performed in Milan four years before Filippo Taglioni's famous Paris production. In 1837, when Carlo Blasis was installed as director of La Scala's Imperiale Regia Accademia di Danze (founded in 1813), the city's position as one of the international focal points for ballet was assured.

As director Blasis developed ballet techniques and teaching methods which irrevocably altered the state of the art, to such an extent that their influence is still felt today. Under his guidance the La Scala Academy became the most important ballet training ground in the world; a hundred years after his death Italian ballerinas still had a technical edge over any of their rivals, as a direct result of the systems he established.

Blasis's two most important technical innovations were the *attitude* and expansion of turnout. Both were based on his studies of anatomy and geometry. The *attitude*, now one of the standard positions, was based on Giovanni Bologna's statue of Mercury. The importance of turnout had been recognized ever since ballet performances were transferred from court halls to proscenium arch theaters as a way to display the individual dancer's body to its best advantage and also to improve execution and elevation. Much of Marie

Camargo's success, for example, was based on her good turnout, and Noverre had written, 'in order to dance well, nothing is so important as the turning out of the thigh . . . (it) gives ease and brilliancy, it invests steps, positions and attitudes with grace.' However, the standard turnout of the period was only 45 degrees. It was Blasis who widened it to 90 degrees and made it an essential ingredient of ballet.

Students at La Scala were not offered an easy path to success. Girls between the ages of eight and 12 and boys between eight and 14 were accepted only after they had passed a test to confirm their physical fitness and freedom from any hereditary diseases. Each signed an eight-year contract and worked for the first three years as an unpaid apprentice. Everyone was required to practice dance for at least three hours a day, and mime for one; older pupils were given more experience in productions at the theater. These guidelines were adopted by most European schools and to some extent are still followed in the Soviet Union today.

It was a rigorous life, but Milan graduates were guaranteed financial security for the rest of their lives, and students came from all over Europe to be able to study there.

The first generation of Blasian dancers included the famous 'Pleiades': Pasquale Borri (1820–44), who became a *premier danseur* and choreographer at both La Scala and the Kaertnerthor Theater in Vienna; Marietta Badarina; Augusta Domenichettis; Flora Fabbri (1830–1904), who went on to an illustrious career in Turin, London, Paris and finally Russia; Sofia Fuoco (1830–1916), later nicknamed 'La Pointue' because of her skillful *pointe* dancing; and Carolina Granzini. Other students who eventually became famous included Amina Boschetti (1836–81), Claudina Cucchi (1834–1913), Giovannina King and Carolina Pochini, along with stellar dancers Fanny Cerrito, Carlotta Grisi and Carolina Rosati.

One of the best-known Romantic choreographers in Milan was Antonio Cortese (1796–1879), who is credited with over 100 ballets. In addition to his versions of *La Silfide* and *Giselle*, he is best remembered for his *Beatrice di Gand* (1845).

Of course, all the great dancers of the day appeared in Milan. Fanny Cerrito was prima ballerina at La Scala from 1838–40; though none of the productions she appeared in was particularly distin-

guished, she was taking the first steps in what was to become a long and illustrious career. Other dancers with the company at the time included: Pallerini, past her prime technically, but still excellent in mime roles; Francesco Rosati, Cerrito's partner at her debut; Louis Bretin; and Luigi Mabille (who later, as Charles Louis Mabille, married the first international American star, Augusta Maywood). Carlotta Grisi and Louis Perrot were frequent visitors, as were Fanny Elssler and Marie Taglioni.

In January 1841 Cerrito opened a very successful version of *La Silfide* by Cortese, and that same spring Taglioni made eight guest appearances in her father's version of *La Sylphide* and also in *La Gitana*. Both ballets were received very well, and Taglioni's ethereal style apparently made as big a hit in Milan as it had in Paris. In 1843, when both Cerrito and Taglioni were engaged for the same season, Milan eagerly chose sides, even though Cerrito was appearing in a mediocre five-act *Giselle* and Taglioni in her father's equally dull version of *La Péri*. Both the theater and the piazza outside were packed for their first appearance together; as the curtain fell the 'contest' ended in a battle of flowers and both sides declared themselves winners. Taglioni also staged a version of Perrot's *Pas de Quatre* in 1846, starring herself, Fuoco Rosati and Caroline Vente, while Perrot himself produced *Faust* in 1848.

Milan held on to its position as one of the two great ballet capitals long into the second half of the nineteenth century, but ballet in Italy, as in most of Europe, was beginning to decline. The school system kept Milan going; Blasis's methods were still producing excellent dancers like Rita Sangalli, Virginia Zucchi and Pierina Legnani. Naples had three excellent teachers in Ernesto Mascagno, Raffaele Grassi and Nicola Guerra. In Genoa's school the instructors included Paganini, Carlo Felice, the acrobatic dancer Giovanni Carbone and Guiseppe Bonfiglio. Rome also had an excellent school, while Florence, Turin and Catania, though perhaps not in the same league as the other four, produced their own quota of first-rate dancers.

The 'Italian technique' still emphasized speed and spectacular exhibitions of technical skill, as it had done since the eighteenth century. Some critics, like Serge Lifar, sneeringly called them 'acrobats,' but no one could deny that in the late 1800s almost all the world's out-

standing dancers were Italian.

Unfortunately, few were dancing in Italy. The opportunities were far greater on the touring circuit in Europe or America. Marietta Bonfanti (1847–1921), one of Blasis's pupils and a principal dancer at La Scala by 1861, embarked on a tour of the United States in 1869 – and never returned. Sangalli (1850–1909) had made her debut at La Scala in 1865, but by 1872 she had settled in Paris where her talent, great beauty and intelligence soon made her the toast of the French capital. Malvina Cavallazzi (d 1924) left La Scala to dance in London in 1872 at the Alhambra and Empire theaters. The rest of her career was spent in England and America, where she was not only first ballerina during the New York Metropolitan Opera's first season in 1883, but also founder of that theater's ballet school in 1909 and its director until 1914. Legnani, Zucchi and a host of others spent the major portions of their dancing lives outside their own country.

The situation was especially difficult for male dancers, who had seen their role in ballet dwindle in importance during the Romantic era until they had become little more than animated balance beams. In the aftermath of the 'Golden Age of Ballet,' in addition to their rigorous physical training, they had to fight the prejudices of the age – an atmosphere in which the vociferous critics, who considered dance an 'unworthy' (if not unnatural) pursuit for men, were almost preferable to the overwhelming indifference of the public and even the ballet world itself.

The last two decades of the nineteenth century were dominated by the choreography of Luigi Manzotti, whose 'colossal' productions were masterpieces of baroque vulgarity. *Pietro Micca*, for example, featured 'the charge of the ballerinas' who, dressed as soldiers, performed their routines to the accompaniment of 64 drums. *Excelsior* (1881) had a cast of over 500 people and almost as many animals; *Amor* (1886) and *Sport* (1897) were overwhelming, grandiose concoctions featuring battles, triumphs, catastrophes and tributes to the glories of heroism and work. The whole genre, with its huge casts, spectacular stage effects, and elaborate productions, had very little to do with dance as such and even at its height never managed to topple its great rival, opera. Nor could traditional ballet compete with either. Carlotta Brianza's visit to Milan in the 1890s to appear in *Sleeping*

Beauty, the role she had created for Marius Petipa in St Petersburg, made little or no impression. The decline was irreversible.

In 1900 La Scala was still turning out excellent dancers and teachers, but for the first time a foreigner, the Spaniard Guiseppe Mendez, was director of the famous academy. Though he was an avid Italophile and had been a very good dancer, he was not of the same caliber as former directors like Blasis or Giovanni Casati (1811–95). In 1902 he was succeeded by Caterina Beretta, who arrived from Russia with a great reputation as one of the most famous teachers of her time. She was over 60, however, and even though ballerinas still came from all over the world to study with her, she could not make a dent in the tremendous atmosphere of apathy that hung over Italian ballet.

As the century progressed the last great stars like Cecilia Cerri (1872–1931) and Carlotta Zambelli (1875–1968) left the country. The older nineteenth-century choreographers, Manzotti and Carlo Coppi, died – while others, like Alfredo Curti and Giovanni Molaso, deserted ballet altogether for the music-hall stages of London and New York. Younger audiences began listening to jazz and going to popular revues, while older ones nostalgically recalled the days of the great classical ballerinas. The silence was broken only by the fireworks on the stage of La Scala, where the repertory was still dominated by works like *Sieba* and *Excelsior*. Eventually the very word ballet became a synonym for futile pomposity and Italian choreography, after five centuries of excellence, was on the verge of total collapse.

The opening of Diaghilev's Ballets Russes in Paris in 1909 – a group which developed new themes and new combinations of sight and sound from the exciting changes that had been taking place in music, art and design – was the last straw for Italian ballet in Europe and it suffered considerably.

Ettore Caorsi's debut in Turin in 1909 was the only bright spot in the period of stagnation that preceded World War I. The elegant, virile dancer with superb technique not only managed to overcome Italy's antipathy toward ballet in general and male dancers in particular, he also resisted joining the hordes of dancers on their way to New York, Paris and Russia, preferring to join with his friend Nicola Guerra in their 20-year battle to preserve

Liliana Cosi as Odette/Odile from Swan Lake. *Pierina Legnani created this role, turning an unprecedented 32* fouettés *in the ballroom scene.*

Italy's ballet heritage.

During World War I many important Italian artists returned to their native land and ballet in Italy began, albeit slowly and painfully, to be revitalized. In 1916 the great impresario Diaghilev arrived in Rome to spend the winter working in a studio in the Piazza Venezia. Soon Leonide Massine, Léon Bakst, Jean Cocteau and Pablo Picasso joined him, bringing with them the outline and music for *Parade*, one of three important ballets they were to work on that winter.

To thank the Romans for their hospitality, Diaghilev staged a production of *Les Femmes de Bonne Humeur* at the newly reopened Costanzi Theater in April 1917. His choice of this particular ballet – based on a comedy by Goldoni, with music by Scarlatti – was a graceful compliment which his Italian audience

was quick to appreciate. The all-star cast featured the famous Enrico Cecchetti and his wife Giuseppina as the old couple, along with Massine himself, the Polish dancers Idzikowski and Woizikowski, and the enchanting ballerinas Tchernicheva and Lopokova.

In Milan in the autumn of 1918 a new production of *Carillon Magico* choreographed by Cia Fornaroli, promised a breath of fresh air at La Scala as well. Radical reforms in 1921 were followed by the appointment of the famous teacher Olga Preobrajenska as director in 1922. She was succeeded by Nicola Guerra, whose volatile creativity did much to dispel the turgid aura that still surrounded ballet. In 1925 the old maestro, Cecchetti, returned at the age of 75. Despite his hard work in the three years left to him, he did not make much pro-

gress and when Fornaroli took over after Cecchetti's death in 1928 choreography and public taste in Italy were still years behind the rest of Europe. Diaghilev, one of whose greatest dreams was a triumph at La Scala, had visited twice, in 1920 and 1927, to be met on both occasions with cool indifference and half-empty houses. Milan, home of Viganó and Blasis, had no time for upstarts, however sophisticated.

Still, the period between the wars was one of steady improvement. Massine spent time at La Scala in the 1930s, while in Rome the school attached to the Teatro dell'Opera (formerly the Costanzi) was consolidated and stabilized under Boris Romanoff and Aurel von Milloss, who alternated as directors between 1934 and 1960.

Italian ballet has continued to grow

Prince Siegfried is enchanted by the wiles of Odile, believing her to be the white swan princess, Odette.

Carla Fracci as Giselle.

since 1945; if Italy cannot be considered a major center for ballet, it is still making important contributions on a more modest scale.

The two most important centers of activity are Milan and Rome. Both cities have seen a rapid turnover in ballet masters and choreographers, with most of the major figures in modern ballet working in one or the other at some time. Naples has also been the scene of continuing activity, although on a smaller scale. Venice, Florence and, most recently, Palermo occasionally attract a famous ballet director, but in the absence of an established tradition they have had a difficult time maintaining any continuity. On the other hand, annual summer festivals at Florence, Genoa-Nervi, Spoleto and, to a lesser extent, Verona attract many foreign companies and much acclaim.

The greatest dancers of the postwar generation have all travelled abroad in search of performance opportunities. Carla Fracci (b 1936) came from the La Scala school. She became the company's prima ballerina in 1958. Best known for her romantic roles, Fracci was regarded as a supreme *Giselle*. She appeared with the American Ballet Theatre (1967–76), partnered by Bruhn, Nureyev and Paolo Bortoluzzi.

Born in 1938, Bortoluzzi made his début at the Nervi Festival (1957). He was a star of Béjart's Ballet of the Twentieth Century (1960–72). He created many major roles, notably *Firebird* (1970) and *Songs of a Wayfarer* (1971). He and Nureyev have performed this compelling male duet around the world. He now runs a school in Turin. He is also director of the Deutsche Oper Ballet in Düsseldorf.

Elisabetta Terabust (b 1946) studied in Rome. She joined the Rome Opera Ballet in 1964 and was promoted to prima ballerina two years later. Terabust has regularly appeared with the London Festival Ballet since 1973. She performed *Giselle* with Nureyev (Rome, 1981) and *La Sylphide* for Teatro Communale (Florence, 1983).

Aterballeto, based in Regio-Emilia, is the liveliest new company in Italy. During the 1980s, a roster of international dancers and choreographers have been lured to northern Italy by a dynamic policy of creative experimentation. Stars, such as Terabust and Peter Schaufuss, have created roles choreographed by the likes of MacMillan and Tetley.

BARBARA CAMPANINI
'La Barbarina'
1721–99

From the fifteenth century onward, many of the greatest Italian dancers and choreographers seldom, if ever, worked in Italy. Instead they travelled the world, adding to the fame of Italian technique if not to the development of the art in Italy itself. La Barbarina, as she was universally known, was therefore not the first (nor certainly the last) to carve out an international career far from home.

La Barbarina was born in Parma and studied in Italy with Rinaldo Fossano. Eventually the two, now partners, set off for the capital of the ballet world – Paris. In July 1739 audiences at the Paris Opéra were in the mood for someone new. La Barbarina,' a young woman, well trained in the dazzling Italian style, with its emphasis on speed and acrobatic techniques, became an overnight sensation. Confident and precise, with excellent elevation, she amazed Parisians with her turns and *entrechats huits*, and delighted them with pirouettes and *jetés battus*.

In 1740 John Rich, director of London's Covent Garden, made a personal visit to Paris to hire the new star for his theater. There La Barbarina scored if possible, an even greater success, enchanting the royal family, who attended nine of her 75 performances. For the next few years she danced in Paris, London and Dublin.

She was as famous for her offstage life as she was for her dancing; her list of lovers included Prince Carignan, Lord Arundel, the Marquis de Thebouville and the Duke of Durfort. In 1744 she accepted an engagement in Berlin. However, when the time came to leave, she was having such a good time in Venice with her current lover, Lord Stewart MacKenzie, that she announced she would not be able to make it. Frederick the Great immediately forced Venice to deport her (by jailing the Venetian ambassador until they did so), and then had her escorted to Germany.

Once in Berlin, La Barbarina accepted defeat gracefully, immediately captivating the king and the citizens of the capital. In fact, Frederick was so taken with her performance at her debut on May 13 that he hired a *corps de ballet* and established a respectable salary scale for dancers – making La Barbarina, in effect, the 'mother' of ballet in Germany. Soon she was also installed as Frederick's mistress – a purely honorary position, since the king's tastes ran in other directions. However, it was a thoroughly satisfactory arrangement for both parties: Frederick maintained his respectability and in return kept La Barbarina in an appropriate style, indulged her whims and allowed her any number of lovers.

Finally, in 1749, she married one of them – Frederick's privy councillor, Charles-Louis de Cocceji. Within 10 years they were separated, though they were not divorced until 1788. Then, as a last favor, Frederick made her Countess de Campanini and endowed a convent on her estates. This she ran as a refuge for impoverished ladies of noble birth, serving as its prioress until her death.

LOUIS XAVIER STANISLAS HENRY
1766–1836

Louis Henry, a native of Versailles, trained at the Paris Opéra school with Deshayes, Pierre Gardel and Coulon. He made his debut as a dancer in 1803 and was much praised for the purity of his style. His first ballet was choreographed for the Théâtre de la Porte-Saint-Martin in 1805.

In 1807 he emigrated to Italy where, free from the overpowering egotism of Auguste Vestris and Gardel, he responded to the influence of Viganó and Gioia by becoming an innovative, creative choreographer. He was fond of experimenting with new dance forms, for example, Amalia Brugnoli demonstrated some of the first toe dancing in his ballet *Dircea*, and his version of *La Silfide* in Milan predated Taglioni's by four years.

A great success in Italy, in later years he produced several ballets in Vienna and in smaller theaters in Paris. He returned only once to the Opéra but *L'Ile des Pirates*, produced there just before his death, was not a success.

Henry is credited with more than 125 ballets, of which the best known are *Otello* (Naples, 1808), *Hamlet* (Théâtre de la Porte-Saint-Martin, 1816), *La Silfide* (Milan, 1828) and *William Tell* (Milan, 1833).

SALVATORE VIGANO
1769–1821

Salvatore Viganó, the greatest producer of heroic ballets in the early 1800s, was born in Naples, into a musical family. His parents were dancers and encouraged the development of his musical talent. His first music teacher was his uncle, the composer Luigi Boccherini. Later he studied with Dauberval, who introduced him to Noverre's theories, which were to have a great influence on his later work.

Viganó began dancing in Italy, then accepted an engagement in Spain where he met and married the beautiful dancer Maria Medina. Between 1793 and 1803 the two toured Europe and became enormously popular (due in part, perhaps, to Mme Medina's daring costumes); clothes, food, hairstyles, even cigars were named after them. In Vienna Beethoven composed his only ballet score for Viganó's first important work, *The Creatures of Prometheus* (1801).

Most of his early ballets stressed mime. As he incorporated more of Noverre's theories he moved toward mime-dance, as in his adaptation of Shakespeare's *Coriolanus* (Milan, 1804).

In 1812 he arrived in Milan to take up a post as a dancer at La Scala but when one of his admirers died and left him a fortune he gave up dancing altogether and turned to his first love, choreography. It was in Milan that he produced his greatest ballets: *Prometheus* (1813), a remake of the Vienna production which retained only four of Beethoven's original numbers; *Psammi, Re d'Egitto* (1817); *Otello* (1818); *Dedalo* (1818); *La Vestale* (1818); and *I Titani* (1819), for which Rossini wrote most of the music. Other popular works from this period include *Gli Ussitti* and *Numa Pompilio* (both 1815), *Mirra* (1817), *Allessandro nelle Indie* (1820), and *Giovanna d'Arco* and

Didone (both 1821).

Viganó called his works 'coreodrammi.' They had a tremendous impact; not only were they heroic in both size and subject matter, but they took dramatic technique much further than Noverre had ever imagined.

The most outstanding characteristic of Viganó's ballets was his use of a style somewhere between normal gesture and pure dance. Though some critics complained that the gestures were getting in the way of the dancing, the technique did allow him to tell complex, exciting stories coherently, without breaking them up into alternating mime and dance scenes. He also was fond of constructing tableaux (groups posed in a statuesque way) and contrasting them with ensemble scenes full of intricate movement.

All the movement in his ballets was controlled by the music, which was usually a medley of pieces by various composers; if he could find nothing that suited him, he would write it himself.

The novelist Stendhal called Viganó 'the Shakespeare of the dance.' The title is appropriate, for he did more than any choreographer before him to extend and develop the inherent dramatic qualities of ballet.

FILIPPO (PHILLIPE) TAGLIONI
1777–1871

Filippo Taglioni is another famous figure in ballet history who was born and trained in Italy and then spent most of his career in other parts of the world.

In 1797, at the age of 20, he landed in Paris, but, like Louis Henry before him, he soon realized that no outsider had a chance while Vestris and Gardel controlled the Opéra. So when he was offered the job of ballet master in Stockholm in 1803, he accepted gladly. There he married Sophia, daughter of one of Sweden's leading opera singers and in 1804 their daughter Marie was born.

For several years the family lived in Vienna and Kassel, Germany, then, to escape the danger of Napoleon's incessant warfare, Taglioni settled everyone in Paris while he set off again on his freelance career through Italy, Sweden, Denmark, Germany and Austria.

In 1821 he was given a three-year contract at the Kaertnerthor Theater in Vienna. As soon as he was settled he sent for Marie, who had been studying in Paris. When she arrived he was dismayed to discover that her dancing was positively dreadful; immediately he set her on a strict training program (practicing six hours a day for the first six months).

His teaching methods, which bore some resemblance to those developed later by Enrico Cecchetti, were unique for his time and produced a unique ballerina. The *danseurs nobles* of France (Vestris, et al) were concerned with elegance and worldly sophistication. Taglioni, on the other hand, wanted a modest, light, delicate style and therefore he put most emphasis on elevation (*ballon*) and *pointe* technique.

In Stuttgart, where he worked from 1824 to 1828, he continued to perfect Marie's technique. When she was finally ready he took her back to Paris for her debut. By 1831 she was so popular he was able to negotiate a six-year contract for both of them

The year 1832 saw the culmination of all his years of effort, with the triumphant opening of *La Sylphide*. Marie became the prima ballerina of the Romantic period and her father its most renowned choreographer; for several years he accompanied her on her tours of Europe and Russia.

As he grew older, Taglioni became more and more eccentric – at one point losing all of Marie's carefully amassed fortune in unwise speculations. However, nothing in his later life can detract from his achievements as the creator of the archetypal Romantic ballerina and as a pioneer in the ballet style that was to alter the very nature of the art.

CARLO BLASIS
?1797–1878

Carlo Blasis, one of the greatest theorists and teachers in the history of ballet, came from a noble Neapolitan family. Thus his father could afford to give him an extensive education in the arts and sciences. It was not wasted, since from all accounts Blasis was something of a universal genius. His interests ranged beyond dance to anatomy, geometry and sculpture; he was a composer and poet in addition to being a choreographer, and wrote not only on dance, but also on other aspects of music and even on politics.

Much of his early life was spent in France. He made his debut as a dancer in Marseilles at the age of 12; from there he

went to Bordeaux to study with Dauberval and to Paris where he worked with Pierre Gardel. In 1817 he was back in Italy as a soloist for Viganó at La Scala, and in 1820 he published his first technical work: *Traité Elementaire, Theorique et Pratique, de l'Arte de la Danse*.

From 1826 to 1830 he was employed as soloist and choreographer at King's Theatre, London, and it was there, in 1830, that he published his most important book, *The Code of Terpsichore*. In it, for the first time, he outlined ballet technique as we know it today – based not on trial and error, but derived from his pet disciplines, anatomy and geometry, as well as from a sound knowledge of the arts in general and a well-developed esthetic sense.

Blasis was a prolific choreographer, credited with more than 70 ballets and many *pas de deux*, and is said to have been one of the first to use Biblical themes for his works. His most important achievements came after 1837 when, following an accident which ended his dancing career, he was appointed director of La Scala's Imperial Academy of Dance. Though he was arrogant and a dreadful snob, Blasis was also a dedicated thorough teacher. His technical innovations, like the widening of the turnout and invention of the *attitude*, changed the whole look of ballet. His teaching methods produced pupils like Cerrito, Rosati, Maywood, Andreyanova and dozens of other first-rate dancers, who in turn went on to shape the history of ballet from Russia to the United States. His work in Milan established that city as a leading ballet center throughout the Romantic period, and solidified Italy's reputation as the source of technical excellence for over a century.

FANNY (FRANCESCA) CERRITO
1817–1909

Fanny Cerrito, whose fame was to become second only to Marie Taglioni's, was the daughter of a middle-class Neapolitan family. She was trained in Naples and made her debut at the Teatro San Carlo, in *L'Oroscopo*, in 1832.

After four years touring Italy and dancing in Naples, Rome, Milan and Turin, she set out for Vienna and an 18-month engagement at the Kaertnerthor Theater. There her admirers gave her the

Fanny Cerrito in Alma (*or* La Fille de Feu) *in 1842. This tambourine dance, the 'Pas de Fascination,' was one of her greatest successes.*

nickname Fanny, which she used thereafter. From 1838 to 1840 she was prima ballerina at La Scala. Though none of the productions she appeared in was outstanding, she was a great favorite with the public. The stage experience, and also her work with Carlo Blasis, did much to improve her style and self-confidence.

In May 1840 Cerrito made her debut in London, where her English admirers found her ample voluptuous figure and vivacious dancing an irresistable combination. Her spectacular leaps and brilliant *pointe* work transformed the most mediocre ballets and, for the next 17 years she was a familiar and popular figure during the London season. Even the arrival of Marie Taglioni could not shake her confidence.

The year 1843, however, marked a turning point in her career. It was the year in which she and Taglioni appeared together in Milan, exciting great interest and dividing the city into two factions. It was also the beginning of her collaboration with Jules Perrot in London, where her performance in *Ondine* (for which she herself arranged several dances) brought down the house. That year she also danced an extraordinary *pas de deux* with her other great rival, Fanny Elssler, at the express request of Queen Victoria. Finally, she renewed an old acquaintanceship with Arthur Saint-Léon and began a dancing partnership that would culminate in marriage two years later.

For the next six years the two danced their way through Europe. Saint-Léon choreographed many ballets for her; one of their greatest successes, *Le Violon du Diable* (Venice, 1848), featured Saint-Léon on the violin.

Unfortunately, the combination of two tremendous egos was too volatile to last long and in 1851 they went their separate ways. In October 1853 Cerrito's daughter Mathilde – the result of a liaison with a young Spanish nobleman – was born. Though she was 36 years old, Fanny never thought of retirement and 1855 found her in Paris, creating the lead role in *Gemma*, which she had choreographed to a libretto by Gautier.

Later that year she began an engagement in St Petersburg. It was not a success; at that time native Russian dancers were in favor with the public, and in any case Cerrito was no longer in her prime. In 1857 she returned to England where, after a farewell performance at the Lyceum, she retired to raise her daughter in peace and quiet. In 1909 she died in Paris – just as Diaghilev's Ballets Russes was opening an entirely new chapter in the history of ballet.

Grisi's death-defying leap from Coralli's La Péri. *She fell from a cloud into her lover's arms.*

CARLOTTA GRISI
1819–99

Carlotta Grisi's parents were not musicians, though almost everyone else in her family sang in the opera. She, too, had an excellent voice, but dancing was her first love from the time she entered the La Scala academy at the age of seven.

By the time she was 10 she was being given her own roles, and in 1833 when she was 14, her parents gave her permission to tour Italy. It was in Naples that she met Jules Perrot who, attracted not only to her talent but also to her quiet, gentle personality, took her in hand. Perrot began as her teacher – as relentless and demanding a teacher as Taglioni – but he soon became her lover as well. (Their marriage has never been definitely established, although she appeared on a few occasions as Mme Perrot.)

Perrot secured them engagements in London, Vienna, Munich, Milan and finally at the Théâtre de la Renaissance in Paris, where Grisi danced and sang in *Le Zingaro* in 1840. A year later, in February 1841, she made her debut at the Opéra, and a few months after that appeared in her most famous production, *Giselle*.

She and Perrot had been drifting apart for some time and, when his contributions to *Giselle* were not even acknowledged, he departed, leaving Grisi to carry on alone in Paris. However, her dancing in her next major role, *La Péri* (1843), which was choreographed by Coralli to a story by her devoted admirer, Théophile Gautier, was as good as ever. Six months later the Opéra extended her contract for three years – at four times her original salary.

During the next few years Grisi appeared in two excellent productions at the Opéra, both by Mazilier – *Le Diable à Quatre* (1845) and *Paquita* (1846). In the meantime she had also become a favorite at Her Majesty's Theatre in London, where her working relationship with Perrot was as good as it ever had been. In 1844 she created the title role in *La Esmeralda* (often cited with *Giselle* as the two best Romantic ballets), and in 1845 she appeared with Taglioni, Cerrito and Lucile Grahn in the famous *Pas de Quatre*. In 1847 she danced Fire in *Les Eléments* and the following year portrayed Summer in *Les Quatre Saisons*. After Perrot left for Russia and was replaced by Paul Taglioni, she was seen in *Electra, ou la Pléiade Perdue* (1849). In 1850 she gave her last performance in the West, in *Les Métamorphoses*.

Soon she was reunited with Perrot in St Petersburg where her popularity grew slowly but surely (especially after he was appointed ballet master in 1851). In 1854 she left for Warsaw, where she intended to continue dancing. But she was pregnant, and the child's father, Prince Radziwell, persuaded her to retire while she was still at the height of her fame.

Happily settled on the property he gave her at Saint-Jean, near Geneva, she spent her last 46 years in quiet retirement, bringing up her daughter Ernestine and keeping in touch with a few old friends like the ever-devoted Gautier. Grisi died in 1899, a month before her eightieth birthday; like many others, unmourned by the thousands who once adored her.

CAROLINA ROSATI
1826–1905

Rosati was another of the great Italian dancers who trained at La Scala under Blasis and then left to make her reputation abroad. A *terre à terre* dancer, with an acting talent that was, if anything, greater than her dancing, she was tremendously popular in London. There, in 1847, she appeared twice in Grahn's role in *Pas de Quatre* and in 1849 she danced with Paul Taglioni in his *La Prima Ballerina, ou l'Embuscade*, a ballet based on his sister Marie's encounter with a highwayman in Russia.

In 1853 Rosati travelled to Paris, where she soon managed to oust Cerrito in the hearts of Opéra audiences – not, however, because of her beauty (she was just as overweight as Cerrito had become), nor her technical skill (she was not as good a dancer), but because of her superb acting ability. For the next few years she continued to dance in both Paris and London, appearing in *Le Corsaire* (1856), a spectacular, action-packed epic full of harems, pirates and shipwrecks, and in *Marco Strada* (1857), with Amalia Ferraris.

Following the path beaten by other Romantic ballerinas, she left in 1859 for St Petersburg, where for three seasons she delighted the Russians – again, more with her acting than her technical skill as a dancer. Following Grisi's example, she retired in 1862, at the age of 36, before her presence began to pall. After a triumphant farewell performance in Marius Petipa's first big success *La Fille du Pharaon*, she returned to Paris. There she remained a familiar and beloved figure on the ballet scene until her death at the age of 79.

Her tremendous personality, which captured audiences wherever she went, was summed up by an admirer who wrote: 'If La Rosati no longer had feet she would continue to dance with a smile or a curl of her hair.'

LUIGI MANZOTTI
1835–1905

Italy has always been the home of dance extravaganzas, from the Renaissance court ballets through the heroic epics of Viganó, but the grand master of the spectacular must be Luigi Manzotti. Manzotti began his career as a mime-dancer in Rome, where he was enormously popular

Enrico and Mme Cecchetti's class reads like a ballet hall of fame. Left to right: 1, Madame Cecchetti, 2 Dovbrovska, 3 Markova, 4–7 unknown, 8 de Valois, 9 Sokolova, 10 unknown, 11 Sovmorokova, 12 Chamil, 13 Woizikowsky, 14 Lifar, 15 Tcherkas, 16 Nikitina, 17 Dolin, 18 Danilova, 19 unknown, 20 Savina, 21 Cecchetti.

and where he choreographed his first ballets: *La Morte di Misaniello, Moro delle Antille, Michaelangelo e Rolla, Cleopatra* and *Pietro Micca*.

In 1872 he moved to Milan where his 'colossal' productions, like *Sieba* (first produced in Turin, 1878), *Excelsior* (1881), *Amor* (1886) and *Sport* (1897), made him – and his genre – world famous.

Strictly speaking, his productions were not ballets at all. Rather, they consisted of episodes in mime combined with both incredible processions of dancers and animals, and with simple dances suitable for the huge choruses. It is easy to poke fun at these rather mindless pageants, but they had a lasting effect on the popular theater, if not on ballet itself. Many features of the music hall – vaudeville acts, revues and even, one might say, aspects of the great movie epics of only 25 years ago – can be traced back to Manzotti's work.

CATERINA BERETTA
1839–1911

Caterina Beretta studied in Milan, but made her debut at the age of 14 in Paris, appearing in the first production of Verdi's *Les Vêpres Siciliennes*. Rapidly becoming one of the most famous ballerinas of her time, by 1858 she was dancing again at La Scala, billed as *prima ballerina assoluta de rango francese*. She danced there off and on for the next 18 years.

In 1877 she was given the post of ballet mistress at the Maryinsky Theater in St Petersburg. There she found a new, even greater career as a teacher in Cecchetti's classical style.

Returning to La Scala in 1902, she was soon acknowledged as one of the most celebrated teachers of her time, with pupils like Trefilova, Pavlova, Legnani and Karsavina to her credit. Aspiring dancers flocked from all over the world to study with the 'ludicrous little figure . . . fat and short, her pyramidal shape emphasized by a very small head with a meager blob of hair on top.'

ENRICO CECCHETTI
1850–1928

Enrico Cecchetti, one of the greatest and best loved teachers in ballet history, was a true child of the theater. The son of two dancers, he was born in a dressing room in

Nicola Guerra, premier danseur at the Scala by 14, partnering Marie Taglioni in Filippo Taglioni's L'Ombre.

Rome's Teatro Tordinonia, made his first stage appearance at the age of five in Genoa, and his adult debut in 1879 at La Scala.

A fine dancer, he toured for the next 11 years, and was welcomed in all the ballet centers of Europe. In 1890 he accepted an appointment as second ballet master at the Imperial Theater in St Petersburg; two years later he began teaching at the school. There he developed his teaching methods (based on the Milanese system and later codified by Idzikowski and Beaumont), which were to have a tremendous impact on twentieth-century ballet.

In 1902, after a short time in Warsaw, he opened his own school in St Petersburg and settled down, apparently, to a long, peaceful retirement. However, in 1910 Diaghilev persuaded him to join Ballets Russes as ballet master, and he was on the road again, soon becoming the company's guiding spirit. Finally at the age of 68 he left the troupe and he and his wife opened a school in London, which was instrumental in producing some of the top British dancers of this century.

In 1925 the 75-year-old Maestro returned to La Scala, and he directed the school there until his death in 1928. The list of Cecchetti's pupils reads like a Who's Who of ballet: Trefilova, Egorova, Pavlova, Sedova, Vaganova, Kschessinska, Preobrajenska, Karsavina, Gorsky, Legat, Fokine, Nijinsky; then Massine, Bolm, Lepokova, de Valois, Danilova, Markova, Dolin, Lifar. In short, there are very few top-rated dancers in the first half of the twentieth century who do not owe a great deal, directly or indirectly, to his teaching.

Thanks to the work of organizations like England's Cecchetti Society (founded in 1922 and incorporated into the Imperial Society of Teachers of Dancing in 1924) and the Cecchetti Council in the United States (in existence since 1939), his famous system has been preserved and is still a strong influence on Western ballet today.

NICOLA GUERRA
1865–1942

A native Neapolitan trained at San Carlo, Nicola Guerra's talent as a dancer surfaced early. By the time he was 14 (in 1879) he had been appointed principal dancer at La Scala. Though he was devoted to the advancement of Italian ballet, his difficult personality led him into constant feuds with various managements (especially in Italy) and as a result he seldom stayed in one place long enough to effect any lasting changes.

In 1896, after dancing in Paris, London, New York and St Petersburg, he was hired as principal dancer at the Vienna Court Opera. There he stayed until 1902, when he began a 13-year stint as ballet master at the Budapest Opera (for which he created 19 ballets).

At the outbreak of World War I he returned to Italy and founded Balli Italiani di Nicola Guerra. Unfortunately, wartime Italy was not interested in supporting ballet and the company folded; the end of the conflict found him back in Paris, where he staged a revival of Jean Phillipe Rameau's opera *Castor et Pollux* (1918), as well as choreographing *La Tragédie de Salomé* (1919) and *Artemis Troublée* (1922).

On occasion he did obtain more or less stable positions: a few months at La Scala in 1922; leader of La Compagnia dei Nuovi Balli Italiani, the largest ballet company ever seen in Italy at that time; a two-year engagement as director of the Paris Opéra Ballet School; one year as director of the Rome Opera's school. For the most part he travelled incessantly, teaching and creating new ballets, until his retirement to Cernobbio, on Lake Como, where he died at the age of 80 – the last of the great Italian choreographers.

CIA FORNAROLI
1888–1954

Cia Fornaroli, one of the great, if not the greatest, Italian ballerinas of her generation, graduated from La Scala in 1909, and left Italy for New York as soon as she could. There she danced with the Metropolitan Opera Ballet until 1913, but when World War I broke out she gave up her steady job for the touring circuit.

After the war, in 1921, Fornaroli returned to Italy as *prima ballerina assoluta* at La Scala, where she was one of Cecchetti's favorite dancers. In 1928 she took over his post as director of the ballet school. The appointment, unfortunately, did not last long. In 1933 she married Dr Walter Toscanini, an ardent anti-Fascist, and Mussolini immediately saw to it that she was fired. Without more ado the couple left the country and settled in New York City, where Fornaroli opened a school which operated from 1943–50.

FRANCE

A lavish costume design by Jean Berain for the Paris Opéra production in 1681 of Le Triomphe de L'amour, with music by Jean Baptiste Lully.

France was introduced to *balli* in 1494 when Charles VIII invaded Italy. On their return the French princes were soon eagerly producing their own court ballets, usually with the assistance of Italian dancing masters.

However, all the productions were on a fairly small scale until the arrival of Catherine de Medici, who came to France in 1533 as the bride of the duc d'Orleans, later Henry II. In 1555 she acquired a new valet – a compatriot, named Baldassarino di Belgiojoso – who soon became the unofficial organizer of all the parties at court. Between them, the showman (he was also a violinist) and the daughter of the Medicis had a finely developed sense of how to produce a magnificent spectacle and use it to best advantage. When Catherine became regent for her son, Charles IX, in 1560, Belgiojoso's entertainments became an important tool of the monarchy as well as occasions for having a good time.

Their first important *ballet de cour*, *Le Ballet des Polonais*, was staged in the Palace of the Tuileries in August 1573 to celebrate Henry III's election as King of Poland. It was a pattern woven of music, dance and song, at the end of which the spectators joined the performers for a general dance.

Their most ambitious – and best known – production was *Le Ballet Comique de la Reine*, which Belgiojoso (who later changed his name to Balthasar de Beaujoy-

eaux) staged in the Salle Bourbon of the Louvre Palace in October 1581. The occasion was the marriage of Marguerite of Lorraine, Mlle de Vaudemont (Queen Louise's sister), to the duc de Joyeuse and Catherine was determined that it be the most magnificent, spectacular affair of its kind ever seen in Europe.

Money was, of course, no object and Belgiojoso did not let his patron down. In a production that lasted over five hours, he told the story of Circe, who became queen of the seasons through sorcery, only to be defeated at the end by the gods. The end of the pageant contained a graceful tribute from Athena to the Queen of France (who had also been one of the performers in the ballet). As a finale Louise gave her husband, Henry III, a medal engraved with a picture of a dolphin and the words *delphinium ut delphinium rependat* (a dolphin is given to receive a dauphin, that is, an heir to the throne).

Belgiojoso had spent more than three million francs, but Catherine and the rest of the audience (said to have numbered about 10,000) were more than happy with the result. The Queen Mother was so pleased, in fact, that she had illustrated accounts of the affair prepared and circulated all over Europe. As its fame spread, other monarchs were inspired to produce similar spectacles.

The intricate, sophisticated and mannered world of the French court was a

Le Ballet Comique de la Reine *staged in 1581 by Belgiojoso for Catherine de Medici at the Louvre was the most important to date.*

perfect breeding ground for ballet, and the art flourished. The first French book on dancing, *Orchésographie*, which concentrated mainly on court dances of the

Jacques Patin's design for the Four Virtues from Le Ballet Comique de la Reine.

period, was written by Thoinot Arbeau in 1588.

Court ballets continued to be popular after Catherine's death, though it was not often that the kings could afford to produce anything that rivalled *Le Ballet Comique de la Reine*. The approximately 80 court ballets performed during Henry IV's reign were, for the most part, more informal. The most usual format was for a series of entrées (separate dances by small groups) followed by a grand finale (Grand Ballet), in which everyone danced together, and which usually contained some compliment to the guest of honor.

Louis XIII, who reigned from 1610–43, had a decidedly gloomy disposition and preferred ballets that were fantastic or even grotesque. Each ballet was still a collection of entrées, but as time went on there was more of a tendency to group them into acts and relate them to a central theme. For example, in *Ballet de Madame Soeur de Roi* (1613), Act I consisted of entrées titled Snow, Hail, Ice, Fog and Dew; Act II presented Comet, Thunder and Lightning; while in Act III the guests saw Clouds, Shooting Star and Rain. The King himself made frequent appearances in these productions, usually

in dignified roles. It has been said, however, that among friends he enjoyed dancing comic or even female parts as well.

During the first few years of Louis XIV's reign (1643–1715) his mother, Anne of Austria, acted as regent. She preferred opera (another Italian import) to ballet, and for a while dance took second place. But the young king, who, like all other well-born children, took dancing lessons as a matter of course, soon came to love the art. His first public performance was in *Cassandre* in 1651 when he was only 13. It was to be but the first of many. In fact for almost 20 years he appeared in all the court productions.

Court ballet, by definition, was dependent on the policies and preferences of the ruling monarch. As Louis became Europe's greatest king and archetypal aristocrat, so dance was transformed into a respectable, even dignified art form, which reflected the spectacle (and artifice) of the glittering French court. It lost none of its value as a political tool in the process; Louis's chief minister, Mazarin, encouraged him to appear in impressive roles in public to help consolidate his position as absolute monarch.

His appearance in 1653 in *Le Ballet Royale de la Nuit* is a case in point. Between 1648 and 1653 France had been torn by bitter civil war, but by 1653 the rebels had almost been defeated. Thus the ballet's story, which records the course of the hours of the day, conceals a political allegory obvious to audiences at the time. As the 15-year-old king, portraying the Rising Sun, drove out the demons and robbers who ruled the night, so would he triumph over the rebels who threatened to bring everlasting darkness to France.

Pierre Beauchamps, Louis's dancing teacher and, after 1650, the choreographer of his court ballets, was an important influence on the development of ballet at this time. Previously there had been no formal vocabulary of steps for performers; it was Beauchamps who codified dance movements, formalized them and began to establish ballet as an art form distinct from ballroom dancing.

As the monarchy became more firmly established, ballet lost its political role,

A design for a choreographic composition from a ballet de cour, circa 1660. An early form of notation, the dancers are drawn in position.

but the court ballet, or *ballet à entrée*, continued to rise in popularity. Opera-ballets were being developed by the composer Jean-Baptiste Lully and others, partly because the influential Mazarin preferred opera, but mainly because ballet was not yet far enough advanced to tell a story without words. As long as entertainments were still being performed in ballrooms or gardens like Versailles, formations and patterns were all-important, leaving little scope for depicting human emotion.

As the 1660s wore on, Louis danced in public less and less. He had gained quite a bit of weight and he was increasingly aware of the need to maintain the dignity of his position. Another factor probably was the ever-more demanding nature of ballet, which was steadily requiring greater skill from its performers. Though many court ballets were still little more than excuses for the nobles of the court to dress up in elaborate costumes and masks, professional dancers had been part of the dance scene since 1630. As the king became less interested in dancing, so did his court. After his last performance, in *Flora* in 1669, ballet performances moved from the palace ballroom to the royal theater (constructed by Cardinal Richelieu in the Italian style, with a raised stage and proscenium arch).

It is difficult to overemphasize the importance of this change. The increased distance between dancers and audience removed much of the amateur quality and camaraderie, which had been a feature of the court productions and encouraged an atmosphere of greater professionalism. In addition, the audience's entire perspective changed, instead of surrounding and looking down on the performers, they had a one-sided view. Thus choreographers had to begin emphasizing individual dancers rather than group patterns and the dancers themselves had to move from side to side across the stage rather than back and forth.

Though Louis had retired from public performance, he had by no means lost interest in the dance. In 1661 he had established the Académie Royale de Danse, 'to increase the said art as much as possible.' It remained in existence until just before the French Revolution, but was mainly concerned with social dancing; its 13 dancing masters spent more time in taverns than on the business at hand, and the academy had little influence on the development of ballet.

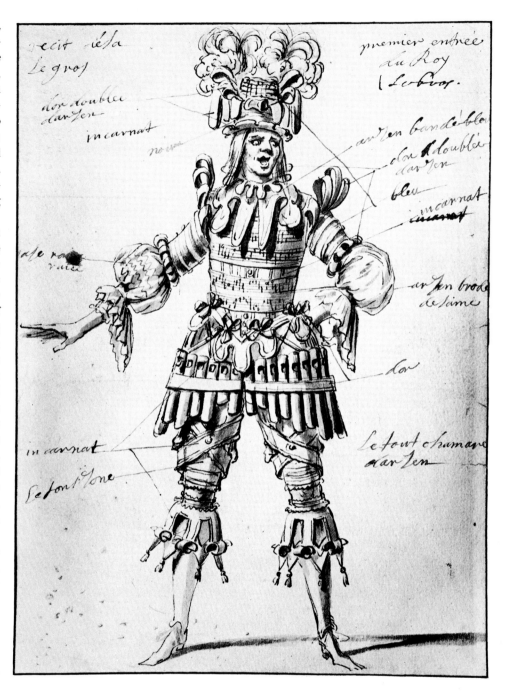

More important was Louis's founding, in 1669, of the Académie Royale de Musique, which was known almost from the beginning as the Paris Opéra (the oldest ballet company in the world). The year 1672, when a school of dance was attached to the company, marks the end of the noble amateur as ballet dancer.

Under the direction of Lully, who was a virtual dictator at the Opéra from its early years until his death in 1687, opera-ballet continued to develop – as did a newer form, *comédie-ballet* (an ancestor of today's musical comedies). The combination of Lully's elegant music, Beauchamp's choreography and dramatist Jean-Baptiste Molière's witty scripts was unbeatable. Perhaps their best known collaboration was *Le Bourgeois Gentil-*

An elaborate costume for the first entrance of the Louis XIV as the embodiment of Music, from a ballet de cour, circa 1660.

homme (1670), in which Lully himself danced as The Mufti in Molière's story of middle-class M Jourdain and his unfortunate attempts to mimic the aristocracy by taking singing and dancing lessons, which still amuses audiences today.

With the new technical resources available in a theater, scenery – which had been elaborate even for court productions – became incredibly complex and ornate. Designers like Jean Berain and, later, Claude Gillot created gorgeous sets and even ingenious machines which lowered dancers from the flies to the stage in

clouds or chariots. Costumes were equally beautiful to look at, though they seemed designed to make dancing as difficult as possible.

In 1681 the first professional female dancers appeared on stage, in Lully's *Le Triomphe de l'Amour*. Women had appeared in court ballets, of course, at least in private performances. But propriety would not permit noblewomen to dance in public, especially if the king happened to be dancing as well. Thus Mlle Lafontaine and her colleagues, Mlles Fanon, Lepeintre and Roland – all graduates of the new Opéra school – were the first real ballerinas.

In time Mlle Lafontaine (1665–1738) was succeeded by Marie Subligny (1666–1736), who in turn was followed by Francoise Prévost (1680–1741) as the Opéra's leading ballerina. Prévost is remembered today more for her two famous pupils, Marie Camargo and Marie Sallé, than for her dancing.

In general, however, men still held center stage – as they would throughout most of the eighteenth century. In addition to Beauchamps, the list of early dancers includes: his nephew Nicolas Blondi; André Lorin, who also invented an early system of dance notation; Louis Pécourt (1655–1729), considered the best *danseur noble* of his day; and Jean Balon (1676–1741), whose name has become a synonym for lightness and elevation.

In 1687, when Lully died, Jean-Phillipe Rameau was appointed director of the Opéra. In the same year Beauchamps retired, to be succeeded as ballet master by Pécourt. In 1713 a new school was established at the Opéra, marking the further separation of social and professional dance. Several steps that we would recognize today, like the *entrechat*, *cabriole*, *coupé* and *chassé*, had already been incorporated into the standard technique. Under Rameau opera-ballet reached its zenith with *Les Indes Galantes*, a typical piece for the period, consisting of a series of more or less independent scenes based on a common theme, with spectacular stage effects, including, in this case, an erupting volcano.

New ways of creating ballets were also being explored in the early 1700s. One was sponsored by the Duchess of Maine, an eccentric noblewoman who compensated for her physical deformity (she was a dwarf) by cultivating her intellect and wit, and for her insomnia by staging late-night entertainments at her chateau. For one of these, dancers from the Opéra produced a mime version of one act from Corneille's *Horace* – perhaps the first attempt at *ballet d'action*.

In the early 1700s ballet in France was dominated by Louis Dupré, 'the god of the dance,' famed for his grace and noble posturing; after 1739, when he took over as ballet master, he produced students like Gaetano Vestris and Jean Noverre. But though male dancers were still paramount, women were beginning to make progress. Two of them, Camargo and Sallé, not only began a rivalry that sparked public interest in ballet, but were also early pioneers for long-needed reforms in both costumes and technique.

As in the previous century, men's costumes included elaborate masks, plumed helmets and short tunics (tonnelets), which by this time had been wired to project from the hips, often as far as the dancer's outstretched arms. Awkward they might have been, but at least they left the legs free. Women were still trying to dance in long, heavy, hooped skirts, usually decorated with tiers of ruching in lace or feathers, and at the same time balance towering wigs (perukes). Since all the costumes were tightly fitted (which made breathing difficult at the best of times) and all dancers wore high-heeled shoes, it is little wonder that few attempted to do much more than strike a series of graceful or impressive poses.

Camargo, who made her debut at the Opéra in 1727, was an outstanding technician. She shortened her skirts so that audiences could better appreciate her quick steps and flashing *entrechats* and donned heelless slippers so that she could jump higher. Her greatest rival, Marie Sallé, the toast of London and Paris in the 1730s, relied on dramatic expressiveness rather than technical virtuosity, and insisted that costumes should be changed to reflect character. Audiences fought to see her in London, but in Paris the Opéra management refused to give her the freedom to act as she liked which she desired.

Despite the technical advances – such as new, difficult types of *entrechats* and *jetés* – introduced by Camargo and others (like Louise Lany and Marie Lyonnois), ballet under Louis XV (reigned 1715–44) was becoming more and more refined and elegant – so much so that it was strangling itself. By 1760 the Opéra had reached a state of acute artistic stagnation. The management's blind adherence to outdated, artificial conventions and unsuitable costumes left the dancers with little scope for creativity. They found an outlet only in intrigue – competing for promotion or new lovers. In the forefront of all this activity was Gaetano Vestris, head of the close-knit Vestris clan and leading *danseur noble* of his day. The only dissenting voice, heard faintly through the stultifying fog surrounding the Opéra, was that of another of Dupré's pupils, the French choreographer Jean-Georges Noverre.

Noverre believed strongly that the future of ballet lay in its development as an art form independent of opera. He also realized that technical skill alone would not be sufficient, that ballet would have to rid itself of the cumbersome conventions and costumes of the seventeenth century and begin to incorporate dramatic action if it was to have a chance for survival.

In 1758 in Lyons Noverre produced the first ballet without words: *Caprices de Galatée*. In 1760 he published his theories in *Lettres sur la Danse et les Ballets* (Letters on Dancing and Ballet), a cry for reform which had a tremendous impact in the ballet world. He argued for the abolition of 'hideous masks . . . ridiculous perukes . . . clumsy panniers . . . and inconvenient hip pads'; instead he advocated light, unconfining costumes that would allow dancers to move freely. He insisted that every ballet have a plot, a simple theme developed without words through the coordination of dramatic, expressive dance and mime with music, setting and costumes. This new concept came to be called *ballet d'action* and was publicized throughout Europe, not only by Noverre himself and others working along the same lines (like Hilferding and Angiolini, in Vienna), but also by younger choreographers like Noverre's pupil Jean Dauberval and, in turn, Salvatore Viganó in Milan.

In 1772 at least one of Noverre's reforms was adopted at the Opéra. One evening Gaetano Vestris was too ill to dance the part of Apollo in a performance of *Castor et Pollox*, a role he performed in the usual wig and mask. His rival, Maximilien Gardel, agreed to appear in his place, but only if he could dance without the mask so that his fans would recognize him. By 1773 ego had triumphed completely over tradition and masks were not worn by any dancers.

The major female dancers at the Opéra during this period included the charming, gay Marie Allard, who was also an excellent actress, the German dancer, Anne Heinl, Marguerite Peslin and Madeleine Guimard. The men included Dauberval, Jean Lany (1718–86), Charles LePicq (1744–1806), Maximilien Gardel and, of course, Gaetano Vestris. Vestris has often been described as all-powerful in the complicated, intrigue-ridden world of the Opéra at that time, but there were limits, as he discovered when he had the popular Anne-Marguerite Dorival imprisoned on a trumped-up charge following a quarrel. His next appearance on stage was greeted by a chorus of boos, catcalls and shouts of 'La Dorival!' As the pandemonium threatened to grow into a full-scale riot, Vestris dashed offstage and rushed to Fort-l'Eveque prison, where he found Dorival and a crowd of friends having a congenial champagne supper. It took Vestris an hour to convince her to leave the party, but the patient audience welcomed their slightly unsteady return with enthusiasm.

In 1776 Noverre was appointed ballet master at the Opéra, through the influence of Marie Antoinette. Gardel, the logical choice for the job, deeply resented being pushed aside and did all he could to sabotage Noverre's work, from performing badly on stage to stirring up dissension among the dancers. Things went from bad to worse when the popular and well-protected Guimard turned against Noverre as well.

The atmosphere rapidly became unbearable. In 1778 Noverre choreographed Mozart's *Les Petits Riens*. It was an excellent effort, combining mime and dance in expressive choreography, and was much enjoyed (especially the climactic scene in which the shepherdess bares her bosom to prove she is not a boy) but Noverre was furious at what he considered deliberately bad dancing. Meanwhile, Mozart, who had discovered that someone had added some French songs to his score, walked out in a huff, swearing he would never again compose anything for the Opéra.

The newly installed director, Jacques de Vismes, was having an equally difficult time with his temperamental staff (led by Guimard). Eventually the leading performers presented an ultimatum: if the position of director was not abolished they would either go on strike or, if necessary, resign. At this, even the king

One of Jean-Georges Noverre's greatest ballets d'action *was* Jason et Medée, *seen here with Gaetano Vestris, top male dancer of the day.*

(who, one suspects, got much amusement from his spies' tales of Opéra infighting) lost his patience. Guimard, who had many powerful friends, was immune to punishment, but Gaetano's son, Auguste Vestris, was clapped in prison. In addition Mlle Duplant, a singer, was fired and deprived of her pension and Dauberval was forbidden entrance to the theater. The musicians struck in support of the dancers and, just at the worst possible time, a long-standing feud between the Italian composer Piccini and the Austrian Gluck erupted into open warfare, with inflammatory articles in the newspapers and even street demonstrations. The battle ended when Gluck stormed out of Paris, vowing never to return.

Eventually, in 1780, both de Vismes and Noverre resigned, and Maximilien Gardel finally got the position he coveted. The change did little to improve the situation. In June 1781 the Académie Royale de Musique et de Danse burned down (for the second time), killing or injuring several people. The architect, Lenoir, promised to build a new opera house in 90 days, but in the meantime the harassed management had to find a way to keep the singers and dancers from leaving Paris for better positions in Stuttgart or London. Not surprisingly, many made plans to escape when they found out that the police were shadowing them. One popular dancer, Nivelon, actually did manage to slip over the Belgian border and spent a year in England before returning to Paris.

During the years after the fire, the directors, including Pierre Gardel (who succeeded his brother as ballet master in 1787), had to cope with Guimard, who became more and more difficult. She would refuse to dance – and the ballet would be cancelled; she demanded equal pay with Auguste Vestris – and got it; she required unlimited funds for costumes – and the Opéra paid. Finally, in 1789, to everyone's relief, she announced her retirement.

By that time, on the eve of the French Revolution, ballet was becoming increasingly popular with the general public. In response, choreographers began using stories from ordinary life in addition to the traditional plots based on classical mythology. One of the best ballets of the time was produced by Dauberval in 1789 in Bordeaux's large, luxurious theater. *La Fille Mal Gardée*, a two-act ballet/ pantomime, is a simple, happy story, in which a scheming mother's attempts to marry her pretty daughter to a wealthy fool are foiled by the girl and her lover. It put Noverre's theories into practice, in fact, going much further than the master himself had ever been able to. Although Dauberval's choreography has long been lost, his scenario has inspired a constant series of versions throughout the intervening years, including: Viganó's 1792 production in Italy; Petipa's St Petersburg version in 1882; and finally Frederick Ashton's excellent ballet, first seen at Covent Garden in 1960.

The philosophy of the French Revolution (1789–99) affected every aspect of life, including, of course, ballet. Its influence was most visible in costuming. The old-style costumes, so reminiscent of the aristocracy, disappeared completely, to be replaced by simple tunics inspired by the Greek and Roman republics. The material – what there was of it – was slightly transparent, to better display the beauty of the human body, and only the introduction of tights stood between the dancers and complete exposure. The trend toward stories from everyday life continued and ballet – like the other arts – was even used to some extent as political propaganda. In 1792 Pierre Gardel set one ballet to the stirring strains of the *Marseillaise* and in 1794 he produced another patriotic piece, *La Fête à l'Etre Suprême*.

As always, there were administrative problems. In 1794 the Committee of Citizens of the Republic ordered the Opéra to move from Lenoir's theater to another on the Rue de la Loi (now Rue de Richelieu), changing its name to Théâtre des Artes and then to Théâtre de la Republique et des Artes. The citizens had little feel for the difficulties involved in handling temperamental artists, catering to public tastes and at the same time remaining financially viable. There was a flood of resignations, and chaos reigned among those who remained.

At the end of the eighteenth century France was still the world leader in both dancers and choreography and Frenchmen were in evidence in ballet all over Europe and Russia. But in Paris itself – despite two more official name changes (to Académie Imperiale de Musique et de Danse and finally back to Académie Royale) – the Opéra remained the same stagnant backwater, crushed under the egotism and political maneuvering of Auguste Vestris (who retired in 1816) and Pierre Gardel (who retired in 1829). While choreographers like Viganó, Didelot and Henry were producing new, exciting ballets elsewhere, Vestris and Gardel continued their series of cold, formal, mediocre productions.

For the most part the ballerinas who remained at the Opéra had little to do on stage but show off the unexpressive, dull technique demanded by these productions, leaving them free to use their creative energies elsewhere. Mme Gardel, the former Marie Miller, a fixture in Opéra ballets for 30 years (from 1786–

1816), showed far more creativity backstage, jealously making trouble for any younger dancer who seemed to threaten her position. Mme Clotilde took her dancing more seriously and was very good at it, but her amazing beauty and adventures with her many lovers were her real claims to fame. Fanny Bias (1789–1825), who danced at the Opéra from 1807–25, was noted for her lightness and precision, and had such an extraordinarily thin, supple body that she was nicknamed 'La Désossée' (the boneless one). Unfortunately, she was also so temperamental that no one was ever sure whether she would appear or not. Geneviève Gosselin (1791–1818), a talented young dancer, seemed just on the brink of achieving stardom despite all Mme Gardel's intrigues, when she died suddenly in childbirth at the age of 27.

In contrast to the Revolution, which had a drastic impact on ballet, the Napoleonic era went by virtually unnoticed. The Corsican general rose to power, was defeated at Leipzig in 1813, retired to Elba, escaped, marched north and was defeated again at Waterloo, all without causing a ripple at the Opéra.

One of the few bright spots in the interminable series of pompous productions was Louis-Jacques Milon's ballet *Nina, ou la Folle d'Amour*, the harrowing tale of a young girl who goes mad when her lover is banished and she is threatened with marriage to another man (though of course there is a happy ending). Emilie Bigottini sent audiences weeping from the theater with her portrayal of Nina, and in many respects the ballet itself was a precursor of the Romantic era.

In December 1815 Didelot returned from Russia to give a performance of his *Flore et Zéphyre*, despite Gardel's strenuous attempts at sabotage. Parisian audiences loved the ballet, with its exciting aerial effects, as much as their counterparts in London and St Petersburg had done. Having made his point and humiliated Gardel, Didelot immediately returned to more congenial territory.

Meanwhile, in 1814 a young woman who was to become one of the Opéra's most important personalities was hired – not as a performer, but as concièrge. Over the next 40 years (during which time she was never absent from her post for a day), Mme Crosnier became loved, feared and an indispensable part of everyone's lives. Officially she was the doorkeeper, controlling the entrance of the hundreds of people who worked at the

Opéra, as well as their friends, relations and lovers. Unofficially she was an advisor on strategy and an ally (or enemy) in countless love affairs; she even fed the youngsters in the *corps de ballet* when they were hard pressed. She retired much against her will in 1854 when her son became director of the Opéra.

Another influential figure at the Opéra during the early part of the century was Auguste the *claqueur*, the leader of a group of hired applauders. He was never on the Opéra's payroll, but on the afternoon of each performance he would meet with management, discuss the amount and timing of the applause, and receive a block of tickets. Some went to the *claque* and the money taken from sales of the rest, along with fees paid by the performers themselves, amounted to a very comfortable living. His relations with the performers were not always amicable (Fanny Elssler managed to have him replaced for a short time), but most soon found that they needed him. Once an overconfident Mme Duvernay announced that her daughter Pauline did not need Auguste's 'protection'; but when the young woman's solos were received in total silence she quickly changed her mind.

In February 1820 the Opéra had to move from the theater on Rue de Richelieu, but not, for once, because of a fire. One night the young duc de Berry was fatally stabbed in the street and carried inside to die. The Archbishop of Paris agreed to give him absolution, but only on condition that the building was never used again for theatrical performances. The theater closed immediately and, while construction was proceeding on a new opera house, the Opéra performed in temporary quarters on the Rue Favart.

In August 1821 the company moved into their new home on the Rue de Peletier, where they would stay for the next 52 years (until it, too, burned down in 1873). The building was located in the middle of a narrow street which became completely blocked by carriages, theater goers, scalpers and pickpockets every time there was a performance. From the outside it was not impressive; in fact, one critic claimed that it looked like a 'substantial stable.' Another, noting that there were statues of only eight Muses on the flat roof, speculated that poor Polyhymnia (the muse of sacred song) had 'flung herself down in an excess of despair brought on by the wretched singing of M. Duprez.'

The interior, however, was more satisfactory. The house was elegantly proportioned, beautifully decorated, with excellent acoustics and a seating capacity of 2000. The stage itself was large and, best of all, lit by gas – a technological innovation that would soon make possible the magical effects so necessary in Romantic ballets. Just offstage there was a large room called the Foyer de la Danse. During the day it was a classroom; at night it was the room in which performers not only warmed up, but also met their admirers and friends. In years to come it became famous all over Europe as one of the places to see and be seen in.

In 1827 Filippo Taglioni and his daughter, Marie, arrived in Paris and in 1828 she began dancing at the Opéra, with great success. That year, after her sixth performance in *Le Sicilien*, someone tossed a wreath of flowers on to the stage for the first time in the history of the Opéra.

At about this time, French Romanticism, spurred by similar revolts against Classicism in England and Germany, was becoming a well-established movement. Meanwhile, M Lubbert, director of the Opéra, was assembling a stellar collection of talented singers, dancers, choreographers and designers. In 1831 he commissioned the opera *Robert le Diable* from the composer Giacomo Meyerbeer, entrusting Taglioni with the choreography.

The opening of the opera was plagued by a series of near-disasters. A piece of scenery fell from the flies, barely missing

Marie Taglioni in the title role of her father Filippo's great triumph of the Romantic ballet, La Sylphide, *first performed in Paris in 1832.*

Patrice Bart danseur étoile of the Paris Opéra and Elisabetta Terabust from Italy in the London Festival Ballet's production of La Sylphide.

Marie Taglioni; another dancer escaped a falling gaslight by inches; and the lead tenor, M Nourrit, unexpectedly disappeared through a trap in the stage just before the wedding scene. But none of this bad luck affected the tremendous reception given the production in general, and Taglioni's 'Dance of the Nuns' in the third act in particular. The ballet sequence was like nothing before seen, as the ghosts of nuns who had been unfaithful to their vows danced amid the ruined cloister in eerie 'moonlight.' Marie seemed to float rather than dance, seducing not only the unfortunate hero, but the entire audience as well.

In March 1832 Filippo followed this early Romantic divertissement with the two-act *La Sylphide* and took Paris by storm. This archetypal Romantic ballet tells the story of a young Scotsman's meeting with a beautiful nymph on the eve of his wedding, his abandonment of his fiancée to pursue her, and her death when he tries to bind her to him. Its theme, man's yearning for an unattainable ideal, is one of the most basic tenets of the Romantic movement. The designer, Pierre Ciceri, created a mystical, otherworldly effect with the new gas reflectors and constructed apparatus to float dozens of sylphs through the air. Taglioni's own ethereal style was enhanced by Eugene Lamy's costume: a long, bell-shaped *tutu* of white muslin, pale pink tights and satin slippers (still the standard uniform for all Romantic ballerinas). *La Sylphide* even contains the travelogue element popular in many later Romantic ballets,

with its Scottish dances in the early scenes. The emphasis on the ballerina, at the expense of the male lead, was shown in the choice of Joseph Mazilier as James. Mazilier, an astoundingly handsome – if mediocre – dancer, was probably given the part over Jules Perrot, whose excellent dancing was matched only by his ugliness.

Within a month an outbreak of cholera in Paris had led Dr Véron, the Opéra's new director, to send most of his leading performers away. The passion for the new style was too great to be damaged by a mere epidemic and when the stars returned they found their audiences as eager as ever.

In 1834 a new dancer made her debut at the Opéra. Fanny Elssler epitomized the 'other' side of Romanticism – the earthy, pagan nature of man, as opposed to his supernatural, spiritual characteristics. Véron, who had an unerring eye for publicity, soon promoted a highly effective 'feud' between Elssler and Taglioni. His tactics increased box-office receipts, but distressed Taglioni, who reacted by becoming increasingly temperamental. The last straw came when the ballerina developed a mysterious *mal du genou* (disease of the knee) which kept her bedridden for six months and at the end of which she produced a child. At the end of 1836, by mutual consent, her contract with the Opéra was dropped.

Taglioni's great rival and one of the greatest dancers ever, Fanny Elssler in La Volière. *Her sensual style earned her worldwide popularity.*

Véron's successor, Henri Duponchel, who had little patience with arrogant ballerinas, stuck to his decision to let Taglioni go, despite a vehement campaign by her supporters which culminated when hundreds of 'mourners' gathered in the Opéra courtyard to commemorate his 'death.'

Elssler continued to be a popular attraction, though she had no spectacular successes until her appearance in January 1839 in *The Gypsy*, followed six months later by another success, *La Tarantule*. That same year the Danish dancer, Lucille Grahn, gave a performance of *La Sylphide* so good that it made Elssler's version look vulgar. Elssler threatened to leave and Duponchel, true to form, said 'good riddance.' However, just before the 1840 season opened, with Elssler on her way to New York, his plans for the year fell apart: Grahn injured her knee (a real injury this time); the American, Augusta Maywood, eloped, never to return; and Fanny Cerrito, for whom he had been negotiating, decided instead to go to London.

The year 1841, however, marked the high point of Romantic ballet with the premier of *Giselle*, a masterpiece which remains one of the few Romantic ballets in the repertory today, and which is considered, along with *Swan Lake*, the ultimate test of any ballerina's dancing and acting skills. The production, which seemed to send everyone who saw it into a state of ecstacy, could hardly have failed. The scenario was written by Théophile Gautier in collaboration with the talented, eccentric Vernoy de Saint-Georges, to music by Adolphe Adam (a popular composer, who also wrote the carol 'O Holy Night'); Ciceri designed the sets. Jean Coralli is credited with the choreography, but most of the dances were created by Jules Perrot. The rising young ballerina, Carlotta Grisi, starred in the title role opposite Lucien Petipa (one of the few male dancers able to achieve any recognition during the Romantic era) and Adele Dumilâtre (1827–52) portrayed the beautiful but cruel Myrthe, Queen of the Wilis.

Giselle's plot is much more substantial than that of *La Sylphide* and manages to combine in one production both the pagan and spiritual faces of Romanticism. The first act takes place at a village festival where the young peasant girl, Giselle, falls in love with a mysterious stranger. On learning that he is really a nobleman and engaged to another, she goes mad and dies. In the second act Myrthe and the Wilis (the ghosts of women who died un-

Above: Margot Fonteyn in the title role of La Péri *in the Ashton version of Jean Coralli's ballet in which Carlotta Grisi made such an impact.*

Below: Claire Motte, étoile of the Paris Opéra in a pas de deux from Giselle, *with a member of Les Jeunes Danseurs de l'Opéra de Paris*

Act I of Coralli and Perrot's great classic Giselle *with Marguerite Porter and David Wall, Royal Ballet.*

Emma Livry as Papillon. Her career was cut tragically short when her tutu *caught a gaslight during rehearsal and she died from burns.*

happy in love) call Giselle's spirit from the grave, their eerie dance contrasting with the robust peasant romps of the first act. The penitent Albrecht appears and Giselle is ordered to dance him to his death, but she refuses, managing to shield him until dawn breaks and the Wilis' spell is broken.

La Péri (1843), choreographed by Coralli from a story by Gautier, had an Egyptian setting. Like *La Sylphide*, it showed man in search of an unattainable ideal. The most exciting part of the ballet came when Grisi, as the Péri, fell from heaven into Petipa's arms – a height variously described as anywhere from six to 20 feet. Though most of the time Petipa caught and held her in a graceful pose, she risked life and limb every time she attempted the feat.

After 1850, ballet began to decline in France, though less rapidly than in England or Italy, primarily owing to the continued presence of the 'old guard': Saint-Georges, Maxilier, Saint-Léon and Adam. In 1853 Carolina Rosati arrived, upsetting the current favorite, Cerrito. But Cerrito continued to retain most of her popularity and in 1855 she choreographed and starred in *Gemma*. The ballet was set in Naples and was one of the first productions to deal with the very popular subject of hypnotism. Though not an inspired creation, it was well received.

In 1856 the newcomer, Rosati, ap-

peared in *Le Corsair*. This stirring tale of pirates and slave girls even included a sinking ship among its stage effects and was a tremendous success in both London and Paris, remaining in the repertory for half a century. In 1857 Amalia Ferraris replaced Rosati as the Opéra's leading ballerina.

Marie Taglioni returned to Paris in 1859 as the Opéra's Inspectrice de la Danse and teacher for the most advanced classes. By this time the Opéra school was producing few notable dancers; most of the principal dancers in the company were Italian. One notable exception was Emma Livry (1842–63), Taglioni's favorite pupil. Even though she was French (a decided handicap at the time) and not at all pretty, she compensated by developing a light, airy style reminiscent of the great Romantic ballerinas. The contrast with the flashier Italian dancers appealed to audiences, but before she could fully realize the benefits of her increasing popularity, Livry's career was cut short by a tragic accident.

The gaslit stages were, of course, terribly dangerous. The management, well aware of the problem, ordered all dancers to dip their costumes into a flame-proofing solution. But Livry refused, claiming that it made her *tutus* look dingy. During a rehearsal on 15 November 1862 she brushed up against a gas jet and immediately her flimsy garment burst into flames. Despite the heroic efforts of the rest of the cast, she was horribly burned and died in July 1863, eight agonizing months later.

After Livry's accident there were no great ballerinas dominating the Paris scene, except fleeting appearances by

guest stars like the German-born Adele Grantzow (1847–77) and Marsha Mouravieva (1838–79), a much-admired Romantic ballerina from St Petersburg, whose creation of the leading role in Saint-Léon's *Diavolina* in 1863 marked the first new production at the Opéra in nearly two years.

In 1866 a young accompanist named Leo Delibes, who had been composing operettas as a sideline, collaborated with Leon Minkus on the score for Saint-Léon's new work, *La Source*. The tunes he created were so well received that soon he was commissioned to write *Coppélia*. One of the biggest problems with *Coppélia* (which was some three-and-a-half years in preparation) was finding a suitable star to dance the lead role, Swanilda. Emile Perrin, the director of the Opéra, first hired Grantzow, but she fell ill. Next he considered Leontine Beaugrand (1842–1945), an excellent dancer with extraordinary elevation, but she was French and therefore not glamorous enough. After searching all over Europe, Perrin finally found his Swanilda in the Opéra's own school. Giuseppina Bozzacchi, a 15 year old who had come from Milan to study with the Opéra's world-famous teacher, Mme Dominique, turned out to be perfect for the role of the mischievious heroine – warm and gay, with a natural spontaneity tempered by the dignified French style.

Coppélia (subtitled 'The Girl with the Enamel Eyes') is the story of young Franz, who deserts his girlfriend, Swan-

Below and left: Arthur Saint-Léon's ever-popular ballet Coppélia *deals with the eccentric Dr Coppelius's attempts to instil life into his puppet creation.*

ilda, when he becomes infatuated by Coppélia. Swanilda sneaks into the house Coppélia shares with her father, an eccentric inventor, and discovers that her rival is, in fact, a doll. To her horror Franz appears and is drugged by the doctor. The scientist is determined to make Coppélia really live by transferring Franz's 'life force' to the puppet. Quickly Swanilda changes places with Coppélia and then pretends not only to come to life, but to go berserk upsetting everything in the laboratory. Eventually, of course, Franz revives and all ends happily.

Though the plot reads like a modern horror movie, Saint-Léon's production was a clever commentary on the dangers of infatuation. When the ballet finally opened in Paris in May 1870 it seemed, with its freshness and vitality, as if the art had been reborn in France. But in mid-July the Franco-Prussian War began and at the end of August the Opéra closed. Saint-Léon died on 2 September and on the 18th the Germans besieged the French capital.

During the Siege of Paris, dancers – like everyone else – coped as best they could. Some continued studying as long as they were strong enough and Mlle Beaugrand even installed a sloping floor in her apartment so that she could practice every day. She also organized groups to collect food and money for those in greater need, while others, like the re-tired ballerina Delphine Marquet, worked in a soldiers' hospital established in the basement of the Comédie Française. At the end of November, on her 17th birthday, Bozzacchi died of hunger and illness.

The end of the Siege in January 1871 was followed by an equally difficult time during the Paris Commune. Luckily, the Opéra managed to survive the holocaust which destroyed most public buildings when the insurrection was finally repressed in May. Soon after, the indefatigable Beaugrand opened in *Coppélia* – and did an excellent job after all.

The cult of the ballerina had grown to ridiculous proportions (to such an extent that the part of Franz in *Coppélia* was danced by a woman – Eugenie Fiocre). Not only male dancers but even music and choreography were subordinated to the creation of a vehicle for the prima ballerina. Neither the opening of the huge, sumptuous Palais Garnier in 1876 (after the old theater burned down in 1873), nor the lively dancing of a series of ballerinas, like Rita Sangalli, Rosita Mauri, Carlotta Zambelli and Aida Boni, could hide the fact that ballet had become a one-dimensional art form. The decline was exacerbated by the tremendous growth of ballet in Russia, which siphoned off many of France's best dancers and choreographers.

Then in 1909 a young Russian impre-

Adolph Bolm is chiefly remembered for his creation of the role of Prince Igor in Fokine's ballet for the Ballets Russes in 1909.

sario named Serge Diaghilev presented his new ballet company, Ballets Russes, for the first time. Though he had been coming to France since 1906 (with Russian art exhibitions, concerts and even operas), this was his first attempt to sell ballet. While his choreographer, the talented Michel Fokine, rehearsed the company, Diaghilev wrestled with constant financial crises and oversaw the cleaners, painters, electricians and decorators who were refurbishing the Théâtre du Châtelet. He also publicized the program in his own inimitable fashion, even sending complimentary tickets to the most beautiful actresses in Paris to add a glamorous touch to opening night.

On 18 May it seemed as if all Paris was on hand for the opening performance. Used to the insipid, dull Opéra programs, the audience was a bit skeptical, but by the end of the evening it was wildly enthusiastic. The program was a series of short ballets and the very first item, Fokine's revised version of *Le Pavillon d'Armide*, with Tamara Karsavina, Michel Mordkin and Vaslav Nijinsky, received a standing ovation. As the last number – the Polovtsian act from *Prince Igor* – ended, the crowd rushed the stage,

Vassilie Trunoff in a typically athletic leap from the London Festival Ballet production of Fokine's Prince Igor *to Borodin's music.*

David Wall and Jennifer Penney in the Royal Ballet production of Fokine's tribute to the Romantic era, Les Sylphides.

Julian Hosking and Monica Mason of the Royal Ballet in Fokine's Firebird *set to Stravinsky's first ballet score for Ballets Russes in 1910.*

tearing down the orchestra rail in its eagerness to congratulate the dancers. Fokine's vital choreography and Adolf Bolm's splendid performance in the warriors' dance had put the capstone on a night that heralded the rebirth of ballet in Western Europe.

For the next 20 years Ballets Russes toured Europe, outshining all other activities in the dance world. Diaghilev assembled an extraordinary collection of painters, composers, choreographers and dancers; collectively the company had a tremendous influence on all aspects of modern art.

Over the years almost all the great dancers of the period worked with Ballets Russes. Even Anna Pavlova danced with the troupe, appearing as Armida and in Fokine's *Les Sylphides* and *Cléopâtre*. Her presence was an important factor in Ballets Russes's early success, though she soon left the company to strike out on her own. The dancers who contributed most to the group's popularity in those first years were the charismatic Nijinsky and Karsavina, whose technical skill and talent for both poetic dancing and mime made her the perfect partner.

Diaghilev's skill in finding and developing exciting new choreographers was another big reason for his success. The first of his finds was Michel Fokine, whose exotic productions lured the first audiences to the Théâtre du Châtelet. In St Petersburg the young man had been bitter and discontented, chafing against the restrictions of the hidebound Imperial Theater system. In Paris his creativity burst out, resulting in works like the mysterious *Firebird*, set to Stravinsky's first ballet score; *Schéhérazade*, with Léon Bakst's extravagant, scandalous costumes and settings; *Cléopâtre*, in which the Egyptian queen entered in a sarcophagus, wrapped in veils like a mummy; the pathetic story of the puppet *Petrouchka*, told against the backdrop of a gay carnival; and his tribute to the Romantic era, *Les Sylphides*, one of the first abstract ballets.

Fokine did more than arouse new interest with his ballets, he also made substantial contributions to the development

Alexander Grant as Petrouchka, Nadia Nerina as the ballerina and Keith Rosson as the Moor in the Royal Ballet production of Fokine's ballet.

Fokine's Schéhérezade *caused a furore with its sensuous choreography and Bakst's risqué designs which had a great effect on fashion.*

Leon Bakst's sumptuous design for the costume of the Firebird which Tamara Karsavina wore on the opening night partnered by Fokine himself.

his own dances, reminiscent of some primitive animal.

In May 1913 *Jeux*, starring Nijinsky, Karsavina and Ludmilla Schollar, was produced. This work was based on a modern theme, exploring the relationships between three tennis players. That same year Paris was scandalized again, this time by Nijinsky's masterpiece, *Le Sacre du Printemps*. Diaghilev had encouraged him to compose a ballet to Stravinsky's score, even hiring a bright young student from the Dalcroze School of Eurythmics, Marie Rambert, to help him work out the movements. The ballet depicts a ceremony in which the 'Chosen Maiden' dances herself to death as a sacrifice to the gods. It had a prehistoric setting and a pagan atmosphere emphasized by Nijinsky's strange, non-classical movements. During its four Paris performances it sent many in the audience walking back up the aisles. The great Cecchetti, when Diaghilev asked his opinion about the work, bluntly replied: 'I think it is the work of four fools: M Stravinsky, M Bakst, M Nijinsky and M Diaghilev, who spent so much money on it.' The choreography has long been completely lost, though Richard Buckle has tried to reconstruct what it must have been like in his book, *Nijinsky*. Diaghilev, who was an avowed homosexual, made no secret of his infatuation

of the art as a whole. In his productions men returned to an equal level with ballerinas and the *corps de ballet* became an integral part of the action. He combined dancing, music and choreography to develop themes that expressed complex emotions rather than just a plot.

Fokine did not stay with Ballets Russes for long, primarily because he did not like having to compete with Diaghilev's protégé, Nijinsky. Nijinsky was more interested in exploring Russian prehistory than in aping Fokine's sumptuous spectaculars. In 1912 Paris was shocked by his 11-minute ballet, *L'Après-midi d'un faune*. The dance tells the story of a group of nymphs who meet a faun, flirt with him, then become frightened and run away as he becomes aroused. As they flee, the principal nymph drops her veil and the episode ends as the faun lowers himself on it – an ending many considered obscene. All the dancers except the two main characters were barefoot in this production and moved in profile to the audience along a narrow path, like Greek friezes. Nijinsky himself devised a strange, flat-footed, jerky movement for

Apollo, one of the two ballets by George Balanchine from his time with Ballets Russes which is still performed today. This is the Royal Ballet version.

Vaslav Nijinsky in L'Après-midi d'un Faune. *His ballet caused a scandal with its frieze-like choreography and sexual connotations.*

with Nijinsky and when the dancer had the temerity to marry while on an overseas tour, he was immediately fired. His place was taken by Leonide Massine, a good character dancer, who blossomed into a gifted choreographer under Diaghilev's guidance, ushering in an era of witty, cosmopolitan ballets. Some of his best works include: the eighteenth-century-style comedy *Les Femmes de Bonne Humeur* (1917); *Le Tricorne* (1919), which tells the old story of a lecherous duke foiled by a virtuous wife; and *La Boutique Fantasque* (1919), another tale of dolls come to life. *Parade* (1917) set out to prove that ballet could be fun. Jean Cocteau's story and Erik Satie's score (which included the sound of typewriters and steamship whistles) were modern and clever; Picasso's sets and huge cubist costumes added an extra dimension to Massine's burlesque of the circus and music hall. The ballet became a landmark in the history of the company, setting the tone for many of its future productions and also sparking Picasso's lifelong interest in ballet.

Massine was succeeded by Nijinsky's sister, Bronislava Nijinska (1891–1972). The first performance of *Les Noces* in July 1923 – a moving enactment of a Russian peasant wedding, set to words and music by Stravinsky – established the already well-known dancer as an exciting choreographer. In 1924 the com-

pany performed three more of her ballets. *Les Biches*, a parody of the Riviera smart set, was first performed in Monte Carlo; another sophisticated comedy, *Le Train Bleu*, was written by Cocteau and starred Anton Dolin and *Les Fâcheux*, based on Molière's *comedie-ballet*, was designed by Georges Braque.

George Balanchine was Ballets Russes's last choreographer, joining the company in 1924 after Diaghilev had lured him away from a touring Soviet dance troupe. In his four years with the company he choreographed 10 ballets, including *Le Triomphe de Neptune* (1926) and *La Chatte* (1927). The only two that are still performed, however, are *Les Fils Prodigue* and *Apollo*.

In 1929 Diaghilev died in Venice and Ballets Russes died with him. Almost unaided, the impresario had pulled ballet out of the doldrums and reestablished it as a vital, serious art. But without him the company could no longer exist, and its dancers soon scattered all over the world. In the long run, this proved to be a good thing; a significant number of today's ballet troupes were begun by dancers who started their careers with Ballets Russes.

The august Paris Opéra, like any other long-established official institution, had been slow to react to the exciting new developments begun by Ballets Russes in 1909, even though the Opéra Ballet did regain some popularity as a side effect of Diaghilev's success. In 1914 Jacques Rouché was appointed director of the Opéra and, as soon as World War I ended, he set out to build a new, revitalized ballet program. He invited Pavlova to star in *La Péri* and revived *Giselle* for Olga Spessivtseva, who overwhelmed audiences with her intense portrayal of

the title role. He had two excellent resident choreographers, Fokine (who produced *Daphnis et Chloë* in 1921) and Nijinska.

By 1929 Rouché's efforts were beginning to bear fruit; the Opéra Ballet was much stronger, though it could not yet compete with the Opéra itself. Immediately after Diaghilev's death, therefore, the director hired Balanchine to choreograph a new ballet to Beethoven's *The Creatures of Prometheus*. However, Balanchine became ill and after the first few rehearsals the production was taken over by the principal male lead, another Ballets Russes alumnus named Serge Lifar. His efforts were so successful that he remained permanently at the Opéra as both dancer and choreographer until 1959, stabilizing and strengthening the company, adding new numbers to the repertory and restoring much of its traditional prestige.

Paris's position in the ballet world was further enhanced after the Russian Revolution when several notable teachers emigrated and opened schools there, among them Mathilde Kschessinska, Vera Trefilova (1875–1943), Lubov Egorova (1880–1972) and Olga Preobrajenska.

Eventually many of the best Ballets Russes members made their way to Monte Carlo, where René Blum (1884–1944) and Colonel Wassili de Basil (Wassili Gregorievitch Voskresensky, 1888–1951) were running the tiny Monte Carlo Opéra. With this nucleus, plus new dancers from the Paris schools, the two formed Ballets Russes de Monte Carlo in 1932.

Balanchine, their first choreographer, prepared two productions for that first season – *La Concurrence* and *Cotillon* – then departed for New York. He was re-

Nathalie Goncharova's design for Bronislava Nijinska's Les Noces, *a ballet set to Stravinsky's score of four pianos and a chorus.*

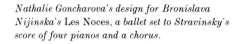

placed by Massine. The company was especially famous in its early years for its star, Alexandra Danilova, and the 'baby ballerinas' – Irina Baronova, Tatiana Riabouchinska and Tamara Toumanova – whose youth (they were only 14 to 15 years old) and technical ability made them overwhelmingly popular, especially when combined with the Colonel's publicity campaign.

Blum and de Basil were never able to build a ballet empire that matched Diaghilev's – not only because they were trying to imitate the inimitable, but be-

Left: In 1966 Nijinska, at Ashton's invitation, revived Les Noces *for the Royal Ballet with the original decor and Svetlana Beriosova in the lead.*

Below: l to r Rudolf Nureyev, Vergie Derman (kneeling), Vyvyan Lorrayne and Svetlana Beriosova in Balanchine's Apollo, *Royal Ballet.*

Tamara Toumanova, one of de Basil's original three baby ballerinas, in La Esmeralda. *She danced with many companies and made several films.*

cause they lacked his organizational ability. The company's history is a long series of disputes between cliques, jealousies and legal battles. In 1938 Blum and Massine broke off and formed Le Ballets Russes de Monte Carlo, while de Basil and Fokine carried on with Les Ballets Russes du Colonel de Basil.

De Basil soon changed the name of his company to Original Ballet Russe and set off for South America. After the war the group returned to Europe and soon dissolved. Ballets Russes de Monte Carlo, meanwhile, went to the United States where it soon became virtually an American company (a transition marked by the production of Agnes de Mille's *Rodeo*, to music by Aaron Copeland, in 1942). Blum (brother of the French Socialist leader, Léon Blum) returned to Europe during the war and died in a Nazi concentration camp. The company, however, continued to tour in America until 1963.

Surprisingly, ballet flourished in France during World War II. At the Opéra Lifar was at his most creative, showing works like *Le Chevalier et la Demoiselle* (1941), *Joan de Zarissa* (1942) and *Suite en Blanc* (1943) to capacity houses. Much of his success was due to the appearance of three excellent ballerinas: Yvette Chauviré (b 1917), whose sensational performance in Lifar's *Istar* rocketed her to

Right: Yvette Chauvire, greatest French dancer of this century, premiere danseuse étoile *of the Paris Opéra and holder of the* Legion d'Honneur.

stardom as the greatest French classical ballerina of her time; the blond, athletic Lysette Darsonval (b 1912); and Solange Schwartz (b 1910), a specialist in *demi-caractère* whose best remembered role is Swanilda in *Coppélia*.

Many other dancers gathered in Monte Carlo where, in 1942, they formed Les Nouveaux Ballets de Monte Carlo. The dancers included the elegant Ludmilla Tscherina (b 1924), Genevieve Kergrist, Marie-Louise Dideon and Gerard Mulys (b 1915). Classes were run by Julia Sedova (1880–1970) and Gustave Ricaux (1884–1961). In 1944 the company was reorganized as Nouveau Ballet de Monte Carlo, with Lifar as artistic director, choreographer and dancer. With the addition of other dancers, like Chauviré, Renée Jeanmaire (b 1924), Janine Charrat (b 1924) and the dark, romantic Wladimar Skouratoff (b 1925), the troupe prospered. In 1947 Lifar and Chauviré returned to the Opéra, while the Marquis de Cuevas took over the company.

Far right: Janine Charrat, French dancer and choreographer who started her own company, in Pavlova's immortal role, The Dying Swan.

Lifar's second stay at the Opéra (1947–59) produced several important ballets. *Les Mirages* (1947) is the story of a young man who pursues riches and love, only to find himself, at the end, alone with his shadow; *Phaedre* (1950) is a tragic tale based on an outline by Jean Cocteau; while *Les Noces Fantastiques* (1958) is a brooding Celtic drama.

In 1951 the Dane, Harald Lander, joined the Opéra as choreographer-in-residence and in 1959 he took over directorship of the school. Since Lifar's departure there has been a succession of directors and choreographers, including George Skibine, Michel Descombey (who produced a controversial new version of *Coppélia*) and Roland Petit (whose 1965 presentation of *Notre Dame de Paris* was very successful).

In 1972, Cuban ballerina Alicia Alonso staged a new *Swan Lake*. Heinz Spoerli, director of Switzerland's Basel Ballet, staged a rollicking rendition of *La Fille Mal Gardée* in 1981. Nureyev mounted a new *Don Quichotte* in the same year.

American-born, former ballerina Rosella Hightower was director of the Opéra (1981–83). Her new productions included

The Can-Can scene from the revival of Leonide Massine's Gaîté Parisienne *for the International Ballet of the Marquis de Cuevas in 1958.*

an elaborate multimedia version of *The Sleeping Beauty* and an unfortunate, failed version of *The Nutcracker*.

Since his 1983 appointment as artistic director, Rudolf Nureyev has rejuvenated the Opéra. His new stagings include a delightful *Cinderella* (1986) which transports the fairy tale to Hollywood in the 1930s. Cinderella's pumpkin turns into a golden Cadillac and the Prince becomes a matinée idol searching for a new leading lady.

Pierre Lacotte (b 1932) is a specialist in nineteenth-century ballets. He mounted *Marco Spada* (originally choreographed for the Opéra in 1856) in 1984. A tale of bandits, kidnappings and true love, Lacotte's production brims over with authentic mid-nineteenth-century set pieces.

Contemporary ballet at the Opéra has been featured in works by Tetley, Béjart, Neumeier and Merce Cunningham. Several Balanchine ballets continue to enhance the repertory.

In 1981 a modern offshoot of the Opéra was formed to foster experimentation. Known as GRCOP (Groupe de Recherche Choreographic de l'Opéra de Paris), this company of a dozen dancers is under the direction of Jacques Garnier. Leaders of the international avant-garde (Cunningham, Lucinda Childs, Michael Clark) and young French choreographers, such as Maguy Marin, have all contributed inventive new works.

Since the war, however, most of the interesting work in France has been done by smaller companies. Les Ballets des Champs Elysées was founded in 1945 by Boris Kochno (who had been Diaghilev's secretary). Cocteau and Christian Bérard, and gave a start to two young choreographers – Roland Petit and Janine Charrat. One of Petit's most successful early ballets was *Le Jeune Homme et la Mort*. Lichine's *Creation* (1950), which was danced in practice clothes, in total silence, was one of the group's biggest successes, just before it disbanded. Ballets des Champs Elysées's bright, sophisticated

Left: Diagramme, *an abstract ballet choreographed by Janine Charrat to Bach music for de Cuevas's company.*

Right: André Prokovsky, *ex-Charrat dancer, and his wife, Galina Samsova, in John Taras's* Piège de Lumière, *first performed in 1952.*

productions were very popular in both Paris and London; dancers included Petit, his wife Jeanmaire, Jean Babilée, Youly Algaroff, Vyroubov, Colette Marchand and Irene Skorik.

The International Ballet was owned by the Marquis de Cuevas, who strengthened the former Nouveau Ballet de Monte Carlo with new ballets and new dancers, like Rosella Hightower, Marjorie Tallchief, André Eglevsky and George Skibine, and the company soon became a fixture of the Paris ballet season. The company concentrated mainly on new ballets by choreographers like Massine, Nijinska, Balanchine, Lichine, Lander, Charrat and John Cranko. Some of its best productions were John Taras's *Piège de Lumière* (1952) and Skibine's *Annabel Lee*, *Idylle* and *Prisoner of the Caucasus*. Unfortunately this company, like Diaghilev's, was too much the creation of its flamboyant owner and did not last long after the Marquis's death in 1961.

Far left: Marjorie Tallchief, American dancer of Indian descent with husband George Skibine in his version of Fokine's Daphnis and Chloë.

Left: Colette Marchand and Milorad Miskovitch, the Yugoslav dancer, in Antony Tudor's one-act ballet, Soirée Musicale.

Below left: Rosella Hightower, great American dancer of Red Indian descent who danced with Ballets Russes and de Cuevas. She now runs a school in Cannes, France.

Ballets de Paris de Roland Petit, founded in 1948 after Petit left Ballets des Champs Elysées, opened in Paris with Les Demoiselles de la Nuit (featuring guest artist Margot Fonteyn as a cat). Soon the group's sophisticated, sensual productions had all Paris buzzing, and Carmen, which used parts of Bizet's opera score, made Jeanmaire an overnight sensation. Another successful production was Le Loup, the story of a werewolf and the girl who loves him.

Roland Petit (b 1924) became the director of the Ballet National de Marseille in 1972 and firmly consolidated his position as France's most popular (and prolific) choreographer. His evening-length works are highly theatrical spectacles, supported by stunning designs.

Petit's most successful recent works include Proust – Les Intermittences de Coeur (1974). Filled with dream sequences inspired by episodes from Remembrances of Things Past, this is an elegaic and often erotic personalized vision of la belle époque. In 1980 Petit created The Phantom of the Opéra for the Paris Opéra Ballet. The original production featured Peter Schaufuss in the title role.

Petit was one of the few Western choreographers to work behind the Iron Curtain; his La Rose Malade (1973) was staged for Maya Pliesetskaya of the Bolshoi Ballet.

Since the late 1960s there has been increasing activity in the provinces, especially in Nancy, Amiens, Lyons, Grenoble, Strasbourg and Angers. Paris is still one of the most important cultural centers in Europe and continues to attract both traditional and modern companies. One of its most popular events is the annual Festival International de Danse (begun in 1963).

Right: Roland Petit's Carmen, a production for his own Ballet de Marseille, with Danielle Jossi as Carmen and Denys Ganio as Don Jose.

Suzanne Farrell in Maurice Béjart's Ballet of the 20th Century production of The Rite of Spring.

Jorge Donn, premier danseur *of the Béjart company as Nijinsky in* Nijinsky, Clown of God.

Suzanne Farrell and Jorge Donn in Nijinsky, Clown of God, *in which all his greatest roles are embodied – the Faun, the Golden Slave and so on.*

Far left: Ballet Theater Contemporain's work Bakyla with choreography by Felix Blaska and decigns by Karel Appel.

Left: Petit's Ballet de Marseille production, La Rose Malade with Maya Plisetskaya of the Bolshoi to music by Mahler and decor by St Laurent.

Below: Hopop a pop art ballet for the now defunct Ballet Theater Contemporain (1968–78) with choreography by Dirk Sanders and costumes after Guy Pellaert set to pop music.

CATHERINE DE MEDICI
1519–89

Catherine de Medici was only 14 when she arrived in Paris as the bride of the duc d'Orleans (who became Henry II), but it was not until 1560, after the death of her husband and eldest son (Francis II) that this daughter of the Medicis came into her own as regent for her son, Charles IX.

The daughter of Lorenzo, Duke of Urbino, and great-granddaughter of Lorenzo the Magnificent, Catherine had all her forebearers' skill for intrigue and power politics. For almost 30 years she was the virtual ruler of France while Charles IX and Henry III succeeded each other on the throne.

Catherine was a remarkable woman; autocratic, self-indulgent and highly intelligent, she devoted most of her energy toward preserving the power of the monarchy in the midst of the religious conflicts of the time. With her Italian love of spectacle and her almost instinctive knowledge of its uses, she was also an enthusiastic patron of *balli*, or lavish court entertainments.

These pageants, produced by her dancing master, Baldassarino de Belgiojoso, marked important events and impressed visiting dignitaries with the power and magnificence of the French court. For example, in 1573 *Le Ballet aux ambassadeurs Polonais* celebrated the accession of Henry III to the throne of Poland, while in 1581 the famous *Ballet Comique de la Reine* was part of the festivities surrounding the marriage of Queen Louise's sister, Marguerite of Lorraine.

Another reason for having Belgiojoso stage these and many smaller affairs was to keep her sons' minds occupied with something other than the business of governing the country – a task which, from all accounts, was not at all difficult.

BALDASSARINO DI BELGIOJOSO
d 1587

Belgiojoso was an almost penniless Italian immigrant when he arrived in Paris in 1555 with a group of Piedmontese violinists, all in the service of the Maréchal de Brissac. But his knowledge of music and dance – and most of all his organiza-tional ability – soon brought him to the attention of the queen, Catherine de Medici. Within a short time he had become one of her personal servants and, when she attained real power after the death of Henry II, he was placed in charge of all court entertainments.

We know that he participated in a masquerade called *Défense du Paradise* in 1572, but his most famous productions are *Le Ballet aux ambassadeurs Polonais* (1573) and *Ballet Comique de la Reine* (1581). Though these works would have been considered old-fashioned in Italy, they made a great impression on the other princes of Northern Europe, enhancing the reputation of both the French monarchy and, of course, Belgiojoso himself.

In 1584 the dancing master, who had some years previously changed his name to the more French-sounding Balthasar de Beaujoyeaux, retired to rest on his laurels for the three years remaining in his life.

JEAN BAPTISTE LULLY
1632–87

Lully was born Giovanni Battista Lulli in Florence in 1632. As a boy he became an excellent comic dancer and taught himself to play the violin. By the time he arrived in France at the age of 14, he was already well versed in composition and dance, as well as in the standard characters from *commedia del l'arte* like the

Jean Baptiste Lully, favorite of Louis XIV.

acrobatic Arlecchino (Harlequin), the greedy Brighella, Pedrolino (Pierrot) the dreamer, and the dwarfish, cruel Pulcinella (Punch). In 1652 he entered the service of Louis XIV, who, it is said, would laugh till he cried when Lully danced.

Within a very short time he had ruthlessly worked his way into a position of extraordinary power at court, dominating almost all musical activities as leading dancer, chamber composer, conductor of one of the king's orchestras and, in due course, director (or dictator) of the Opéra from 1672.

His work, in collaboration with Beauchamps, Molière, Phillipe Quinault and many others, had a tremendous effect on virtually every aspect of French theater: music, opera, drama and, of course, ballet. His demand for increasingly sophisticated and difficult dancing in his productions also fostered the increased use of professional rather than amateur dancers.

PIERRE BEAUCHAMPS
?1631 – 1705

Pierre Beauchamps, Louis XIV's dancing teacher and one of the most famous dancer/choreographers of his day, was only a few years older than his powerful pupil, and was just 19 in 1850 when the young monarch put him in charge of all court ballets and entertainments.

At that time there was no formal dance vocabulary, but by the 1660s Beauchamps had begun to codify the popular court ballroom steps. The result was the development of the five standard foot positions which have been used in ballet since at least 1700. Although the steps bore little resemblance to any movements we see today, they are the direct ancestors of the modern *danse d'école*. In 1672 he was appointed director of the Opéra's dancing school, where his efforts produced France's first professional dancers. He resigned the post in 1687, after Lully's death, but continued to do research and to teach.

As a dancer, Beauchamps was noted for his noble carriage and for his technical skill (he is said to have been among the first to perform *tours en l'air*). He was also an important choreographer, whose career spans the transition from ballroom presentations, with their emphasis on patterns and formations, to stage productions. Much of his work was done in collaboration with Lully and Molière; their best-remembered work is *Le Bourgeois Gentilhomme* (1670).

LOUIS DUPRE
1697–1774

Louis Dupré began his career in Mans as a dancing teacher before moving to Paris, where, from 1715–51, he was the most acclaimed soloist at the Opéra.

His imposing manner, graceful carriage and splendid physique – qualities he retained into his sixties – earned him the title 'Le Grand Dupré'; he was also known, only half-mockingly, as 'the god of the dance.' Until 1743 he was in charge of the Opéra's school, counting Vestris and Noverre among his pupils.

One of his greatest admirers was Casanova, who has left us the following description of one of his performances:

'Advancing with measured tread and having reached the footlights, slowly raising his rounded arms . . . moving his feet lightly and precisely, taking small steps, battements on the calf, a pirouette, and then disappearing like a zephyr. All this had lasted half a minute.'

It may sound rather odd to admirers of Nureyev or Baryshnikov, but no doubt the crowds were enthusiastic.

MARIE SALLE
1707–56

Marie Sallé was a true child of the theater, born into a large family of travelling animal trainers, puppeteers, jugglers, singers, actors and dancers. She made her official debut in October 1716, dancing with her brother at Lincoln's Inn Fields in London.

When the family moved back to France, Sallé was enrolled in the Opéra school, where she studied with famous dancers like Prévost, Balon and Blondi. In 1725 she and her brother began another two-year engagement at Lincoln's Inn Fields,

dancing in pantomimes or entertaining audiences between acts.

In 1727 she returned to Paris, but her stay was not a success. She missed her brother, and her personality – quiet, reserved and sincere – was not at all suited to the competitive, backbiting, backstage world of the Opéra. Though she had a devoted following in Paris (which included Voltaire), she was extremely unhappy about the furore over over her much-publicized rivalry with Camargo.

Sallé's art was all-important to her, and here again she found the Opéra lacking. Her complaints about the restrictive, unsuitable costumes then in vogue, with their long, heavy skirts, corsets and high-heeled shoes, fell on deaf ears. At the end of 1732 she resigned from the Opéra in disgust.

Her popularity in England had never waned and the 1733–34 season found her back in London where John Rich, former manager at Lincoln's Inn Fields, had just taken over a new theater at Covent Garden. The engagement was a total triumph, with Sallé not only dancing, but

An engraving from a painting by Lancret of Marie Sallé, great French dancer of the 18th century.

arranging dances as well, thus becoming one of the first female choreographers. Crowds fought in the streets to see *Pygmalion* and her next creation, *Bacchus and Ariadne*. Much of the excitement was caused by her costume rather than her dancing; for *Pygmalion* she was able to finally abandon her heavy skirts and appear in a simple muslin shift and heelless slippers, with her hair falling about her shoulders.

The 1734–35 season began well, with her arrangement of Handel's only complete ballet, *Terpsichore*. But then scandal erupted when her relationship with another dancer, Mlle Manon Grognet, was discovered. Most of her audience, and even her friends, were enraged to find that her famous chastity was the result of her sexual preferences rather than a high moral character, and her appearance in April 1735 in *Alcina*, dressed as a boy, drew hisses and boos.

In August she began her last engagement in Paris. In many respects the situation had improved: Camargo was in temporary retirement; Sallé acquired the best partner of her entire career in David Dumoulin; and she was able to dance in ballets by Jean-Phillipe Rameau, including *Les Indes Galantes*, even incorporating some of her own choreographic ideas.

Despite a more satisfactory working atmosphere and rekindled popularity, Sallé still found the Opéra management rigid and devoted to mediocrity. In 1740 she settled down in an apartment on the Rue Saint-Honore with her friend Rebecca Wick and – but for occasional appearances – enjoyed a quiet, happy retirement.

MARIE-ANNE DE CUPIS DE CAMARGO
1710–70

Marie Camargo was born in Brussels; her father, the son of a well-known Roman family which had fallen on hard times, was a successful dancing master and violinist at the court. (Camargo is a Spanish name, taken from her maternal grandmother.) Like her rival, Marie Sallé, Camargo was a child prodigy. When she was only 10 the ladies of the Belgian court collected money to send her to Paris to study with the famous Françoise Prévost.

On her return she danced with the

Marie-Anne de Cupis de Camargo, great rival of Marie Sallé, noted for her lightness of style.

Brussels Opera until 1726, when she made her debut in Paris, where Prévost, ever mindful of dangerous young rivals, placed her in the back row of the *corps de ballet*. But at the first opportunity, when one of the Dumoulin brothers failed to appear on cue, Camargo came forward and danced his part, with an élan that brought the audience to its feet.

Unlike Sallé, Camargo (whose spirit was as fiery as her dancing) had no trouble making her way in the decadent, worldly atmosphere of the Opéra; she probably enjoyed the trumped-up rivalry and managed to juggle the usual long string of lovers. In 1733 she became the mistress of Louis de Bourbon, Comte de Clermont. The two were devoted to each other and Camargo even retired for six years at his request. By 1741, however, he had found another ballerina and she was back at the Opéra, where during the next 10 years she appeared in 78 different ballets. She was the darling of the capital, and hairstyles, fashions, even culinary creations were named after her.

Camargo was an outstanding technician, especially celebrated for her *entrechats*, and her dancing had a speed and virtuosity that had never been seen in a woman before; the quick brilliance and gaiety of her performances made onlookers forget her rather unsatisfactory figure and lack of real grace. Not surprisingly, she was unwilling to hide her light steps and high jumps under the Opéra's regulation costumes. Audiences were properly scandalized when she shortened her skirts (even though she wore a *calecon de precaution* – rather like

bloomers) and donned heelless slippers, but they came in even greater numbers to watch her dance.

In 1751 Camargo retired to an apartment on the Rue Saint-Honoré, where she lived for the next 19 years with the last of her lovers and a menagerie of pets. Despite her unconventional life and the disapproval of the church where dancers were concerned, her death was marked by a magnificent funeral at the Eglise Saint-Roch, which included a eulogy praising her as 'a model of modesty, charity, and decent conduct.'

JEAN-GEORGES NOVERRE
1727–1810

Jean Noverre, one of the most influential figures in the early history of ballet, was unusual in that his parents did not guide him into dance as a career. His Swiss father was anxious for him to become a soldier, though he himself was determined from an early age to become a dancer.

As a young man he studied with Louis Dupré at the Opéra, then instead of joining the company, set out to wander Europe. In Berlin he did imitations of famous ballerinas for a hugely amused Frederick the Great; in the French provinces (especially Marseilles and Lyons) he danced, choreographed and began developing his theories about what ballet was and what it should be.

Eventually he wound up back in Paris,

Jean-Georges Noverre, great reformer of ballet.

where he obtained the position of ballet master at the city's second opera house, the Opéra Comique. There, in 1754, he had his first big success with the exotic *Les Fêtes Chinoises*. The next year David Garrick invited him to London to stage the production at Drury Lane. Unfortunately, the timing could not have been worse. It was the beginning of the French-English War and the loyal Londoners, who could not stomach anything French (or even half-French), rioted. On the fifth and sixth nights of the run they caused so much damage that the production was finally withdrawn.

In 1757 Noverre was in Lyons again, where he wrote and published his *Letters on Dancing and Ballet* (1760). By this time he was able to argue clearly and concisely for what he called *ballet d'action* – productions in which every element contributed to the overall dramatic theme. For example, he maintained, technical exhibitionism should be replaced by expressive and realistic dancing; the inappropriate costumes of the time should give way to 'light and flowing draperies' and heelless slippers; masks, of course, were barriers that had to be removed.

In 1760, soon after publication of his treatise, he was invited to Stuttgart to act as the Duke of Württemburg's ballet master. There, with a good theater, competent dancers, composers and designers, and plenty of money, he was able to produce several excellent ballets, including *Medée et Jason*. He remained in Stuttgart until 1767, when he moved to Vienna. There he did much to reform the Austrian company and also had a chance to work with Gluck (choreographing the dance scenes for the opera *Alceste*).

Then in 1776 he achieved his ambition.

At the insistence of a former pupil, Marie Antoinette, he was named ballet master of the Paris Opéra. In October he mounted his first production, *Apelles et Campaspe*, with the magnificent Anne Heinl, whose performance even managed to gloss over most of the errors perpetrated by Maximilien Gardel (who was angry that he had not been given the job). It was only the beginning of an exasperating five-year term, which turned into a continuous battle with his enemies.

Finally in 1781 he resigned the post and for some years commuted to London from his home in St Germain en Laye, outside Paris. But during the Revolution (1789) he lost all his money as well as his pension. For the rest of his life he remained at St Germain, writing, commenting on affairs at the Opéra and gardening.

THE VESTRIS FAMILY

The name Vestris dominates the history of the Paris Opéra for more than half a century, from Louis XIV to Napoleon. Although the most famous members of this dancing dynasty were Gaetano and his son Auguste, the Vestris' were such a close-knit clan that even today they can only be considered together.

Their story begins in 1747 when Mme Vestris arrived in Paris from Italy with

Gaetano Vestris, head of the Vestris clan.

five of her eight children: Gaetano, Thérèse (Marie-Francoise Thérèse, 1766–1808), Angiolo, Jean-Baptiste and Violante. While Jean-Baptiste (whom his siblings called 'The Cook') stayed at home and kept house, the others were soon gainfully employed. Violante sang in court concerts, while Gaetano, Thérèse and Angiolo found jobs as dancers at the Opéra.

Angiolo did not stay long. Four years after his debut he resigned and in 1761 moved to Württemburg as *premier danseur*. There, away from the overwhelming competition with his older brother, he was able to work productively and happily with Noverre.

Thérèse's talents as a ballerina were minimal, but her capacity for intrigue was enormous – and both qualities were outshone by her skill in the bedroom. In fact, her main career was that of a courtesan. Though her position as Gaetano's sister guaranteed her a job at the Opéra for as long as she wanted, she gave up the stage in 1766 and devoted her energy to her lovers, often juggling up to four or five at a time.

Their elder brother, Gaetano (1729–1808), quickly became enormously popular in serious, heroic roles; his light, precise and above all noble dancing made everyone else look second-rate. His talent was matched only by his vanity, which was phenomenal, and his quarrelsome nature; his Opéra career was a constant series of pitched battles with the management and the other dancers. Periodically, when their scheming grew intolerable, he and Thérèse would be banished, but he was always allowed to return.

Gaetano's private life was a series of liaisons, notably with Marie Allard, who bore his son Auguste. In 1776 he was replaced as Opéra ballet master by Noverre; in 1782 he finally retired to live with his former rival, the German ballerina Anne Heinl. Their son, Apollon, was born in 1791 and the following year the two were married.

Auguste (1760–1842), meanwhile, was well embarked on a career that would span 35 years as *premier danseur*. He inherited his father's arrogance as well as his sensitive musical ear, but his dancing style was quite different. Though he was short, his technique was excellent, featuring remarkable elevation and notable *entrechats* and pirouettes. He was also very adaptable to varying moods or styles and, best of all, he made it all look easy; there was never a suggestion of effort or strain in his performance. Soon he was recognized as the world's greatest dancer – a situation even his prickly father was able to accept with equanimity. 'Of course,' said Gaetano, 'Gaetano Vestris was his father – an advantage that was denied me.' In 1816 he retired officially and devoted his time to teaching, although in 1835, at the age of 75, he made his last appearance on stage partnering the 31-year-old Marie Taglioni.

The Vestris family's most notable characteristic was devotion – to each other and probably to no one else. They presented a united front in public and even in private preferred each other's company. When Gaetano was imprisoned in Fort l'Eveque for a month, Thérèse boycotted the Opéra and visited him every day. And when Auguste was sent to jail (also for insupportable insubordination), his uncle Jean-Baptiste actually went along to keep him company.

The group even managed to stay together in death. Gaetano, his wife and Thérèse all died within a few months of each other, and Angiolo passed away soon after.

THE GARDEL BROTHERS

The two Gardel brothers, Maximilien (1741–87) and Pierre (1758–1840), were also a force to be reckoned with at the Opéra in the late eighteenth and early nineteenth centuries.

Their father was ballet master to Stanislas, King of Poland, so both boys grew up in the world of court ballet. Maximilien is most famous for having been the first male dancer to appear on stage without a mask (in 1772) to show the audience that he was dancing in place of his great rival, Gaetano Vestris. He expected to be rewarded for his long service to the Opéra by being appointed ballet master after Vestris, and his resentment at Noverre's appointment was bitter and implacable. In 1781 he and his allies (especially Madeline Guimard) managed to force Noverre's resignation and Maximilien finally got the post of ballet master, which he held until his death in 1787.

In addition to dancing, he also choreo-

Maximilien Gardel, ballet master of the Opéra.

graphed many ballets for the company, including *La Chercheuse d'Esprit* (1777), *Ninette à la Cour* (1778), *Mirza et Lindor* (1779), *Le Deserteur* and *Le Rosière* (both 1784), *Le Premier Navigateur* (1785) and *Le Coq du Village* (1787).

When Pierre took over his brother's post in 1787 he had already been a soloist with the Opéra for seven years. He was to remain as ballet master for 40 more, in addition to running the school from 1799–1815.

He was a respected teacher (with pupils that included Carlo Blasis) and the works he choreographed were an important part of the repertory. Some of the most popular were: *Télémaque dans l'Ile de Calypso* (1790), *Psyche* (1790), *Le Jugement de Paris* (1793), *La Dansomanie* (1800), *Achille à Scyros* (1806) and *Paul et Virginie* (1806).

MARIE ALLARD
1742–1802

Although Marie Allard is best remembered today as the mother of Auguste Vestris, she was also a well-loved ballerina in her own right. Her life had an inauspicious start in the slums of Marseilles with her poor, corrupt, greedy parents. When she was only 10 her mother sold her to an elderly rake, but four years later she turned up in Paris where she found a job at the Comédie Française.

Her great ambition was to become a ballerina, so as soon as she could she began studying with Gaetano Vestris.

Auguste Vestris's career lasted over 35 years.

The great dancer was enchanted, not only by the girl's dancing, but by her personality; against all odds she was gay, warmhearted and totally charming. Her many affairs usually ended in friendship and were never tainted by obvious commercialism.

In 1760 (at the age of 17) she gave birth to Vestris's son, which meant that her debut had to be postponed for a year. But when she finally appeared (in *Zaïs*, 1761), the audience fell in love with her sparkling style and vivacious personality.

For the next 10 years she continued to cheer Parisians, appearing in some 35 different rôles; she was also increasingly busy helping Gaetano train Auguste. In September 1772 they watched from the wings as the boy, now 12½, made his debut. With them was Jean Dauberval, another of her lovers, who exclaimed, 'What talent! He's Vestris's son, not mine. Alas, he missed being mine by a mere fifteen minutes!'

As her son's career began to rise, Allard's started to decline; a lack of will power when it came to both sex and food led to several more pregnancies and a serious weight problem. Eventually she was simply too fat to dance, even in an age that admired plumpness; and in 1780 she retired to the suburbs. There she became tremendously obese and died in 1802 of a stroke caused by overweight.

JEAN DAUBERVAL
1742–1806

Jean Dauberval, who was born Jean Bercher, graduated from the Paris Opéra school in 1761 and rose rapidly in the company; he was made *premier danseur demi-caractère* in 1763, *premier danseur noble* in 1770 and *maître de ballet* in 1771. He cultivated a humorous, flirtatious dancing style that was very popular and which was described by Noverre as having 'wit, taste and intelligence.'

His career as a dancer in those early years was equalled only by his career as a lover – in which he was so adept that Parisian wits credited him with a 'masters degree in philandering.'

If Noverre admired Dauberval's dancing, he in turn was strongly influenced by Noverre's theories on *ballet d'action*, especially the importance of naturalness in both mime and dance. Though he remained with the Opéra after Noverre's unhappy departure, he was soon persuaded by his wife, Mlle Theodore, to seek

Jean Dauberval, dancer, teacher and choreographer.

his own fortune elsewhere. (Once he was finally married he proved to be a loyal, devoted husband.)

In 1785 the two moved to Bordeaux where, in 1789, he produced his most famous ballet. *La Fille Mal Gardée*, a two-act ballet-pantomime, is one of only two eighteenth-century productions in the modern repertory, and was one of the first ballets about ordinary people in real situations. Dauberval was also an influential teacher, including Salvatore Viganó and Charles Didelot among his pupils.

MADELINE GUIMARD
1743–1816

Despite her pockmarked face and unfashionable thin figure (she was nicknamed 'The Skeleton of the Graces'), Madeline Guimard became one of the most popular dancers of her time.

Guimard had a poor, rather unhappy childhood, with a mother who seems to have devoted herself solely to finding lovers for her daughter. She began her dancing career at the Comédie Française, where she became friends with Marie Allard; in 1762 she made her first appearance at the Opéra, substituting for Allard (who had hurt her foot).

It was the beginning of a long, successful career, in the course of which she came to wield enormous power at the Opéra; like Dauberval, her talent for dancing was combined with an equal facility in bed. With her long list of prominent lovers, she was able to make life exceedingly difficult for anyone who offended her. Though she sided with Noverre in 1776, she switched sides later on, swinging the balance against him and virtually forcing his resignation in 1782. (However, the two soon made up and within a few years Guimard was happily dancing for Noverre during the summer in London.)

Perhaps because of her deprived childhood, Guimard was determined to live well. She managed to dispose of several sizeable fortunes and her two homes (the 'Temple of Terpsichore' in Paris and a country home at Pantin) saw a continuous series of parties with crowds of princes, intellectuals and all her friends from the theater. But she was also a familiar sight in the Paris slums, carrying baskets of food and clothing to those in need. Her generosity even extended to her ex-lovers when they found themselves in financial difficulties.

In 1789 her career came to an abrupt

Madeline Guimard, Jean Dauberval and Marie Allard.

end – not because of age, sickness or the politics of the French Revolution, but fittingly, for love. For the next 27 years, through all the difficulties of the Revolution, she and her husband, Jean-Etienne Despreaux (who was 18 years her junior), led a contented if poor existence in Paris.

MARIE-MADELEINE CRESPE, MLLE THEODORE
1760–96

Mlle Theodore was one of the most popular dancers at the Opéra from 1777–82. She had a quick, precise technique and was famous for her *ballon*; Noverre (for whom she worked at King's Theatre, London, in 1882–83) said that she danced with 'ease, facility and brilliance, and had the resilience of a ball.'

She is worthy of special mention if only because her moral outlook and intellectual ability are in such contrast to most other eighteenth-century ballerinas; she so impressed Paris that she was called 'the philosopher in ballet slippers.' She fell deeply in love with Dauberval despite his promiscuity, of which she strongly disapproved; putting affection aside, she steadfastly refused to join his long list of mistresses. Eventually he gave in and married her and the two moved to Bordeaux. There, though they occasionally missed the excitement of Paris, they were quite happy – she as prima ballerina, he as dancer, choreographer and ballet master. Her most famous role was that of Lise in Dauberval's ballet *La Fille Mal Gardée*. Dauberval settled down quite happily with his witty, intelligent wife and was heartbroken when she died at the age of only 36.

LOUIS ANTOINE DUPORT
1783–1853

Little is known of the origins of Louis Duport, one of the most famous dancers of his day. A child prodigy by the same name was popular in the United States during the early 1790s and disappeared in 1796, but no connection has ever been definitely established.

Wherever he came from, Duport was a tremendous success at the Opéra between 1797 and 1808. This placed him in direct competition with Auguste Vestris, whom he rivalled not only in talent and audience appeal, but also in arrogance.

Eventually even his admirer Napoleon became disgusted with his posturing and intriguing, and Duport was forced to flee Paris disguised as a woman. After a brief stop in Vienna (where he appeared in *Figaro, or the Barber of Seville* in 1808), he moved to St Petersburg. During the next four years he danced 150 performances, mostly in Didelot's ballets, to enthusiastic audiences. He then returned to Vienna where he choreographed many ballets for the Kaertnerthor Theater; he also made regular guest appearances in Naples and London.

In 1837 Duport returned to Paris, where he retired and was not heard from again.

EMILIE BIGOTTINI
1784–1858

Emilie Bigottini, one of the earliest dancers to link *danse noble* and Romantic ballet, was the daughter of a perpetually struggling Italian actor who had drifted to France 30 years before she was born.

She studied at the Opéra school, making her debut with the company in 1801. In 1804 she was promoted to soloist and by 1812 was *première danseuse*. Much of this early success was due to her connection with her teacher and patron, Louis Milon, Gardel's assistant, who was married to her half-sister, Louise.

Thanks to Milon she was able to remain aloof from the petty intrigues and scandals of the Opéra, and though she had the usual compliment of distinguished lovers and admirers (including, at one time, Napoleon), she was invariably gentle, kind and generous.

She was a good dancer and popular with the audience, but she showed no signs of extraordinary talent until 1813 when she was given the title role in Milon's *Nina, ou la Folle par Amour*, a sentimental tale that was one of the earliest forerunners of Romantic ballet. Suddenly it was discovered that her acting was as good as her dancing and audiences left her performances with tears in their eyes.

She continued to be popular in Paris and was a guest artist for Jean Aumer during the Congress of Vienna in 1814. It was not until 1820, when Milon came up with *Clari, ou la Promesse de Mariage*, that she was able to repeat her previous

Emilie Bigottini in La Lampe Merveilleuse.

triumph. Her portrayal of the unfortunate Clari, overcome with shame at being the mistress of the Duke, was even greater than her Nina had been.

In December 1823, after several more years of charming but undistinguished performances, she made her farewell performance, as Nina. She was almost 40, with four children, and thought it was time to retire. Since she had invested her money wisely she was able to live comfortably and quietly for the next 35 years.

MARIE TAGLIONI
1804–84

Marie Taglioni's biography appears in this chapter because she had her greatest triumph in Paris. Born in Sweden to an Italian father and Swedish mother, trained in Vienna and Stuttgart and with a career that included more appearances in the other great cities of Europe than in Paris, she was, in fact, a truly international ballet personality.

Taglioni began studying dance in Paris when she was almost 12 with Jean-Francois Coulon; but her father, Filippo, was away most of the time and the thin, round-shouldered little girl did not take her lessons very seriously. That all changed in 1820 when Filippo had her join him in Vienna. For the next two years she worked six hours a day for six days a week, often until she was on the verge of collapse.

In June 1822 she made her debut in *La Reception d'une Nymphe au Temple de Terpsichore*; it was the beginning of five years of performances to enthusiastic audiences in Vienna, Munich and Stuttgart, with partners that included her brother Paul and the handsome Anton Stuhlmüller.

By 1827 her father finally considered her ready for the greatest ballet stage of all. Her Paris tryouts were successful, and in 1828 she began dancing at the Opéra. During the next few years she became increasingly popular, both in Paris and in London during the summer season at King's Theatre, where her performance in *Flore et Zephyre* (1830) made her almost a cult figure.

Years of Filippo's gruelling training had given her a style that no one had seen before. She cultivated a chaste, ethereal stage personality which was emphasized by her technique: skillful *pointe* dancing and amazing elevation. Her ability to remain suspended at the highest point of her jumps had been matched only by Auguste Vestris – and would not be seen again until Vaslav Nijinsky. It was not long before the verb 'taglioniser' (to move with the lightness of Taglioni) had become part of the French vocabulary. Auguste Bournonville, who danced with her several times in 1827 and 1828, wrote, 'She seemed to lift you up from this earth; her divine dancing made you weep, and I saw Terpsichore realized in her lovely person.'

The story of Taglioni's triumph in *La Sylphide*, which opened on 12 March 1832, and the mass hysteria it occasioned, has been told many times over. It catapulted her to the very top of her profession as the epitome of the spiritual ideals associated with the Romantic movement.

During the next few years the management at the Opéra found her increasingly difficult to work with, despite her continued popularity; box-office receipts at this time were increased still more by her rivalry with the 'pagan' Fanny Elssler – mainly a publicity stunt organized by the Opéra's director, Dr Véron.

In March 1836 her daughter Marie (Nini) was born, the result of a temporary reconciliation between Marie and her seldom-seen husband, Gilbert de Voisins. The next year her contract was not renewed and she began the peripatetic life of a freelancer, accompanied by a retinue of family, lovers and friends.

Her first stop was St Petersburg, where the Russians reacted with as much enthusiasm as Paris had done five years before. One of the highlights of that first visit was a banquet featuring 'toe shoe soup,' in which a pair of Taglioni's slippers took the place of the chicken. As she was returning to Europe, at the end of the 1837–38 season, her coach was stopped by bandits. The terrified party resigned themselves to losing their jewels and money, but soon learned that the raiders wanted neither their lives nor their possessions; they only wanted to see Taglioni dance. Rugs were spread beside the road and, after an impromptu recital, the party continued on its way – losing only the rugs, which the bandit leader kept as souvenirs.

After 10 years on the touring circuit,

Taglioni retired to a villa on Lake Como. The quiet life did not suit her for long and in 1858 she returned to Paris where she was soon dancing again with Mazilier (her original partner in *La Sylphide*). The next year she was appointed Inspectrice de la Danse at the Opéra – a post she held until 1870, when she discovered that her increasingly eccentric father had lost all her considerable fortune.

Undaunted, Taglioni resigned her post in Paris and moved to London, where she opened a school at 6 Connaught Square. She continued to teach – and maintain an active social life – until 1880. Then her son, George Gilbert de Voisins, persuaded his 76-year-old mother to come and live with his family in Marseilles, where she died four years later.

JULES JOSEPH PERROT
1810–92

Jules Perrot, one of the few male dancers to achieve recognition during the Romantic era, was the son of a Lyons carpenter and began his career as a child acrobat and clown with a travelling circus. But by

Jules Perrot and Carlotta Grisi in his ballet La Esmeralda.

the time he was 13 he had decided to become a classical dancer and had settled in Paris to study with the great Auguste Vestris.

Vestris quickly developed an appreciation for the boy's talent and agreed he had potential as a dancer, but also told him that he would have to keep moving on stage so that the audience would not notice how ugly he was. Perhaps as a result of this advice Perrot developed a technique which combined the dramatic skills from his circus years with Vestris's traditional *danse noble* tradition to derive a unique, fast and flashy style. He was especially noted for his *ballon*, which earned him nicknames like 'l'aerien' (the aerialist) and 'the male Taglioni.' At his Opéra debut in 1830 Gautier declared him 'the greatest dancer of our times.'

During his five years at the Opéra he was one of Taglioni's best partners, but as he became more popular she became more jealous. By 1835 the situation had become intolerable and Perrot officially left the Opéra to embark on a European tour. By this time he was already involved with the young Carlotta Grisi (whom he had met in Naples in 1834), and he was beginning to experiment with choreography. His first major production was *La Nymphe et le Papillon* for the Kaertnerthor Theater in Vienna in 1836; by the end of 1840 he was already famous as a choreographer.

Early in 1840 he and Grisi were in Paris, where they scored a success with *Le Zingaro*. But this second Paris stay was to be no happier than the first. By the time the famous *Giselle* was premiered four months later, he and Grisi were separated and credit for the choreography went to Jean Coralli.

For the next seven years (1841–48) Perrot worked for Benjamin Lumley at Her Majesty's Theatre, London. There he produced some of his best work, in collaboration with Carlo Pugni, and made London one of the great ballet centers of the time.

Perrot was one of the most dramatic and expressive choreographers of the Romantic era. Able to create characters from all social classes, he took care with every part, from the prima ballerina to the last member of the *corps de ballet*. He had a natural feeling for theater, and his ballets were fast-moving and entertaining.

La Esmeralda (1844), an adaptation of Hugo's *Notre Dame de Paris*, is one of Perrot's most famous ballets. Another is

Pas de Quatre (1845), a 'trifle' which brought together on one stage at the same time the four greatest ballerinas of the day: Taglioni (with whom he had become good friends), Fanny Cerrito, Fanny Elssler and Lucille Grahn. Other popular works from this period included *L'Aurore* and *Ondine* (both 1843), *Caterina* and *Le Jugement de Paris* (both 1846) and *Les Quatre Saisons* (1848).

In 1848 he left London, stopped off at La Scala in Milan (where he choreographed *Faust*), and set out for St Petersburg, where he had a contract to partner Elssler on her Russian tour. Once there, he decided to stay on and in 1851 he was appointed ballet master. During the next eight years he produced about 20 ballets, in addition to making guest appearances in Berlin, Warsaw, Brussels, Lyons and Paris. But he was never quite able to fit in with the Imperial Theater system, and in 1859 he was forced to leave.

After several unsuccessful attempts to stage a comeback in France and Italy, he and his wife, the Russian ballerina Capitoline Samovskaya, retired to an obscure village in France where he lived – unhappy, idle and forgotten – until his death some 30 years later.

ARTHUR SAINT-LEON
1821–70

Arthur Saint-Léon, born Charles Victor Arthur Michel, was a child prodigy on the violin, but once he turned to dancing he developed so rapidly that soon he was second only to Jules Perrot. His energetic, almost acrobatic dancing attracted an unusual amount of attention in an age devoted almost entirely to the ballerina. He was also a composer, but his greatest

Arthur de Saint-Léon, choreographer of Coppélia, *seen here in a scene from Perrot's* La Esmeralda.

gift was for choreography.

He first encountered Fanny Cerrito in Vienna in 1841; they worked together again in London in 1843, married and spent several years touring the capitals of Europe. In 1851, however, after an engagement in Madrid, they agreed to go their separate ways.

By 1859 Saint-Léon was tremendously successful, commuting between St Petersburg and Paris and choreographing a series of popular ballets. *Diavolina* was produced in Paris in July 1863; in February 1864 he showed *Fiammetta* in St Petersburg and in July of the same year he staged an adaptation, called *Néméa, ou l'Amour Venge*, in Paris. By December 1864 *The Little Humpbacked Horse* was ready to be performed in Russia. The year 1866 saw the premiere of *La Source* in Paris, and in 1870 audiences at the Opéra were overwhelmed by *Coppélia* – Saint-Léon's best work and still a favorite in the modern repertory.

Unfortunately, in 1870 he suffered a stroke, brought on by overwork and overweight, and died at the early age of 49.

SERGE DIAGHILEV
1872–1929

Serge Diaghilev, one of the towering figures in ballet during the twentieth century, was born in a barracks in Novgorod Province in Russia where his father, a Colonel in the Imperial Guard, was stationed. Most of his youth was spent in Perm and even as a boy he showed a notable self-confidence and ability to get his own way.

In 1890 he moved to St Petersburg, ostensibly to study law, and was soon drawn into a group of promising young artists. His main interests were music and painting rather than ballet, and in 1897 he began a series of annual art exhibitions. His success in 1905 with an exhibit titled 'Historic Russian Paintings, 1705–1905' inspired him to look further than the confines of Russia for his next venture.

In 1906 he was in Paris with another Russian art exhibition; the following year he was back with a concert series, 'Russian Music Through the Ages,' and the year after with an opera, *Boris Gudunov*, starring the incomparable Chaliapin. By 1909, when he arrived with his feverishly recruited ballet troupe, his 'Saison Russe' was an established feature of the Paris season. The trials and tribulations of preparing for that first season – recurring financial crises and the struggle to get the Théâtre du Châtelet ready on time – are well documented. That year he stormed Paris; in the years before World War I he would conquer the rest of Europe as well.

During those halcyon years, when Ballets Russes was attracting the greatest artistic talents in Europe and overshadowing anything else on the ballet scene, Diaghilev could afford to be offhand with his artists. In 1912 Fokine left the company; in 1913 Nijinsky married and the mortally offended Diaghilev (who had once chided a male colleague for having 'a morbid fascination for women') fired him immediately. In 1914 he found a new young choreographer whom he carefully instructed, encouraged and introduced to the 'right people.' Leonide Massine remained with the company for seven years before he married.

When World War I broke out Diaghilev moved the company to Switzerland, where he somehow managed to keep the group together. In 1916, while most of his troupe was on tour in the United States, he took a small group with him to Rome; that winter saw the birth of the first cubist ballet, *Parade*, with a libretto by Jean Cocteau, design by Picasso, music by Erik Satie and, of course, Massine's choreography.

In general, however, the years after the war were increasingly unstable. Despite an impressive string of choreographers (Nijinska, Cecchetti, Balanchine), composers (including Stravinsky, Prokofiev, Ravel, Debussy, Strauss, Satie, Milhaud and Poulenc), and artists (like Picasso, Bakst, Braque, Utrillo, Miro and Matisse), the company was as often as not on the edge of financial disaster.

Through all the triumphs and trials Diaghilev stalked, larger than life, sophisticated and eccentric, with his monocle, cape and white-streaked hair. But the 20-year struggle to overcome the never-ending series of financial and administrative problems finally took its toll. In 1929, at the end of the London summer season, he retired to his favorite city, Venice. There he died on 19 August and was buried on the island of San Michele.

Diaghilev was the first impresario – an 'outsider', who was not himself skilled in any of the arts but who had the ability to inspire, combine and direct the artistic talents of others. His entire career was based on striking a delicate balance between his own excellent taste and that of the public, and on a constant race to keep his productions in the forefront of the avant garde. During his lifetime he *was* ballet.

MICHEL (MIKHAIL) FOKINE
1880–1942

Michel Fokine, the choreographer Jack Anderson calls 'the father of modern ballet,' received his training in the Imperial school in St Petersburg and upon graduation joined the company at the Maryinsky Theater. There he became the

Diaghilev, Lifar (right) and designer Nouvel.

Tamara Karsavina and Michel Fokine in Firebird.

Vaslav Nijinsky and Tamara Karsavina in Fokine's Spectre de la Rose *of 1911.*

became *Les Sylphides*; *Le Pavillon d'Armide* (1907); and *Une Nuit d'Egypte* (1908), which he later revised into *Cléopâtre*.

These short ballets, however original, could make little impression in conservative Russia. In 1908, when Diaghilev invited him to join Ballets Russes for its opening season in Paris, he – and many of his colleagues – accepted gladly.

That opening night in May 1909 marked the beginning of Fokine's most prolific period, as Diaghilev's chief choreographer. The 1909 season produced revisions of the three short ballets mentioned above, plus *Le Festine* and a series of dances from *Prince Igor*. In 1910 he produced *Le Carnaval*, to music by Schumann, and the gorgeous, oriental *Schéhérazade*, in which Nijinsky created the role of the Golden Slave (sets for both were designed by Léon Bakst). That year he also composed *Firebird*, to Igor Stravinsky's first ballet score. In 1911 his works included: a *pas de deux* for Karsavina and Nijinsky titled *La Spectre de la Rose*; *Narcisse*, with Bakst's Grecian setting; and the greatest ballet of its time, *Petrouchka*, a masterpiece that featured excellent choreography, an excellent score by Stravinsky and superb dancing by Nijinsky, Karsavina and Cecchetti. His later ballets for the company included *Le Dieu Bleu*, *Thamar* and *Daphnis et Chloë* (all 1912).

Fokine's later years with Ballets Russes were a time of increasing tension (he especially resented Diaghilev's determination to encourage Nijinsky's experimental choreography), and in 1912 he left the company. For the rest of his life, except for a few years in the 1930s with René Blum and his Ballets Russes de Monte Carlo, he worked as a freelance artist, producing ballets at most of the major theaters in Europe and America.

In addition to being remembered as a fine dancer and choreographer who played a leading role in bringing audiences back to ballet, Fokine is also known as one of the great reformers of ballet. Like Noverre and Blasis he felt that all aspects of a production – choreography, music, costumes and design – should be integrated into the dramatic action, without which they had no meaning. He looked for plots with real significance rather than simple vehicles for the prima ballerina, and he did much to bring democracy to the ballet hierarchy, as well as restoring male dancers to a more equal position after many years of neglect.

leader of a group of young dancers, all eager to break away from Marius Petipa's standardized formulas and start creating new, more modern ballets – a desire reinforced by Isadora Duncan's visit to the city in 1904.

One of Fokine's early ventures into choreography was the creation of *The Dying Swan* in 1907, a solo for Anna Pavlova to dance at a charity performance. The work, set to the music of Saint-Saëns, has been associated with the great ballerina ever since and is generally considered the ultimate test of a dancer's technical skill. Other early works included: *Chopiniana* (1906), which

LEONIDE MASSINE
1895–1979

Leonide Massine, whom *Dancing Times* has called 'one of the greatest dancers and choreographers of this century,' was a graduate of the Moscow Bolshoi school. He had been dancing with the company for two years and was just about to abandon dance in favor of acting when he was discovered by Diaghilev in 1913.

While Massine studied with Cecchetti and danced Nijinsky's roles with Ballets Russes, Diaghilev himself worked on expanding the young man's cultural and social horizons, grooming him to be the company's next great choreographer. He proved to be a quick student (Diaghilev once claimed that Massine was the only dancer he knew who was his intellectual equal), and by 1917 he was producing charming, sophisticated comedies like *Les Femmes de Bonne Humeur* and exuberantly modern pieces like *Parade*. A tour in Spain and Portugal gave him the material for *Tricorne* (The Three-Cornered Hat) and *La Boutique Fantasque*, both of which were successfully premiered in London during the 1919 season. In 1920 he scored again with *Le Chant du Rossignol* (Song of the Nightingale), *Pulcinella* (another collaboration with Picasso) and a new version of *Le Sacre du Printemps*.

In 1921 he married the English dancer Vera Savina and, like Nijinsky, was forced to leave the company, returning only occasionally as guest artist. As a freelance, he worked all over the world

Massine in conversation with Colonel de Basil.

and became one of the most influential choreographers on the international scene. He worked with Soirées de Paris in 1924, the London Cochrane revues in 1925–26, and as soloist and ballet master at New York's Roxy Theater from 1927–30.

During the 1930s his symphonic ballets for Blum's Ballet Russe de Monte Carlo (the allegorical *Les Présages*, to Tchaikovsky's Fifth Symphony, and *Choreartium*, an abstract work set to Brahm's Fourth Symphony, both 1934) caused a furore among those who were shocked by his 'presumption.' For the next three decades he produced many new ballets and revived old ones. The story of his

travels and many productions is told in his sometimes suspect autobiography, *My Life in Ballet* (London, 1960).

Massine never stopped thinking of himself as a dancer as well as a choreographer and almost all his ballets contained major roles for himself – though he choreographed equally well for other men. Though no longer considered the giant he was in his lifetime, his place in ballet history is assured, not only as the originator of the symphonic ballet, but also because of his many contributions to comedy ballet, stemming from his firmly held belief that ballet should be fun as well as an intellectual or aesthetic experience.

SERGE LIFAR
b 1905

Serge Lifar was another Russian-trained dancer who joined Diaghilev in Paris, then found himself at a loose end once the company disintegrated in 1929. Soon after Diaghilev's death, however, he was offered an engagement at the Paris Opéra, as a lead dancer in a production of *The Creatures of Prometheus*, which was to be choreographed by George Balanchine. When Balanchine fell ill, Lifar – already an excellent dancer – proved himself to be an equally good choreographer. His version of the ballet was so popular that he was offered a permanent job at the Opéra.

For almost 30 years Lifar dominated ballet in Paris. His virile, exciting dancing and his inventive choreography – of both old and new ballets – caught the public's imagination, while his administrative reforms completely transformed the Opéra Ballet.

In 1934 he published *The Manifesto of Choreography*; just as he himself had to be the center of attention at all times, so he insisted that choreography was the center of ballet, existing independently of music and design. As an example, in 1935 he composed the powerful *Icare*, creating the ballet first and then sending the rhythms to a composer who wrote a percussion score to them.

During the Nazi occupation of Paris any distraction from day to day life was a relief and ballet, like the other performing arts, was extremely popular. Every Wednesday evening the Opéra would be packed, even though in winter both dancers and spectators had to bundle up against the cold. This was the period when

Leonide Massine in his ballet Le Tricorne *with Tamara Toumanova and David Lichine (left).*

Serge Lifar in his version of Prometheus, *1929.*

Lifar was at his most creative, producing the romantic *Le Chevalier et la Demoiselle* (1941); *Joan de Zarissa* (1942), depicting all the refinement and brutality of the Middle Ages; and *Suite en Blanc* (1943), a plotless display piece.

In 1944 he was accused of collaboration with the Germans and left the Opéra; bringing his two best ballerinas (Yvette Chauviré and Solange Schwartz) with him, he joined Les Nouveaux Ballets de Monte Carlo. During his three years with the company he produced several new ballets including *Drama per Musica, Chota Roustaveli* and *Nantéos.*

By 1947, however, he and Chauviré were back in Paris, where he remained with the Opéra until 1958. Some of his many ballets from this period are *Les Mirages* (1947), *Phédre* (1950) and *Les Noces Fantastiques* (1958).

Since 1958 he has worked as a freelance, occasionally for the Opéra. His ballets continue to be popular in Paris, although many modern critics consider them superficial and rather self-conscious, and for the most part they have fallen out of favor. None of this, however, alters Lifar's position as one of the chief architects of modern French ballet. He published more than 25 books between 1935 and 1967, and remains an active and vocal commentator on the ballet scene.

ROLAND PETIT
b 1924

Roland Petit was born in Villemomble, France. He studied at the Paris Opéra Ballet and joined the company in 1940 when he was only 16. Even as a young man his dancing displayed great personal magnetism and he was soon considered one of the Opéra's most promising dancers.

In 1945 he left this secure position, however, and formed his own company. Ballets des Champs Elysées attracted a group of talented young dancers; with Petit as ballet master, principal dancer and chief choreographer, they presented several excellent ballets. One of the productions that caused the most stir was *Le Jeune Homme et la Mort,* which Petit composed in collaboration with Jean Cocteau. The ballet, which tells the story of a young artist scorned and driven to suicide by a mysterious woman, was rehearsed to a jazz score; only on the night of the performance did the cast discover that it would be danced to a Bach passacaglia. Petit spent the entire evening in the wings, nervously wondering if the piece would be long enough; it worked perfectly and the production, starring Jean Babilée and Nathalie Philippart, was a resounding success. Petit's *Les Forains* and his revival of *La Sylphide* to Schneitzhoeffer's original music were two more of several memorable productions.

In 1948 he formed yet another company, Ballets de Paris de Roland Petit, which opened its first season in the Théâtre Marigny with *Les Demoiselles de la Nuit.* Most of the ballets he produced for this company were sensual, almost risqué; two of the most famous were *Carmen* – starring his wife, Renée (Zizi) Jeanmaire – and *Le Loup.* Ballets de Paris was disbanded and re-formed several times over, and toured extensively both in the United States and Europe.

Petit has also choreographed revues, television programs and films – with credits that include *Hans Christian Anderson* (1951) and *Daddy Long Legs* (1953). In 1970 he bought the Casino de Paris, where he staged several revues for his wife during his five years as director; at the same time he also worked for the Opéra (*Turangalia*) and other troupes. Since 1972 he has also directed Ballet de Marseille. Though his choreography has often been criticized for being too light and theatrical, he has always produced attractive, entertaining and sometimes provocative pieces.

Cyrano de Bergerac as portrayed by Roland Petit.

RUSSIA

Dedicated young students at the Kirov school practicing pliés before class begins.

Ballet was introduced in Russia much later than in other European countries. The Renaissance – with its wealth of exciting new political, economic, intellectual and artistic developments – had never penetrated Muscovy; at the end of the seventeenth century Russia was still a medieval state.

However, in 1697–98 the young Czar Peter I (Peter the Great) made an extended tour of Europe and returned determined to pull his country into the modern world – and the European community. On the day after his return he personally cut off the beards of his nobles and ordered them to dress in Western fashion instead of their traditional long robes and fur hats. It was the beginning of an era of intensive Westernization that would drastically affect all the arts as well as the political, economic and social structures.

In 1734 a Frenchman, Jean-Baptiste Landé (d 1748), arrived in the new Russian capital, St Petersburg. After dancing in Paris and London and working as ballet master in Stockholm, he was hired to teach dancing to the cadets at the military academy. To supplement his income, he opened a private dance academy. It was so successful that in 1738 the Empress Anna granted the establishment Imperial support. As the St Petersburg School of Ballet, its primary purpose was to train the children of servants at the court for appearances in royal entertainments. Ballet quickly became popular and many serfs were trained to appear in private productions on isolated estates, ensuring that familiarity with and love of dance were never limited in Russia to just the ruling classes.

One of the earliest visitors to this ballet outpost was the Austrian ballet master Franz Hilferding, who probably did as much as Noverre to promote the development of expressive choreography. His pupil Angiolini followed a few years later, and the French dancer Charles LePicq worked in St Petersburg from 1786–98.

Catherine II (Catherine the Great), who reigned from 1762–96, was a great patron of all the arts. In 1766 she established the Directorate of the Imperial Theaters, giving it control over ballet, drama and opera, and so beginning a long tradition of Imperial patronage.

A ballet school was established at the Moscow Orphanage in 1774 by Filippo Beccari, another imported dancing master. In 1780 he began supplying dancers to the Petrovsky, forerunner of today's Bolshoi Theater; in 1794 the school was put under the theater's management. Both theater and school were made part of the Imperial system in 1806.

In 1801 Charles Didelot arrived in St Petersburg to take up a temporary appointment and stayed to establish the foundations of Russian ballet. His arrival sparked the first great period of ballet activity in the capital. An acknowledged master of stagecraft and dramatic action, he produced ballets at St Petersburg's Bolshoi (Big or Grand) Theater, which made full use of his famous techniques such as wires to lift the dancers above the stage or mirrors arranged so that the audience could see the same dancer from several angles. With his connections in Paris, he was also able to import skilled dancers like Louis Duport, who became a tremendously popular attraction.

Perhaps Didelot's most valuable contribution during his two stays in Russia (1801–11 and 1816–37) was his reorganization of the Imperial schools and revision of their teaching methods. The children who entered his academy (usually at the age of eight or nine) were subjected to a rigorous program of ballet training, in which the smallest error resulted in instant punishment. Although not a pleasant experience, the system produced excellent dancers including: Maria Danilova; Eugenia Kolossova (1780–1869), who was Didelot's favorite ballerina; and the dark-haired beauty Avdotia Istomina, an excellent dancer noted for her elevation and pirouette technique, whose skill, combined with her acting ability and Latin good looks, inspired poems by Pushkin as well as several duels.

The first Russian ballet master to gain a measure of fame was Ivan Valberkh, director of the St Petersburg school from 1794. He strongly supported native Russian dancers, and though he drew inspiration for his ballets from many sources, the most popular were his patriotic works, like *Love for the Fatherland*, produced in 1812 after Napoleon's invasion of Russia.

Meanwhile, in Moscow the old Petrovsky Theater had burned down in 1805 and the company was operating from 'temporary' quarters in the Arbat Theater; in fact, the new (present) Bolshoi Theater did not open until January 1825.

The first Russian ballet master in Moscow was Adam Gluszkowsky (1793–c1870), one of the first to base his ballets on works by Pushkin and other Russian writers. One of Didelot's favorite pupils, he had come to Moscow in 1812 and remained as ballet master at the Bolshoi until 1839. He also taught at the school, adding much to its reputation. During the 1820s and 1830s Yekaterina Samkovskaya (1816–78) was also a central figure in the growing movement to develop a national ballet tradition.

By the end of the first quarter of the century Moscow was already well on its way to developing its own style. Moscow audiences may not have been as sophisticated as those in St Petersburg – they were certainly not as stylish and preferred their dancing lively and acrobatic instead of refined and elegant – but they were knowledgeable and had high standards for both their own and for visiting performers.

During the nineteenth century the Czars exercised complete control over all theatrical activities, including ballet. Though this sometimes led to uncomfortable situations, as when Paul I (reigned 1796–1801) banned men from the stage and insisted they be replaced by women *en travesti*, on the whole it was beneficial.

Marie Taglioni in Charles Didelot's Flore et Zéphyre. *She was an instant sensation in St Petersburg and was booked for four more years.*

At least the theaters and schools never lacked for money or support from the royal family.

Despite its periodic bursts of enthusiasm for Westernization, Russia was still a mystery to most Europeans. Dancers who had toured Russia returned with fabulous stories of luxurious theaters, tremendous salaries paid to guest artists and elegantly dressed audiences, who showered gifts upon them. Thus it is not surprising that Didelot was followed by a veritable flood of the best ballet talent in Europe. Louis Duport, Jules Perrot and Arthur Saint-Léon were among the choreographers; and all the great Romantic ballerinas – Taglioni, Grahn, Cerrito, Elssler, Grisi – danced in Russia.

The first of the ballerinas was Marie Taglioni, who appeared in St Petersburg in 1837. She arrived accompanied in regal style by an entourage consisting of her father, her daughter, her lover Eugene Demares (who was also her manager, publicist and librettist), her dog and an unbelievable amount of luggage. Her first performance had the usually restrained St Petersburg audience on its feet, shouting and cheering. Members of the royal family left their boxes to get a better view from the orchestra and even went up to the stage to congratulate her after the show – an unprecedented compliment. At the end of the season her contract was extended for four more years, with an arrangement that left plenty of time free during the spring and summer for appearances in London, Vienna and Poland.

In 1842, Taglioni's last season in Russia, she arrived with a new partner, a Swedish dancer named Christian Johansson. She left when her contract expired, but he remained to become one of Russia's leading dancers. Soon he was also teaching, and his methods, based on those he had learned from August Bournonville, did much to improve the quality of ballet in Russia. Johansson was also responsible for ensuring that Russian schools did not neglect male dancers, even at the height of the Romantic era – a situation that did much to keep ballet viable in Russia when it was on the decline in the rest of Europe.

Though the craze for foreign dancers was to continue well into the 1860s, the Imperial schools in St Petersburg and Moscow continued to produce excellent dancers. In the state academies pupils studied and trained in virtual seclusion until they were deemed ready to appear at one of the theaters. As much time was devoted to men as to women (especially after Johansson's influence began to make itself felt), which prevented many of the worst excesses of ballerina worship afflicting the art in the West, and helped Russian ballet avoid the decline into a stilted, one-dimensional vehicle for a prima ballerina.

Two of the best dancers to emerge from the St Petersburg academy were Tatiana Smirnova and Elena Andreianova, who became the first Russian Giselle in 1842. Both learned much from watching Taglioni. Smirnova probably came closest to being the ideal Romantic ballerina, but her modest, retiring nature was a handicap both on and offstage. In 1844 she was one of the first Russian ballerinas to appear at the Paris Opéra, but she did not make much of an impression. After a more successful engagement in Brussels she was happy to return to St Petersburg and a more comfortable, if less distinguished, career.

Andreianova, on the other hand, had a much more forceful character and was, in addition, the mistress of Alexander Guedenov, Director of the Imperial theaters. Her dancing style was flashier and more self-confident, and her engagement in Paris in 1845 received a much better reception. Upon her return she became all-powerful in St Petersburg until Fanny Elssler's arrival in 1848 overshadowed her, along with everyone else,

Elssler's appearance took the emotional Russians by storm in St Petersburg and especially in Moscow; her beauty and dramatic dancing were an irresistible combination. With her on her first trip was Jules Perrot who, like Johansson before him, stayed on to work in Russia where he choreographed some of his best ballets.

Elssler's return visit to Russia in 1849 was followed by four seasons in which Carlotta Grisi danced the leading roles (1850–53). In 1855, however, Russians were swept by a wave of intense patriotism in response to the Crimean War. When Fanny Cerrito arrived to take her place in the parade of foreign ballerinas she had a disappointing reception, with heavy competition from Russian dancers like Martha Mouravieva and the superficial, but popular, lyrical ballerina Nadehda Bogdanova (1836–97).

Perrot found it more and more difficult to work under the strict supervision of the Imperial family, and in 1859 he was replaced by Arthur Saint-Léon. Mouravieva soon became the new ballet master's special favorite and many of Saint-Léon's restagings of old works, as well as his new productions, were created especially for her.

Her biggest rival was Marie Petipa, wife of Saint-Léon's assistant, who has been described by a contemporary writer as 'a very graceful dancer whose figure rivalled that of Venus.' Marie's husband, Marius, had come to Russia from France in 1847 and worked his way up from dancer to his present position. Saint-Léon kept him very much in the background and no one at the time could have predicted that within a few more years he would be leading Russia to a position of glorious supremacy in the ballet world.

In the 1860s, while ballet was declining more or less rapidly in Western Europe, it was still alive and growing in Russia. Its strong position there was due in large part to support from the Czar; since employees of the theaters and schools were servants of the court, they commanded a measure of respect that was noticeably absent in the rest of Europe. In fact, students at the Imperial ballet academies were considered on the same level as cadets at the military and naval schools. The company attached to Moscow's Bolshoi Theater was flourishing, while St Petersburg supported two theaters: the imposing Bolshoi and the elegant Maryinsky, which was packed for every performance with courtiers, diplomats and prominent businessmen. The rivalry between the two cities, which continues to this day, was already well established. Residents of the self-consciously elegant capital looked down their noses at what they considered crude, flamboyant Moscow productions; Moscow, on the other hand, despised St Petersburg's cold, 'academic' style.

Toward the end of 1861 Petipa, who had been able to do very little choreography under Perrot and Saint-Léon, was finally given his opportunity when Saint-Léon ordered him to create a vehicle for a distinguished guest artist, Carolina Rosati. The result was *The Pharaoh's Daughter*, which he created in six weeks and premiered in St Petersburg in 1862. Petipa's years of watching and waiting in the wings had paid off handsomely; his choreography lifted the ballet above an extremely silly plot (about a Victorian gentleman's opium dream) and turned it into a production that remained popular for many years.

An amusing caricature of the great French choreographer Marius Petipa by the Russian dancer and teacher Nicholai Legat.

The great ballet maestro Enrico Cecchetti, teacher of the greatest dancers of all time, seen here teaching Pavlova privately in Russia.

From then on there was no stopping him. While Saint-Léon commuted between Russia and France, Petipa consolidated his own position and in 1870 he was officially appointed ballet master. It was the beginning of a dictatorship that lasted more than 30 years and changed the face of Russian ballet, establishing it as an entity distinct from the French, Italian and Danish traditions that were its roots.

Petipa virtually created the style we now consider 'classical' ballet. His productions were long (five or six acts), lavish and varied, combining classical dances with folk dances, mime and dramatics. Each work would contain, somewhere near the end, a divertissement and a *pas de deux* for the two principal dancers; the latter had its own formula: an adagio, or lyrical duet for both partners, solos for first the man then the woman and finally a coda which brought them back together for the grand finale. The plot was simply a vehicle for displaying the dancers' technical skill. Despite the sumptuous productions, the major characters' costumes were always the same, with only their accessories hinting at the locale or historical period in which the action took place.

Though Petipa's approach was popular with audiences and produced some excellent ballets, it inevitably became stale and hackneyed through overuse. The process was hastened by his extremely mechanical production methods. In his

attempt to unify dance and music, he would block out the stage action at home ahead of time, using miniatures to help his planning and plugging in prearranged dances. His composers were then expected to write their scores to rigid specifications regarding length, type of music and even orchestration. Sometimes, of course, a truly great composer like Tchaikovsky or Glazunov would be able to rise above these restrictions and produce a masterpiece, but for the most part the music tended to be mediocre.

Petipa was obsessed with technique – for the entire company, not just the soloists. A brilliant teacher, he united all the various foreign styles creating what is now called the Russian technique and the high standards he set for the *corps de ballet* established a strong foundation for the entire Russian ballet organization.

His favorite ballerina for 20 years, between 1864 and 1884, was Ekaterina Vazem (1848–1937), an impeccable, if somewhat cold, technician. She taught in St Petersburg for many years following her retirement from the stage, her most famous pupil being Agrippina Vaganova. Vazem's greatest rival was Eugenia Sokolova (1855–1926), an enchanting dancer

The Italian ballerina Virginia Zucchi rekindled the interest of Russian ballet goers, bored with Petipa's repetitive offerings.

who, after her own retirement in 1886, also produced some stellar pupils, notably Tamara Karsavina and Anna Pavlova.

As time went on the public became bored with Petipa's repetitious productions; attendance at the performances declined and the number of shows per week was cut. However, in 1885 the appearance of the brilliant Italian ballerina, Virginia Zucchi, brought the audiences flocking to the theater once more.

Zucchi, whose vital, flashing virtuosity was such a welcome contrast to the cold perfection of the reigning Russian ballerinas, heralded the last great foreign invasion of Russian ballet. The stream of Italian ballerinas, mostly products of Carlo Blasis's system at the Milan academy, included: the young, exquisitely beautiful Antonietta dell'Era; Emma Bessone, who remained for several years in Moscow; and Carlotta Brianza, who arrived in 1887 and stayed for four years, dazzling audiences with her portrayal of Princess Aurora in *Sleeping Beauty* (1890). In addition to reviving public interest, the competition from the Italians inspired Russian dancers to greater efforts. For example, Pierina Legnani's introduction of 32 *fouettés* in *Cinderella* (1893) and later *Swan Lake* (1895) not only astounded balletomanes, but also frustrated the Russian ballerinas who tried to emulate her, until finally Mathilde Kschessinska discovered the key to the technique

The magnificent Imperial box in the vast Maryinsky (now Kirov) Theater in Leningrad, scene of countless milestones in ballet history.

(focussing on one point during each turn).

The most important difference between the wave of Romantic ballerinas that swept Russia during the second quarter of the nineteenth century and the dancers who came at the end was that most of the former came, danced, and left again. Many of the latter, however, stayed on to teach and influence future generations. Caterina Beretta, for example, was already more famous as a teacher than as a dancer when she arrived in St Petersburg in 1887, and commanded so much respect that many dancers followed her to Milan when she left in 1902. Of tremendous importance was the arrival of the great maestro Enrico Cecchetti, who came to dance Carabosse in *Sleeping Beauty* in 1890 and stayed to develop a whole new career in Russia, adding his special genius to the already excellent Imperial school system, and turning out a stellar list of dancers like Serafina Astafieva, Lubov Egorova, Mathilde Kschessinska, Anna Pavlova, Olga Preobrajenska, Julia Sedova, Vera Trefilova and Agrippina Vaganova.

Petipa's *Sleeping Beauty*, premiered in January 1890, was a major event. The old Bolshoi Theater had finally been declared unsafe and the performance was held in the elegantly remodelled Maryinsky (now called the Kirov), with its glamorous white, gold and pale blue decorations. The costumes were designed

by the director of the theater, the cultured, charming Ivan Alexandrovich Vsevolozhsky (1835–1909); Tchaikovsky's music (his favorite ballet score) was magnificent. The cast was more than equal to the occasion. Brianza danced Princess Aurora, partnered by the famous Russian *danseur noble*, Paul Gerdt, as Prince Charming; Cecchetti created both the wicked witch Carabosse and also Bluebird, providing demonstrations of his skill at mime and his superlative technique. Petipa's daughter, Marie Petipa II, portrayed the Lilac Fairy. Her part in

Irina Kolpakova, member of the Praesidium, as Aurora and her husband Vladilen Semyonov as Florimund in The Sleeping Beauty.

Above: Irina Kolpakova in the Kirov production of Petipa's Raymonda *to music by Glazunov. It was first performed in St Petersburg in 1898.*

the original production involved very little dancing; the variation we see today was staged some years later by Feodor Lopukhov for Egorova. All this was tied together by Petipa's choreography, which included an unequalled series of superb dances with not one, but two *pas de deux* at the finale.

The Czar did not like *Sleeping Beauty*, but even that fact did not damage its reception. Rather its success encouraged Vsevolozhsky to commission Tchaikovsky to write *The Nutcracker*. Though today it is an international favorite, its premiere in December 1892 was not auspicious. The choreography, by Petipa and his assistant, Lev Ivanov, could not overcome the silly libretto about a little girl's Christmas fantasy; Tchaikovsky did not enjoy writing the music and was less than enthusiastic about the final score. It was little wonder that its first performances received a lukewarm reception.

Tchaikovsky's first ballet score, *Swan*

Above left: Ekaterina Maximova in a 1966 Bolshoi restaging of The Nutcracker *(1892), choreography by Grigorovitch. The original by Ivanov/Petipa was not a success.*

Left: The corps de ballet *from the Bolshoi* Swan Lake. *This most-famous of all ballets also proved a failure when first performed in 1877.*

Lake, had not been successful either when it was produced in Moscow in 1877; the choreography had not been equal to the music, which the conductor considered 'too difficult' in any case. But after the composer's death in 1893, Vsevolozhsky decided to restage the second act as part of a memorial performance. Ivanov was assigned the task and in February 1894 Legnani starred in what was to become one of ballet's most enduring masterpieces.

Swan Lake is the story of Prince Siegfried, who meets the Swan Queen, Odette, while on a hunting expedition; she is under a spell that will be broken only if a man remains faithful to her. On his return home, Siegfried attends a ball, where he is tempted by Odile, a magician's daughter disguised as Odette. Despite his promise to the Swan Queen, he agrees to marry Odile, but of course discovers the deception in the nick of time. For the full production, given in January 1895, Petipa and Ivanov collaborated on the choreography; Petipa devised Acts I and III, which take place in the real world of the glittering court; while Ivanov composed the romantic, other-worldly lakeside scenes (Acts II and IV). At last, the ballet, with Legnani as Odette-Odile, enjoyed the success it deserved.

Although Petipa continued to produce some good ballets after *Swan Lake* (including *Raymonda* in 1898, to Glazunov's excellent music), he faced increasing dissatisfaction among many of the younger dancers, who were becoming restive under the restrictive, old-fashioned Imperial system. In 1899 his friend and colleague, Vsevolozhsky, was replaced as director by Colonel V A Telyakovsky. A strong mutual antipathy developed between the two, and in 1903, after a performance of *The Magic Mirror* drew boos and cat-calls (said to have been instigated by the Colonel), Petipa bitterly resigned.

In 1904 Isadora Duncan gave a series of performances that aroused a tremendous controversy in St Petersburg between the reactionaries, who saw her bare feet and emotionalism as a degradation of the art, and the reformers like Michel Fokine and his friends (including Tamara Karsavina and Anna Pavlova), who saw in her dancing reinforcement for their vision of a new dance form that had meaning beyond its value as purely visual entertainment. But the young radicals, whose thirst for reform was as desperate as that of their contemporaries in the political arena, ran up against a stone wall of traditionalism. Petipa recognized Fokine's talent and sent him a note after the performance of *The Vine* in 1906, saying, 'You will be a great ballet master.' But by that time the old man's support meant nothing. In 1909 Diaghilev had little trouble recruiting a host of gifted dancers away from Russia to join his new company, Ballets Russes.

With many of its most promising dancers gone, ballet in Russia – demonstrably the best in the world only a few years before – was dangerously weakened. Economic difficulties, World War I and finally the October Revolution in 1917 brought it to the edge of disaster. Most of the greatest dancers (many of whom had strong associations with the

Above: A scene from Rotislav Zhakarov's The Fountain of Bakhchisaray, *showing Khan Girei upheld by his Tartar warriors.*

Imperial family) fled. Those who remained faced a desperate battle to save classical ballet, which the new government tended to view as decadent and not suited to a mass audience. That ballet survived at all is due to the efforts of a few people like Anatoly Lunacharsky, the first Soviet Commissar of Education, and dancers like Agrippina Vaganova, Yekaterina Geltzer and Vassily Tikhomirov, who refused to join the flood of émigrés. The emergence in Leningrad of two new dancers, Marina Semyonova and the brilliant Galina Ulanova, was also a big boost for the classicists.

After the Revolution, Russia's capital was moved to Moscow, which hitherto had always taken second place to St Petersburg, in ballet as in everything else. Though the shift in political power helped strengthen the arts in the city, ballet had been improving its position there for several years. Ever since the turn of the century the committed reformer Alexander Gorsky had been working at the Bolshoi, trying – like Fokine – to break the chains of the old traditions and, under his direction, ballet in Moscow soon had a new lease of life.

George Zoritch the Russian-born dancer in the 'Ribbon Dance' from the first important Soviet ballet, The Red Poppy, *premiered in 1927.*

In the 1960s Maya Plisetskaya performed Juliet in Leonid Lavrovsky's ballet Romeo and Juliet, first shown with the legendary Galina Vlanova at the Kirov Theater in 1940.

Working with dedicated artists like Geltzer (his most popular ballerina), her husband, Tikhomirov, and Mikhail Mordkin, he reorganized the company completely. *The Red Poppy*, produced in 1927 by Tikhomirov and Lev Laschilin, became the first important Soviet ballet. Despite its obvious propagandist overtones and conventional choreography, the ballet (the story of a group of Russian sailors who assist Chinese workers in an uprising against their masters) was very popular, and its success represented a triumph for classicism over modernism. In 1935 Yelisaveta Gerdt (daughter of the famous Paul Gerdt) arrived from Leningrad; until her retirement in 1960 she was one of Moscow's most influential teachers. Important dancers at the Bolshoi during the second half of the decade included the great technician Olga Lepeshinskaya (b 1916), her partner Vladimir Preobrajensky (b 1912) and the outstanding character dancer Serge Koren (1907–69).

In Leningrad, meanwhile, the old Maryinsky's name had been changed to the State Academic Theater of Opera and Ballet, known by its Russian initials, GATOB. (In 1935 it received its present name, the Kirov State Academic Theater of Opera and Ballet, after the Soviet hero, Serge Kirov.) During the 1920s GATOB was the center for much experimental ballet activity; in 1923 the young George

Balanchine appeared in Feodor Lopukhov's abstract *Dance Symphony*, and during the same period Kasyan Goleizovsky was producing avant-garde cubist and constructivist ballets. Lopukhov, known as 'the choreographer's choreographer,' also played an important role in preserving the classical repertory at the theater. Some noteworthy productions during the 1930s were: Vassily Vainonen's *Flames of Paris* (1932), with its exciting, realistic mob scenes; Rotislav Zakharov's *Fountain of Bakhchisaray* (1934), another realistic production based on a Pushkin poem, about a Polish girl (originally danced by Ulanova) kidnapped by a Tartar and later stabbed by one of his jealous wives; and Vakhtang Chaboukiani's *Laurencia* (1939), with its Spanish folk dances.

Leonid Lavrovsky produced an elaborate *Romeo and Juliet*, with music by Prokofiev, in 1940. Ulanova gave a brilliant performance as Juliet, and the work is still considered to be in the top rank of Soviet ballets.

During World War II there was little ballet activity in Russia. Dancers from both the Kirov and the Bolshoi were evacuated, and the elegant old Kirov was badly damaged during the Siege of Leningrad. After the war, when Ulanova was transferred to Moscow and Lavrovsky was appointed ballet master (1944–56 and 1960–64), the center of Soviet ballet finally and definitely shifted to the capital. In 1945 Zakharov created a splendid *Cinderella* to Prokofiev's second ballet score, starring Lepeshinskaya in the title role. Lavrovsky's original version of *The Stone Flower* (again, to Prokofiev's music) premiered in 1954. But despite stellar performances by Ulanova and the great Maya Plisetskaya, the production was not very successful; Yuri Grigorovich's 1957 production for the Kirov has become the standard version.

The major dancers in Moscow during the postwar period – in addition to Plisetskaya (b 1925), an extraordinary technician with an amazingly supple body and excellent acting ability – include: her favorite partner, Nicolai Fadeyechev (b 1933); the popular Raissa Struchkova (b 1925); Nina Timofeyeva (b 1935), who came from Leningrad to become one of the Bolshoi's best-known ballerinas; the brilliant character dancer Georgi Farmanyantz (b 1921); Maris-Rudolph Liepa (b 1936); and Yaroslav Sekh (b 1930).

Above left: Maya Plisetskaya, prima ballerina assoluta, *in* The Little Humpbacked Horse.

Above: Two spectacular jumps from Maris Liepa as the Roman general Crassus in the grandiose Bolshoi production of Grigorovitch's Spartacus.

In 1956 the Bolshoi company made its first appearance in London and in 1959 they appeared in New York. In 1960 Sophia Golovkina was made director of the school, and in 1964 the gifted Grigorovich (b 1927) was transferred to Moscow as chief choreographer and artistic advisor, bringing with him a new elegance and grace to enhance the acrobatic Moscow style. Some of the most popular dancers at the Bolshoi in recent years include Natalia Bessmertnova (b 1941) and her partner Mikhail Lavrovsky (b 1941), Yekaterina Maximova (b 1939), and the internationally popular Vladimir Vasiliev (b 1940).

The Grigorovich years at the Bolshoi have been dominated by a series of huge epic creations that stress the athletic vigor of the male dancers in contrast to the fleet, polished flexibility of the ballerinas. The favorite Grigorovich ballet is the heroic

Left: Raissa Struchkova in the Bolshoi production of Walpurgis Nacht, *a divertissement from* Faust *choreographed by Lavrovsky in 1941.*

and bombastic *Spartacus* (1968, following earlier versions by other choreographers in 1958 and 1963).

Here Grigorovich devised a pattern that has remained consistent throughout his other major ballets. Large crowd scenes are set against intimate solos and duets for the main characters. Grigorovich refers to them as 'dialogues.' This alteration of focus allows the sweep of historical events, so loved by the Soviet realist school, to be juxtaposed with psychological portraits of the individuals caught up in the grand schemes of history.

Spartacus leads a slave rebellion against Crassus, a depraved Roman general of the first century BC. The characters are depicted in extreme black-and-white contrast: noble Spartacus and his saintly wife, Phrygia; the wicked Crassus and his evil-minded consort, Aegina. All of them are set in high relief by stampeding hordes of soldiers and rebellious slaves.

Grigorovich continues the same formula in *Ivan the Terrible* (1975). The locale is Russia in the sixteenth-century. The story centers on a boyar conspiracy to dethrone the young czar. The quiet interludes focus on the doomed love of Ivan and his bride Anastasia. Massive crowds of the Russian populace surge through the ballet in complex and energetic crowd scenes.

The Golden Age (1982) may be the most successful of Grigorovich's ballets. Set in the roaring 1920s, it is more frothy and less heavy-handed than the historical epics. The flimsy story concerns a night-club dancer, named Rita, who falls in love with an upright working youth named Boris. The entire company celebrates a People's Festival in the first act, slinks through some funny nightclub routines in the second act, and gathers for a rousing happy-ending finale. It's all presented with a lively cartoon-strip flair.

All of these ballets have featured Natalia Bessmertnova (Grigorovich's wife). Dark and delicate, and with an ethereal manner, she has become the leading Russian ballerina of her generation. Recently she has found an ideal new partner in the dynamic Irek Mukamedov (b 1960). His prodigious energies are tempered with a lyricism unknown in other Bolshoi males. Already dancing many leading roles, Mukamedov is set to become one of the greatest of all Russian dancers.

Despite the Bolshoi's growth, the Kirov has by no means drifted into insignificance. In 1944 the theater was rebuilt and Natalia Dudinskaya (b 1912) replaced Moscow-bound Ulanova as prima ballerina. She and her husband, Konstantin Sergeyev (b 1910), were the Kirov's leading couple in the 1950s, and have since held varying positions in the theater's administrative hierarchy, depending on the political climate. Some of the noteworthy productions at the Kirov since the war are: Zakharov's *The Bronze Horseman* (1949); Leonide Yacobson's *Shuraleh* (1950) and *Spartacus* (1956); Sergueyev's *Path of Thunder* (1957), which was based on South Africa's racial problems; Igor Belsky's *Coast of Hope* (1959); and Grigorovich's *Legend of Love* (1962).

The most important dancers include: Mikhail Baryshnikov (b 1948); Irina

Left: The Mistress of the Copper Mountain (Alla Osipenko) helps the Stone Cutter (Igor Chernishev) in his quest for Katerina.

Kolpakova (b 1933); Gabriella Komleva
(b 1938); Natalia Makarova (b 1940);
Rudolf Nureyev (b 1938); Valerie Panov
(b 1938); Alla Shelest (b 1919), who has
been ballet mistress of the company since
1970; and Yuri Soloviev (b 1940). Unfortunately the sterility of the Kirov's
repertory and the rigidity of its system,
which has not changed much since the
early part of the century, have led to
rebellion and an exodus by some of the

*Top: Princess Aurora has just pricked her finger
on the fateful spindle in this Bolshoi performance of
Sleeping Beauty with Natalia Bessmertnova.*

*Above: Natalia Dudinskaya great prima ballerina
of the Kirov and disciple of Vaganova, and her
husband Konstantin Sergeyev famous danseur noble.*

*Right: Top Bolshoi star, the internationally
acclaimed Vladimir Vasiliev in the title role of the
Bolshoi's spectacular ballet Spartacus.*

Above: The Bolshoi Ballet's current style is seen in the populist jazz-age romp The Golden Age *choreographed by Grigorovich in 1982.*

Above right: The world-famous Russian star Natalia Makarova in her most famous role, Giselle, in the Kirov production.

Below: As well as a great dancing career Konstantin Sergeyev has long been involved in the company's administration, albeit with stormy patches.

Mikhail Baryshnikov, pictured here in a pas de deux *with Alla Sizova before his defection.*

Irek Mukhamedov, a new star for the 80s, in the Bolshoi's Spartacus with Natalia Bessmertnova, reigning ballerina since 1965.

Left: One of Makarova's last performances of Giselle *with the Kirov. She is partnered by Yuri Soloviev in Act II of the ballet.*

Below left: An extremely rare shot of Nureyev demonstrating his prowess while a senior student at the Kirov school.

best dancers. Nureyev, Baryshnikov and Makarova all broke away to the West. Panov and his wife, after a widely publicized, two-year struggle, were allowed to emigrate to Israel. However, Panov's individualism has made it difficult for him to accept Western standards.

Panov's major work in the West has been done in Germany, where he is now artistic director of the Berlin Ballet. His choreography tends towards the grandiose. In 1979 he translated Dostoevsky's *The Idiot* into ballet. In 1981 he brought Tolstoy's *War and Peace* to the stage. Opinions continue to be sharply divided on Panov's large-scale projects.

The Moscow Classical Ballet was created in 1968. With only 50 dancers, it is much more portable than either the Kirov or the Bolshoi. Under the direction of former dancers Vladimir Vasilev and Natalia Kasatkina, this company has toured throughout the USSR and abroad.

The repertory ranges from the standard classics to Pierre Lacotte's 1980 reconstruction of *Nathalie, or the Swiss Milkmaid*. This is a charmingly inconsequential bit of fluff originally choreographed by Filippo Taglioni in Vienna (1821). The company's most popular ballet is *The Creation of the World*, a 1971 comedy by Vasilev and Kasatkina that retells Genesis in a style that mixes Hollywood, music-hall and classical ballet together.

The continuing success of Russian ballet is based on the excellent dancers turned out year after year by the Soviet school system. Students are admitted to the state academies at the age of 10, after passing a physical examination that not only checks their health and coordination, but even takes into consideration details like delicate hands and long necks for girls. For the next nine years, every hour of their lives is regulated by the school. Smoking and drinking are not allowed and long hours of dance classes (including classic, character and historical dance, adagio and mime) alternate with academic courses, emphasizing the history of art and music.

Right: Valery and Galina Panov with the Israeli Batsheva Dance Company, after their long struggle to emigrate there from Russia.

Training at all schools is carried out under a standard method developed by Agrippina Vaganova, and this continuity has done much to ensure the consistently high quality of the graduates. Though few Westerners could make the enormous commitment required by the Soviet system, especially at such an early age, it does produce dancers with extraordinary elevation, strength and fluidity, and avoids the worst pitfalls of the American 'catch-as-catch-can' situation, which often results in dancers whose training has been superficial and disconnected.

Once the Soviet government finally decided to accept ballet as both a valid art form and the perfect goodwill instru-

Above and top: The Moiseyev Folk Dance Ensemble was founded in 1937 by Igor Moiseyev, former Bolshoi soloist. The dances they perform are adapted from folk dances and from events in everyday life. One of the examples here is a Cossack-style dance, the other a work aptly-named Football.

ment (since there is no language barrier), Russian ballet flourished. By the mid-1960s there were 34 ballet companies in 31 cities in the Soviet Union. Some, like the companies in Kiev or the Georgian capital of Tbilissi (now directed by Chabukiani), have traditions dating back to the nineteenth century, while others are of more recent origin. Kiev's Genrik Maiorov (b 1936), Nikita Dolgushin (b 1938) of Leningrad's Maly (Little) Theater, and Perm's Nicolai Boyartchikov (b 1935) are three of Russia's most noteworthy choreographers. Moscow's Stanislawsky Theater company, directed by Vladimir Bourmeister, has had great success abroad, as has the State Folk

Dance Ensemble, which specializes in a dance form somewhere between folk dancing and ballet.

The recent development of ballet in the Soviet Union is very different from that in the West. The isolation that followed the Revolution meant that many of the old traditions survived. That, plus the commitment to make ballet acceptable to as wide an audience as possible, has led to a concentration on full-length, dramatic ballets with strong stories, lots of action and realistic stagecraft to carry them. Folk dances are incorporated into Russian productions much more than in the West.

The continuity of the Russian ballet tradition is one of its greatest strengths, but often the weight of that tradition stifles experimentation and growth. Despite many visits from Western ballet and modern dance troupes, the creative climate in the Soviet Union has become increasingly stale.

IVAN VALBERKH
1766–1819

Ivan Valberkh, the first famous Russian ballet master, graduated from the St Petersburg academy, where he had studied with Angiolini and Canziani in 1786.

As a choreographer he obtained most of his plots from literature, operas and plays. He was fiercely devoted to the cause of advancing Russian dancers, and his patriotic ballets were his most popular productions. The story has it that one, *Love for the Fatherland* (1812), was so inflammatory that many in the audience left the theater and immediately enlisted in the war against Napoleon.

He succeeded Cenziani as director of the school in 1794, and later also reorganized and ran the academy in Moscow.

CHARLES DIDELOT
1767–1837

Charles Didelot studied with his father at the Royal Theater, Stockholm, then in Bordeaux and Paris with Auguste Vestris, Noverre, Lany and Dauberval. In 1790 he joined the Paris Opéra and partnered Guimard, but within a few years he had struck out on his own and was working in theaters throughout Europe.

Didelot was a good dancer and an excellent choreographer, who put Noverre and Dauberval's theories concerning dramatic clarity and expressiveness to good use. However, his European reputation was even more the result of his genius for stagecraft. In *Flore et Zéphyre* (first seen in London in 1796), for example, dancers flew high above the stage on invisible wires, gently landing on the tips of their toes (ballet slippers with blocked toes had not yet been invented). He also was an advocate for unconfining costumes and tights, to give dancers more freedom of movement.

Didelot is best known, however, as one of the founders of Russian ballet. During his two engagements in St Petersburg (1801–11 and 1816–37) he choreographed over 20 productions, described by Pushkin as having 'more poetry than in all of French literature.' His most lasting contribution was his amplification and organization of the curriculum at the ballet school. He ran the institution with harsh, almost military discipline, but in so doing he established a strong foundation for Russian ballet training that endures to this day and has had a significant effect on ballet.

MARIA DANILOVA
1793–1810

Maria Danilova was sent to the Imperial ballet academy in St Petersburg in 1801. Though she was only eight years old, her talent soon attracted Didelot's attention. She made her first appearance on stage at the age of nine; by the time she was 15 she was dancing with prestigious partners. like Louis Duport in *Les Amours de Venus et d'Adonis, ou La Vengeance de Mars*.

When she graduated from the academy in 1809, Danilova was Russian ballet's brightest hope for a ballerina of international stature. Her dancing was so light and elusive that it almost took her audience's breath away. But Danilova was too delicate to withstand the tremendous physical and emotional pressures of professional ballet and a short, unhappy love affair with Duport undermined her constitution still further. Tragically, she died of consumption before her official debut, when she was only 17.

AVDOTIA ILYINITSHNA ISTOMINA
1799–1848

Avdotia Istomina graduated from the St Petersburg academy in 1815 and by 1820 held the important rank of *première danseuse mime*.

In addition to her great beauty (she had jet-black hair and a perfect figure), she had a self-confident, accomplished technique with especially good elevation and pirouettes, and was also an accomplished actress. Her most popular roles were in Didelot's *Flore et Zéphyre, The African Lion or Heroism of a Mother, The Caliph of Baghdad, Ruslan and Ludmila* and *Prisoner of the Caucasus* (1823), which Pushkin wrote with her in mind as the Circassian woman.

Unfortunately, her career was cut short by a foot injury in 1829. Following the accident she danced less and less, finally retiring altogether in 1836. She unfortunately died in a cholera epidemic 12 years later.

CHRISTIAN JOHANSSON
1817–1903

Christian Johansson began his training at the Royal Swedish Ballet school in Stockholm, where he showed so much promise that the theater sent him to Copenhagen to work with August Bournonville. On his return in 1837 he was made *premier danseur* and was considered one of the company's most promising dancers.

When Marie Taglioni came to Stockholm in 1841 as a guest artist, she formed an equally high opinion of Johansson's ability. In fact, she was so impressed that when it was time for her to set out for her next engagement in St Petersburg, she 'kidnapped' her Swedish partner and took him with her. Though she departed after her performances there, he decided to remain, taking a post as *premier danseur*.

In 1860 Johansson began teaching as well as dancing and soon discovered that it was his true vocation. In 1869, though he was still very popular as a dancer, he gave up the stage entirely.

As a teacher, Johansson is one of the most important figures in Russian ballet history. He was well-versed in the Bournonville method and was especially good at coaching the male dancers; his highest compliment was always, 'Now you may do that in public.' Paul Gerdt, Kschessinska and Preobrajenska are just a few of his many famous pupils. Perhaps his greatest accomplishment was to ensure that in Russia, as in Scandinavia, male dancers were never pushed into the background as they were in the rest of Europe during the Romantic era.

Johansson's daughter Anna (1860–1917) carried on the family tradition, becoming a ballerina in St Petersburg and later a much respected teacher in her own right.

MARIUS PETIPA
1818–1910

Marius Petipa, one of the great choreographers of the nineteenth century and a towering figure in Russian ballet, was born in Marseilles into a family of travelling dancers. He began studying dance at the age of seven while the family was based in Brussels, and his childhood was spent touring Europe. He danced his first

solo in Nantes, when he was 16. The Petipas even managed an engagement in the United States, but the tour turned into a disaster when their dishonest manager decamped with all the box-office receipts.

Back in Europe his family settled in Paris, where, while Marius studied with Auguste Vestris, his older brother Lucien joined the Opéra company. Lucien was an excellent dancer and was soon made *premier danseur*. His fame rose to even greater heights when he created the role of Albrecht, as Grisi's partner in the first *Giselle*.

Marius grew more and more unhappy working in his brother's shadow in Paris. Finally he set out on his own to create an independent career, spending a year in Bordeaux and four more in Madrid before taking a position in St Petersburg in 1847.

Petipa had a long apprenticeship ahead of him before he reached the heights of his later years; for 12 years he danced, taught and acted as assistant ballet master to Jules Perrot and Arthur Saint-Léon — neither of whom was inclined to share his glory with a lowly aide. In 1854 he married the dancer Marie Sourovschikova and was able to do much to advance her career. But by 1861, after a tour to Riga, Berlin and Paris, he was much more interested in a new protegée, Ekaterina Vazem.

He did not achieve his first major success until 1862 when, against all odds, he produced a new, five-act ballet in only six weeks for the visiting Carolina Rosati. *The Pharaoh's Daughter* was a tremendous success, and the resulting sensation finally made an impression on the management. When Saint-Léon left for good in 1869, Petipa was made ballet master at the St Petersburg Bolshoi Theater.

As director, he proved adept at the difficult business of pleasing the public, dealing with the bureaucracy that controlled the Imperial Theaters, and at the same time maintaining some measure of artistic integrity. During the next 30 years he ruled unchallenged in St Petersburg, producing more than 50 new ballets, reviving 17 old ones and arranging dances for some 35 operas.

Some of his best known works include: *Le Roi Candaule* and *Don Quichotte, or Don Quixote,* (both 1869); *La Bayadère* (1877); *La Belle au Bois Dormant, or Sleeping Beauty,* and *Le Lac des Cygnes, or Swan Lake,* (both 1890); and *Raymonda* (1898). Most of his works were five- or six-act productions, with elaborate sets and intricate dances, interspersed with mime, beautiful groupings and long, imposing processions. Petipa did much to promote the unity of dance and music in ballet; the problem was that once he had hit upon a successful formula he applied it mechanically, long after it had become hackneyed and extremely predictable.

Much of Petipa's success was due to his excellent rapport with Ivan Vsevolozhsky, director of the Imperial Theaters, who consistently gave him wholehearted support. When Vsevolozhsky was replaced in 1901, the entire situation changed. His successor, Colonel Telyakovsky, was anxious only to get rid of Petipa and establish his own administration. In 1903, after Petipa's production of *The Magic Mirror* was received badly, he resigned and, as a final insult, was forbidden even to enter the theater that had been his world for more than half a century. Though he remained in St Petersburg until his death seven years later, watching and commenting on ballet from afar, he died a bitter and unhappy old man.

ELENA ANDREIANOVA
1819–57

Elena Andreianova graduated from the Imperial Theater school in 1837 and was one of the many Russian ballerinas watching jealously from the wings while Marie Taglioni took St Petersburg by storm that same year.

Soon, however, Andreianova achieved a considerable amount of power in the Imperial system, partly because of her popularity with audiences and partly because her friend and lover, Alexander Guedenov was the director of the Imperial Theaters. In 1842 she was the first Russian to portray Giselle; in 1845 Guedenov arranged for her much publicized and highly successful Paris debut (audiences at La Scala in Milan were less impressed).

The arrival of Fanny Elssler in 1848 forced everyone, including Andreianova, into the background and, to avoid a major explosion, Guedenov sent her to Moscow. However, Moscow audiences were jealous of their own ballerinas and did not take kindly to invasions from St Petersburg; on Andreianova's opening night, instead of flowers someone threw a dead cat onto the stage. Shocked and appalled, the ballerina fainted, upon which the audience relented and gave her a standing ovation.

In 1862 she set out on another foreign tour. This, too, was successful, but on her return she discovered that Guedenov had found another protegée. Although she was only 34, Andreianova was forced to retire. Unable to bear St Petersburg any longer, she moved to France, where she died three years later.

MARFA (MARTHA) NICOLAYEVNA MOURAVIEVA
1838–79

Martha Mouravieva was a graduate of the St Petersburg academy, making her first appearance on the Bolshoi stage when she was 10 years old.

Her official debut was at an outdoor performance of *The Butterfly, The Rose and the Wolf*, presented on the estate of Prince Oldenburg. Oldenburg had written the music for the ballet, choreographed by Marius Petipa (then assistant to Arthur Saint-Léon) and co-starring his wife, Marie Petipa. With her striking beauty and slim figure, Mouravieva soon became a popular attraction both in St Petersburg and Moscow.

Though her technique was good, her acting ability was minimal, and her first appearance abroad – in an elaborate production of *Giselle* at the Paris Opéra – was not a resounding success. However, with Saint-Léon's backing, she became quite popular in subsequent appearances; she was especially admired in *Diavolina*, which he choreographed especially for her.

In December 1864 she danced in Saint-Léon's *Little Humpbacked Horse* in Russia; though she was only 27, it was to be her farewell performance before her resignation.

PAVEL (PAUL) ANDREYEVICH GERDT
1844–1917

Paul Gerdt studied with Petipa and Johansson in St Petersburg and graduated from the school there in 1864. Within two years he had been made *premier danseur*, a rank he held for the next 50 years.

Rimma Karelskaya in the Bolshoi production of Arthur Saint-Léon's the Little Humpbacked Horse.

Tall, blond and handsome, Gerdt was the most famous Russian dancer of his day. He was especially admired for his grandeur and noble bearing, and every ballerina considered it an honor to appear with him.

Gerdt created the leading male roles in many of Petipa's and Ivanov's productions, including *Sleeping Beauty* (1890), *Kalkabrino* (1891), *The Nutcracker* (1892), *Cinderella* (1893), *Halte de Cavalerie* (1896), *Raymonda* (1898) and *Swan Lake* (1895). He considered his creation of Rudolf in Petipa's *La Fille du Danube* his greatest role. In addition to his other talents, he had a gift for mime which enabled him to continue working long after he had passed his prime as a classical dancer; his farewell performance was as Gamache in *Don Quixote* at the age of 72.

He was also a teacher at the academy from 1909 and his classes in *pas de deux* and mime attracted many of the best Imperial dancers, including Pavlova, Karsavina, Fokine, Legat and Tikhomirov.

Gerdt's daughter Elizaveta also became a popular dancer at the Maryinsky and, like her father, she was especially admired for her pure, clean, classical technique. She remained in Russia after the Revolution and moved to Moscow in 1934 where she in turn taught many later Bolshoi stars, like Maya Plisetskaya and Raissa Struchkova.

VIRGINIA ZUCCHI
1847–1930

Virginia Zucchi was a graduate of La Scala in Milan where she studied with Blasis and Lepri, and spent the first 20 years of her working life touring the provinces of Italy and the capitals of Europe.

Her arrival in St Petersburg in 1885 revived the Russians' declining interest in ballet, heralding the third and last 'invasion' of that country by foreign dancers. In addition to her flashy, dazzling technique, she was an excellent actress, whose portrayal of the much-tried heroine in *Esmeralda* had the little girls from the ballet school sobbing in the balconies. Her other greatest successes were in Manzotti's *Brahma* and Petipa's versions of *La Fille Mal Gardée*, *Pharaoh's Daughter*, *Paquita* and *Coppélia*.

Following two highly successful seasons in Russia she made one last tour of the other European capitals, then retired and established a school at Monte Carlo, which she ran until her death.

PIERINA LEGNANI
1863–1923

Pierina Legnani was one of the great Italian ballerinas produced by La Scala during its heyday in the mid-nineteenth century, who, like many of her colleagues, spent the first part of her career touring the world – Europe, England, even the United States.

Her greatest successes, however, came in Russia when she introduced 32 *fouettés* into her début performance as Cinderella. Nothing like it had ever been seen in Russia before and the feat was an even greater success when she repeated it as Odile, in the *pas de deux* in the third act of the 1895 revival of *Swan Lake*. Her other ballets included leading roles in *The Pearl* (which commemorated the coronation of Nicolas II in 1896), *Bluebeard* (1896), *Raymonda* (1898), *Ruses d'Amour* (1900) and innumerable revivals of classics like *Coppélia* and *The Talisman*.

Along with Mathilde Kschessinska, she is the only dancer in the history of the Maryinsky to receive the title *prima ballerina assoluta*. It is a tribute to her that, although younger Russian ballerinas breathed a sigh of relief when her retirement in 1901 ended her virtual monopoly of the ballet stage, they could all agree that, in addition to being a great dancer, she had been a charming, kind person, liked by everyone.

NICOLAI GUSTAVOVICH LEGAT
1869–1937

Nicolai Legat, one of the most distinguished teachers of the twentieth century, was born in St Petersburg and studied at the Imperial school there with Gerdt and Johansson. He graduated in 1888. An excellent dancer with an impeccable technique, he soon became one of the Maryinsky's most respected principal dancers. In addition to his skillful classic dancing, he was an expert at *caractère* and mime and appeared in some 70 ballets in 20 years.

In 1903 Legat succeeded Petipa as ballet master, but though he choreo-graphed a few ballets, he far preferred teaching. After Johansson's retirement he took over as director of the school, where he taught a distinguished list of pupils, including Preobrajenska, Egorova, Sedova, Vaganova, Karsavina, Fokine, Nijinsky and Bolm.

Diaghilev lured him away in 1923 to replace Cecchetti as ballet master for Ballets Russes. In 1926 he and his wife opened a school in London, where he trained a whole new set of dancers like Danilova, Lopokova, Margot Fonteyn, Ninette de Valois, Anton Dolin and Serge Lifar. His wife continued to run the school after his death; it is now headed by Eunice Bartell and Derek Westlake.

OLGA JOSIFOVNA PREOBRAJENSKA
1870–1962

Olga Preobrajenska graduated from the St Petersburg academy in 1889 and the tiny, adorable dancer with the sparkling personality became one of the city's best-

Olga Preobrajenska, a great dancer and teacher of the Imperial Ballet era.

loved prima ballerinas (a rank she achieved in 1900).

She was an excellent technician and danced in some 700 performances in Russia, in addition to several tours after 1895. Her best roles included *Coppélia, Raymonda, The Seasons, Le Corsaire, Sleeping Beauty, Paquita, The Nutcracker, The Talisman, Sylvia* and *Don Quixote*. All in all, she dominated the Russian ballet scene during the first two decades of the twentieth century.

Preobrajenska began her teaching career in St Petersburg in 1914 and continued after she left the country in 1921. After two years spent travelling and teaching in Milan, London, Buenos Aires and Berlin, she settled in Paris, where she opened the famous Studio Wacker. There she attracted virtually every exceptional dancer of the time, continuing to teach until she was 90. By the time she finally retired in 1960 she had been responsible for forming several generations of the best dancers in Europe.

ALEXANDER ALEXEIEVICH GORSKY
1871–1924

Alexander Gorsky, a contemporary of Fokine at the Maryinsky, graduated from the Imperial school in 1889 and be-

Kschessinska, prima ballerina assoluta.

came a soloist with the company in 1895. In 1896 he also began teaching and was instrumental in introducing the Stepanoff system of dance notation into the curriculum.

In 1900 he moved to Moscow, where his production of *Don Quixote* proved him to be a master of *ballet d'action* on the grand scale. In addition to playing a major role in Moscow's rise from second to first place in the Russian artistic establishment, he proved to be an influential reformer, breaking up Petipa's stiff formations and applying Stanislavsky's emphasis on dramatic expression to ballet. His many productions show him to have been an important pioneer of dramatic, realistic ballet. His last ballet was *The Grotto of Venus* (1923–24).

MATHILDE FELIXOVNA KSCHESSINSKA
1872–1971

Mathilde Kschessinska studied with Ivanov and Johansson, and graduated from the ballet academy in St Petersburg in 1890. Like her father (the popular Polish character dancer Felix Kschessinsky), brother and sister, she joined the Maryinsky company.

Kschessinska was one of the first Russians to try to meet the challenge posed by the visiting Italian ballerinas at the end of the nineteenth century; she was the first Russian to dance Brianza's Aurora in *Sleeping Beauty* and the Sugar Plum Fairy in *The Nutcracker*. Her greatest talent was for *demi-caractère*, and her favorite role was Esmeralda, which she danced in Zucchi's style. After Legnani had amazed Russian audiences with her famous 32 *fouettés*, native ballerinas struggled to discover her secret. Finally, after many hours of work and experimentation, Kschessinska discovered the technique: to keep from losing her balance it was necessary to focus on the same fixed spot through each turn. That night she fixed her eyes on the medals decorating the chest of a baron who occupied the same seat for every performance. As she twirled away the crowd erupted into thunderous cheers; at last a Russian ballerina had reached the heights of the Italians.

Kschessinska, the only dancer other than Legnani to be titled *prima ballerina assoluta* at the Maryinsky (in 1895), was

the last of the great Czarist ballerinas. She had beauty (her waist was so slim that a man could span it with his two hands), a flawless technique, an acting talent that ranged from comic to tragic roles and a personality commonly described as charming.

She wielded great influence, not only at the theater, but also in the city's political and social life, first as the mistress of Czarovich Nicolai (later Nicolas II) and then as the morganatic wife of his cousin, Grand Duke Andrei. Her elegant house on Kronervsky Prospect was one of the focal points for St Petersburg's upper crust and Lenin used her balcony to address the crowds when he returned from exile to take power in 1917.

Kschessinska gave a few performances with Ballets Russes in Paris in 1911, but most of her dancing was done in Russia. She left the country in 1920, marrying the Grand Duke the following year and settling on the Côte d'Azur. In 1929 she opened a school in Paris. The last time she danced in public was in 1936 when, at the age of 64, she performed her famous Russian Dance for a charity event at London's Covent Garden.

VASSILI DIMITRIEVICH TIKHOMIROV
1876–1956

Vassili Tikhomirov graduated from the Moscow ballet school in 1891, then moved to St Petersburg to study with Gerdt and Johansson. Returning to the Bolshoi in 1893, he soon became the company's leading principal dancer, with a unique, acrobatic, extraordinarily plastic style. Though he toured with Pavlova in 1914, most of his dancing was in partnership with his wife, Yekaterina Geltzer.

After the October Revolution he and Geltzer worked with Gorsky and Mordkin to reorganize the company, and fought long, hard and often bravely to preserve the classic tradition in Russian ballet. From 1925 to 1930 he succeeded Gorsky as director of both the Bolshoi Ballet and its school, continuing to teach until 1937.

In addition to distinguished careers as both dancer and choreographer (*The Red Poppy*, produced in 1927, is generally considered to be the first good Soviet ballet), Tikhomirov is also known as one of the greatest teachers in the history of Russian ballet.

YEKATERINA GELTZER
1876–1962

Almost from the day of her debut in 1894 until her retirement in the late 1920s, Yekaterina Geltzer was Moscow's most important ballerina.

Her rare combination of strong technique and outstanding acting talent made her equally at home in traditional roles or in *demi-caractère*. She was also famous as a teacher; and, as one of the few prima ballerinas who elected to stay in Russia after the Revolution, she and her husband Vassili Tikhomirov were major protagonists in the battle to maintain the classics after 1917.

In 1927, at the age of 51, she created the leading role of Tao-Hoa in the first successful Soviet ballet, *The Red Poppy*. She and Tikhomirov are two of the most distinguished members of the first generation of Soviet dancers.

AGRIPPINA JACOVLEVNA VAGANOVA
1879–1951

Agrippina Vaganova graduated from the Maryinsky school in 1897. She had a

Agrippina Vaganova, author of Basic Principles of Classical Ballet, *takes class.*

superb technique; but without beauty or influential friends, she achieved the rank of ballerina only in 1915, the year before she retired.

If she never quite made it as a dancer, she did leave a mark on Russian ballet history as a teacher. In 1921 she received an appointment to the Petrograd State Choreographic School, and was soon the most famous instructor on the staff. In 1934 she was named director of the institution.

Her teaching method was a synthesis of the most important schools and styles from all over the world, both old and new. These she meticulously analyzed and developed in her book, *Basic Principles of Classical ballet*.

The Vaganova System is now the basis for instruction in ballet schools throughout Eastern Europe and in many schools in the West. There can be little doubt that her methods and unstinting dedication have made possible the continuing excellence of Soviet ballet and of Russian dancers.

ANNA PAVLOVNA PAVLOVA
1881–1931

The 'Immortal Pavlova,' as she was known throughout the world, was born in St Petersburg to poor parents. Though she was a sickly child, she managed to

The legendary Anna Pavlova in quadruplicate from the ballet La Fille Mal Gardée, *1912.*

gain entrance to the ballet academy in 1891 and soon her talent was obvious to her teachers: Gerdt, Johansson, and her favorite, Cecchetti. She joined the Maryinsky company in 1899 and was given the rank of ballerina in 1905.

By the time she set out on her first tour in 1908 (to Stockholm, Copenhagen, Prague and Berlin) she was already a great ballerina, experienced in most of the classics and recognized by her colleagues and audiences alike as a genius. Her tours became longer and more frequent; though officially an employee of the Maryinsky until 1913, she was rarely seen on its stage.

Diaghilev managed to sign her for his first Paris season in 1909 and her presence on the program did much to ensure Ballets Russes's initial success. However, she disagreed with the impresario in many areas – especially his preference for male dancers – and she could not share Ballets Russes's attachment to the new and novel. Fokine's *Firebird* was originally composed with her in mind, but when she heard Stravinsky's music she pronounced it 'nonsense' and refused to consider dancing to it.

In 1910 she formed the Anna Pavlova company. At first it consisted of only eight dancers from St Petersburg, but when she was offered a contract to tour America in 1913 she enlarged the company with English dancers and also expanded the repertory. It was the beginning of an incredible 15-year tour, virtually without a break, which took her to every continent, from Australia to Africa, to South America and all over North America and Europe – some 300,000 miles and more than 4000 performances in all.

Pavlova's taste was not impeccable (in fact, it was often over-sentimental and sometimes actually tacky) and her company was seldom more than mediocre. None of that mattered. Wherever she went she became the very personification of ballet, even for those who never managed to see her. She lived only to dance and her obsession lifted her light, graceful, seemingly effortless technique above criticism. Her *Dying Swan* (a solo choreographed for her by Fokine during their early days in St Petersburg) reduced audiences to tears, and whoever saw her dance never forgot the experience.

Although Pavlova composed some of her own arrangements, her major choreographer was Ivan Clustine. Alexander Volinen (1882–1955), a former *premier*

danseur at the Bolshoi in Moscow, toured with the company for 13 years; he then opened a school in Paris which became known as one of the best in the world for male dancers. Mikhail Mordkin also travelled with the troupe for a time.

In 1931, just before her fiftieth birthday, she caught a chill in The Hague and soon it developed into pneumonia. As she lay dying she whispered, 'Prepare my swan costume.' The next night her company danced as usual, but when the time came for the *Dying Swan*, the curtain rose to an empty stage. During her lifetime Pavlova had inspired thousands of young dancers and had probably done more to bring ballet to the world than any other single dancer before or since.

TAMARA PLATONOVNA KARSAVINA
1885–1978

Tamara Karsavina, the daughter of Platon Karsavina, danced and taught at the Maryinsky; she made her own debut at the theater in 1902 in *Javotte*.

Karsavina attained the rank of ballerina in 1909, the year she joined Diaghilev's Ballets Russes with Fokine and other disaffected young dancers. Although she officially remained with the Maryinsky company until 1918, she is best known for her dancing abroad. She

The great Tamara Karsavina rehearsing a young dancer in her role of Columbine.

had great sympathy for Fokine's ideals and gave stellar performances in his Ballets Russes productions (her portrayal of the Ballerina puppet in Petrushka has never been equalled), as well as in Nijinsky's *Jeux* (1913) and Massine's *Le Tricorne* (1919) and *Pulcinella* (1920).

In 1918 she married an English diplomat, Henry Bruce, and moved to London, continuing to dance on an occasional basis for Diaghilev. However, these appearances grew less frequent over the years, since she was not comfortable with many of the modern ballets of the 1920s. In 1930–31 she danced for a season with Ballet Rambert in London.

Karsavina remained active in British ballet long after she had retired from the stage: she was Vice President of the Royal Academy of Dance until 1955; acted as advisor for revivals of many classic and Diaghilev ballets; and occasionally taught mime classes. Her autobiography, *Theatre Street* (London, 1930) is worth reading as a portrait of one of the outstanding (and most intelligent) ballerinas of our century.

FEODOR LOPUKHOV
1886–1973

Feodor Lopukhov was part of a dancing family which included his brother Andrei (1898–1947) and his sisters Yevgenia (1884–1941) and Lydia (b 1891). He graduated from the St Petersburg academy in 1905 and, apart from a short stay in Moscow (1907–09), remained with the company until his retirement in 1970.

During the difficult years immediately following the Revolution, he was instrumental in preserving the old classics and was considered one of the world's experts on classical techniques. He was known as 'the choreographer's choreographer,' and during the 1920s was one of the Soviet Union's leading experimentalists. Apart from revivals his ballets include a version of *Firebird*, the abstract *Dance Symphony*, (set to Beethoven's Fourth Symphony, 1923), *The Red Whirlwind* (1924), *The Bolt* (music by Shostakovich, 1935), *Taras Bulba* (1940) and *Pictures from an Exhibition* (to music by Mussorgsky, 1963). He also created the best-known Lilac Fairy variation (*Sleeping Beauty*) for Lubov Egorova in the early 1900s. Lopukhov was fond of introducing acrobatic techniques into his ballets, like the high lifts in *Ice Maiden*; all the leading choreographers in Russia

today studied with or have been strongly influenced by him.

In addition to his contributions to choreography, Lopukhov served as director of GATOB/Kirov in 1922 to 1930, 1944 to 1947 and 1955 to 1958, in addition to being the founder and first director (1931–36) of Leningrad's Maly Theater. He is the only holder of the title Honored Ballet Master from the Soviet Government.

VASLAV NIJINSKY
1890–1950

Vaslav Nijinsky, one of the greatest male dancers of this century, was already well regarded in St Petersburg when Diaghilev hired him to dance with Ballets Russes in 1909.

Nijinsky was not a prepossessing figure at first meeting: he was short, stocky and, offstage, rather shy and quiet. In front of an audience, however, he came alive. His classical technique was excellent – especially his elevation and *ballon* – while his affinity for character dancing and mime was equally noteworthy. His fondness for unusual roles added to his reputation as an almost mythical being. Soon his fame was as great as Taglioni's had ever been, based on performances in Fokine's ballets like *Les Sylphides* and *Spectre de la Rose* (in which his final leap through a window became one of the most famous in ballet history). He danced with most of the famous ballerinas of his day, including Pavlova, but his most famous characterizations were created in partnership with Karsavina. He also danced with Isadora Duncan in Paris – an experience which had a definite effect on both his dancing and his choreography.

Diaghilev encouraged him to try his hand at choreography; he found it a slow, painful business, and his results were, to say the least, unusual. His dances were based on classical ballet movements, but they contained elements of modern dance in their angularity and broken rhythms; he was also fond of striving for a two- rather than three-dimensional quality in his productions. In general, these were received with shock and controversy in Paris and with serious consideration in London. In *L'Après-midi d'un Faune* (1912) audiences were first taken aback

Nijinsky's role of The Golden Slave in Schéhérazade, faithfully reproduced by Dudley van Loggenburg.

A tribute to Nijinsky's role in l'Après-midi d'un Faune *from Béjart's* Nijinsky, Clown of God.

(by the bare feet of the dancers and the contrast between Debussy's opulent score and Nijinsky's odd, jerky choreography), then scandalized by the closing scene with its hint of masturbation. The next year his contemporary ballet *Jeux* was eclipsed by *Le Sacre du Printemps*. The Paris audience reacted so vocally to Stravinsky's modern score and Nijinsky's strange choreography that he had to stand in the wings and pound out the rhythm because the dancers could not hear the music. Unfortunately, almost all of his choreography has since been lost.

In 1913 Ballets Russes sailed for South America, without Diaghilev, who had a superstitious fear of dying on water. During the voyage Nijinsky married Hungarian-born dancer Romola de Pulszky. Diaghilev – in a jealous rage – fired them both.

After World War I (during which he was interned), Nijinsky signed on with Ballets Russes again. His last choreography, *Tyl Eulenspiegel*, was premiered at the Metropolitan Opera House, New York, in 1916. It was abandoned before the company returned to Europe.

By this time he was already showing signs of mental illness; he became afraid of other dancers, worried about falling through trap doors and sometimes refused to dance at all. In 1917 he, his wife and daughter settled in St Moritz. In 1919 he was hospitalized for the first time. Nijinsky spent the rest of his life moving from one mental hospital to another. In 1947 Romola took him to London, where he died of a kidney disease in 1950. His body is now in the Montmartre cemetery in Paris.

GALINA SERGEYEVNA ULANOVA
b 1910

Galina Ulanova, who has become in her own lifetime the symbol of Soviet ballet in the eyes of the world and who is already considered one of the great figures in ballet history, saw her first ballet when her mother took her to a production of *Sleeping Beauty* at the Maryinsky Theater in St Petersburg. She entered the academy during the difficult years just after the Revolution and her first teachers were her mother and then Vaganova, the greatest of all Soviet instructors.

Ulanova graduated from the academy in 1928 and joined GATOB. The poetry

Galina Ulanova being presented with a bouquet.

and expressiveness of her dancing were apparent almost from the beginning. Her style, which was extraordinarily smooth, even and flowing, was shown to perfection when she danced Maria in the *Fountain of Bakhchisaray* (1934): it was an unparalleled performance which proved to be a turning point in her career. Her interpretation of Giselle is universally recognized as one of the greatest of all time.

In 1940 she starred in Lavrovsky's *Romeo and Juliet* and the resulting triumph marked the start of her greatest period as a dancer. Prokofiev composed all his ballets for her (*Romeo and Juliet*, *Cinderella* and *The Stone Flower*), and her transfer to Moscow in 1944 was a major factor in the rise of ballet there. Her fame had spread far beyond Russia long before she made her first outside appearance in Vienna in 1945.

In 1956 Ulanova went into semi-retirement, dancing only occasionally, and in 1962 she retired altogether. But retirement only meant the beginning of yet another distinguished career, as a teacher. Ulanova is no romantic; she talks of hard work before inspiration and takes a consciously intellectual approach to dance, which she describes as 'that which makes music visible.' She is a frequent guest of honor at ballet festivals in Eastern Europe and has come to be an articulate spokeswoman for Soviet ballet to the rest of the world.

The Dying Swan, *Pavlova's most famous role interpreted by the great Ulanova.*

The Scottish Ballet's spectacular Beauty and the Beast, *with choreography by its former director Peter Darrell and decor by Minshall.*

The reign of the Tudors (1485–1603) has often been described as one of the most fascinating periods of English history, and, of all the Tudor kings, the much-married Henry VIII (1491–1547) is probably the best remembered today. Many of the new ideas and art forms of the Renaissance made their first appearance in England during Henry's reign. Furthermore, his second wife, Anne Boleyn, came from a family still attached to its French roots. Anne had spent several years in France before moving to the English court in 1522 and, after she had replaced Katherine of Aragon in the king's affections (about 1530), the latest European fashion – court ballet – became popular in England as well. Her love of these entertainments was shared by the king, who was an expert musician and dancer.

Henry's daughter Elizabeth I (reigned 1558–1603) also loved dancing. Every morning, ignoring disapproving churchmen, she would leap through six or seven lively galliards. Court spectacles became more elaborate under Elizabeth, but they reached their peak when James I (reigned 1603–25) united the thrones of England and Scotland.

Masques, as the productions were called in England, combined court ballet from the continent with mummery, a form of entertainment popular in the early sixteenth century, in which disguised guests, bringing presents, would burst into a party and then join their hosts for a ceremonial dance. By the early seventeenth century, these masques had evolved into magnificent, colorful productions, performed outdoors on huge wooden platforms; they combined music, acting and dance, and for a time were the envy of Europe. Much of their development was due to the great theatrical architect Inigo Jones (1573–1652), whose elaborate costumes, sets and effects greatly enhanced their popularity.

Jones also wrote the occasional masque, but the major poet/playwrights were Samuel Daniel (The Twelve Goddesses, 1604) and Ben Jonson (1572–1637). Beginning in 1605 the arrogant, witty Jonson wrote 37 masques (12 designed by Jones) that were mixtures of dance, song and speech. Unfortunately for ballet, the words were so well written that dancing became relatively less important in the productions. Many of Jonson's masques have been lost, but two titles remain: The Masque of Blackness (1605) and The Masque of Beauty (1608). Shakespeare included a masque in The Tempest (writ-

ten about 1611) and John Milton wrote one called Comus (1634) for Lord Bridgewater, to music by the noble's music tutor, Henry Lawes.

Alfonso Ferrabosco was one of the most popular composers for these court productions; early choreographers included Thomas Gates and Hieronimus Herne.

The last masque on record is Samacida Spolia, presented at Whitehall in 1640. The show – which featured a bevy of nymphs who spelled out 'Anna Regina' in honor of Charles I's mother, Anne of Denmark – was enjoyed by all (despite Francis Bacon's sour remark that 'turning dancers into figures is a childish curiosity'). But court entertainments were, by definition, dependent on the fortunes of the monarchy, and as Charles I's power declined, so did ballet. With the advent of the Civil War in 1642 the masque died.

After the restoration of the monarchy in 1660, social life began to revive. In 1661 Sir William D'Avenant, one of Charles II's most loyal supporters, opened the Lincoln's Inn Fields theater; in 1663 another old comrade, Thomas Killigrew, obtained a royal charter and built the Theatre Royal in Drury Lane. From 1682 to 1695 the Drury Lane Theatre was managed by Thomas Betterton (1635–1710), a former member of D'Avenant's company, and considered the greatest English actor of his day.

Betterton was keenly interested in theater on the Continent and made several trips to France to examine theaters there and scout likely talent. In 1699 he brought back two of the most noted French dancers, Marie Subligny and Jean Balon; although they were well received, Balon, who was idolized in Paris, was a little disappointed at London's more objective reaction to his dancing.

Betterton reopened Lincoln's Inn Fields in 1695, then in 1705 he moved his company over to the new Haymarket theater, which soon became the city's principal venue for opera and ballet. A few years later, in 1717, Drury Lane audiences were unwitting spectators at a milestone in ballet history – the first serious attempt to tell a story using only dance and pantomime, without words. John Weaver's The Loves of Mars and Venus was composed of separate segments of mime and dance, and featured an all-English cast with the exception of Mars, who was portrayed by the most famous French dancer of the day, Louis

Dupré. Neither George I nor George II was interested enough to give Weaver the patronage he needed to develop the genre, but the work remains the earliest example we have of ballet d'action, predating Jean Noverre's efforts by some 50 years.

John Rich (1692–1761) is another important figure in English theater history. He is credited with introducing pantomime to the English stage, appearing himself in the role of Harlequin every year from 1716 to 1760. As manager of Lincoln's Inn Fields he regularly hired Marie Sallé and her brother to entertain audiences with their dancing during pantomimes or between the acts of operas. In 1728 he garnered some working capital from the very successful production of John Gay's Beggar's Opera and used the money to build a new theater at Covent Garden. In 1733 he hired Sallé, who had just resigned from the Paris Opéra. Unlike the managers of the French opera house, Rich was willing to give the dancer her way when it came to costumes and production. His gamble paid off handsomely; crowds fought to see her in Pygmalion, which she not only choreographed, but also danced the lead in, wearing a simple, unconfining tunic instead of the usual tight, heavy costume and with her hair streaming down her back. She also was able to produce another triumph, Bacchus and Ariadne, and arrange the dances for Handel's only complete ballet score, Terpsichore, before scandal forced her to return to France in 1735.

Though English audiences of the mid-eighteenth century included more than a sprinkling of aristocrats, their behavior was anything but refined. Bottles, fruit and vegetables flew through the air at regular intervals and riots (caused by either approbation or disapproval) sometimes seemed to be the rule rather than the exception. Not surprisingly, they found the dignified classics with mythological themes rather dull; far more popular were comic productions with titles like The Laundress's Visiting Day, Maggots, or The Drunken Peasant; or 'exotic' pieces like Turkish Dance, The Italian Peasants, or Tambourine. Thus, when David Garrick invited Jean Noverre to produce his Paris hit Les Fêtes Chinoises at Drury Lane in 1755, it seemed destined for certain success.

In addition to being the greatest actor in England at the time, Garrick (1719–79) was also an influential theater reformer.

During his tenure as manager of Drury Lane (1747–76), for example, he instituted concealed stage lighting and put a stop to the practice of allowing part of the audience to sit on the stage. Though his theatrical instincts were sound, his engagement of Noverre was badly timed. The colonial rivalry between England and France, which was about to erupt in the Seven Years War, had brought anti-French sentiments in London to boiling point. Though Garrick did his best, emphasizing Noverre's Swiss background, pointing out that two-thirds of the cast were English and even getting George II to attend the opening, it was to no avail. The never-stable audiences rioted on the fifth and sixth nights, breaking furniture, trying to tear down the sets and throwing dried peas and nails onto the stage. A mob even attempted to destroy Garrick's house. Not surprisingly, the production was withdrawn.

Garrick and Noverre remained friends, however, and in 1781 Noverre was appointed ballet master at King's Theatre, a post he held, commuting from his home outside Paris, until the theater burned down in 1789. One of his most popular dancers was his old enemy, Madeleine Guimard, who would arrive at the beginning of each summer season in a whirlwind of excitement. Her dancing kept the theater filled, while her amusing anecdotes and fashionable Paris wardrobe made her the toast of the London salons.

The outbreak of the French Revolution in 1789 and the subsequent war against Napoleon, meant that French dancers were not seen in England for some years; one notable exception was Charles Didelot, whose 1796 production of *Flore et Zéphyre* was a revelation in terms of imaginative stagecraft. Soon after the restoration of the French throne in 1815, however, English entrepreneurs were busily scouring the Continent, and within a few years foreign dancers were arriving in ever-increasing numbers. King's Theatre established a permanent *corps de ballet* and in 1826 Carlo Blasis was appointed choreographer and principal dancer. Though he was hard at work on his monumental thesis, *The Code of Terpsichore*, he was also able to do much to strengthen and organize the company. By the time his contract expired in 1830 ballet was more popular than opera, not only at King's Theatre, but also at the Haymarket and Covent Garden.

The Elssler sisters, Thérèse and Fanny, were the major attractions during the 1833 and 1834 seasons at King's Theatre. Thérèse was not only an excellent dancer (tall enough to partner her sister), but was also a choreographer, reviving *La Fée et la Chevalier* (1833) and *Armide* (1834). Fanny, meanwhile, was well on the way to developing her charming, vivacious style which would rival Taglioni's in a few years.

Another stalwart of the London scene between 1833 and 1837 was Pauline Duvernay. Her dancing career ended abruptly when an Englishman, Stephen Lyle-Stephens, bribed her mother and convinced Pauline to retire and become his mistress. The couple lived happily together for several years before they married; in later years the former dancer became one of the pillars of British society.

King's Theatre was renamed Her Majesty's Theatre in 1837 when Queen Victoria ascended the throne. The queen loved romantic ballet, and her approval – plus the shrewd management of Benjamin Lumley at Her Majesty's Theatre – lifted London to new heights in the ballet world. Though Elssler had been one of the first, eventually all the great Romantic ballerinas appeared in London; many, like Cerrito, Grisi, Rosati and Ferraris, appeared there before they danced in Paris. For a time, indeed, the traffic was reversed, with Opéra talent scouts covering London.

Lumley's perspicacity was never better demonstrated than in his decision to hire Jules Perrot in 1841. Perrot was one of the greatest choreographers of the Romantic era and some of his finest ballets were produced in London. Ballets like *Ondine* (1843), *La Esmeralda* (1844) and *Lalla Rookh* (1846) were big, grandiose productions that had everything: drama, excitement, hints of the supernatural and exotic dances from faraway places. By 1844 Perrot and his favorite composer, Carlo Pugni, controlled virtually all ballet in London, creating works for all the leading international stars of the day.

The vast majority of these dancers were foreigners, and the infant British ballet suffered a great blow when its most promising artist, Clara Webster, died tragically in 1844. Webster brushed against a gas lamp during a performance of Filippo Taglioni's *Revolt in the Harem* at the Drury Lane Theatre. Her *tutu* burst into flames in a moment; a stage hand caught her, as she rushed back and forth across the stage under the horrified gaze of the audience, and extinguished

Dame Margot Fonteyn in the role of Ondine, from Ashton's Royal Ballet production, after the early Romantic ballet by Jules Perrot in 1843.

the blaze, but it was too late. The unfortunate ballerina died two days later – at that, luckier than Emma Livry, who lingered for eight months after a similar accident in Paris in 1862.

In 1845 Lumley came up with what seemed at first to be an impossible scheme: he suggested that Perrot and Pugni devise a ballet that would star the four greatest ballerinas of the day – Taglioni, Grisi, Cerrito and Grahn – together on one stage. It was a fantastic idea; British enthusiasm for ballet was at its height and each of the four had her own group of fierce partisans. But how to get four spoiled, temperamental stars to work together at all, much less dance harmoniously in the same piece? The London *Times* predicted a terrible collision and during rehearsals that prediction seemed only too sound. The biggest battle was over the penultimate solo (all four ballerinas having decided that Taglioni deserved the honor of dancing last); Lumley, thinking fast, ordered that they appear in order of age, with the youngest first, and from then on the production ran smoothly.

Pas de Quatre, a divertissement with

no story line, was an instant, overwhelming success. The audience cheered from beginning to end and at times the flowers covered the stage, leaving hardly enough room for the dancers. The ballet was danced only five times by the original cast, but it was the talk of London; Queen Victoria and Prince Albert attended one of the few performances and found it as charming as everyone else did.

Pas de Quatre's success led to a whole series of 'steeplechases' (as Arthur Saint-Léon unkindly dubbed them). Taglioni, Cerrito and Grahn appeared the following year in *Le Jugement de Paris* and *Pas des Déesees*; the latter also featured Saint-Léon (Cerrito's husband) as Paris and Perrot himself as Mercury. Taglioni officially retired in 1847, but Cerrito, Grisi and Rosati carried on in *Les Eléments*; in 1848 the three were joined by Marie Taglioni II for *Les Quatre Saisons*.

Perrot left London in 1848 and was replaced by Paul Taglioni, who produced several excellent ballets starring his daughter Marie (1833–91). Grisi remained in England for a time, appearing in

Below: Jules Perrot's great triumph Pas de Quatre, *performed here by Carla Fracci, Rosella Hightower, Margrethe Schanne and Nathalie Krassovska.*

Above: Paul Taglioni's Electra *in 1849 with Carlotta Grisi dancing the leading role, was the first ballet to use the far safer electric lighting.*

Taglioni's *Electra, ou la Pléiade Perdue* (the first ballet to use electric light) in 1849 and in *Les Metamorphoses* (1850). The latter was her last appearance in Western Europe before joining Perrot in Russia.

However, Romantic ballet was, to all intents and purposes, finished in England. Grisi's departure was symbolic of the drift toward Russia. In addition, the emergence of the popular Jenny Lind in London was drawing audiences from ballet to opera once more. There were still many talented dancers left besides Taglioni and Rosati, including: Flora Fabbri, a dynamic ballerina with amazing *ballon*; the elfin Amalia Ferraris (1830–1904); Sofia Fuoco (1830–1916), who was famous for her *pointe* work; and Adeline Plunkett (1824–1910) from Belgium. But by the time Covent Garden burned down for the last time in 1856 (not to be rebuilt until 1858), ballet was no longer very popular in London.

Native English ballet still suffered greatly from the lack of adequate training facilities; Leon Espinosa (1825–1904), who opened a school in 1872, and the Austrian Katti Lanner, who became director of the National Training School in 1876, were two of the very few good teachers working in London before the turn of the century.

Ballet was kept alive only by the

Alhambra and Empire Theatres; though they specialized in vaudeville shows, they used ballet extensively and kept public interest alive to some degree. Most of the emphasis, however, was on pageantry and astounding stage effects. Manzotti's 'colossal' productions were standard favorites and the lavish spectacles were, for the most part, choreographed and danced by Italians. Only a few French or Russian, let alone English, names were seen in the programs.

In 1887 Lanner was appointed ballet mistress at the Empire. Soon it was London's strongest ballet company, especially after the arrival of Adeline Genée in 1897. Genée, who was to become one of the three real founders of British ballet, not only reigned supreme at the Empire for over a decade, but also took one of the first touring companies to Australia.

In 1910 *Dancing Times* was founded and the same year Anna Pavlova arrived in England after her rather unsatisfactory season with Diaghilev. Pavlova holds a special place in English ballet history. The troupe she employed consisted mainly of English dancers; they were far below her standard, but they excited renewed interest in ballet and gave younger dancers important models to emulate, simply by their association with the great ballerina. Diaghilev brought Ballets Russes to London for its first season in 1911; that tour and sub-

This playbill from the London appearance of the Ballets Russes in 1911 reads like a who's who of ballet, every other name is now a legend.

Serafina Astafieva taught the Russian technique at her Chelsea school, opened in 1916. Her pupils included Markova, Dolin and Fonteyn.

sequent appearances, were popular, but throughout the teens they remained outside the national consciousness. Ballet outside the music halls was still an exotic Russian art form, not something that could be transferred to England.

The Russian ballerina Serafina Astafieva (1876–1934) opened a school in London in 1916 and was soon turning out some of the best dancers in England (including Markova, Dolin and Fonteyn); in 1920 a young Polish dancer, Marie Rambert, who had worked on the Continent with Ballets Russes, established her own academy in Notting Hill Gate. In July 1920 Diaghilev took the city by storm with two new Massine ballets, which he produced at the Alhambra Theatre in Leicester Square. The first success, *La Boutique Fantasque*, was followed hard upon by *Le Tricorne* (The Three-Cornered Hat), a comedy about a virtuous wife seduced by a lecherous old man, with a superlative score by Manuel de Falla and design by Picasso. It is still considered one of Massine's masterpieces.

In 1920 ballet had made some headway and a few people, at least, began seriously to consider the possibility of eventually forming a national company. To that

Above: The lively choreography of Massine's Le Tricorne, *coupled with Picasso's designs and an amusing plot, made for an instant success.*

Above left: Dame Marie Rambert, one of the founders of British ballet, rehearsing her company in a production of the great classic Giselle.

Left: The Sadler's Wells Royal Ballet production of Massine's La Boutique Fantasque, *a fantasy set in a toyshop of the 1860s, with decor by Derain.*

distant end, Edouard Espinosa, son of the famous teacher and himself one of the leading instructors in England, collected some like-minded friends and formed the Association of Operatic Dancing (later to become the Royal Academy of Dancing). Genée was its first president (a post she held for over 30 years) and its board members represented the major national academies: Danish, French, Italian and Russian. This organization, along with the Cecchetti Society (formed in 1922 to codify and maintain the great teacher's methods), played an enormous role in improving the standard of instruction in England.

For his 1921 season at the Alhambra, Diaghilev presented a showcase revival of Petipa's *Sleeping Beauty*. The choreography was reconstructed by Nicolas Sergeyev, who had notebooks full of notations taken at the old Maryinsky, while Nijinska composed several additions. The designs, in the great Imperial tradition, were magnificent and the cast was extraordinary: Egorova danced Aurora; Vilzak was Prince Florimond; and Carlotta Brianza, the first Aurora,

Dame Ninette de Valois, brilliant and determined founder of the Vic-Wells Ballet which was destined to become the Royal Ballet in 1956.

portrayed Carabosse. One of the pages was a young dancer named Patrikeef, who was later to become famous as Anton Dolin. *Sleeping Beauty* was performed every night for three months (November 1921 through January 1922) and was a great success. But Londoners were not used to long runs and box office receipts began to taper off long before Diaghilev had begun to recover his expenses.

In 1926 Ninette de Valois arrived in London after an engagement with Ballets Russes and the trio of women – Genée Rambert and de Valois – who were to become the prime movers in establishing modern British ballet was complete. In addition to opening a school in South Kensington (The Academy of Choreographic Art), de Valois also began working with several small companies. One of these was housed at the Old Vic Theatre run by Lilian Baylis (1874–1937); de Valois staged the dances for plays and operas at the theater.

In 1931, when Baylis reopened the Sadler's Wells Theatre, she included a ballet studio in the remodelled building. De Valois moved her school and small company (seven dancers in all) to the new location and became director of the Vic-Wells Ballet. The first years were difficult ones for the little company, which was often kept going only by de Valois's stubborn determination and refusal to let it die. She managed to get help from a few patrons and organizations

like the Camargo Society (formed in 1930 to encourage British ballet), which turned all its funds over to the Vic-Wells in 1933. Soon her company began not only to grow, but to attract some of the best talent in England. From individual dances they expanded to entire programs of short ballets and by 1933 could begin producing full-length classics.

In those early years the first great British ballerina, Alicia Markova, and her partner, Anton Dolin, provided a solid base for the troupe's dancing; Constant Lambert (1905–51), the great British conductor and composer, served as musical director until 1951; and de Valois was also able to secure the assistance of Sergeyev and his invaluable notebooks. In 1933 the Vic-Wells staged *Coppélia* and also commissioned their first ballet: Frederick Ashton's *Les Rendezvous.* The following year saw them dancing in *Giselle, Swan Lake* and *The Nutcracker,* all starring Markova; in 1935

Dame Alicia Markova as Taglioni in Pas de Quatre. *Markova's poise and ethereal grace made her Britain's first truly great ballerina.*

came the production of de Valois's *The Rake's Progress*, derived from Hogarth's illustrations.

In 1935 Baylis decided to use the Old Vic entirely for drama and the dance company became known as the Sadler's Wells Ballet. That same year Markova and Dolin left to form their own company (named, logically, the Markova-Dolin Ballet), but by that time enough good, younger dancers were available to fill the gap. Two Ballet Club alumni, the beautiful Pearl Argyle (1910–47) and Harold Turner (1909–62), a brilliant *demi-carac-*

Far left : Coppèlia performed by the Royal Ballet School. Each year top students give a performance preparatory to entering the company itself.

Left : A scene from Act IV of the Royal Ballet's Swan Lake, with the great Nadia Nerina as Odette and Erik Bruhn as Prince Siegfried.

Below: Fiona Chadwick and guest artist Mikhail Baryshnikov in the Royal Ballet's atmospheric Ashton masterwork A Month in the Country.

Above: Anton Dolin as Petrouchka. *Dolin has performed the world over and his partnership with Markova is part of ballet history.*

Above right: The Sadler's Wells Royal Ballet production of The Rake's Progress, *with Alain Dubreuil as the Rake and Margaret Barbieri as the Maiden.*

Right: Act II of the Royal Ballet's production of Swan Lake *with Merle Park as Odette and Anthony Dowell as Prince Siegfried.*

Left: Dame Alicia Markova with Erik Bruhn, the Great Danish star, in Act II of Giselle, *set in the forest beside Giselle's tomb.*

Below: The famous dramatic solo of The Dying Swan, *immortalized by Anna Pavlova, is vividly re-created here by Alicia Markova.*

Sir Frederick Ashton's ballet Les Patineurs, *as performed by students of the Royal Ballet School, a young Anthony Dowell among them.*

tère dancer, joined Sadler's Wells; two other stellar performers emerged as well, Margot Fonteyn and her partner, a young Australian named Robert Helpmann (b 1909). From 1935 on, Ashton was the group's principal choreographer, producing works like *Apparitions* (a romantic ballet set to music by Liszt and designed by Cecil Beaton), *Nocturne*, *Les Patineurs* and *Horoscope*. In 1939 de Valois achieved a long-standing ambition when she produced *Sleeping Beauty*, with Fonteyn and Helpmann in the leading roles.

While de Valois was building her company along standard, conventional lines, the vital, restless Marie Rambert was exerting an equally profound influence on British ballet, but usually from outside the establishment. During the 1930s her Ballet Club productions on the tiny stage of the Mercury Theatre in Notting Hill Gate gave many young people their first experience in ballet, and proved to the ballet public that English choreographers, designers and dancers could compete with Europe when it came to devising and executing beautiful, clever and sophisticated ballets.

Rambert possessed a special talent for discovering and encouraging young

Sir Frederick Ashton and Dame Ninette de Valois during a rehearsal at the Royal Opera House, Covent Garden.

choreographers. For example, she was responsible for the production of Ashton's first ballet, *A Tragedy of Fashion*, at the Lyric Theatre, Hammersmith, in 1926. His *Capriol Suite* was seen at the Mercury in 1930 and in 1936 Antony Tudor both choreographed and danced in the subtle *Jardin aux Lilas*, the first 'psychological ballet,' which is still a standard in both the Royal Ballet and the American Ballet Theatre repertories. Tudor's powerful *Dark Elegies* was also first produced at the Mercury. In 1939 another new choreographer, Andrée Howard, produced *Lady into Fox*, based on a novel by David Garnett.

In addition, Rambert has trained some extraordinary dancers. The group of talented young people at the Mercury in the early days included Argyle, Sally Gilmour, Diana Gould, Maude Lloyd, Peggy van Praagh, Walter Gore, Hugh Laing and Turner.

During the 1930s London audiences also saw the glamorous Ballets Russes de Monte Carlo productions, featuring the famous 'baby ballerinas,' along with favorites such as Alexandra Danilova and Leonide Massine. In 1938 there were two companies in town, since de Basil and Blum had parted company; balletomanes had to race hectically between Drury Lane and Covent Garden to catch first one group, then the other. But during World War II both companies left England. Blum's group remained in America; de Basil's Original Ballet Russe returned in 1947, but the company was obviously in

Beryl Grey was a child prodigy who danced the lead in the full length Swan Lake *at the age of only 15. She was appointed CBE in 1973.*

Dame Margot Fonteyn and Sir Robert Helpmann discussing a point during a break in rehearsal on stage.

decline and soon disbanded altogether.

The Ballet Club evolved into Ballet Rambert in 1939 and spent the war years on tour, entertaining both fighting men and civilians. De Valois and the Sadler's Wells Ballet were caught in Holland when the Germans invaded during the summer of 1940 and barely made it back to England, leaving their costumes, scenery, even their music behind. During the weary, tension-filled war years London audiences, like their French counterparts, flocked to ballet as an escape – at first to Sadler's Wells, then (after the building was bombed) to the New Theatre. Two new ballerinas, the beautiful red-haired Moira Shearer and Beryl Grey, a child prodigy who danced the lead in *Swan Lake* on her 15th birthday, emerged during this period. Though the male half of the company was seriously reduced, Helpmann held the dancing together. He also choreographed several original ballets, including *Hamlet* and *Miracle in the Gorbals* (a story set in the notorious slums of Glasgow).

Several other companies sprang up during the war, in response to public demand. One, the International Ballet, was formed in 1941 by Mona Inglesby. During the war it produced revivals of the Russian classics, with help from Sergeyev. The company toured throughout Britain, then after the war expanded to include the Continent as well, before

Right: A great partnership, Anthony Dowell and Antoinette Sibley, in Anthony Tudor's Jardin aux Lilas, *the first 'psychological' ballet.*

Margot Fonteyn as Princess Aurora and Michael Soames as Prince Florimund in the Royal Ballet's production of The Sleeping Beauty.

disbanding in 1953. Another interesting company was the Anglo-Polish Ballet (1940–47), organized by Polish refugees, which specialized in incorporating lively folk dances into the ballets.

Michael Coleman and Jennifer Penney in Sir Frederick Ashton's Scènes de Ballet. *First performed in 1948, it is a work of pure dancing.*

Another Ashton ballet, Symphonic Variations, *with Marguerite Porter, Wayne Eagling and Wendy Ellis.*

Act I of the Royal Ballet's The Sleeping Beauty. *Maidens perform a floral dance on Aurora's birthday.*

Above: Merle Park and Anthony Dowell as Cinderella and the Prince incur the disdain of the ugly sister in the ballroom scene.

Above left: Daphnis and Chloë, a popular Ashton ballet with Dowell and Sibley in the title roles. It deals with Chloë's kidnap by pirates.

Left: London Festival Ballet's Schéhérazade remains faithful to Diaghilev's original production, using Léon Bakst's stunning designs.

Above right: Antoinette Sibley, a great ballerina of the 1960s and 1970s, danced many Ashton roles, such as this 'Scènes de Ballet.'

Right: Margot Fonteyn as Cinderella, David Blair as the Prince in the Royal Ballet's Cinderella. Ashton and Helpmann play the ugly sisters.

Below right: John Gilpin as Peer Gynt from the London Festival Ballet production with choreography by Vaslav Orlikowsky and music by Grieg.

In 1946, as soon as possible after the war, the Royal Opera House, Covent Garden, was reopened with state support; the Sadler's Wells Ballet became its resident company, which made it, in effect, the state ballet company. Their opening production that season was a new version of *Sleeping Beauty*; it was followed by Ashton's new abstract work, *Symphonic Variations*. Since the company's old home was now without a dance troupe, the Sadler's Wells Theatre Ballet also was formed; by 1955, under the able direction of Peggy van Praagh (b 1910), it was producing John Cranko's and Kenneth Macmillan's first ballets. Both companies were supported by the two Sadler's Wells schools: a junior school in Richmond Park and a senior school in West London.

In 1949 Sadler's Wells Ballet made a

Violetta Elvin the Russian-born and trained ballerina who left the Bolshoi at the end of the war and came to England to join the Royal Ballet.

triumphant first visit to New York. Ashton's ballets continued to dominate the repertory after the war, including earlier works like *Apparitions* along with later compositions such as *Scenes de Ballet* and *Cinderella* (both 1948), *Daphnis and Chloë* (1951) and *Sylvia* (1952), almost all written for Fonteyn, with whom he had an extraordinarily sympathetic working relationship.

Finally in 1956 Queen Elizabeth II granted a royal charter, uniting the entire Sadler's Wells Ballet organization – both companies and both schools – together into the Royal Ballet: Britain finally had its national ballet company, led until 1964 by de Valois.

The Royal Ballet has enjoyed the services of many excellent dancers throughout its history, including Violetta Elvin, Moira Shearer, Beryl Grey, Nadia Nerina, Lynn Seymour, Svetlana Beriosova and Antoinette Sibley; male dancers along with Dolin, Helpmann and Turner, include Michael Somes, David Blair and Anthony Dowell. But all have been overshadowed by Margot Fonteyn, who succeeded Markova and became one of the greatest dancers of her time. Her tremendous contribution to British ballet was recognized in 1956 when she was made a Dame of the British Empire – the first ballerina ever to receive such an honor while she was still dancing.

In 1961 Rudolf Nureyev defected from the Soviet Union, where he had been dancing at the Kirov, and de Valois offered him a position as permanent guest artist with the Royal Ballet. He made his first appearance with Fonteyn at Covent Garden in February 1962; it

Beryl Grey as the all-conquering Black Queen in the Royal Ballet production of one of Ninette de Valois's best ballets, Checkmate.

Nadia Nerina as Aurora from The Sleeping Beauty. *Born in South Africa, Nerina enjoyed great success and popularity with the Royal Ballet.*

was an historic event that marked the start of a new era in British ballet, as well as the beginning of one of the most fabulous partnerships in all ballet history.

Nureyev's virile, athletic style and magnetic personality soon made him a cult figure not equalled since Nijinsky. His dazzling virtuosity, with its overwhelming feeling of strength perfectly controlled, contrasted with and enhanced Fonteyn's exquisite, refined technique. Despite the 20-year difference in their ages and the vast dissimilarity in their cultures, backgrounds and temperaments, their amazing physical rapport and mutual professional respect resulted in a magical affinity that soon came to

A legend in our own time, the partnership of Margot Fonteyn and Rudolf Nureyev culminated in Frederick Ashton's Marguerite and Armand.

epitomize not only the Royal Ballet, but even ballet itself. Their appearances together became less frequent as the 1970s progressed, but in 1979 Fonteyn made an unexpected appearance in a revival of Nijinsky's *L'Après-midi d'un Faune* at the Nureyev Festival in London, and also danced the last two performances of *La Spectre de la Rose*. Perhaps their best-loved ballet was Ashton's *Marguerite and Armand*, a short work created for them in 1963, with costumes and settings by Cecil Beaton.

In addition to inspiring younger dancers and greatly enhancing the regard in which male dancers were held all over the world, Nureyev added several important works to the Royal Ballet repertory. For example, in 1963 he staged the Kingdom of the Shades scene, from Pepita's *La Bayadère*, in the traditional manner he learned during his years at the Kirov.

Left: Svetlana Beriosova in Les Biches, *a satire on the 1920s with choreography by Nijinska, who revived this production for the Royal Ballet.*

Below: Anthony Dowell and Antoinette Sibley in Giselle. *The heroine, just crowned 'Queen of the Harvest,' is as yet unaware of her fate.*

Rudolf Nureyev and Merle Park as the Prince and the Sugar Plum Fairy, in a spectacular leap from Nureyev's own version of The Nutcracker.

By the time de Valois retired as director of the Royal Ballet in 1964, Ashton, recognized all over the world as a genius, was her logical successor. His version of *La Fille Mal Gardée* (1960) is an acknowledged masterpiece. As director of the company he established a strong repertory consisting not only of his own works, but those of many others as well. For his first season he commissioned a version of *Romeo and Juliet* from Kenneth Macmillan, produced Jerome Robbins's *Dances at a Gathering* and had Nijinska revive her *Les Biches* and, two years later, *Les Noces.* Balanchine, Petit and Tudor

Top: Ashton's dramatic Marguerite and Armand, *taken from Dumas's* La Dame aux Camelias, *was the first ballet created for Nureyev in the UK.*

Above: The pairing of the formidable talent of Margot Fonteyn and Rudolf Nureyev made for a partnership that enraptured audiences worldwide.

Right: A rare shot of Nureyev at the Kirov School, learning the role of Sergeyev (center), while his teacher Alexander Pushkin looks on.

Below: Thaïs was specially created by Ashton for Antoinette Sibley and Anthony Dowell.

Above: Desmond Kelly and Brenda Last as Colas and Lise in the ribbon dance from Ashton's La Fille Mal Gardée *for the Royal Ballet.*

Left: Margot Fonteyn and Rudolf Nureyev in Kenneth Macmillan's Romeo and Juliet.

Below left: Nijinska's ballet Les Noces, *which she revived for the Royal Ballet at Ashton's invitation, with the original designs by Goncharova.*

have been among the many distinguished guest choreographers who have contributed to the company over the years.

In 1964 Ashton contributed to the national celebration of Shakespeare's 400th birthday with *The Dream*. This joyous one-act version of *A Midsummer Night's Dream* remains one of the Royal Ballet's most enduring hits. It also marked the first flowering of the glorious partnership between Anthony Dowell (b 1943) and Antoinette Sibley (b 1939).

Other major Ashton ballets followed. *Enigma Variations* (1968) is a series of evocative Edwardian character studies based on Edward Elgar's score of the same name. Filmed in 1969, this ballet is greatly enhanced by its accurate, minutely detailed designs from Julia Trevelyan Oman. She also served as designer on Ashton's late masterpiece, *A Month in the Country* (1976). Based on Turgenev's 1850 play, this sad tale of entangled lives caught in a web of unrequited loves ranks as one of the very finest story ballets ever created. Not a moment is wasted and every gesture is brimming with dramatic truth. The music is by Chopin. The original cast was headed by Lynn Seymour (b 1939), the company's finest actress, and Dowell.

Members of the Royal Ballet make up the cast of the 1970 EMI film *Tales of Beat-*

Page 118, top: Anthony Dowell, Michael Coleman and Davis Wall in Dances at a Gathering, *the Jerome Robbins' work Ashton produced in 1970.*

Page 118, center: Davis Blair as Colas from Ashton's La Fille Mal Gardée. This ballet is one of the most popular in the Royal Ballet's repertory.

Page 119, top: In Act I of this amusing ballet, Lise's mother, the Widow Simone, performs a famous comic clog dance.

Page 118–119, bottom: The kingdom of the Shades scene from the Royal Ballet's La Bayadère, *staged by Nureyev, with Michael Coleman and Merle Park.*

rix Potter. Ashton not only provided the choreography, he also appears as the industrious Mrs Tiggy-Winkle. He retired as artistic director in 1970.

Kenneth MacMillan was his successor (1970–77). His major works during this period include full-length productions of *Anastasia* (1971) for Seymour and *Manon* (1974). The latter provided an impressive showcase for Sibley and Dowell. *Elite Syncopations*, his popular comedy to the ragtime music of Scott Joplin, was premiered later that year.

Norman Morrice (b 1931) was the next artistic director (1977-86). Morrice had been dancer, choreographer and eventually director of Ballet Rambert (1952–74). Unlike Ashton and MacMillan, Morrice contributed no works of his own to the repertory.

In 1978 MacMillan produced his violent, operatic, full-length *Mayerling*. The tortured history of Austria's Crown Prince

Rudolf, this remains one of his most powerful and disturbing creations. It is loaded with *fin de siècle* sex, drugs and violence.

Ashton choreographed *Rhapsody* (1980) for guest artist Mikhail Baryshnikov and joined forces with David Hockney for another Sibley-Dowell vehicle, *Varii Capricci* (1983). Guest choreographer Glen Tetley received the Queen Elizabeth Coronation Award in 1981 for *Dances of Albion*, set to two Benjamin Britten compositions.

Young British choreographers were brought to the fore, beginning in 1982, when Michael Corder staged *L'Invitation au Voyage*. Lusciously designed by Yolanda Sonnabend and sung to Duparc's indolent, sensual song cycle, it featured a soprano who wandered among the characters of the ballet. Richard Alston (of Ballet Rambert) and company dancers Ashley Page, Wayne Eagling and Derek Deane all contributed works to the repertory (1983-87).

The most successful young choreographer to emerge during the 1980s has been dancer David Bintley (b 1957). He has turned out an impressive and diverse list of works for both Sadler's Wells Royal Ballet and the Covent Garden company. They range from the bright and brisk abstractions of *Chorus* (1983) to the dark drama of Kafka's *Metamorphosis* (1984). His *Flowers of the Forest* (1985) celebrates the Highland clans; while *The Sons of Horus* (1985) evokes the ancient Egyp-

tian deities of the dead. Bintley's full-length ballets have been inspired by Scandinavian legends: *The Swan of Tuonela* (1982) and *The Snow Queen* (1986). He was appointed resident choreographer for the Royal Ballet in 1986.

A lavish new production of *The Nutcracker* (designed by Trevelyan Oman) premiered in 1984. It was staged by Peter Wright, director of Sadler's Wells Royal Ballet. He also mounted the Royal Ballet's impressive new version of *Giselle* (1985).

Anthony Dowell took over as the Royal Ballet's artistic director during the 1986-87 season. He staged a new production of *Swan Lake* (designed by Sonnabend) in 1987. The Royal Ballet returned to Russia in 1987 for the first time since 1961.

The largest and best known of England's 'other' companies is London Festival Ballet. It was founded by Markova and Dolin in 1950 to coincide with the 1951 Festival of Britain. Though Markova left in 1952, Dolin remained as artistic director until 1961. His succesor was longtime company dancer John Gilpin (1962-64). Ballerina Beryl Grey was director from 1968 to 1979. John Field held that position until 1985, when Peter Schaufuss was appointed to head the company.

Throughout its history, London Festival Ballet has performed extensive tours both at home and abroad. Its regular London seasons are at the Royal Festival Hall and the Coliseum. The company's goal has always been one of broad-based popular appeal.

Right: The beautiful and ethereal ballerina Belinda Wright, in a spectacular jêté from London Festival Ballet's production of The Snow Maiden.

Below: Margot Fonteyn and Rudolf Nureyev in Paradise Lost, *a ballet specially commissioned for them by the French choreographer, Roland Petit.*

Major guest artists have included Alexandra Danilova, Toni Lander, Eva Evdokimova, Elisabetta Terabust and Natalia Makarova. The repertory has included Harald Lander's *Etudes* (first added in 1954 and still seen regularly in the 1980s) and several Ballets Russes classics, such as Massine's *Parade* and *The Three-Cornered Hat*.

Full-length ballets have played a big part in the company's success. Maurice Charnley devised *Alice in Wonderland* in 1953. Nureyev produced both *The Sleeping Beauty* (1975) and *Romeo and Juliet* (1977). Ronald Hynd staged *The Nutcracker* (1976) and *Coppélia* (1985). Cranko's *Onegin* entered the repertory in 1983.

Schaufuss, who had been a guest dancer with the company since 1973, staged *La Sylphide* (1979) and *The Nutcracker* (1986). A diverse repertory of shorter works ranges from Balanchine and Paul Taylor to Petit, Béjart and British punkster Michael Clark. In 1986 Christopher Bruce was appointed associate choreographer.

Perhaps the crowning achievement of Schaufuss's first years as director has been the resurrection of Ashton's *Romeo and Juliet*. Originally staged for the Royal Danish Ballet in 1955, it starred Mona Vangsaae (Schaufuss's mother) as Juliet. Ashton's version was the first Western production to use the now-famous Prokofiev score. Considered a 'lost' ballet for more than 20 years, it was effectively brought back to life thanks to members of the original cast and with the help of an amateur silent film that had been shot by one of the Danish company. This is the most intimate and personal of the many versions of the ballet. It has both delicacy and ease, yet never loses sight of the central tragedy. Ballet Rambert's recent history is discussed in the European Modern Dance chapter.

Elsewhere in Britain, the Scottish Ballet (before 1974 the Scottish Theatre Ballet) now numbers about 30 dancers. The company had its origins in Bristol, where Elizabeth West (1927–62) founded the Western Theatre Ballet in 1956. West firmly believed that drama was as important as dance in ballet, and hoped to establish Britain's first regional ballet company. Despite the desperate struggle

Right: At Riverside Studios in London, Ballet Rambert holds 'workshops' in which young dancer/choreographers present new-style works.

to stay afloat during the early years, the company developed into an excellent group and began building an international reputation in the 1960s. It moved to Glasgow in 1969 after dancing for four years at the Sadler's Wells Theatre. The chief choreographer and director until 1986 was Peter Darrell, whose works range from *The Prisoners* (1957) and *Chiaroscuro* (1959) to *Mods and Rockers*, set to music by the Beatles (1963), *Beauty and the Beast*, with music by the contemporary composer Thea Musgrave (1969), *Mary, Queen of Scots* (1976) and *Carmen* (1985). The repertory also contains other dramatic ballets by choreographers like Béjart, Macmillan and Flindt. Gordon Aitken is currently ballet master.

Beauty and the Beast *based on the story by Mme de Villeneuve, was presented by the Scottish Theatre Ballet as a full-length work in 1969.*

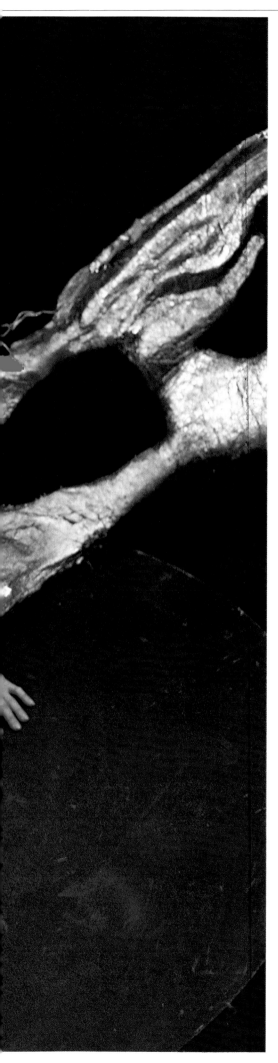

Gianfranco Paoluzi as the sprite Ariel in Ballet Rambert's production of The Tempest.

Christopher Bruce's Night of the Waning Moon *for Ballet Rambert.*

JOHN WEAVER
1673–1760

John Weaver, a native of Shrewsbury, was perhaps the earliest serious proponent of what we now call *ballet d'action*.

As dancing master at the Drury Lane Theatre, Weaver staged several works that told a story without songs or recitations, using only dance, mime and music. One of his earliest – and certainly most famous – attempts was the *Loves of Mars and Venus* (1717); others included *Orpheus and Eurydice* (1718), *Perseus and Andromeda* (1726) and *The Judgement of Paris* (1732).

Unfortunately, Weaver was too far ahead of his time; neither the king nor any other potential patron was interested in the new ballet form, and after Weaver's death it was left to a Frenchman, Jean Noverre, to carry on the campaign.

KATTI (KATHARINA) LANNER
?1829–1908

Katti Lanner, daughter of the famous Viennese waltz composer Joseph Lanner, studied at the Vienna Court Opera School. She made her debut at the Kaertnerthor Theater in 1845 (Elssler and Cerrito were working there at the same time).

Following her engagement in Austria she began travelling and working throughout Europe: dancing in Berlin, Dresden and Munich; choreographing 10 ballets as ballet mistress in Hamburg (1862–63); and touring Scandinavia, Russia and Western Europe. She even sailed to New York and toured the United States in 1872.

Finally, in 1876, she settled in London, where she became the director of the National Training School of Operatic Dancing. In addition she worked at several London theaters, including Her Majesty's Theatre, where she choreographed ballets for the Italian opera seasons between 1877 and 1881.

By 1887 she had been appointed leading dancer, choreographer and ballet mistress at the Empire Theatre. Along with dancing and training other dancers, she choreographed 33 ballets for the theater. Some of the most popular were *The Sports of England* (1887), *Cleopatra* and *The Paris Exhibition* (both 1889), *Orfeo* (1891), *Versailles* (1892), *On Brigh-*

ton Pier (1894), *Faust* (1896), *Alaska* (1898), *The Milliner Duchess* (1903), *The Dancing Doll* (1905) and *Sir Roger de Coverley* (1907).

During her stay at the Empire as ballet mistress (1887–97), she turned the theater into London's ballet center; one of her most far-reaching acts was the hiring of Adeline Genée in 1897. Lanner is one of the major figures in the long transition period between Romantic and modern ballet.

DAME ADELINE GENEE
1878–1970

Adeline Genée, one of the most influential figures in British ballet, was born Amina Jensen in Hinnerup, Jutland (Denmark). As a child she studied dance with her aunt and uncle, M and Mme Alexandre Genée, making her stage debut at the age of 10, when she danced a polka in Christiania (now Oslo), Norway.

In 1893, when her uncle was hired to manage the Centralhallen Theater in Stettin, Germany, Genée went along as a dancer with the company; in 1896 she made her adult debut at the Court Opera in Munich.

Katti Lanner hired her for the Empire Theatre in London in 1897, and for the next 10 years the tiny, delicate ballerina had the city at her feet as she appeared in

Dame Adeline Genée as Coppèlia.

both Lanner's ballets and other theater productions. Her popularity helped keep ballet alive in London during a particularly difficult period; her excellent technique kept standards high and her respectable private life helped counter the low regard in which most dancers were still held.

In 1907 Genée formed her own company and set out on an extended tour of the United States; she returned briefly to London in 1910 to work at the Coliseum and Alhambra theaters, then in 1913 made an immensely successful tour of Australia and New Zealand. In 1917 she retired in order to marry, making her farewell performance at the Coliseum. Years later she was persuaded to return to the stage and appear in a charity matinée in 1932 – a performance she repeated in Copenhagen and again in London in 1933 (with Anton Dolin).

For the most part, however, she worked behind the scenes. In 1920 she was elected Founder President of the Association of Operatic Dancing, a post she continued to hold after the organization became the Royal Academy of Dancing in 1935, until her retirement in 1954. She was also a founding member of the Camargo Society; in 1950 she was awarded the DBE (Dame of the Order of the British Empire) for her many years of service and her effective championship of British ballet.

DAME MARIE RAMBERT
1888–1982

Marie Rambert, a vivid, exciting lady with the strange habit of turning cartwheels at the most unexpected times and in the oddest places, was born Cyvia Rambam, in Warsaw. Her parents sent her to dancing school when she was quite young, hoping to alleviate the restlessness that was her hallmark even then; later, as she grew older and began to divert her energies to radical politics, they sent her off to study medicine in Paris.

Once in the French capital, however, she attended several modern dance concerts and fell under Isadora Duncan's spell; soon she began studying eurythmics with Jacques Dalcroze, eventually becoming one of his assistants. This experience led to a job with Diaghilev, who engaged her to work with Nijinsky,

LYDIA VASILIEVNA LOPOKOVA, LADY KEYNES
1891–1981

Lydia Lopokova received her training in St Petersburg, graduating from the Imperial ballet academy in 1909. But instead of joining her brothers, Feodor and Andrei, and her sister, Yevgenia, at the Maryinsky, she left Russia with Ballets Russes in 1910 and never returned.

During her stage career she was known as a brilliant *demi-caractère* ballerina. Her most important roles include Mariuccia in *Les Femmes de Bonne Humeur* and Acrobat in *Parade* (both 1916), Can Can Dancer in *La Boutique Fantasque* (1910) and Street Dancer in *Beau Danube* (1924). In later years she also created Tango in Frederick Ashton's *Façade* (1931) and danced Swanilda in the Vic-Wells production of *Coppélia* in 1932.

In 1925 Lopokova married the famous British economist John Maynard, Lord Keynes. After Ballets Russes disbanded she settled permanently in London, where she worked long and hard for the fledgling British ballet movement. She was one of the original members of the Camargo Society, and in 1936 she and her husband founded the successful Cambridge Arts Theatre.

Lydia Vasilievna Lopokova, Lady Keynes.

DAME NINETTE DE VALOIS
b 1898

Ninette de Valois, born in Ireland as Edris Stannus, danced with Diaghilev for several years before leaving the company and setting up her own school in London in 1926. To help make ends meet she talked Lilian Baylis into letting her stage dances at the Old Vic Theatre. At the same time she also was working at the Abbey Theatre, Dublin, (with W B Yeats)

Dame Marie Rambert, founder of Ballet Rambert.

as rhythmic advisor for *Le Sacre du Printemps* (1913). Soon she was working as a regular member of the *corps de ballet* and studying with Cecchetti.

A few years later Rambert moved to London, where she studied ballet further with Astafieva, opening her own school in Notting Hill Gate in 1920. From the very beginning the small woman with the big temper proved adept at discovering and encouraging young choreographers, like Frederick Ashton, who, prompted by her, choreographed his first ballet in 1926.

Early in 1931 Rambert and her husband, the dramatist Ashley Dukes, converted an old building into a tiny theater, called the Mercury. There the Ballet Club gave its performances; a great number of Britain's best dancers gained their first experience on its stage before moving on to larger companies.

Rambert's interest in modern dance continued through the years, keeping her always on the leading edge of ballet activity. In 1966 the company made a radical policy shift and turned from classic to contemporary ballet and modern dance. Rambert remained intimately involved with the company until her death in 1982.

Rambert was awarded the DBE (Dame of the British Empire) in 1962, in recognition of her pioneering work for British ballet; her autobiography, *Quicksilver*, was published 10 years later.

Dame Ninette de Valois takes a class at the Royal Ballet School in London.

De Valois's Checkmate, *with Robert Helpmann as the Red King and Beryl Grey as the Black Queen.*

and at the Festival Theatre in Cambridge.

When Baylis reopened the Sadler's Wells Theatre in 1931, de Valois and six other dancers moved in as the resident ballet company. Soon her genius for organization and her virtually unlimited capacity for hard work in pursuit of clearly defined goals were paying dividends. The tiny company grew both in strength and numbers, producing first short and soon full-length ballets.

In 1935 the company was finally able to afford a resident choreographer, and young Frederick Ashton got the job. Together de Valois, Ashton and conductor Constant Lambert built up the great organization known today as the Royal Ballet.

Also a choreographer of note, de Valois produced three ballets that still survive: *Checkmate* (a battle between love and death, fought on a chessboard), *Job* (based on the Biblical story as illustrated by William Blake) and *The Rake's Progress* (from Hogarth's series of prints). De Valois's iron will and gift for administration carried the Sadler's Wells Ballet through the difficult war years and on to even greater heights thereafter. In 1951 she was made a Dame of the British Empire and in 1955 became the first director of Britain's new national ballet company. After her retirement in 1964 she was made Life Governor of the Royal Ballet. Her publications include *Invitation to the Ballet* (1937) and her autobiography *Come Dance With Me* (1957).

MARY SKEAPING
1902–1984

Mary Skeaping, an important figure on the international ballet scene since World War II, was born in Woodford, Essex. She studied with Laurent Novikov, Cecchetti, Trefilova, Egorova and Margaret Craske before making her debut with Pavlova in 1925.

During World War II Skeaping found herself stranded in South America, so she

A production by the Royal Swedish Ballet.

spent the war years teaching and giving recitals there. Returning to England in 1948, she spent three years (1948–51) as ballet mistress for the Sadler's Wells Ballet before making a two-year tour of the United States, Canada and Cuba.

Between 1953 and 1962 she directed the Royal Swedish Ballet, where she became an authority on seventeenth- and eighteenth-century ballets. She was responsible for reviving several historic *ballets de cour* at the Drottingholm Court Theater, outside Stockholm; one example was her 1956 production of *Cupid out of His Humour*, danced in a rococo setting to music by Purcell. In 1965 Skeaping re-created the seventeenth-century *Atis et Camilla* at Drottingholm and she has also directed a series of television programs on the history of dance.

Skeaping's later works, as a freelance choreographer, include a new production of *Giselle*, composed for the London Festival Ballet in 1971.

SIR FREDERICK ASHTON
b 1904

Frederick Ashton was born in Guayaquil, Equador, and grew up in South America; his ballets, however, are usually regarded as being most thoroughly British.

As a young man he studied first with Massine, then with Rambert, who immediately spotted his talent for choreography and encouraged him to develop it, urging him to produce his first work, *A Tragedy of Fashion*, for a revue at the outstanding Hammersmith Lyric Theatre in 1926.

In 1935, after some years choreographing for Ballet Club and the Camargo Society, Ashton joined the Vic-Wells Ballet as chief choreographer. He remained with the group from then on, through its years as the Sadler's Wells Ballet and after it had become the Royal Ballet.

Appointed de Valois's associate director in 1952, he succeeded her as director in 1963 and held the post until 1970. Since then he has continued working as a freelance choreographer and advisor. During his long career he has choreographed ballets for most of the top companies in the world, including Ballets de Paris, the London Festival Ballet, the New York City Ballet, the Royal Danish Ballet and La Scala.

Sir Frederick Ashton on stage at rehearsal for one of his many successful ballets, Façade.

SIR ANTON DOLIN
1904–1983

Anton Dolin, the first British male dancer to earn an international reputation, was born in Slinfold, Sussex, where he was christened Sydney Francis Patrick Chippendall Healey-Kay. He studied dance with Astafieva and Nijinska, but made his first appearance as a child actor (playing Michael in *Peter Pan*).

In 1921 he was a member of the *corps de ballet* in Diaghilev's production of *Sleeping Beauty* at the Alhambra Theatre and he later joined the company. During his two seasons with Ballets Russes (1924–25 and 1928–29) he created roles in Nijinska's *Le Train Bleu* (1924) and in Balanchine's *The Prodigal Son* and *Le Bal* (both 1929).

Dolin paid a brief visit to New York after Diaghilev's death, then returned and settled in London, where he helped form the Camargo Society in 1930. From 1931 to 1935 he was a soloist with the Vic-Wells, partnering Markova in her first *Giselle* in 1934.

In 1935 the two dancers struck out on their own, forming the Markova-Dolin Ballet. The group disbanded after three years, however, and in 1940 Dolin accepted an engagement as *premier danseur* with Ballet Theater in New York and

Ashton is without doubt a choreographer of rare distinction; his ballets range from witty comic pieces like *Façade* (1931), *A Wedding Bouquet* (1937) and *La Fille Mal Gardée* (1963) to the lyrical, abstract *Symphonic Variations* (1946) or the graceful, sensitive *Enigma Variations* (1968). His fantasies include *Cinderella* (1948), *Ondine* (1958) and *The Dream* (1964). Two of his best-loved romances are *Marguerite and Armand*, choreographed for Fonteyn and Nureyev in 1963, and the late masterpiece, *A Month in the Country* (1976). His *Romeo and Juliet* was originally created for the Royal Danish Ballet in 1955. After some 20 years out of the repertory, it was brought back by the London Festival Ballet in 1985. Whatever their style, whether new works or historical adaptations, Ashton's ballets are invariably tasteful, straightforward and musical, depicting a wide range of emotions in an impeccably classic style. In addition to contributing a great deal to the Royal Ballet's worldwide reputation for exellence, he also helped create one of the greatest ballerinas of our time, Margot Fonteyn.

Anton Dolin as Petrouchka in the London Festival Ballet's production of the work.

remained with the company until 1946.

He and Markova founded the London Festival Ballet in 1950. Dolin remained as principal dancer and artistic director until 1961. The last 20 years of his life were spent as a freelance choreographer, teacher and ballet master. He worked all around the world, including Leningrad and Tokyo. Dolin was knighted in 1981 and died in 1983. He wrote several ballet books and two volumes of memoirs.

DAME ALICIA MARKOVA
b 1910

Alicia Markova, whose original name was Lillian Alice Marks, was born in London and studied with Astafieva, Legat, Cecchetti and Vincenzo Celli.

In 1925, when she was still only 14, Markova joined Ballets Russes (changing her name to comply with Diaghilev's ironclad rule). She remained with the troupe until it disbanded in 1929; back in England she danced with Ballet Club, the Camargo Society and the young Vic-Wells Ballet. Her appearances with the latter, at a time when she could have been making far more money with more prestigious groups elsewhere, were instrumental in helping establish itself.

Markova's dancing was incredibly light and delicate, making her performances in the Romantic repertory (*Giselle*, *Pas de Quatre*) unforgettable events. In addition, she had a crisp, precise technique that was a delight in other classic roles, notably that of the Sugar Plum Fairy in *The Nutcracker*. Her partnership with Dolin is one of the most famous in ballet history.

After three years spent touring Britain (1935–38) with the Markova-Dolin Ballet, she joined Ballet Russe de Monte Carlo on their American tour, where she was an immediate and overwhelming success. She and Dolin renewed their partnership from time to time; in 1945 they toured Mexico and Central America, the United States and the Philippines, and in 1949 took a company on a successful tour of South Africa.

In 1950 that company became the London Festival Ballet, a group that still exists, though Markova left in 1952 to spend 10 more years dancing as a guest artist with many companies all over the world. After her retirement from the stage she worked as ballet mistress at the New York Metropolitan Opera House from 1963 to 1969. Since 1971 she has been Visiting Professor of Ballet at the University of Cincinnati and since 1973 has served as Governor of the Royal Ballet.

DAME MARGOT FONTEYN
b 1919

Margot Fonteyn, who holds a secure position as the Royal Ballet's greatest ballerina, was born Margaret (Peggy) Hookham in Reigate, Surrey. Her mother was half Brazilian, which perhaps accounts for some of the extra sparkle that marks this most typically British ballerina.

Fonteyn began taking dancing lessons at an early age, and her mother soon realized that the child had real talent; when the family moved temporarily to the Far East she kept a watchful eye on her daughter's training. In Hong Kong young Peggy took first two, then three lessons a week; in Shanghai she met with George Goncharov every day.

Back in London in 1933, when she was 14, Fonteyn studied with Astafieva for a year before transferring to the new Sadler's Wells Ballet School. Within a year she was dancing Odette in *Swan Lake* and in 1936, when Markova and Dolin left the troupe, she was made principal ballerina.

From that point Fonteyn's career was one of smooth, steady, upward growth. Her dancing, with partners like Robert Helpmann, Michael Somes and David Blair, was superb, and Ashton choreographed many ballets to take specific advantage of her graceful, elegant artistry: notably *Apparitions* (1936), *Symphonic Variations* (1946), *Cinderella* (1948) and *Ondine* (1958).

In the early 1950s she married a Panamanian diplomat, Dr Roberto Arias; in 1956 he was appointed ambassador to London and Fonteyn was made a Dame of the British Empire. A minor scandal erupted in 1959 when both were mentioned in connection with revolutionary activities in Panama. Fonteyn was given Guest Artist status at the Royal Ballet; she was 40, and the time seemed to have come for her to begin gently fading into retirement.

But in 1962 her career took off again and she was soon soaring to even greater heights with a partner 20 years her junior. Together, she and Rudolf Nureyev created perhaps the greatest dancing partnership of our time.

The two most famous examples of this legendary partnership have been captured on film: MacMillan's *Romeo and Juliet*

Markova rehearsing dancers of the Festival Ballet in her own great role as the Sugar Plum Fairy.

Alicia Markova in Don Quixote.

(1965) and Ashton's *Marguerite and Armand*. The latter is part of the 1972 Nureyev movie *I am a Dancer*.

Margot Fonteyn: An Autobiography was published in 1975. In 1979 she hosted a six-part BBC television series, *The Magic of Dance*.

RUDOLF NUREYEV
b 1938

Rudolf Nureyev, considered the greatest male dancer in the world in the 1960s and early 1970s, was born on a Russian train, three months after Fonteyn made her début in *Swan Lake* at Sadler's Wells. His family, which was very poor, lived in Ufa, a town near the Ural Mountains.

Unlike Fonteyn, Nureyev had to fight hard for every step he took in his career. He deceived his father as a child in order to take his first lessons in folk dancing and eventually he managed to get permission to study at the Ufa opera house, where, after some years he was allowed to dance in a few productions.

In 1955 he was finally included in a group that was travelling to Moscow to participate in a folk dance festival. The moment they arrived the young man went straight to the Bolshoi school and auditioned for a place. Though he was accepted, he declined the school's offer and bought himself a one-way ticket to Leningrad. A week later he was accepted by the examining board of the Kirov school, with the comment, 'Young man, you will either become a brilliant dancer or a total failure, and you will probably be a failure.'

Nureyev's apprenticeship in the Lenin-grad Choreographic School was not a particularly happy one. The many years of having to fight for everything had made him difficult to get along with and, as a poor country boy, he felt defensive and totally estranged from the artistic and social atmosphere of the school. Only the support he received from his teacher and mentor, Alexander Pushkin, enabled him to stay the course.

By 1958 Nureyev had been appointed a soloist with the Kirov company. But again his prickly personality and refusal to conform to the theater's authoritarian regulations kept him at loggerheads with the management. During a tour in Paris he openly broke all the rules, staying out past curfew and socializing with foreigners. At the end of their engagement, when the company gathered at Orly airport to fly on to London, Nureyev was told that he was being sent back to Leningrad. Realizing that he would never be allowed to leave Russia again, he simply turned on his heel, walked over to two nearby policemen, and demanded asylum.

He spent the first year after his defection touring France and Italy with the Grand Ballet du Marquis de Cuevas; he was in Copenhagen, getting acquainted with Erik Bruhn and taking lessons with Vera Volkova, when Fonteyn telephoned to see if he would take part in a gala benefit performance for the Royal Acade-my of Dancing.

Though the two dancers developed an immediate rapport when they met in London to discuss the performance, Fonteyn at first refused to dance with the young Russian. She felt that the difference in their ages would make them both look ridiculous and Nureyev appeared first in England with Rosella Hightower. But after the show Fonteyn changed her mind. De Valois offered him a job with the Royal Ballet, and in February 1962 the most famous partnership of the age was born.

As early as 1963, Nureyev began to stage the Russian classics for Western companies. His first major production was 'The Kingdom of the Shades' from *La Bayadère* for the Royal Ballet. He has since staged virtually all of the major nineteenth-century works around the world. His original choreography includes *Manfred* (1979) for the Paris Opéra and a one-act version of *The Tempest* (1982) for the Royal Ballet.

In 1972 he starred in the film *I am a Dancer* with Fracci, Seymour and Fonteyn. His film acting début was in Ken Russell's *Valentino* (1977).

Nureyev was appointed artistic director of the Paris Opéra Ballet in 1983. It is difficult to overemphasize the impact he has had on making ballet interesting and for a wider audience and, especially, on improving the image of male dancers.

Rudolf Nureyev and Margot Fonteyn in the tomb scene from Macmillan's Romeo and Juliet.

CANADA

Kettentanz *as performed by the National Ballet of Canada, choreographed by Gerald Arpino of the City Center Joffrey Ballet of the USA.*

Ballet in Canada belongs wholly to the twentieth century. In fact, the first organized Canadian ballet activity was the founding of the Winnipeg Ballet Club by Gweneth Lloyd and Betty Farrally in 1938. The group gave its first performance in 1939, made the transition from amateur to full professional status by 1949, and in 1953 was granted a royal charter – becoming the Royal Winnipeg Ballet.

Arnold Spohr, who took over as director after Lloyd's departure in 1958, has built up a company that is equally at home in classic and modern works. The repertory ranges from Ashton's ebullient *Les Patineurs* to de Mille's cowboy hoedown *Rodeo* and the Kurt Jooss anti-war ballet, *The Green Table*. Canadian choreographers Brian Macdonald and Norbert Vesak have each contributed several works.

In the mid-1970s Winnipeg developed a close relationship with the Argentinian choreographer Oscar Araiz. For several seasons his intense, sometimes brutal works dominated the repertory. *Family Scenes* (first created for Hamburg, 1976) is a claustrophobic dissection of a family's neuroses. During the 1980s, Dutch choreographers Rudi van Dantzig and Hans van Manen have replaced Araiz as the major contributors.

Winnipeg's first full-length ballet, other than the perennial holiday favourite *The Nutcracker*, premiered in 1981 with van Dantzig's rendition of *Romeo and Juliet*. In 1982 Peter Wright, director of Sadler's Wells Royal Ballet, produced *Giselle* specifically to highlight the talents of Evelyn Hart, the company's first home-grown ballerina of international stature.

Compact and cheerful, the Royal Win-nipeg Ballet continues to have a roster of under 30 dancers. It is a company dedicated to a life of touring across Canada and the USA, as well as abroad.

The National Ballet of Canada was established in Toronto in 1951, to balance the western company. The group, which is modelled strictly on Sadler's Wells, was directed until 1974 by Celia Franca; the British artist and writer, Kay Ambrose, served as artistic advisor from 1952 to 1961 and designed over 30 productions.

British dancer Alexander Grant was artistic director from 1976 until 1983, when the leadership passed on to Erik Bruhn. His links with the company go back to 1964 when Bruhn produced *La Sylphide* there. This was followed in 1966 by his *Swan Lake* (1966). This controversial production, designed by Desmond Heeley, included a quirky psychological twist: the parts of the Prince's mother and his magician tormentor, von Rothbart, were combined into a single role. The character became something like the Wicked Queen in Disney's *Snow White*. Bruhn staged *Coppélia* (1975) and the company also performs Ashton's *La Fille Mal Gardée* and Cranko's *Onegin*.

Rudolf Nureyev and Peter Schaufuss have both had ongoing associations with the company as guest dancers. In 1973 the Russian staged *The Sleeping Beauty*. The Dane produced a full-length *Napoli* (one of the very few outside Copenhagen) in 1981.

Glen Tetley created *Alice* for the company in 1986. He blends the childhood visions of Wonderland with the adult reality of the grown-up Alice. Fancifully designed by Tetley's regular collaborator, English designer Nadine Baylis, the ballet has a score by American avant-garde composer (and *Alice* fanatic) David del Tredici.

Local choreographers have been greatly encouraged during recent seasons. Chief among them is Constantine Patsalas, a Greek who has danced with the National since 1972. He was appointed company choreographer in 1980 and became a part of Bruhn's artistic staff in 1983. Among the young Canadians who have contributed ballets to the repertory are James Kudelka and Danny Grossman.

Bruhn's tenure as artistic director brought the company to new heights of polish and increased international stature. His untimely death, early in 1986, was an unexpected blow which the company had to surmount.

Les Ballets Chiriaeff, begun by Ludmilla Chiriaeff in Montreal in 1956, became Les Grands Ballets Canadiens the following year. Fernand Nault, a French-Canadian native of Montreal, became resident choreographer in 1966. *Tommy* (1970), his ballet to the rock opera by the pop group The Who, was one of the company's biggest successes. When Chiriaeff retired in 1974, another Montrealler, Brian Macdonald, was appointed as artistic director.

The company's varied repertory ranges from classics to contemporary ballet. The troupe also performs a complete trilogy by the German composer Carl Orff – *Carmina Burana*, *Catulli Carmina* and *Trionfo di Afrodite* – all choreographed by Norman Walker.

Bottom: Karen Kain, top principal of the company, as Aminta and Thomas Schramek as Catalinon, Don Juan's servant in Neumeier's production.

GWENETH LLOYD
b 1901

Gweneth Lloyd was born in Eccles in 1901. She studied dance at the Liverpool Physical Training College and the Ginner-Mawer School of Dance and Drama in London. In 1938 she went to Canada and with Betty Farally established Canada's first professional company, the Winnipeg Ballet. In 1953 Queen Elizabeth granted it a charter to become the Royal Winnipeg. From 1939–50 she choreographed 30 ballets for the company including *The Wise Virgins* (1942), *Chapter 13* (1947), *Visages* (1949) and *Shadow on the Prairie* (1952). The company mostly performs revivals of modern ballet but also short extracts from classical ballets. The company tours extensively and its lighthearted, folksy approach is widely enjoyed.

Lloyd opened a school in Toronto in 1950 but remained a director of Winnipeg until 1958, when Arnold Spohr took over. In 1961 she won a Senior Fellowship Award from the Canada Council.

ARNOLD SPOHR
b 1920?

Born in Rhein, Saskatchewan, just after World War I, Arnold Spohr grew up in Winnipeg. He had a degree as a physical education teacher and was even considering a career as a concert pianist long before he became involved with ballet. He joined the Winnipeg Ballet in 1945 and was eventually promoted to principal dancer. He began choreographing in 1950 and left the company in 1954.

In London he danced with Alicia Markova in *Where the Rainbow Ends* (1956–57) and also worked in Canadian television before returning to Winnipeg. The company was on the verge of collapse when the board asked Spohr to step in as a temporary director. He has now held that position for more than a quarter of a century. Soon after being named to his post, Spohr abandoned his choreographic career to concentrate instead on building a first-rate ensemble with an eclectic repertory of classics and modern works by both established and young choreographers.

In 1983 the Canadian Conference of the Arts awarded Spohr a *Diplome d'Honneur*. The citation dubbed him as 'the best-loved man in Canadian dance.'

CELIA FRANCA
b 1921

Celia Franca was born in London in 1921 and studied at the Guildhall School of Music. She received a Scholarship to the Royal Academy of Dance, where she studied under Anthony Tudor and Stanislaus Idzikowski. She first appeared in the chorus of *Spread it Around* in 1935. She joined Ballet Rambert in 1937 and danced in *The Lilac Garden* and *Les Sylphides*. She danced with Sadler's Wells from 1941–46. She created the Queen in *Hamlet* and the prostitute in *Miracle in the Gorbals*. When Sadler's Wells Theatre Ballet was organized in 1946, she choreographed *Khadra* and *Bailemos* (1947).

In 1948 she became leading dancer and ballet mistress of the newly formed Metropolitan Ballet, but in 1951 she founded the National Ballet of Canada and the National Ballet Summer School. The Summer School expanded to become the National Ballet School in 1959 and now teaches both academic and dance subjects. During the company's early years she performed, creating the ballerina role in the Canadian production of Tudor's *Offenbach in the Underworld*. In 1968 Franca choreographed *Cinderella*. She resigned as artistic director in 1974.

LUDMILLA CHIRIAEFF
b 1924

Ludmilla Chiriaeff was born in Riga, Latvia. Her family moved to Berlin after the Revolution where she studied under Alexandra Nicolaieva, formerly of the Moscow Imperial Ballet. In 1936–37 she danced with Ballet Russes and continued to study under Michel Fokine and Leonide Massine. She joined the Berlin Opera Ballet in 1939 but her career was interrupted by the war.

After the war she was *premiere danseuse*, choreographer and ballet mistress for the Lauanne Theater and opened her own school in Geneva in 1948, and her own company, Les Ballets des Arts.

She went to Montreal in 1952 and was quickly asked to produce ballets for Radio-Canada Television, working with producer Jean Boisvert. This fruitful partnership led to the formation of Les Ballets Chiriaeff, renamed Les Grands Ballets Canadiens. She retired in 1974.

Carmina Burana, *first part of Carl Orff's Trionfi trilogy, performed by Les Grands Ballets Canadiens founded by Ludmilla Chiriaeff.*

AUSTRALIA

Sir Robert Helpmann, great Australian dancer and choreographer, pictured here in the role of the doomed Red King from Checkmate.

The history of Australian ballet begins in 1833, when a school was opened in Sydney by Mr Cavendish de Castell from the Paris Conservatoire. During the 1840s dance presentations were very popular at the Royal Victoria Theatre and the Melbourne Royal Theatre; some of the more memorable titles included *Polinchinelle Vampire*, *Mountain Ape* and *Tawny in a Galloping Consumption*. Foreign companies began touring the country in the 1850s. Lola Montez was, as usual, a scandalous sensation; another popular attraction was 'Tomato, the three-legged dancer.'

The quality of dance in Australia had begun to improve, however, by the time Adeline Genée and a troupe of Russian Imperial dancers arrived in the early 1900s. They were followed by the modern dancer Maude Allan, who was very popular. By the 1920s several excellent teachers were based on the Australian continent and their work was reinforced by Pavlova's visits in 1926 and 1929.

During the 1930s and 1940s the stream of visitors continued; Pavlova's husband, Victor Dandré, toured with a large company, and the various Ballets Russes troupes were great attractions in 1934, 1938 and 1940. The number of teachers increased too: Gertrude Bodenweiser (1886–1959) came from Vienna in 1939; Helene Kirsova (c.1911–62) stayed in the country after one of de Basil's tours, establishing a school and a small company; and Edouard Borovansky and his wife founded a school in Melbourne. This last became the Australian Ballet in 1940, predecessor of the present organization, which was established in 1962.

The Australian Ballet, under the direction of Peggy van Praagh and with much support during its formative years from Robert Helpmann, is now the leading classical troupe in the country. Its repertory ranges from Bournonville to Cranko, including works by Ashton, Balanchine, Massine, Nureyev, Petipa, Tetley and Tudor.

Former ballerina Maina Gielgud (b 1945) became the company director in 1981. The niece of actor Sir John Gielgud, she made her début in France with Roland Petit (1961), and danced with Béjart and London Festival Ballet (1972-75) among others. Under her leadership the company is producing a whole new generation of Australian dancers. The repertory continues to depend on the full-length classics for its major strength.

Sydney Dance Theatre is Australia's most-travelled international ensemble. Originally organized in 1965, the troupe came to prominence with appointment of Graeme Murphy as artistic director (1976). Since that time, the company has specialized in evening-length spectacles that blend dance and theater into a dazzling experience that sometimes appears dreamlike and at other moments descends into nightmare. Murphy's flair for theatrics and the company's overt sexual stance combine to produce a lush (for some tastes much too lush) *mise en scène* of colorful and elaborately designed productions.

The modern-based Australian Dance Theatre is located in Adelaide and plays host to a biennial international arts festival of impressive stature. There are also several other smaller ballet and modern companies throughout Australia.

Right: Gary Norman and Alida Chase in Gemini *a work commissioned from choreographer Glen Tetley by the Australian Ballet.*

SIR ROBERT HELPMANN
1909–86

The most-famous Australian dancer, choreographer and director is undoubtedly Robert Helpmann. He trained with the Anna Pavlova company in Australia and began his dancing career in 1926. In 1933 he moved to London, joining the Vic-Wells company and his abilities attracted attention from the beginning. The following year he became *premier danseur* with the company (then renamed Sadler's Wells and to become Royal) and he was to remain with them until 1950.

Noteworthy among the roles he danced were the Red King in *Checkmate*, Orpheus in Ninette de Valois's *Orpheus and Euridice*, the White Skater in *Les Patineurs*, the title roles in *Don Juan* and *Don Quixote*, the Stranger in *Miracle in the Gorbals* (his own ballet), and Doctor Coppelius in *Coppélia*. During this period he also appeared in the theater as an actor, playing Oberon in *A Midsummer Night's Dream* at the Old Vic and the title role in *Hamlet* at Stratford-on-Avon. His talent extended to the cinema, with appearances in *The Red Shoes* (1948) and *The Tales of Hoffmann* (1950).

Although Helpmann left Sadler's Wells Ballet in 1950, he did not entirely sever his connections with the company, with which his name will always be associated. His guest appearances as a dancer included a tour of Australia with the Royal Ballet in 1958–59. Yet by this time he was chiefly working as a director and choreographer with such success as *Le Coq d'Or* (1954) to his credit. In 1963 he collaborated with Frederick Ashton in a new production of *Swan Lake* and in 1965 the two men danced together as the stepsisters in a revival of Ashton's *Cinderella*.

In 1964 he returned to his native Australia to work with the Australian Ballet. He choreographed *The Display*, based on an Australian legend about the lyrebird, and *Yugen*. In 1965 he became joint director with Peggy van Praagh. While retaining links with the Royal Ballet, Helpmann became increasingly associated with ballet in Australia. He choreographed *Sun Music* in 1968 and in 1974 became sole director of the Australian Ballet. During his long career Helpmann has gained many honors, which include the Queen Elizabeth II Coronation Award of the Royal Academy of Dancing in 1961

Sir Robert Helpmann in The Rake's Progress.

Robert Helpmann partnered by Nadia Nerina.

she was invited back to Australia to direct the new Australian Ballet. Dancers from Berovansky Ballet formed the nucleus of the new company. The company follows the style of the Royal Ballet, performing many classic ballets such as *Swan Lake* and *Coppélia*, but it also produces ballets with an Australian flavor, such as *Melbourne Cup* which was choreographed by Rex Reid.

The company appeared in London in 1965 as part of the Commonwealth Art Festival and for a three-year-old company gave a very assured performance. The company tours extensively. Peggy was awarded the OBE in 1966 and the DBE in 1970. She is a leading member of the Cecchetti Society and has written *How I Became a Dancer* and coauthored *The Art of Choreography* and *Ballet in Australia* with Peter Brinson.

She retired in 1974 and then returned as director for a single season (1978–79).

Dame Peggy van Praagh, first director of the Australian Ballet.

and the CBE in 1964, culminating with his knighthood in 1968. His vast experience as a performer, choreographer and director has made a great contribution to the success of Australian ballet.

DAME PEGGY VAN PRAAGH
1910

Peggy Praagh studied under Aimée Phipps and Margaret Craske. She danced with Anton Dolin in 1929. In 1930 she

joined Ballet Rambert and in 1938 became *principal danseuse* at Antony Tudor's London Ballet. In 1941 she joined Sadler's Wells, dancing soloist roles. On the formation of Sadler's Wells Theatre Ballet she became ballet mistress, and from 1952–55 was assistant director. She created roles in *Jardin au Lilas*, *Dark Eulogies* and *Gala Performance*. From 1955 she has mounted ballets in Canada, Munich, Copenhagan and so on for the Royal Ballet.

In 1960 she went to Australia as artistic director of Berovansky Ballet. She left to teach with Cuevas' company but in 1962

SCANDINAVIA

Flemming Flindt and his wife Vivi in The Miraculous Mandarin, *choreographed by Flindt in 1967.*

DENMARK

As the last quarter of the sixteenth century began, the new wave of the Renaissance, which had been steadily pushing north from Italy through France, began making its influence felt strongly in Denmark. Dancing had been popular since the early days of Frederick II's reign (1559–88); the first recorded court production, however, appears in 1577 when a dance entitled *Morain Dance of Fools* by the famous poet Martin Børup was presented in the courtyard of the Royal Palace, to help celebrate the christening of young Prince Christian.

The production contained all the traditional Renaissance trappings – dance, song and recitation – but real *ballets de cour* were not introduced until after the young prince had ascended the throne as Christian IV (reigned 1588–1648). While visiting his sister Anne, wife of James I of England, the king had been greatly impressed by the famous masques popular in the English court at the time. In 1634 he ordered Alexander von Kuckelsom, dancing master at the Sorø Academy, to stage the first real Danish court ballet, with the usual procession of *entrées* culminating in a grand finale featuring all the dancers. Later von Kuckelsom was hired to give dancing lessons to the children of the court.

In Denmark, as elsewhere in Europe, the fortunes of dance were dependent on the monarchy. During the reign of Frederick III (1648–70) court ballet attained even greater heights; Queen Sophie Amalie was very fond of the art, even hiring a French dancing teacher, Daniel Pilloy, for the court. Christian V (reigned 1670–99) and Frederick IV (reigned 1699–1730) continued to support court entertainments, especially the opera ballets popular at the French court, which Christian V greatly admired. (During a visit to Paris he attended a performance of Molière's *L'Ecole des Femmes*, in which the author himself portrayed Arnolphe.) English and European touring companies had brought ballet to a wider Danish audience, and the art was becoming more and more popular with ordinary people.

In 1722 a group of Danish actors founded a theater in Lille Grønnegade, only a few hundred yards from the site of today's Royal Theater; though the theater specialized in drama, especially the comedies of Ludvig Holberg, ballet was an integral part of every successful production. In 1726 Jean-Baptiste Landé and his wife were hired to take charge of the dancing. Unfortunately, the theater was never in a stable financial position and in 1728 it was destroyed by fire. The Landés moved on to greener pastures and, before the theater could be rebuilt, Frederick IV died.

Frederick's successor, Christian VI (reigned 1730–46), was dour and puritanical and would allow neither ballet nor drama to be performed at all. His son, Frederick V (reigned 1746–66), had no such scruples, however; with support from the new king and his English wife, Louise, all forms of theatrical entertainment – ballet, opera, music and drama – were soon more prosperous than ever.

In December 1748 all four found a home when the first Royal Theater opened in Kongens Nytorv. Since there were few Danish dancers as yet, foreigners made up the bulk of the company. Some were French, like Des Larches, the theater's first ballet master; others were Italian, including Gaetano Orlandi and Angelo Pompeati. (Pompeati was also responsible for bringing the pantomime to Denmark in the form John Rich used in his harlequinades at Lincoln's Inn Fields, in London – a form that can still be seen in the pantomimes performed today in Tivoli Gardens.)

Antonio Como, a dancer who arrived in Copenhagen in 1756, worked hard to train a Danish *corps de ballet*. He never expanded the repertory beyond short pieces, but his teaching gave his successor, Antonio Sacco, the personnel he needed to produce his own ballets. Sacco was a disciple of Noverre and Angiolini and during his four seasons in Denmark (1763–67), the ballet master gained a reputation as an excellent choreographer of *ballets d'action*.

A private theater was built for the court at Christianborg Castle during the reign of Christian VII (1766–1808), and its stage provided a venue for many visiting troupes from abroad. There were occasional dancers who worked at both the Court and Royal Theaters, but for the most part the two were in competition. Despite serious fires at the castle in 1794 and 1884, the theater survived; today it is one of the most interesting theatrical museums in existence.

In 1771 a regular dancing school was established at the Court Theater. Its founder, Pierre Laurent, had come to Copenhagen in 1752 with a touring company and had remained, eventually becoming the court dancing instructor. He directed the school for its first 10 years,

laying the foundation for the organization that is still the backbone of Danish ballet.

Thus, when the famous Vicenzo Galeoti arrived at the Court Theater in 1775 he found an already-established company, with dancers trained in the French style. Galeoti, who had already established a solid reputation during some 20 years spent working in English and European theaters, had been hired by the conductor of the court orchestra, the composer Scalabrini; his duties included dancing and teaching both the soloists and the *corps de ballet*. During his 40 years in Denmark he was responsible for the first great flowering of Danish ballet.

Though he was 42 when he arrived in Copenhagen, Galeoti was still an excellent dancer and he never really retired from the stage. When he grew too old to perform as a *danseur noble*, he continued to appear in character parts. In 1812 he made his last public appearance, as Friar Lawrence in *Romeo and Juliet*. He was 79 years old.

As the choreographer of over 50 ballets (not to mention many minor works), Galeoti gave his audiences dramatic works in the Italian style – true *ballets d'action* with plenty of dramatic action, kaleidoscopic crowd scenes and pantomime to carry the plot. His stories were drawn from every imaginable source (literature, mythology, his travels, even his competitors) and ranged in mood from serious works to light-hearted divertissements. One of his most popular ballets, *Lagertha* (1801), was the first to use a Nordic story. Music for the production was written by Claus Schall (1757–1835), whom Galeoti discovered in the court orchestra soon after his arrival, and who, with his encouragement, became the first important Danish composer for ballet.

Only one Galeoti ballet survives today. *The Whims of Cupid and the Ballet Master (Amors og Balletmestorens Luner)*, which premiered on 31 October 1786, is preserved in practically its original form and is the oldest ballet available to modern audiences. The lighthearted story of the complications that result when mischievous Cupid mixes up several pairs of lovers from various countries has never been considered special or a work of genius. But for all that, the loosely connected series of folk dances and *pas de deux* continues to delight audiences almost 200 years later, and is still a favorite in the Royal Danish Ballet's colorful and interesting repertory.

The indefatigable Florentine also made an important contribution as a teacher. He ordered every member of the company to attend classes on a regular basis, which improved the quality of the dancing and also gave the school a strong organizational base. In addition, his wide experience with European ballet, his sophisticated outlook and his vibrant personality all helped combat insularity and brought Danish ballet into the mainstream with the rest of Europe.

Anine Frölich was Galeoti's first popular ballerina, but she died at an early age and was succeeded by Margrethe Schall, who remained the company's leading ballerina until 1824. In 1792 Antoine Bournonville, an excellent dancer, arrived from Stockholm to strengthen the male half of the troupe, and in 1799 Laurent returned to Copenhagen, taking over many leading roles as Galeoti grew older and less able to perform to his previous high standards.

Unfortunately, as Galeoti neared the end of his life-time appointment as director of the Royal Theater, his judgment became less certain, and even before his death in 1816 Danish ballet was on the decline. His successor, Antoine Bournonville, had little choreographic talent and was unable to change the trend. The public lost interest, the repertory degenerated and the dancing became shoddy and careless. Altogether, it was a sad time for Danish ballet.

In 1829 August Bournonville, Antoine's son, returned to Copenhagen from Paris to dance as a guest artist on leave from the Opéra. Five months later the talented young man (who had been born in Denmark and received his early training at the Court ballet school) signed an 18-year contract with the Royal Theater to serve as principal dancer, ballet master and teacher. It was the beginning of the second great period in Danish ballet.

When Bournonville took over, ballet in Denmark was a shambles; when he died half a century later he left a well-trained company with an exciting repertory and, most importantly, a strong organization to perpetuate it. In order to pull ballet out of its doldrums he established a dictatorship; though in the long run it accomplished his purpose, it also cost him the services of some excellent dancers. His first major ballerina, Andrea Kraetzmer, walked out in 1832. Her successor, Lucile Grahn (considered the greatest Danish ballerina of the nine-

teenth century and one of the best Romantic dancers in the world), left in 1839, never to return. However the company never lacked good replacements; some of the most popular performers during Bournonville's tenure were Caroline Fjeldsted (1821–81) and Augusta Nielsen (1822–1902), along with Juliet Price (Bournonville's ideal dancer) and her brother Waldemar.

Bournonville is recognized today as one of the great Romantic choreographers; since he himself danced the principal male roles for many years, men retained their importance in Denmark even during the height of the age of the ballerina. The now-famous Bournonville style is graceful and essentially gentle, lacking many of the flashier Italian techniques popular throughout the rest of Europe. Its two main features are elevation, or *ballon*, and a quick, easy lightness. The almost nonstop jumping, with many beats for the legs and feet, gives Bournonville's ballets an almost breathless quality; often the torso remains almost still while the feet flash through a series of fast, intricate steps;

Eva Evdokimova demonstrates the Bournonville style of lightness and ballon *in an excerpt from* Napoli.

A beautifully executed jeté en avant *in the Bournonville style, with the arms extended forward and with good elevation.*

there are unexpected shifts in weight or changes in direction; and throughout the emphasis is on making it all look easy rather than calling attention to the dancers' technical skill.

One typical Bournonville step is a *jeté en avant* that ends with the dancer facing the audience, arms outstretched in a cheerful, embracing gesture. That gesture expresses the Danish concept of *hygge* (coziness and warmth), which is also reflected in the ballets themselves. The supernatural plays a smaller part in Bournonville's works than in French Romantic ballets, while Christianity and domesticity get proportionally more attention. Many other works were 'travelogues,' featuring local color from faraway places.

One of Bournonville's best-loved pieces, *Napoli eller Fiskeren og hans Brud* (*Naples or the Fisherman and his Bride*, 1842), combines several of these elements. *Napoli* is the story of a young fisherman named Gennaro whose fiancée, Teresina, is abducted by the wicked Golfo, a sea creature who rules Capri's Blue Grotto. The opening scenes, full of gay young people, have a warm, southern atmosphere, and the ballet ends with a joyful tarantella to celebrate Teresina's return; Gennaro finally rescues his lover, through faith, with a statue of the Virgin Mary.

Fairy tales were also popular subjects; *A Folk Tale* (1854) is as full of elf maidens and trolls as Bournonville's good friend Hans Christian Andersen could have wished.

Mozart was Bournonville's favorite composer, and he was also responsible for introducing Wagner's music to Denmark (with his production of *Lohengrin* in 1870), but most of his ballets were set to music by Danish composers, which did much to further the development of Danish music.

Perhaps Bournonville's greatest and longest-lasting contribution was organization. His teaching methods, which were codified after his death into a series of set classes or 'schools' for each day of the week, were the basis for all ballet training in Denmark until 1950. The administrative structure he established still exists in modified form and the discipline he insisted on fostered a professional outlook and dedication that remains a hallmark of the Royal Danish Ballet.

In 1874 the Royal Theater moved next door to a grand new building designed by Vilhelm Dahlerup and Ove Petersen. The theater had a much larger stage and all the latest production equipment, but it would be a while before its potential could be fully realized. Bournonville, as he neared the end of his life, lost some of his innovative sense and critical judgment. Artistic development in Denmark began to slow down and, after his retirement in 1877, unfortunately came to a complete stop.

Ludvig Gade, who took over as director of the company, had long been a solid, dependable, but never brilliant member of the troupe. During his tenure and that of his successor, Emil Hansen (1843–1927), ballet was in a rut, stolidly carrying on as before, but without Bournonville's sparkle and sense of atmosphere. Though superficially it looks like a bad period for Danish ballet, in the long term it turned out to be a useful one, as many of Bournonville's ballets, which easily could have been lost, were retained in the repertory out of sheer inertia. Much of Hansen's energy was devoted to recording the choreography in his own system of dance notation – a record which became invaluable in years to come.

In 1879, the day before Bournonville died, a new dancer made his debut at the Royal Theater. Hans Beck was young, virile and an excellent dancer, who began to revive public interest despite the weak management at the theater. In the 1890s he acquired a partner, Valborg Jørgensen (later Valborg Borchsenius), whose youth, vitality and talent matched his own. In 1894 he reluctantly agreed to assume leadership of the company.

Beck was not a brilliant choreographer, and though he revived many Bournonville ballets, as well as Galeoti's *Whims of Cupid and the Ballet Master*, he added few new works to the repertory. His production of *Coppélia* (1896), however, is still considered excellent. *The Little Mer-*

maid (1909), based on Andersen's fairy tale, is another of his creations, and is still a favorite in the company's repertory; Ellen Price, who danced the title role, was the inspiration for the famous statue in Copenhagen. Besides Price and Borchsenius, the most popular dancers in Beck's company were Emilie Smith, Grethe Ditlevsen, Gustav Uhlendorff and Richard Jensen.

In 1909 Diaghilev's Ballets Russes opened a new era in international ballet, but the modern trend had little impact in Denmark. Beck, realizing that ballet was changing and unable himself to adapt to it, retired in 1915.

Following Beck's retirement, Danish ballet went through yet another difficult period. The demand for new ballets and the dissatisfaction with the Bournonville tradition grew, but neither Beck's successor, Uhlendorff (1915–28) nor Kai Smith (1928–30), was able to react adequately. The dancer Emilie Walbom produced *Harlequin's Millions* (1906) and tried adapting two Fokine ballets: *Carnival* (which became *Drommebilleder*, or *Dream Pictures*) and *Cleopatre* (*En Nat i Aegypten*, or *A Night in Egypt*). They were all popular, but none really hit the mark.

Fokine and his wife actually lived in Copenhagen for a year in 1918–19. They were not asked to perform at the Royal Theater, but they did take several pupils, among them Elna Jørgen Jensen, the best ballerina in the company at that time. Fokine returned in 1925 as guest choreographer; his productions of *Les Sylphides* (in Denmark called *Chopiniana*), *Petrouchka* and *Prince Igor* were all tremendously successful, but remained isolated events, not harbingers of any fundamental change.

Several excellent dancers were emerging, however, and to them Fokine's visit was a great inspiration. Besides Jensen, they included: Elna Lassen, a brilliant technician who was considered Denmark's leading ballerina from 1925 until her untimely death in 1930; John Andersen, the company's most promising male dancer, who also died at an early age, in 1926; the talented Ulla Poulsen; Else Merrild; and even the children of the company, like Margot Florentz-Gerhard (later Margot Lander) and Børge Ralov.

In 1929, when Diaghilev's dancers were scattering far and wide after his death, the Royal Theater managed to sign George Balanchine to a six-month contract as guest choreographer. During his stay in Copenhagen he produced six

Technical perfection made to look effortless in this splendid leap by Cyril Atanassof of the Paris Opéra.

ballets: two of Fokine's (*Schéhérazade* and *The Legend of Joseph*), two of Massine's (*Le Tricorne* and *La Boutique Fantasque*) and two of his own (*Apollon Musagete* and *Barabon*).

The third great era in Danish ballet occurred under the leadership of Harald Lander, who assumed the position of director in 1930. Like Bournonville, he established a virtual dictatorship in order to bring the company up to standard in the shortest possible time, then went on to strengthen the repertory and the dancers themselves, setting the stage for the Royal Danish Ballet's current international reputation.

Lander revised several classics from the international repertory and, with the assistance of Beck and Borchsenius, revived several Bournonville works, like *Napoli*, *Konservatoriet* (*The Dancing School*) and *La Ventana*. He was also a prolific choreographer in his own right and his work represented a wide range of styles. Two of his best known works are *Qarrtsiluni* (1942), a fantastical ballet set in Greenland at the end of the long, dark winter, and *Etudes* (1948), which traces the development of a dancer from the first simple barre exercises for children to the *grand allegro* at the end, with its spectacular leaps and turns. After the war came *The Phoenix Bird* (1946), depicting the growth of a dictator and his brutal regime, and then the lyrical *Rhapsody* (1949). Other ballets range from children's pieces (*The Shepherdess and The Chimney Sweep*, 1934) and comic works (*Football*, 1933) to expressionistic ballets like *The Seven Deadly Sins* (1936). Much of his work was done in collaboration with contemporary Danish composers like Fini Henriques, Johan Hye-Knudsen, Emil Reesen and especially Knudage Riisager, who wrote the music for *Qarrtsiluni* and the one-act ballet *Etudes*.

Most of Lander's success was due to his energy and capacity for hard work, but he was also fortunate in having a large group of talented dancers to work with. During the 1930s and 1940s Margot Lander and Børge Ralov (the only two members of the Royal Danish Ballet ever to be given rank of prima ballerina and *premier danseur*) dominated the company. During the 1940s the next generation began to make itself known: Kirsten Ralov, Margrethe Schanne, Kirsten Simone and Mona Vangsaae were among the ballerinas; male dancers included Niels Bjørn-Larsen, Fredbjørn Bjørns-son, Erik Bruhn, Poul Gnatt, Svend Eric Jensen, Henning Kronstam, Frank Schaufuss and Stanley Williams. Later still another crop of talented youngsters appeared, like Toni Lander, Inge Sand and Peter Martins.

In 1950, the year before he resigned his post, Lander made two commitments that had far-reaching consequences. The first was his collaboration with the Danish Travel Bureau to promote an annual Ballet Festival, which soon brought the Royal Danish Ballet to the attention of the world. The second was his engagement of the great teacher, Vera Volkova, who brought the techniques of the Russian school to Denmark for the first time. In addition to adding an important new dimension to the company's training program, Volkova was able to maintain

Above: Eva Evdokimova and Cyril Atanasoff in a pas de deux *from* Napoli, *two dancers who excel in the Bournonville style.*

Below: John Gilpin of the Festival Ballet in Etudes, *which Harald Lander mounted for the company in 1955 at the Royal Festival Hall.*

stability in the school during the years immediately following Lander's departure.

Niels Bjørn-Larsen took over as acting director of the Royal Danish Ballet after Lander's resignation, receiving an official appointment in 1953, the same year that the company made its first venture abroad. Their appearance at the Royal Opera House, Covent Garden, with productions of *Napoli*, *Coppélia* and *La Sylphide* (featuring stellar performances by Margrethe Schanne and Erik Bruhn) was a great success. Until this first tour the company's rich Bournonville repertory had been a well-kept secret from most of the ballet world.

During the early 1950s several members of the company began turning their hands to choreography, including Schaufuss, Bruhn, Bjørnsson, Ralov and of course Larsen, whose *Capricious Lucinda* (1954) is perhaps his best known work. Many foreign choreographers have also worked with the company, like Ashton (who staged *Romeo and Juliet* and *La Fille Mal Gardée*), Lichine (*Graduation Ball*) and Petit (*Carmen*); others include Balanchine, Cullberg, Macmillan, Robbins and John Taras.

In 1965 Flemming Flindt took over as leader of the troupe. Already well known as a dancer, he was a gifted choreographer as well. His best-known ballet is *The*

Lesson (1963), based on a play by Ionesco. His first production as director was *The Three Musketeers*, featuring Kronstam as d'Artagnan and Simone as Milady. During his tenure as director he worked hard to revive and polish the most important Bournonville ballets and also added many modern works to the repertory, including his own ambitious productions and even pieces by modern dance choreographers like Tetley and Taylor.

Danish ballet has long been rich in excellent dancers. Some have remained with the Royal Danish Ballet; many have joined the New York City Ballet (like Ib Andersen, Adam Luders, Peter Martins, Helgi Tomasson and Ulrik Trojabert); international stars include Erik Bruhn, Niels Kehlet, Toni Lander, Peter Martins and Peter Schaufuss.

In June 1980 the troupe made one of its rare appearances in the United States, staging a repetition of its annual Bournonville Festival at the International Festival of the Stars in Chicago. Led by Henning Kronstam and his two current Bournonville experts, Kirsten Ralov and Hans Brenaa, the group presented seven Bournonville ballets: *Konservatoriet, La Ventana,* the *pas de deux* known as *Flower Festival in Genzano,* a *divertissement* from Rossini's opera *Wilhelm Tell* and the full-length ballets *Napoli, La Sylphide* and *A Folk Tale*.

Kronstam was appointed artistic director in 1979. He was succeeded in 1985 by Frank Andersen, one of the leading Danish dancers. Since the mid-1970s Andersen and ballerina Dinna Bjørn have led a small touring ensemble of about a dozen dancers, who specialize in programs that celebrate Bournonville's talents. Bjørn, who is considered to be one of the finest Bournonville authorities in the younger generation, has also created choreography of her own.

The company has never been exclusively devoted to its most famous choreographer. All through the past 200 years, others have also contributed to the repertory. The Danes were among the first companies to add American modern choreography to their repertory. Paul Taylor's *Aureole*, a deceptively simple-looking quintet set to Handel, first appeared in Copenhagen in 1968. Choreography by Neumeier, van Manen, Murray Lewis and Tetley have all helped to round out the company's image as more than just a treasure trove of incomparable mid-nineteenth-century gems.

SWEDEN

Though the development of ballet in Sweden is often overshadowed by the illustrious history of Danish ballet, Sweden too has a long ballet tradition. A French dancing master, Antoine de Beaulieu, produced the first recorded court ballet for the King of Sweden in 1638, and similar entertainments – designed to celebrate weddings, military victories and the like – were soon an established part of life at the Swedish court.

King Gustav III, who not only loved ballet but also wrote his own operas and dramas, opened an opera house in Stockholm in 1773. The company that opened the theater (with a performance of *Thétis et Pélée*) consisted of 24 dancers (mostly French) led by Louis Gallodier of the Paris Opéra. With strong support from the king, ballet flourished; 10 years later the company had grown to 72, and several Swedish soloists had joined the ranks. Antoine Bournonville, a former pupil of Noverre, joined the troupe in 1781 as a dancer/choreographer; he was the driving force behind the change from *ballet de cour* to *ballet d'action* in Sweden, staging works like *Les Meuniers Provençaux* (1785) and *Les Pêcheurs* (1789).

The king also established scholarships to send the most promising Swedish dancers to Paris for further study. One such student was Charles Didelot; but though he returned to Stockholm for a short time as *premier danseur* after his studies had been completed, he soon embarked on an international career and was lost to Swedish ballet.

The beginning of the nineteenth century saw the arrival of Filippo Taglioni, who was a *premier danseur* during 1803 and 1804. Taglioni also married a Swedish dancer, Sophie Karsen, and their daughter Marie was born in Stockholm in 1804. Returning for a short period as ballet master in 1818, he staged two ballets – one, *The Return of Springtime*, especially for a party given by the Spanish Ambassador for the crown prince of Sweden. His most important contribution, however, was redesigning the company's costumes to make them less cumbersome.

Most of the nineteenth century was dominated by French ballet masters and dancers, but in 1833 Sweden acquired its first native dancer/choreographer. Anders Selinder, who has been called 'the Bournonville of Sweden,' brought Romantic ballet to its full flowering and, like Bournonville, was determined to create a national repertory. Selinder was fond of Swedish folk dances and incorporated them into several ballets. He also wrote several musical plays which featured folk dances, and thus did much to preserve them for posterity. Unfortunately, all his ballets have been lost,

Elsa Marianne von Rosen's ballet Pictures at an Exhibition *for the Gothenburg Ballet. It was set to a pop version of Mussorgsky's original music.*

but one of the plays, *Vaarmlaanningarna* (*People of Varmland*, 1846), is still one of the company's most popular Christmas productions.

Marie Taglioni returned to the land of her birth in 1841, and, as everywhere, Taglioni fever swept Stockholm. Her performances in *Le Lac des Fées* and the suite from *La Sylphide* had audiences in an uproar. The nightly mob scenes outside the stage door led the management of the Royal Theater to consider giving her an apartment there for her own safety. But though she did much to popularize ballet during her appearances, in the long run Taglioni did Stockholm a disservice: when she left she took Sweden's most promising male dancer, Christian Johansson, with her to Russia. Johansson spent the rest of his life there, exerting a decisive influence on the development of Russian ballet.

Ballet began to decline in popularity during the 1860s, and even hiring August Bournonville as guest choreographer for three seasons could not stop the drift of the public toward opera. The company at the Royal Theater declined drastically in number, but fortunately training and standards of performance were kept for some time at respectable, if not stellar, levels.

In 1906 a visit from Isadora Duncan helped revive some interest in dance, and in 1908 Pavlova chose Stockholm for her first appearance outside Russia. The tremendous reception by the Swedes encouraged her to continue her tours and her dancing excited renewed interest in the Royal Swedish Ballet.

Michel and Vera Fokine joined the company in 1913; Fokine staged several of his own ballets and also did much to encourage the younger members of the company. Three of the youngsters – Jenny Hasselquist (b 1894), Corina Ari (1897–1970) and Jean Börlin – followed the Fokines to Denmark for further study and later, in the 1920s, became the mainstays of Les Ballets Suédois.

Les Ballets Suédois, a private company formed by Rolf de Maré in 1920, was cast in the same, avant garde mold as the Ballets Russes, by which it was often overshadowed. Nevertheless performances in the major European capitals during its five-year existence were well received. Along with Ari and Hasselquist, dancers with the company included Jolanda Figoni, Margareta Johansson and Ebon Strandon. Jean Börlin was both *premier danseur* and chief choreographer.

His productions were excellent; some were modern, others were based on Swedish folk tales and dances.

But Les Ballets Suédois, though officially a Swedish company, was spiritually a child of Paris and, for the most part, ballet in Sweden itself remained in the doldrums. Interest would flare up during one of Fokine's return visits, then just as quickly subside. The Polish dancer Jan Cieplinski, ballet master from 1928 to 1931, tried staging the classics, but without much success. During the 1940s George Gué tried with an equal lack of success to stage both classics and modern works, but by this time the dancers' training was simply not up to standard, and Gué had to depend on stage effects to carry the productions.

The year 1950 marked the beginning of a new era in the history of the Royal Swedish Ballet. That year Antony Tudor was hired as director; though he only had a one-year appointment, his productions (*Giselle*, *Lilac Garden* and *Gala Performance*) and his wide experience in international ballet inspired many members of the company to work toward higher standards. At about the same time two excellent teachers from Latvia, Albert and Nina Kozlovsky, joined the teaching staff at the academy, bringing with them the famous Vaganova method.

The English producer and choreographer Mary Skeaping came to Stock-

Niklas Ek and Lena Wennergren in Birgit Cullberg's pas de deux from Romeo and Juliet *choreographed for her own Cullberg Ballet.*

holm in 1953 to stage *Swan Lake*, and the performance went so well that the following year she was hired as ballet director. She faced a formidable task with little support from the Royal Theatre, which considered ballet a rather unimportant adjunct to opera.

Skeaping, however, was a vigorous, determined leader who had already amassed a quarter-century's experience with ballet all over the world. Her first step was to build a strong repertory, alternating dancers in the various roles to give them as much experience as possible. She was also a leading expert on seventeenth-century ballets and presented several revivals in Gustav III's Court Theater at Drottingholm Palace, which, with its sets, costumes and stage machinery, is still preserved as a museum.

She made it a policy during her nine years with the company to encourage Swedish choreographers and keep a fair representation of Swedish ballets in the repertory. One of the most important Swedish choreographers to emerge in recent times is Birgit Cullberg, whose production of *Miss Julie* in 1950 has been followed by many successful works, many starring Elsa-Marianne von Rosen (b 1927). During the late 1950s Ivo Cramér

(b 1921) added several ballets to the repertory, including *The Prodigal Son* (1957) and *The Linden Tree* (1958); more recently the modern dancer Birgit Akesson composed three ballets for the troupe.

Cullberg, who was resident choreographer for the company (1952-57), formed her own troupe, the Cullberg Ballet, in 1967. Both of her sons, Mats and Niklas Ek, have been leading dancers with her company. Mats, who began choreographing in 1976, is now regarded as one of the most important Scandinavian dancemakers of the current generation.

Since the 1950s the Royal Swedish Ballet has undertaken a number of European tours and developed a solid repertory, which includes not only the classics, but also ballets by Massine, Tudor, Balanchine, Robbins, Limón, Tetley, MacMillan, Nureyev, Feld and Kylian.

The Canadian, Brian Macdonald, led the company from 1964 to 1966: he was succeeded by an American, James Moore (1972–75), who staged an ornate version of *The Sleeping Beauty* which hid the court of Louis XIV under a welter of silver cobwebs. Ivor Cramer returned to the company as artistic director (1975-80). In 1986, Egon Madsen, one of Cranko's 'magical four' stars from Stuttgart, gave up the post of director to Nils-Ake Haggbom, who has danced with the Royal since 1959.

Ballet is also a growing favorite in cities outside Stockholm. Conny Borg and von Rosen both played important roles in establishing Gothenburg's Stora Theater (now directed by Ulf Gadd), and Borg is currently directing the Municipal Theater Ballet in Malmö.

Mary Skeaping's expertise on the balletde cour *is obvious in productions such as this,* The Return of Springtime *for the Royal Swedish Ballet.*

NORWAY

Norway, which was ruled first by Denmark, then by Sweden until 1905, never developed a court ballet tradition; the history of ballet there does not really begin until after World War II.

The Oslo-based Den Norske Ballet has grown from the six dancers who formed it in 1953 (under co-directors Gerd Kjølaas and Rita Tori) to 40. Nicholas Orloff served as ballet master in 1960 to 1961. He was followed by: Joan Harris (1961–65), who later became director of the company's associated school; Sonja Arova (1966–70); and Anne Borg (1971–76). British dancer Brenda Last was the next artistic director (1977-80). Jens Graff has been in charge of the company since 1980.

The company had its biggest triumph to date when it produced Glen Tetley's *The Tempest* (originally staged for Ballet Rambert a year earlier). Tetley's lush, full-scale

Right: Hedda, *a ballet based on Ibsen's* Hedda Gabler; *choreography by Kari Blakstad, Marthe Saeter as Hedda.*

Below: Members of the Norwegian Ballet demonstrate their prowess. Kari Blakstad is the choreographer and Victor Jara wrote the music.

rendition of Shakespeare's last play featured elaborate designs by Nadine Baylis and a score by the dean of modern Norwegian composers, Arne Nordheim. The production proved so successful that it was selected to open a season-long 'Ballet International' series at the Brooklyn Academy of Music (1983-84).

The repertory is a mix of classic and contemporary works, including several pieces by young Norwegian choreographers, such as Kari Blakstad.

FINLAND

The first state theater opened in Finland in 1879 when the country was still under Russian rule; thus the Alexander Theater (named in honor of Czar Alexander II) was located in Helsingfors (now Helsinki), where the Russian Governor General was based. There has been a school attached to the theater's ballet company since its founding. After Finland declared its independence in 1917 the name of the theater was changed to the National Opera House (*Suomen Kansallisooppera*).

In the beginning, the dance company worked mainly in operas and operettas, with only an occasional short ballet performance; its technical level did not begin to reach a professional standard until George Gué took over as ballet master in 1921. In 1922 Gué had made such progress that he was able to produce the first Finnish *Swan Lake* (the first full-length ballet for the company) with Marie Paischeff as Odette-Odile; in 1923 Senta Will von Knorring danced the leading roles in Gué's versions of *Chopiniana* (*Les Sylphides*) and *Schéhérazade*. Gué was replaced as director of the company by a Russian, Alexander Saxelin, in 1932.

The first Finnish choreographer emerg-

ed in 1955 when Irja Koskinen, who had been a prima ballerina with the company from 1935 to 1959, composed a ballet to Sibelius's *Scaramouche*. In 1966 Elsa Silvesterson, another former dancer, produced *Festivo*, again to music by Sibelius.

Since World War II the company, now 50-members strong, has expanded its repertory considerably. It still has strong connections with Leningrad, in style, teaching methods and even personnel.

Each June, the university town of Kuopio (some 200 miles north of Hel-

Hannu Pekka Holstöm as the shepherd Armen and Ulrika Hallberg as Gayané in the Finnish National production of the same name.

sinki) plays host to an international dance and music festival. Begun in the early 1970s, the event offers a showcase for ballet and modern dance companies from both East and West.

The festival always includes some folkdance ensembles and also features important Finnish creators, such as the experimentalist Jorma Uotinen.

'The Dance of the Young Maidens' from Act 1 Scene 2 of the full-length production of Gayané *by the Finnish National Ballet.*

VICENZO GALEOTI
1733–1816

Vicenzo Galeoti, a native of Florence, received his ballet training in Italy from, among others, Gasparo Angiolini.

Most of the early part of his career was spent travelling and working in Europe. He was very popular in Venice, where he danced and directed ballets at the San Moisé, San Benedetto and San Salvatori theaters. In Stuttgart, probably in the 1760s, he met Noverre, who reinforced Angiolini's theories about *ballet d'action*. In 1769 Galeoti and his wife, the dancer Antonia Guidi, were hired as soloists at King's Theatre, London; the following year he was appointed ballet master. When his contract expired he returned to Venice, where he acted as ballet master for the San Moisé (in competition with Angiolini, who was working in the same capacity at the San Benedetto).

In 1775 Galeoti agreed to come to Copenhagen as *premier danseur* and ballet master. It was soon evident that the peripatetic dancer had found a home at last; he became a Danish citizen in 1781 and remained in Denmark for the rest of his life.

Though, at 42, he had passed his peak as a performer by the time he arrived in Copenhagen, Galeoti continued to dance until he was 79. He was noted for his elegance and style, and later for his ability to portray character parts; his last stage appearance was as Friar Lawrence in *Romeo and Juliet* (1812).

As a choreographer he produced more than 50 ballets in addition to dozens of minor works. They were never lacking in variety. Some plots came from literature, from the works of Voltaire (*L'Orphelin*, 1780, and *Semiramus*, 1787), Ariosto (*Angelica og Medoro*, 1784), Fénélon (*Telemachus on Calypso's Isle*, 1792), Marmontel (*Anette og Lubin*, 1797) and Shakespeare (*Romeo and Juliet*, 1811, and his last ballet, *Macbeth*, 1816). Other works were derived from popular sentimental novels of the day, like *Linba og Walvais*, the story of a London sea captain who elopes with his beloved and their adventures when the are shipwrecked on a cannibal-infested desert island.

Nor was he averse to adapting the work of his colleagues, especially in the early days. *The Gypsies' Camp* (1776) and *The Abandoned Dido* (1777), for example, were virtual copies of two Angiolini ballets, while *Marylebone Garden in London* (1776) has a strong flavor of Noverre's *Les Fêtes de Vauxhall*.

Galeoti's best works were choreographed early in the nineteenth century. His most famous production, *Lagertha*, was premiered in 1801, as was *The Metamorphosis or The Devil is Loose*; another popular piece, *Nina or The Folly of Love*, was first shown in 1802.

It was as a teacher, however, that Galeoti exerted the most lasting influence. His vast experience, vital personality and sophisticated European outlook inspired students to aim for real professional standards. More specifically, he ordered everyone in the company to attend regular classes, which not only developed into a strong, organized system, but also established a sense of discipline and dedication to ballet.

Schall's brother-in-law, Claus Schall (1757–1835), was musical director of the company from 1817 and composed some 20 ballet scores, including *Lagertha*, *Romeo and Juliet* and *Macbeth*.

AUGUST BOURNONVILLE
1805–79

August Bournonville was born in Copenhagen where his father, Antoine, was one of the city's leading dancers. Antoine (1760–1843), a Frenchman, had been trained primarily in Vienna, had worked for Noverre at King's Theatre, London, and had been one of Gustav III's favorite dancers in Stockholm. He had begun to study dance as a very young boy, and later he took his small son with him to the school at the Court Theater as a matter of course.

The lad spent hours mimicking the adults, and before long it was clear that he had extraordinary talent. In fact, for some years he had trouble deciding whether to pursue a career as a dancer, actor or singer. His first dancing role was in 1813 when, at the age of eight, he appeared in a production of *Lagertha*; in 1815 he played the part of Erling in *Hakon Jarl*, a tragedy by Adam Oehlenschlager; and in 1817 he sang in the Danish version of *Le Jugement de Salomon*.

Of all three, however, Bournonville preferred dancing, and in 1820 he and his father set out for Paris where he spent the summer studying with Coulon and

Vincenzo Galeoti, pioneer of Danish ballet.

ANNA MARGRETHE SCHALL
1775–1852

Margrethe Schall was born in 1775, the same year that Galeoti arrived to begin his 40-year sojourn in Copenhagen. As a student and later as a dancer she was one of the maestro's favorites; her debut in *Nina* in 1802 and her many subsequent appearances made her the darling of the audiences as well. Between 1802 and 1824 she was the Royal Theater's leading ballerina, retaining her reputation for many years after her retirement, until she was overshadowed by Lucile Grahn and the advent of Romantic ballet.

August Bournonville's influence survives today.

Vestris, who taught him about French ballet. Back in Copenhagen he was accepted into the company, and as the years went on he became more and more involved with ballet, until it became virtually his whole life.

He soon realized that he would never reach the heights he dreamed of without more study and greater exposure to other groups. Finally, in 1824 he managed to get a two-year leave of absence and sped immediately back to Paris. During his stay at the Opéra's academy, Vestris found him an excellent, hard-working student; when he graduated in 1826 he was offered a job with the company and accepted, despite angry messages from the Royal Theater and even King Frederick VI. Eventually, however, his leave was extended and he was able to spend the next two years dancing in Paris, in smaller French cities, and even at King's Theatre in London. He became increasingly popular and gained much from his contact with dancers like Jules Perrot and Marie Taglioni.

In the early nineteenth century dancers were still not quite respectable, and by 1828 Bournonville was determined to return to Copenhagen where he was anxious not only to upgrade the technical standards, but also to make dancing a respected art and dancers good citizens in the eyes of society.

It took some time to arrange suitable terms, but by 1830 Bournonville was installed as principal dancer and ballet master at the Royal Theater, a post he held, with only a few interruptions, until his death. In order to achieve his objectives as quickly as possible, Bournonville ran the company like a dictator; one break in his tenure occurred when he overstepped the limits of his authority and tried to involve the king in a contract dispute with Lucille Grahn. During his six-month banishment he visited France and Italy, where he got the inspiration for *Napoli*. He also worked for a year in Vienna, in 1855, and in Stockholm, from 1861 to 1864.

As a choreographer, Bournonville was one of the great leaders of the Romantic movement; much of the Bournonville style stems from his own talents – and shortcomings – as a dancer. For example, the style hardly calls for pirouettes, since Bournonville was bad at them; he also had difficulty landing after jumps, so his sequences have dancers taking off into another step immediately rather than holding a pose and then going on into the next step. Since he continued to dance himself until 1848, Denmark was for a time the only place during the Romantic era where men were not completely overshadowed by the ballerinas.

Bournonville retired in 1877 and died two years later, at the age of 74, on his way home from church. After his death his teaching methods were organized into a series of set classes called the Bournonville Schools, which were the basis for all ballet training in Denmark until Vera Volkova arrived in 1950. Each class – one for every day of the week except Sunday – consists of barre exercises, floor combinations and variations from actual ballets. Over the years dancers have given their own names to the various parts. For example, the last combination in Saturday's School is the 'out-the-door' step. And of course, any unfamiliar step in a ballet has to have come from the 'Sunday School.'

ANDERS SELINDER
1806–74

Anders Selinder was trained in Stockholm and became a soloist with the Royal Swedish Ballet in 1829.

In 1833 he became the company's first Swedish ballet master. During his two periods in that position (1833–45 and 1851–56) he brought Romantic ballet to its peak in Sweden. He also did much to preserve Swedish folk dances, which he adapted and used in many of his ballets.

In 1871 Selinder retired and opened a school in Stockholm, which he ran until his death.

Lucile Grahn, the great Danish eighteenth-century ballerina in the role of the bandit's daughter.

LUCILE GRAHN
1819–1907

Lucile Grahn, the most talented ballerina to emerge from Denmark in the nineteenth century and one of the great Romantic interpreters, was the daughter of a customs agent. She showed so much talent as a child at the Royal Danish Ballet school that Bournonville, when he arrived, took over virtually all of her training himself.

In 1834, when she was 15, he took her with him on a trip to Paris, and her first visit to the Opéra left her with the determination to dance there some day herself. In 1835, back in Copenhagen, she was given the leading role of Astrid in Bournonville's historical piece, *Valdemar*; the next year she had her greatest success in Denmark in *La Sylphide*, making such a hit that the royal family invited her to tea with the princesses.

Grahn was a slight, ethereal teenager, but she had inherited a strong stubborn streak from her Jutland farmer-ancestors. She was not about to give up her dream of dancing in Paris and when Bournonville (who by this time was in love with her) refused her application for a travel grant, she bypassed him and went straight to Princess Wilhelmina. Her short stay in Paris in 1873 made life back in Denmark seem even more restrictive and intolerable; Bournonville, she claimed, was a dictatorial, cruel 'old man,' and, of course, as she spurned him, he became so. Finally, in 1838, she obtained royal permission to give six guest performances in Hamburg; she left Denmark in 1839 for ever.

After four months at the Opéra, Grahn's big chance came: Fanny Elssler fell ill and she was given the lead role in a performance of *La Sylphide*. The resulting triumph – for her delicate air better suited the part then Elssler's worldly sensuality – established her as a rising young star and made the older dancer furious. Unfortunately, Grahn injured her knee just before the 1840 season and her next important engagement was not until 1843 in Russia. There she danced Taglioni's roles and, since she was 15 years younger and much prettier, enjoyed a huge success. Her stay in St Petersburg was cut short, however, because of the jealousy of the powerful Andreianova.

In 1844 Grahn began the year in Milan, during the carnival season, then went on to London, where in the next two years she performed the greatest dancing of her career. The culmination was her appearance in the summer of 1845 with Taglioni, Grisi and Cerrito in Perrot's *Pas de Quatre*.

In 1848 she moved to Hamburg and became so fond of Germany that she bought a house in Munich and appeared mainly in various German cities. At the age of 37 (in 1856) she married an English tenor, Frederick Young, and seemed on the verge of a quiet, happy retirement. But in 1863 disaster struck: Young sustained a spine injury in a stage accident, leaving him confined to a wheelchair for the rest of his life.

Undaunted, Grahn immediately began teaching to support them both, eventually securing an official appointment at the school attached to the Munich Hoftheater and even choreographing several ballets and divertissements. Bournonville visited Munich in 1869 and the two met for the first time in 30 years. With the passage of time all the old empity had faded away and the two were able to chat comfortably about the old days and mutual friends like Hans Christian Andersen. In later years Grahn's plump figure, clad in black, was a familiar and much-loved sight in the streets of Munich.

On her death, 23 years after her husband's, Grahn left all her property to the city that had been so kind to her, stipulating that it be used to help talented young artists and Munich returned the compliment by naming a street in her honor.

THE PRICE FAMILY

Price is one of the greatest names in Danish theater history. The founder of the clan, James Price (1761–1805), was a mime and circus rider who came to Copenhagen with a travelling circus and eventually settled there.

James's granddaughter, Juliette (1831–1906), became one of Bournonville's favorite pupils and one of the leading ballerinas of her day. She was the maestro's ideal dancer – elegant and gentle – and created roles in all his important ballets, including *Konservatoriet* (1849), until her retirement. She portrayed the first Danish Giselle in 1862 and was an acclaimed Sylphide. Unfortunately, her career was cut short when an accident in 1865 left her unable to walk.

Juliette's brother, Waldemar (1836–1908), began studying with Bournonville in 1849 and joined the company in 1857. An excellent actor as well as an impeccable dancer, his skill and good looks made him the ideal lover in Romantic ballets. He retired from the stage in 1901.

Other members of the company included Juliette and Waldemar's sister, Sophie, as well as their cousins Amalie and Carl. Another cousin, Julius (1833–93), left Denmark for Austria where he became first soloist at the Vienna Court Opera from 1853 to 1893; he appeared in almost 2500 performances in 25 years and was extremely popular. In addition to dancing, he was a professor at the Vienna Conservatory and an instructor at the Court Opera Ballet School.

Ellen (1878–1968), Juliette and Waldemar's great-niece, carried on the family tradition as soloist at the Royal Theater from 1903 to 1912. In 1909 she created the title role in Beck's ballet, *The Little Mermaid*, inspiring Edvard Eriksen's famous statue at Langelinie in Copenhagen.

HANS BECK
1861–1952

Hans Beck studied in Copenhagen with three of Bournonville's pupils: Georg Brodersen, Ferdinand Hoppe and Gustav Carey. By the time he made his debut at the Royal Theater (on 29 November 1879, the day before Bournonville died) he was already recognized as one of the most promising of the younger dancers. By the 1890s he had risen to the rank of first soloist.

In 1894 he was asked to relieve Emil Hansen as director of the company. During his tenure he rebuilt the repertory, trained a whole new generation of young dancers and rekindled the public's interest in ballet. Beck was unassuming about his talents as a choreographer, but he mounted new productions of the best Bournonville ballets as well as classics from the Romantic repertory, like *Coppélia* (1896), taking pains to remain true to their original choreography and style. His most successful original ballet was *The Little Mermaid* (1909), with Ellen Price in the title role.

Beck realized the importance of the new trends in ballet begun by Ballets Russes in 1909, but felt unable to reproduce them in Denmark. In 1915 he retired from his position as director, though he did continue to work with the company as rehearsal coach and as an advisor to Harald Lander on Bournonville's works.

VALBORG JØRGENSEN BORCHSENIUS
1872–1949

Valborg Borchsenius trained at the Royal Danish Ballet school and became a soloist with the company in 1895. She and her usual partner, Hans Beck, were enormously popular; her portrayal of the lead in *Coppélia* was especially successful, and her superb dancing played a large part in the revival of ballet in Denmark.

In 1918 Borchsenius retired, but she remained active for many more years behind the scenes, helping Lander with his revival of the Bournonville repertory and becoming one of the most important Bournonville teachers at the academy.

JEAN BORLIN
1893–1930

Jean Börlin studied with Gunhild Rosen at the Royal Theater, Stockholm, and joined the company in 1905; in 1913 he was appointed second soloist.

Börlin and several other young dancers were greatly inspired by their contact with Michel Fokine, and in 1918 he left Stockholm to study with the Fokines in Copenhagen. At about the same time he became acquainted with Rolf de Maré, (1898–1964), the noted Swedish patron of the arts.

De Maré financed Börlin's first solo recital in Paris in 1920 and made him the lead dancer and chief choreographer of Les Ballets Suédois from 1920 until the company disbanded in 1925. During this time Börlin choreographed a large number of ballets and also appeared in several more solo recitals. Most of his works incorporated contemporary artistic trends and were produced in collaboration with the leading avant-garde composers and painters of the time.

GEORGE GUE
1893–1962

George Gué (or Gé, originally George Gronfeldt) was born in St Petersburg and studied ballet there with Nicolai Legat, in addition to studying music with Alexander Glazunov.

In 1921 he organized and became the first ballet master of the Finnish National Ballet in Helsinki, a post he held until 1935. During that time he almost singlehandedly established the young company; in 1922 he produced *Swan Lake*, the first full-length ballet in Finland.

In 1935 Gué moved to France where he worked with Fokine and the Ballet Russe de Monte Carlo, also choreographing for several theaters in Paris. From 1939 to 1948 he was ballet master for the Royal Swedish Ballet. Gué retired to Helsinki in 1955 as ballet director for the Finnish National Ballet, a position he retained until his death.

VERA VOLKOVA
1904–75

Vera Volkova began her training at the Imperial academy in St Petersburg with Maria Romanova (Ulanova's mother) and later with Agrippina Vaganova, as well as at Akim Volyasky's private Russian Choreographic School.

For a while after the Revolution Volkova danced at GATOB, but she left Russia within a short time and toured the Far East. In 1929 she settled in Shanghai, dancing and teaching with a former colleague, George Goncharov.

Volkova married the British painter Hugh Williams, and the two settled in London in 1936. There she opened a school and, from 1943 to 1950, taught at the Sadler's Wells Ballet school. Soon her studio was attracting not only the best English dancers, but members of all the major visiting companies as well. She became one of the most important teachers in England and a leading authority on the famous Vaganova system of teaching ballet.

In 1950 she spent a few months teaching at La Scala and then, in 1951, began an engagement as teacher and artistic advisor at the Royal Danish Ballet. Her importance to Danish ballet can hardly be overemphasized; prior to her arrival, the Bournonville system had been the sole basis of training, so the exposure to the classical Russian technique had a great impact.

Volkova accompanied the Danish company on its 1966 tour of the United States, where she had spent the previous two summers as a guest instructor for the Harkness Ballet.

HARALD LANDER
1905–71

Harald Lander virtually grew up in the Royal Danish Ballet school, studying with Bournonville's old students, like Gustav Uhlendorff and the character dancer Christian Christiansen. He danced onstage as a child before making his adult debut in 1925 as Alvar in *Far From Denmark*.

Lander soon came to feel that there was more to ballet than the Bournonville Schools, so in 1927 he embarked on a two-year study program abroad. His first stop was Russia, to obtain a good grounding in the classical style. Then he moved to the United States where he continued his classical training with Ivan Terrasoff, worked with Fokine and also studied the national dances of Spain, Mexico and South America with Juan de Beaucaire y Montalbo.

Back in Denmark in 1929, he soon began to attract increasing public attention. In 1930 he was promoted to soloist; the following year he married Margot Florentz-Gebhardt (who was to become the company's leading ballerina) and choreographed his first production: an Argentinian ballet, *Gaucho*. Its success led to his appointment as ballet master in 1932.

As a dancer, Lander preferred character roles, and usually stayed very much in the background. His greatest impact was as a teacher, choreographer and leader; like his illustrious predecessors, Galeoti and Bournonville, he ran the company almost

Flemming Flindt in Les Sylphides.

single-handedly, setting policies and determining its future with a combination of talent, creativity and sheer physical energy and hard work.

Lander was an inventive choreographer; his most famous work was *Etudes* (1948), which has been restaged many times, for many different companies. Other important ballets include: *Bolero* (1934), *Seven Deadly Sins* (1936), *Thorvaldsen* (1938), *La Valse and The Sorcerer's Apprentice* (both 1940), *Qarrtsiluni* and *Spring* (both 1942), *La Vida Espagnola* (1945) and *Phoenix Bird* (1946).

In 1950 he hired Vera Volkova, one of the greatest teachers in London, to revamp the school's curriculum; he also established the administrative mechanism for an annual ballet festival in Copenhagen. Although Lander had done much to set the Royal Danish Ballet on the road to international success, his dictatorial methods alienated many members of the company. When the number of dancers unhappy with his administration reached a majority, he was pressured into resigning, and in 1951 he, his new wife, Toni Lander, and several others left for Paris.

In 1952 Lander joined the Paris Opéra; the following year he was appointed ballet master, and in 1959 he took over direction of the school, a post he held until his resignation in 1963, when he opened his own establishment. In addition to ballets for the Opéra, he also choreographed for many other companies on a freelance basis: the London Festival Ballet, La Scala, the American Ballet Theatre, the Nederlands National Ballet, the Teatro Municipal in Rio de Janeiro, the Finnish National Ballet and the Marquis de Cuevas's International Ballet. He even returned to Copenhagen in 1962 as guest choreographer, restaging *Etudes* and producing an entirely new version of Lully's old French ballet, *The Triumph of Love*.

BIRGIT CULLBERG
b 1908

Birgit Cullberg, one of the most important figures in the development of modern Swedish ballet, first studied literature at Stockholm University. She then became interested in modern dance, travelling first to England, where she worked at the Jooss-Leeder School, then to America where she studied with Martha Graham.

In 1932 she returned to Sweden and formed her own dance company. From the beginning her ballets have emphasized psychological studies, though many are humorous or satirical as well. Her most important works include *Miss Julie* and *Medea* (both 1950), *The Moon Reindeer* (1957, for the Royal Danish Ballet), *Lady from the Sea* (1960), a *pas de deux*, *Eden* and a television ballet, *The Evil Queen* (both 1961), *Bellman* (1971), and *Revolte* (1973).

In 1946 Cullberg and Ivo Cramér founded the Svenska Dansteater. From 1952 to 1957 she served as resident choreographer for the Royal Swedish Ballet and also as guest choreographer for other companies in Scandinavia, Germany and the United States. In 1960 she became director of the Stockholm City Theater and since 1967 she has directed the state-supported Cullberg-balleter.

MARGOT LANDER
1910–61

Margot Lander, born Margot Florentz-Gebhardt, began her ballet studies as a child at the Royal Danish Ballet school, where she received most of her training from Harald Lander (to whom she was married from 1931 to 1950).

She made her debut in *Far from Denmark* and soon the quality of her dancing, which was poetic and brilliant, set her out from the rest of the company. In 1931 she was made soloist and in 1942 she became the only dancer in the history of the Royal Danish Ballet to be called prima ballerina. Her best performances were in *Napoli*, *Swan Lake*, *Giselle*, *Coppélia* and as Broom in *The Sorcerer's Apprentice*, though she danced all the roles in the standard and Bournonville repertories.

Lander retired from the stage in 1948.

FRANK SCHAUFUSS
b 1921

Frank Schaufuss studied in Paris, London and Copenhagen, entering the Royal Danish Ballet school in 1930 and joining the company in 1941. In 1949 he became a soloist.

In addition to dancing in Copenhagen, he made guest appearances with other groups, like the International Ballet of the Marquis de Cuevas, and served as

Margrethe Schanne as La Sylphide, Danish Ballet.

ballet master for the Royal Danish Ballet in 1956 to 1958. He has choreographed several ballets, including *Idolon* (1952), *Feber* (1957), *Opus 13* (1959) and *Garden Party* (1963).

After his retirement in 1970 he and his wife, Mona Vangsaae, founded the Danish Academy of Ballet, which in turn led to the establishment of the Danish Ballet Theater; both organizations were dissolved in 1974.

Schaufuss's son, Peter (b 1949), also danced with the Royal Danish Ballet but chose to pursue a international career as well. Early guest appearances with the National Ballet of Canada and London Festival Ballet led to the New York City Ballet, where he was a principal dancer from 1974 to 1977. This was followed by several seasons as a freelance dancer with many major companies.

In 1979 he staged *La Sylphide* for the Canadians, followed by a full-length *Napoli* for the same company in 1981. In 1984 he made a four-part BBC television series, *Dancer*. Later that year he was appointed artistic director of London Festival Ballet.

MARGRETHE SCHANNE
b 1921

Margrethe Schanne joined the Royal Danish Ballet upon graduation from its school in 1940; she was named a soloist in 1943.

During her distinguished career she danced both the Bournonville and standard repertories; her dancing was especially known for its lightness and sensitivity. Her most famous role was as La Sylphide; in 1959 she became the first Danish dancer to appear on a postage stamp, in a *grand jéte* from that ballet. In 1966 she made her farewell appearance in the same work.

In addition to her dancing with the Danish company, Schanne appeared as a guest artist with the Ballet des Champs Elysées (1946), the International Ballet (1955), and at the Nervi Festival (1957). She toured South Africa in 1958 and danced in Rome in 1961. Since her retirement she has continued teaching and coaching in Copenhagen.

ERIK BRUHN
b 1928

Erik Bruhn (originally Belton Evers) graduated from the Royal Danish Ballet school in 1947 and was promoted to soloist in 1949.

During his long and productive career he was considered one of the best dancers in the world; his work was stylish and intelligent, his classical technique was superb, and he also had considerable acting ability.

From the mid-1950s Bruhn danced mainly in America, mostly with American Ballet Theatre, where he developed a notable partnership with Carla Fracci. He also spent two brief periods with New York City Ballet. During the 1960s he became one of the most sought-after of international stars. He made guest appearances around the globe, returned to Copenhagen, danced at Covent Garden with the Royal Ballet, in Stuttgart and with many other companies.

His major classic roles included both ballets by Bournonville and the other nineteenth-century masterworks, particularly as James in *La Sylphide* and Albrecht in *Giselle*. His outstanding contemporary roles included the sadistic valet

The great Erik Bruhn, whose flawless technique as a dancer and skills at production have taken him around the world.

in Cullberg's *Miss Julie* and the toreador in Petit's *Carmen*.

Bruhn's interest in technique and teaching led to a pair of books on the subject. From 1967 to 1971 he served as director of the Royal Swedish Ballet.

In 1965 he began his lifetime relationship with the National Ballet of Canada. His productions there included stagings of *La Sylphide* (1965), a controversial *Swan Lake* (1966) and *Coppélia* (1975). He became an associate director of the company before taking over full management in 1983. He remained artistic director until his death (from lung cancer) in 1986.

Balanchine's glittering Diamonds is one of many classical works in the repertory of the Dutch National Ballet.

THE NETHERLANDS

In most European countries the major advances in ballet during the seventeenth and eighteenth centuries were sponsored by the monarch and developed in the protected environs of the court. In Holland, William of Orange did commission a number of French *ballets de cour* during the late 1690s, and travelling French dance and dramatic companies appeared in The Hague throughout the eighteenth century. However, most of the advances in the early history of ballet took place in Amsterdam instead of in the capital.

The first theater in Holland opened in Amsterdam in 1638, and within a few years (by 1642) ballet was sharing the bill with drama and opera. One of the first important moments in the history of Dutch ballet occurred in 1658, with the presentation of *The Ballet of Maidens* – which featured female dancers, more than 20 years before women were allowed on the stage in Paris.

During the seventeenth and eighteenth centuries, Amsterdamers preferred comic ballets to the more rarified, allegorical works popular at court in The Hague, and the transition to *ballet d'action* was an easy one. The first important choreographer in this respect was Pietro Nieri, who worked in the city from 1761–69.

Two Frenchmen, Jean Rochefort and later Le Boeuf, ran the company at the turn of the century. The most popular dancers of the time were Polly de Heus, a former student of Gardel who was prima ballerina from 1801–23, and her partner, Jan van Well.

When Andries Voitus van Hamme took over the company in 1828 it numbered 60 dancers. Van Hamme created some 115 three-act productions during his 40 years with the troupe, in addition to importing all the major Romantic works by choreographers like Taglioni and Coralli (*Giselle* was first seen in Amsterdam in 1844). His son Anton carried on his work after 1868, proving to be an equally distinguished dancer/choreographer.

With the decline of Romanticism in Europe, however, ballet in Holland went into a serious decline. Eduard Witt did choreograph several works (of which the best known is *Coenan*) for the Palace for People's Industry in Amsterdam between 1871 and 1887, but for the most part ballet became an appendage of opera except for occasional appearances by visiting artists.

When dance did begin to make a comeback, with the arrival in 1914 of Gertrude Leistikow (b 1885), it was modern dance, not ballet. Despite visits from Ballets Russes and Pavlova, which aroused sporadic enthusiasm, modern dance continued to lead in popularity for many years.

Pavlova died in the Hotel des Indes in The Hague in 1931, and two members of her company, Alperova and Helden, remained in Holland to try to promote classic dance. They were joined a bit later by Igor Schwezoff (b 1904), a St Petersburg-trained dancer with years of experience in ballet all over the world, who established a classical school, then a company in The Hague in 1933. Things moved slowly, however, until the arrival of Yvonne Georgi in 1934.

Georgi, who had first toured Holland with a troupe from the Hanover Opera, opened a school in Amsterdam. In 1936 she and a few Dutch graduates from the establishment obtained backing from the city's Wagner Association to organize their own company. Within a few years they were able to become a small, independent unit called the Georgi Ballet, with regular summer seasons at Scheveningen and even a brief tour to New York and Washington in 1939 – the first appearance by any Dutch company in the United States.

In 1941 the Wagner Association managed to establish a municipal opera company at the Amsterdam Opera House (Stadsschouwburg), and the Georgi Ballet became the Opera Ballet. As in London and Paris, ballet was very popular in Amsterdam during World War II. Though Jews were not allowed to appear on stage and some other dancers 'retired' in protest, most members of the company remained to do their part in maintaining public morale.

The Opera Ballet presented a varied program of full-length performances, like *Coppélia*, *The Nutcracker*, *Bolero*, *Prometheus*, *Pulcinella*, Voormolen's *Diana* and Wydevald's *Shadows*. In addition, Ballet Parades was established: a series of *pas de deux* and solos, it was designed to give younger dancers more experience and public exposure. Though the group did employ many classical techniques, most of the dancing reflected Georgi's greatest strength – modern dance rather than ballet.

Most of the dancers who were to become leaders in developing the initiatives in ballet that followed the war got their start with the Opera Ballet; the list includes Mascha ter Weeme, Nora de Wal, Marie-Jeanne van der Veen, Lucas Hov-

ing and Karel Poons. Other members of the company included Rini Hopman, Maud Kool, Greet Lintsz, Rita Nauta, Nel Roos, Kyril Alban, Jan Beuchli, Johan Mittertreiner, Bob Nyhuis, Antony Raedt and Corvan Muyden.

After the liberation of the Netherlands in 1945 the state discontinued its support of both ballet and opera, and most artists set out to find work in the cabarets and music halls. That same year Hans (Johanna) Snoek founded the Scapino Ballet, dedicated to introducing children to the art (and thus, in time, creating a knowledgeable, adult audience for ballet). The company – now the oldest in Holland – is still in existence, carrying out its original mission with regular performances in Amsterdam, the provinces and abroad (including the United States), along with frequent lectures and demonstrations at schools and youth centers. Snoek retired in 1970 and was succeeded by Aart Verstegan and Armando Navarro (b 1930), an Argentinian dancer who joined the company as a teacher in 1962 after leaving the Marquis de Cuevas's International Ballet.

The late 1940s saw a resurgence in ballet activity as life in Holland stabilized after the war. In 1946 the Amsterdam Opera was reorganized, and included a small ballet company led by Nel Roos and Max Dooyes. The next year Mascha ter Weeme formed Ballet der Lage Landen (Ballet of the Low Lands), hoping to make the Dutch public – especially outside the big cities – more ballet-conscious. In 1948 Nettie van der Valk formed a semiprofessional group called Ballet Ensemble that showed considerable promise before it disbanded in 1951.

Darja Collin reorganized and developed the Opera Ballet in 1949; the Russian dancer Sonia Gaskell formed her first company, Ballet Recital, that same year. In 1951 Collin left to open a school in Florence and the French choreographer Françoise Adret (b 1920) took over as the Opera Ballet's ballet mistress and choreographer.

The Hague moved back into the ballet picture in 1954 when Het Nederlands Ballet (The Netherlands Ballet) was established, with Ballet Recital as its base and Gaskell as its director. If Gaskell resembled England's Ninette de Valois in her determination and talent for administration, she was like Marie Rambert when it came to discovering and encouraging young talent; Rudi van Dantzig, Hans van Manen and Toer van

Right: Hans van Manen's ballet Grosse Fuge *to music by Beethoven, performed by the Royal Ballet. Scenery by Jean Paul Vroom.*

Opposite: The Dutch National Ballet, as well as performing classical works, has a good repertoire of modern ballets such as Adagio Hammerklavier *by van Manen.*

Below: Moments, *a work by Rudi van Dantzig, director of the Dutch National Ballet and one of the founders of Nederlands Dans Theater.*

Schayk all got their start with her company.

In 1959 ter Weeme's Ballet der Lage Landen and Adret's Netherlands Opera Ballet merged to form the Amsterdam Ballet – which in turn joined with the Netherlands Ballet in 1961 to become the Dutch National Ballet. Gaskell became the group's artistic director, while ter Weeme took over the Opera Ballet division.

After a short time under their joint directorship, Gaskell assumed control of the company, which she ran until 1968. When it was first established, the National Ballet tried to please everyone with a repertory so wide that it was called 'the supermarket of choreography.' Over the years, however, the company has slowly become more discriminating, choosing works that enhance its own character. It still offers great ballets from history, from Galeotti's *Whims of Cupid and the Ballet Master* to several Balanchine productions. In addition, the works of van Dantzig (including *Monument for a Dead Boy*, 1965; *Moments*, 1968; *Epitaph*, 1969; *Colored Birds*, 1971; and *Ramifications*, 1973) along with those produced by van Manen (like *Daphnis and Chloë*, 1972; *Adagio Hammerklavier*, 1973; and *Le Sacre du Printemps*, 1974) have given the repertory an added dimension.

In 1966 Gaskell appointed van Dantzig and Robert Kaesen (b 1931) her co-directors. Kaesen has since left the com-pany, and Gaskell retired in 1968. Van Manen joined the troupe in 1972, and in the mid-1970s van Schayk began choreographing for the group. The three developed a unique cooperative working relationship – so close that on occasion they were even able to work together on the same piece.

The repertory has a strong modernist flair. Van Manen's powerful works often exploit the battle of the sexes and he frequently casts women in an unflattering and domineering mold. One of his favorite devices is to place his ballerinas in high heels. Van Dantzig's dances have a strong element of community. He often uses classical music in juxtaposition with movement that evokes a feeling of folk-dance. His most famous work, *Monument for a dead Boy* (1965), exposes the family and social pressures which drive a young homosexual to suicide. At the time, its frankness and vivid drama were much applauded. The piece entered the repertory of several companies around the world.

The third important dance company in the Netherlands, the Netherlands Dance Theater, was founded in 1959 by Benjamin Harkarvy (b 1930) – an American choreographer who had been one of the original members of The Netherlands

Sylvester Campbell and Marianna Hilarides in a more-classical performance of the Dutch National Ballet, the pas de deux *from* Le Corsaire.

Ballet. After two difficult, uncertain years during which the company lived mainly on hope and good will, it was finally offered a home in The Hague and a handsome subsidy from the Dutch Government. Like Ballet Rambert, the Netherlands Dance Theater is committed to establishing a union between contemporary and classic dance as the only real future for ballet.

In 1960 van Manen joined Harkarvy as artistic co-director. He greatly expanded the scope of the repertory and with aid from American choreographers, notably Glen Tetley, created an eclectic repertory which tried to disregard the distinctions between ballet and modern dance.

The stress was on creativity and the repertory was in constant flux. Among the many important ballets presented were Tetley's *Pierrot Lunaire* to Schoenberg's song cycle of the same name. With only a cast of three, this potent and dramatic work (originally created for Tetley's own American company in 1962) is often singled out as the first ballet seriously to attempt the integration of classical steps with modern dance. Tetley based *The Anatomy Lesson* (1965) on the famous Rembrandt painting. *Embrace Tiger and Return to Mountain* (1969) drew its inspiration from the Chinese martial art of Tai Chi. *Mutations* (co-choreographed by Tetley and van Manen in 1970) achieved great notoriety for its nude scenes.

Other choreographers who contributed to the repertory included Anna Sokolow and another American, Jennifer Muller. Harkarvy resigned in 1969, as did van Manen a year later. The company went into a decline, which was not rectified until 1975 when Juří Kylián was appointed artistic director.

Born in Prague in 1947, he had studied in Czechoslovakia and with England's Royal Ballet School before joining the Stuttgart Ballet in 1968. It was there that he began to choreograph in 1970.

Since taking over the Netherlands Dance Theatre, Kylián has totally revamped the company and turned it into what is essentially a one-choreographer company. His dramatic ballets have had an enormous impact and his work is now

Above right: Mutations *is a complex ballet which blends live dance and filmed dance, grotesque costume and the nude body, the whole to Stockhausen's music.*

Right: Stephen Sylvester showing the need for the dancer to perform in classical and modern styles.

seen in repertories all around the globe. His style is a blend of restless, sinuous movement with a sense of deep, often mysterious, quiet. Several of his pieces are choreographed to Janáček, and it is clear that his fellow Czech strikes a very deep chord of melancholy and loss in Kylián's soul. The sadness in ballets such as *Return to the Strange Land* (1975) is palpable.

Kylián's speciality is the *pas de trois*. While most choreographers make their marks with *pas de deux* (MacMillan is the outstanding contemporary example), Kylián has found a unique manner of choreographing for trios. He has used music by Stravinsky, Martinů, Schoenberg, Ravel and Britten for his ballets. The playful *Symphony in D* is set to Haydn. This exceptionally popular 1976 work is a series of ballet jokes, missed timings and near collisions. Under Kylián, the Netherlands Dance Theatre has become one of the world's leading dance ensembles. It makes regular international tours.

BELGIUM

Although an Academie de Musique was established in Brussels in 1682, and the Théâtre sur la Monnaie opened in 1700, organized ballet did not appear in Belgium until 1705 when an opera company was founded at the theater. A small ballet company was attached to it – four men and five women, including a singing ballerina.

A regular company, consisting of seven soloists, a *corps de ballet* of 40 (20 men and 20 women) and eight children, was founded in 1817. Two years later the Théâtre Royal de la Monnaie opened and Jean-Antoine Petipa (1796–1855), father of Lucien and Marius, was hired as its first ballet master.

Petipa, who served four terms as ballet master (1819–32, 1833–35, 1841–42 and 1843), did much to establish a sound ballet organization in Brussels. In addition to choreographing many productions for the company, he founded the Brussels Conservatoire de la Danse (1826). While he always saw to it that no member of his large family ever lacked a job, he also was able to attract most of the top stars of the Romantic era, such as Taglioni, Cerrito, Elssler, Grisi and Grahn, which helped maintain public interest in his productions.

The theater burned to the ground in 1855, but it was rebuilt immediately and ballet continued to be a popular attraction. The year 1871 saw the first production of *Coppélia* outside France, choreographed in Belgium by J Hansen.

In 1872 Lucien Petipa was appointed to his father's old position, to be succeeded near the turn of the century by G G Saracco and F Ambrosiny. Ambrosiny was another popular choreographer, whose best-known works were *Quand les Chats son Partis* (1908), *Hopjes* and *Istar* (both 1913). Marthe Coeck took over as ballet mistress after World War I. The most notable leader since has been Jean-Jacques Etchevery (b 1916). Etchevery, a Frenchman who was ballet master from 1954–59, is best known for his works inspired by familiar nineteenth-century paintings such as *Les Bals de Paris, Manet* and *Opera-Ballets*. His other works include *Ballade de la Geôle de Reading* (1947).

It was not until 1960, when Maurice Béjart (b 1924 or 1927) founded Ballet de XXe Siècle (Ballet of the Twentieth Century), that Brussels found itself a place on the international ballet map. The company has ballets by other choreographers (like Charrat, Dolin, Massine and Milloss) in its repertory, but for the most part it has been largely dependent on controversial works by Béjart himself. Since the early seventies he has been experimenting with total theater, and the resulting spectacles attract huge, young, enthusiastic crowds to locations that can range from the Opera House to the Royal Circus or the National Forest. Older, more sophisticated audiences tend to view his work as superficial, overly concerned with effect at the expense of substance.

His works show strong Eastern influences and are often exceptionally erotic. The themes are drawn from every aspect of global culture and his ballets have been based on such divergent inspirations as Japanese Noh theater, Indian temple myths and even historic personalities, such as Nijinsky, Isadora Duncan, Edith Piaf and Greta Garbo. Often conceived for large masses of dancers who act as a fraternal community performing some highly personalized ritual, Béjart's ballets pulsate with a life force which few other choreographers can summon up.

His interest in great music led him to Bayreuth, where he choreographed Wagner's *Tannhäuser* and several other operas in the 1960s. For his own company he choreographed Beethoven's *Ninth Symphony* (1964) and a ballet version of Mozart's *The Magic Flute* (1981). His 1960 staging of Ravel's *Bolero* surged along with an undisguised sexual tension. The piece is performed by a single woman atop a gigantic round table that is surrounded by 40 men. In the mid-1970s the piece took on yet a new layer of sexuality when Béjart substituted a man for the female soloist.

Béjart's chief male dancers have been Paolo Bortoluzzi (1960-72) and Jorge Donn, who joined the company in 1963 at the age of 16. Suzanne Farrell was his prima ballerina from 1970 to 1975. During the 1980s, Stuttgart ballerina Marcia Haydée has become a frequent guest artist and one of his chief muses.

He, in turn, is a frequent guest choreographer in Stuttgart and with other companies throughout Europe and Asia. In addition to appearances in Brussels, his company has lengthy annual seasons in Paris and regularly tours internationally. Béjart's work has always been considered controversial, nowhere more so than in America where critics tend to dismiss his elaborate spectacles as the charades of a P T Barnum. In Europe, however, he is often regarded as the century's greatest dance magician.

Outside Brussels, the provinces had little opportunity even to see ballet performed until after World War II. The only notable exception was in Ghent, where the Opera House staged a few ballets between 1835 and 1891. Sonja Korty made an attempt to bring ballet to Antwerp in 1923, and other troupes appeared from time to time, but none made a lasting impression.

The first professional company to attain any real degree of success was the Ballet de Wallonie, established by Hanna Vooss (b 1916) in Charlevoi in 1966, on the foundation of a previous company, Ballet du Hainaut. With the Englishman Tony Hulbert as ballet master and chief choreographer, today it presents a repertory based on the classics to audiences both in Belgium and abroad. Jorge Lefèbre (a Cuban dancer who joined Ballet of the Twentieth Century in 1963 and is now considered one of the most interesting choreographers in Belgium) is a frequent contributor to its programs.

The second successful regional ballet company is Ballet van Vlaanderen (Ballet of Flanders), an Antwerp-based group founded in 1969. Director Jeanne Brabants (b 1920) and chief choreographer Andre Leclair (b 1930) have constructed a wide repertory that ranges from Bournonville to modernists like Jooss and Cullbert. In addition to its performances at home, the troupe also plays in the opera house at Ghent, in other Belgian cities and occasionally abroad.

Below: Maurice Béjart's lavish spectacles for his Ballet of the Twentieth Century have created an avid following in Europe and Japan.

AUSTRIA

In Austria the Holy Roman Emperors were enthusiastic patrons of the arts from the Renaissance onward, and court ballet was an established feature at the court of the Hapsburgs. Maximilian I (reigned 1493–1519), for example, was an enthusiastic and knowledgeable lover of all the arts, and his grandson Charles V, who succeeded him, was especially fond of music. During the mid-seventeenth century even ballets on horseback became very popular; in fact they are still performed at the Hofreitschule in Vienna and attract enthusiastic audiences.

From about the mid-eighteenth century Vienna was one of the great musical centers of the world – and also rapidly became a center for *ballet d'action*. Franz Hilferding, who had been a dancer at the court since 1735, began choreographing

the new ballets in 1744. By the time he left for Russia in 1757 he was able to turn over a well-organized, flourishing organization to his successor, Gasparo Angiolini.

Angiolini, Hilferding's most talented student, carried on the master's work. He is best known for his collaboration with Gluck, which in 1761 produced the tragic ballet-pantomime *Don Juan*. Hilferding returned to Vienna in 1765 and in 1767 Noverre arrived. Soon the two were involved in a bitter dispute over which one was the true inventor of *ballet d'action*. The argument continued even after Hilferding's death the following

An early publication in German, giving written instructions for the dance which is to be performed to the accompanying music.

year, with Angiolini loyally taking his old teacher's part. Though the question was never really resolved, the fireworks did much to enliven the ballet scene in Vienna for several years.

Noverre made significant contributions to Austrian ballet during his seven-year stay in the capital, strengthening and improving the company at the Kaertnerthor Theater and also, of course, choreographing many ballets. One of his private pupils at this time was a young girl named Marie Antoinette. In 1774, as Queen of France, she called him back to Paris to take over directorship of the Opéra.

At the turn of the century, from 1793–95, and again from 1798–1803, Salvatore Viganó directed the company. He too choreographed many ballets in Vienna including his great work, *The Creatures of Prometheus* (1801), set to Beethoven's music. By the time his contract expired and he resumed his travelling around Europe, good ballet had become an established part of Viennese cultural life.

Until the beginning of the nineteenth century the Kaertnerthor held a virtual monopoly on ballet in Vienna, but then other theaters began using dance to attract audiences as well. The dancer Paolo Rinaldi (1781 or 1784–53), a specialist in pantomime and parody, was very popular at the theater in Der Leopoldstadt until 1840, when he moved to Prague.

Children's ballet, which had been popular since Hilferding's day, was featured at the Theater am der Wien, where Freidrich Horschelt (1793–1876) ran a company called The Children's Ballet. Their performances in Horschelt's fairy tales were attractions from 1815 to about 1817. Soon, however, there were so many rumors about their morals that they became notorious. In 1821 there was a scandal involving several of the girls and a pedophiliac prince, and the Emperor ordered the troupe to disband. Horschelt moved on to Munich, where he continued working (with adults) with great success until 1848.

Despite its reputation the Children's Ballet served a useful purpose. It gave a start to many excellent dancers like Therese Heberle. Wilhelmina Schroeder-Devrient, Anton Stuhlmüller and perhaps even Fanny Elssler (though she always denied having been a member). It also provided the basis for a new, all-female troupe called the Danseuses Viennoises. The group's founder, Josephine

Der Scaramutza kombt mit zweyen körben herauß, worinnen zwey kleine Scaramutzen seyn, ü: jetzet solche auf die Erden, ü: nachdeme Er eine gantze Aria außgetantzt, eröfnen die kleinen Scaramutzen die körb, da er nun selbige siehet, erstaunet er darüber, diese aber springe auß den körben ü: geben Scaramutza eins mit den füße vor den hintern, ü: werffen Ihm zu boden, dan tantzen die kleinen Scaramutze die gantze Aria allein, hernach nimbt der wieder aufgestandene Scaramutza, eine nach den andern, ü: jagt sie wieder in die körb hinein, und hierbey Endigt sich die helffte der Aria, bey der andern helffte nimbt Er die körb ü: geht mit langen Schritten hinein .

Weiss (ballet mistress at the Theater in der Josephstadt), began with 20 little girls, mostly from poor families. They became so popular that in 1845 she was able to expand to 35 members and embark on a tour to Paris, London and even Canada and the United States. Everywhere they appeared the critics praised their skill and precision, while the public responded adoringly to their spontaneity and obvious enjoyment. Although at times the authorities treated her like a white-slave trader, Weiss imposed such strict discipline that her girls could never be accused of immorality. In the last analysis, however, they were only a novelty and are heard of no more after their return to Europe in 1848 and made no lasting impact.

In the autumn of 1814 the Congress of Vienna convened and the upper crust of Europe (including four emperors and empresses, four kings, innumerable princes and nobles, and their entourages) gathered for the international conference – which also included a glittering series of hunts, balls, and military and theatrical entertainments. Jean Aumer (1774–1833), newly appointed ballet master at the Kaertnerthor Theater, was more than equal to the challenge, staging spectacular ballets featuring guests like Chevigny, Bigottini and Andre Deshayes. Bigottini, in particular, was the toast of Vienna, gaining a triumph that even outshone

the reception that had been given to Viganó s beautiful wife, Maria Medina. She danced with Emperor Franz I, dined with Talleyrand, and had the gossips chattering about any number of real or imagined affairs with various princes. The management of the theater was so impressed with Aumer's work that he was engaged for another five years, following a brief return to Paris to stage some of his most popular and famous ballets at the Opéra.

In 1821 Domenico Barbaja took over for a seven-year term as director of the Kaertnerthor. Though he was dividing his time between Vienna and Naples, where he also directed the San Carlo, he more than fulfilled his reputation as the best director/impresario in Europe at the time. That same year Filippo Taglioni replaced Aumer as ballet master, with a three-year contract. Under their leadership, ballet in Vienna improved and became even more popular. They also were responsible for the debuts of the two archetypal stars of the Romantic era, Marie Taglioni (in 1822) and Fanny Elssler (1823). Other excellent dancers of the period included Mlle Milliere, Heberle, Amalia Brugnoli, Gaetano Gioja, Louis Henry and Armand Vestris.

During the 1830s and 1840s audiences at the Kaertnerthor watched a constant parade of visiting international stars, along with resident dancers like Fanny

Cerrito (who danced with the company from 1836–38). From 1853 on, Paul Taglioni made regular visits as guest choreographer. It was he who was given the honor of staging the first ballet when the grand new Opera House opened on the Ringstrasse in 1869, replacing the Kaertnerthor after more than 100 years as Vienna's leading center for opera and ballet. Bournonville also served as ballet master, for the 1855–56 season but although he was successful, he did not achieve the overwhelming triumph he was seeking and soon returned to Copenhagen.

As elsewhere in Europe, the public began to drift away from ballet during the last quarter of the nineteenth century, despite the efforts of people like Karl Telle (1826–95). As ballet master at the Opera and director of its ballet school in 1890, Telle staged many ballets – including the first local versions of *Coppélia* (1876) and *Sylvia* (1877).

The time between 1891 and 1920, when Joseph Hassreiter served as ballet master and head of the school, was an excellent period for Viennese ballet. Hassreiter was a talented teacher, who not only instructed the company's soloists, but also gave private lessons to the Imperial

Above : Vaslav Orlikowsky, jovial director of the Vienna Staatsoper from 1966–71 and now a much sought-after freelance choreographer.

Right : One of the cheerful productions of the Volksoper Ballet which specializes in ballets with a folkloric theme.

Below right : A scene from Orlikowsky's truly lavish production of Cranko's Prince of the Pagodas *for the Vienna Staatsoper in 1967.*

family. He gave many promising dancers their start in ballet; the two Weisenthal sisters later became world famous with their interpretations of Viennese waltzes. Two other important figures at the Opera were Heinrich Kröller, who was ballet master from 1922–28, and Margarethe Wallman (b 1904), who led the company from 1934–37.

In 1941 Erika Hanka was invited to the Opera as guest choreographer. Her production of Egk's *Joan von Zarissa* was a tremendous success – so much so that in 1942 she was offered the job of ballet mistress. During the difficult war years and equally hard postwar era, Hanka not only kept the company's morale up, but even strengthened the repertory. When the new State Opera House opened on the Ring in 1955 she turned the classical side of the repertory over to Gordon Hamilton, who produced *Giselle* for the opening performance. Hanka continued to act, as ballet mistress however, until her death in 1958.

After Hanka died, ballet went through a difficult period in Vienna, with many changes in directors: Parlic (1958–61); von Milloss (1961–66); Vaslav Orlikowsky (1966–71); and von Milloss again (1971–74). Gerhard Brunner has directed the company since 1976.

Other companies in Vienna today include the Volksoper Ballet (directed by G Senft), the Theater am der Wien Ballet (Henry Wolejnicek) and the Raimund Theater Ballet (Rein Este). Outside the capital there are companies in Baden (Simenon Dimitrow), Graz (Orlikowski), Innsbruck (Alexander Meissner), Klagenfurt (Fred Marteny), Linz (Anna Vaughn), Salzburg (Leonard Salaz) and St Polten (Norman Dixon).

Training received by pupils at Vienna's State Opera Ballet School is good but despite its potential, ballet in Austria today seems somewhat stagnant.

1980 a Piece by Pina Bausch *illustrates the radical and unorthodox brand of theater that has made her company so popular.*

GERMANY

Ballet began in Germany at the courts of the various German princes: Berlin, Brunswick, Darmstadt, Dresden, Dusseldorf, Hanover, Mannheim and Stuttgart all had their own facilities for producing lavish court ballets. The fierce competition between the princes did much to stimulate development of the art.

Two early examples of German ballets are *Die Befreiung des Friedens* (The Liberation of Peace), an opera-ballet performed at Darmstadt in 1600, and *Ballett von dem Orpheo und der Euridice*, produced by Heinrich Schutz at Dresden in 1638. Note that from the very earliest days German names are found among the usual complement of French and Italian ballet masters. In 1717 in Leipzig Gottfried Taubert wrote the first German treatise on dance, *Der Rechtschaffene Tantzmeister*.

In Berlin Frederick Wilhelm I of Prussia (reigned 1713–40) heartily disapproved of both opera and ballet. His son, Frederick the Great (reigned 1740–86), was determined to create a company as good as that at the Paris Opéra. He engaged Voltaire as his advisor and made Jean-Baptiste Boyer, Marquis d'Argens, his director of court entertainment. D'Argens certainly had experience involving singers and dancers, but it was entertainment of a slightly less public sort, and the company got off to a halting start. The problem was compounded because the king was loath to pay the necessary salaries for first-rate soloists and would not hire a *corps de ballet* at all.

The Royal Opera House opened in 1742, and in 1744 La Barbarina captured not only hearts of her Berlin audiences, but Frederick's as well. Within a few weeks she was firmly entrenched as his mistress (at least in name) and had persuaded him to hire a *corps de ballet*.

After La Barbarina married, the king turned his attention to another dancer, Marianne Cochois, who had joined the company in 1742. Cochois, one of Marie Sallé's cousins, had been trained by Dupré in Paris. She was not as flamboyant as La Barbarina, but after the latter's departure in 1748 she came into her own, remaining Berlin's most popular *première danseuse* for many years. Frederick even wrote a poem to her talent, and in 1764 Casanova noticed portraits of both ballerinas in the king's room at Potsdam Palace.

As he grew older Frederick became more and more like his father. Nevertheless, he still granted La Barbarina a divorce, gave her a title and allowed her to found the convent where she died; Cochois retained a place in his affections even after she married the ballet master, Desplaces. Her sister Babet (or Barbe), however, was not as lucky. A popular dramatic actress and an accomplished musician, painter, poet and linguist, she gave up the stage when she was about 30 to marry the Marquis d'Argens (who was almost twice her age). The king was furious that the couple had not asked his permission first, and began playing increasingly cruel jokes on the hapless old man, eventually forcing him to return to France.

The Berlin Royal Opera House continued to be dominated by French ballet masters for many years. Others who filled the position after Desplaces included Michel Poitier, Bartholome Lany and Etienne Lauchery.

Stuttgart, where the earliest court ballets were performed in 1609, first attracted international attention in 1759, when the Grand Duke Carl Eugen of Württemburg, a great patron of all forms of theater, invited Noverre to serve as his ballet master. The Grand Duke already had established one of the finest opera houses in Europe, and ballet in Stuttgart was as good as anything to be seen in France. When Noverre arrived he was delighted to find that he would be working in an excellent theater, with plenty of money, good designers like Boquet and Servandoni and the freedom he had lacked in Paris to develop his theories about *ballet d'action*. Nor was he lacking in dancers to carry out his plans. All the great dancers of Europe, like Dauberval, Le Picq, Gardel and Angiolo Vestris, were happy to appear in Stuttgart – while the great Gaetano Vestris came every year to help celebrate the Duke's birthday.

With all these advantages, plus knowledgeable, discriminating audiences for his ballets, it is little wonder that Noverre did some of his best work during his years in Stuttgart (1760–67). He expanded the company to include seven male and seven female soloists, along with a *corps de ballet* of 21. He also produced a significant number of *ballets d'action*, including *Rinaldo und Armida*, *Admet und Alkeste*, *Medea und Jason*, *Der Sieg der Neptun* and *Der Raub der Proserpina*.

In 1766, however, the duke was forced to cut back his support for the theater. The next year Noverre moved on to Vienna, and the Stuttgart company continued on a smaller scale under the leadership of Louis Dauvigny. One of the best members of his company was the young Anna Heinl, who at only 14 was already displaying the talent that would lift her to even greater heights a few years later at the Paris Opéra.

In 1824 the arrival of the Taglionis – Filippo, Marie and her brother Paul – heralded a new era in ballet in Stuttgart. Marie was especially taken with the city, she had an excellent partner in Anton Stuhlmüller and her reception was all she could have desired (her gifts from the Royal Family alone included two sets of diamond earrings, a solid gold chain, a golden comb encrusted with amethysts and three gold bracelets). The family stayed in Stuttgart for four years.

Munich also had a strong ballet establishment, if on a somewhat smaller scale. Highlights of the eighteenth century included the first production of Mozart's *Idomeneo*, choreographed by Peter Legrand in 1781, and Viganò's appearance in *La Fille Mal Gardée* in 1795 – which was denounced by some as obscene. A ballet school was founded in the city in 1792 and in 1818 the National Theater opened. The most successful ballet master during the first half of the nineteenth century was Friedrich Horschelt, who came to Munich from Vienna after his notorious Children's Ballet had been dissolved. He

During Kenneth Macmillan's directorship of the German Opera, Berlin, he created Anastasia *as a one-act ballet with Lynn Seymour in the lead. Expanded into a full-length work for the Royal Ballet in 1971.*

The dancers of Tanz Forum Köln are trained in both the classical and modern idiom. Here they are performing Hans van Manen's Situations.

served two terms, 1820–29 and 1831–47. The Taglionis' appearance at the National Theater's grand reopening (after a disastrous fire) in 1825 caused much excitement in the city. Other ballet masters during the nineteenth century were: Johan Fenzl (1848–61); Franz Hoffman (1861–64); Giovanni Golinelli (1864–69); Lucile Grahn (1869–75); who choreographed Wagner's *Die Meistersinger*; Franz Fenzl (1876–90); and Flora Jungmann (1891–1917).

In 1896 the 77-year-old Grahn met a young Danish dancer accidentally, in a shop, and complimented her on her recent performance in *Coppélia*. It was a very minor incident, and neither knew then that Adeline Genée would one day revolutionize modern English ballet and become the first president of the Royal Academy of Dancing.

Paul Taglioni had gone to Berlin in 1828, after the family's engagement in Stuttgart; in 1829 he married the dancer Anna Galster and settled there. Though he made many visits to other ballet centers, like Vienna, Naples, Milan and London, most of his work was done in Berlin. He was a solid choreographer and works like *Ondine* (1836), *Don Quixote* (1839) and *Satanella* (1852) – along with frequent appearances by some of the great Romantic ballerinas – excited great public interest.

Ballet really began flourishing in Berlin when Taglioni took over as ballet master at the Court Opera in 1856. Some of the most popular of his more than 40 ballets were *The Adventures of Flick and Flock* (1858), *Electra, or the Stars* (1862), *Fantasca* (1869) and *Coppélia* (1882). His daughter Marie danced the leading roles in most of his ballets until 1866, when she retired to marry the Prince of Windisch-Gratz. After Taglioni left in 1883, however, ballet in Berlin went into a decline, and did not begin to recover until after World War I.

During the first part of the twentieth century, traditional ballet in Germany had a difficult time competing with modern dance. Heinrich Kröller, who worked at various times in Dresden, Frankfurt, Munich, Berlin and Vienna, was one of the few ballet personalities interested in keeping classic ballet alive. At the same time choreographers like Kurt Jooss in Essen were attempting to synthesize classic and modern dance into a new art form.

After World War II Tatjana Gsovsky developed a sort of hybrid modern ballet in East Berlin, working out a makeshift theater in the Admirals-Palast. Since 1952, when she left for the West, ballet in East Berlin has been dominated by the Russian school. In 1955 the theater in Unter den Linden was rebuilt and Lilo Gruber took over direction of the company, establishing a balanced repertory of both classic and modern works. Since Gruber's retirement in 1970 the theater has been run by a series of temporary directors and guest choreographers.

The East Berlin Comic Opera, which began giving regular ballet performances in 1947, has been thriving since 1965 under the influence of Tom Schilling – the most creative choreographer in East Germany.

Most of the documents detailing Dresden's long and illustrious ballet history (which dates back to the early seventeenth century) were destroyed during World War II. Since then its ballet activity has been controlled by East Berlin, despite efforts by its current ballet mistress, Vera Müller, to establish it as a separate entity. Dresden still has a reputation for excellent ballet, largely because of the presence of the famous Palucca School.

Ballet in West Berlin has been presented since the war in the German Opera, which opened in 1912 as the Charlottenburg Opera House. Gsovsky directed the company after leaving East Berlin, choreographing several works between 1957 and 1966. Kenneth Mac-Millan, who served as director from 1966–

69, reestablished the classics and created *Concerto* (1966) and *Anastasia* (1967) for the company. Guest choreographers have included Balanchine, Cranko, John Taras, van Manen and van Dantzig. The company underwent an equally intense period under the directorship of former Kirov dancer Valeri Panov. Among the several large productions he staged for them are *Cinderella* (1977) and an epic *War and Peace* (1981).

During the early 1960s Cologne became one of the most important German dance centers under the leadership of

Left: Marcia Haydée, prima ballerina of the Stuttgart Ballet in Cranko's time and now director herself, in Kenneth Macmillan's Song of the Earth.

Aurel von Milloss (1960–63) and Todd Bolender (1963–66). Dancers in the Tanz-Forum Köln are trained in both classic and modern dance, with emphasis on the latter. The two-week Summer Academy attracts some 500 students to the city each year. Other companies oriented to modern dance in Germany today are Wuppertal and Bremen.

Stuttgart had a series of ballet leaders after the war, including Anne-Liese Morike, Bernhard Wosien and Robert Mayer. Nicholas Beriozoff (b 1906), who arrived in 1958, established a solid repertory of classic and new ballets; his emphasis on maintaining high technical standards left the company ready to take advantage of its opportunities when John Cranko took over as director in 1960.

Cranko, a South African who obtained his early experience in England, put Stuttgart back on the international ballet map with his full-length, dramatic presentations like *Romeo and Juliet*, *The Taming of the Shrew* and *Onegin*. His works were noted for their fast pace and skillful characterization, and his tragic death in 1973 was a great loss to modern ballet. However, his replacement, Glen Tetley, has continued to produce exciting new works like *Laborinthus*, which combine traditional and modern techniques, and has maintained Stuttgart's reputation as the liveliest, most exciting ballet city in Germany today.

Since 1973 the Hamburg State Opera Ballet has been directed by the controversial American choreographer John Neumeier (b 1942). Neumeier, who danced for Cranko in Stuttgart from 1963–69 and then directed the Frankfurt Opera Ballet, has achieved great success with his lively, theatrical productions which are nevertheless firmly based on the foundation of classical ballet. In 1980 Neumeier was given a new seven-year contract that included directorship of the company's school and also a new theater for the production of experimental ballets.

Neumeier's works have a sense of grand opera about them and are conceived and performed on a scale which would be almost impossible anywhere outside West Germany (where state support of the arts exists on a truly munificent level). He creates two major types of full-length ballets. The first draws inspiration from the thea-

Left: Song of the Earth, *first produced for the Stuttgart in 1965, performed by Haydée for the Royal Ballet with Anthony Dowell and Donald MacLeary.*

ter: between 1977 and 1985 he choreographed *Romeo and Juliet, A Midsummer Night's Dream, Othello* and *Hamlet* (this last for the Royal Danish Ballet, 1985), plus *Camille* and *A Streetcar Named Desire* (both for Marcia Haydée). The second group of ballets draws inspiration from music: in addition to a ritualized version of Bach's *St Matthew Passion*, he has

choreographed abstract ballets to several of the Mahler symphonies. Neumeier has also conceived highly personal, and controversial, interpretations of many of the nineteenth-century Russian classics.

All the major German cities now have ballet companies; standards are high and companies often try to secure the best international talent. The companies in Cologne, Düsseldorf and Frankfurt are among the most impressive.

The major talent to emerge from within Germany in the past quarter of a century

is Pina Bausch (b 1940), director of the Wuppertal Dance Theater. Her elaborate spectacles are neither ballet nor modern dance, but an individualistic hybrid of intensely emotional, physical theater. There is no other single artist anywhere who has had such a pervasive influence on the entire world dance picture in the 1980s. It would not be exaggerating to say that what Martha Graham was to modern dance in the 1950s, Bausch is today. Her work is discussed in further detail in the chapter on European Modern Dance.

Below: The lively Septet *by Uwe Scholz, one of the young German choreographers to emerge from the Stuttgart Ballet.*

CZECHOSLOVAKIA

Ballet has a long history in Czechoslovakia. The first mention of ballet performances occurs in the second half of the sixteenth century. During the seventeenth century foreign touring groups provided much of the entertainment, supplemented by groups of serfs who were trained to perform for the many Czech and Moravian princes.

The first theater in Prague, which opened in 1724, gave occasional ballet performances. The theater in Kotce, opened in 1737, also produced ballets and pantomimes. One of Noverre's pupils, Voiteck Moravek, presented excerpts from the master's ballets there during the second half of the eighteenth century.

Romantic ballet came late to Prague, with the first performance of *La Sylphide* being given at the Tyl Theater in 1850. That same year Lucile Grahn appeared in the city, and after her came several other internationally ranked stars.

In 1862 the first independent theater, the Prozatímni, opened in the city. Its first ballet master was Vaclav Reisinger, who remained with the company until

Modern ballet in Czechoslovakia has received a warm reception uncharacteristic of an Eastern Bloc country and developed great originality.

1881, when he joined the newly opened National Theater.

At the turn of the century, Italian-style extravaganzas (like Manzotti's *Excelsior*) became very popular. Reisinger was succeeded by Augustin Berger and Achille Vicusi. Berger returned from 1912–22 and was followed by Remislav Remislavsky (1922–27). The city was enthusiastic over a visit from Diaghilev in 1927.

During the 1920s and 1930s Czech composers began taking an interest in ballet, and the decades saw choreographers like Jaroslav Hladík and Josef Jenčík producing works to the music of Novák, Martinu and Bořkovec.

Bratislava had had a theater since 1776, but ballet became a major attraction there only after the city became the capital of Slovakia in 1919. Oskar Nedbal became director of the company in 1923 and hired Vicusi as his ballet master,

The Prague Ballet, founded by Lubos Ogoun and Pavel Smok in 1964, spearheaded the modern movement in the country and toured extensively.

thus initiating one of the most flourishing ballet eras in the city's history. Vicusi, who choreographed many Romantic and classic ballets, was followed by Ella Fuchsová, Vladimir Pirnikov, Bohuslav Pelský and Maximilian Froman.

After 1945 the company expanded, producing works by choreographers like Rudolf Macharovský, Stanislav Remar, Josef Zajko, Milan Herényi and Kurd Toth, who, during his tenure as director (1961–72), added many classic contemporary and standard Soviet ballets to the repertory. Boris Slovak, appointed director in 1973, has given the company a definitely contemporary look, but has not in the process neglected the classics.

Vicusi and Jaroslav Hladík were responsible for establishing ballet in Brno after World War I, but the dominant figure in the city's ballet history from the mid-1920s to the early 1950s was Ivováňa Psota. Luboš Ogoun, who directed the city's ballet troupe from 1961–64, gave the company a contemporary bent; his work was continued by his successor, Miroslav Kura. Jiři Němeček has directed the company since 1974, when Kúra took over the National Theater in Prague.

Since the end of World War II the Soviet styles of teaching and choreography have dominated ballet in Czechoslovakia. In addition to native dance companies, Prague audiences have been able to see a large number of foreign companies – including the Royal Ballet from England (1947), the Kirov Ballet (1959), Budapest State Opera Ballet (1964) and the Bolshoi Ballet (1967 and 1975). In addition, the modern dancer Merce Cunningham appeared in Prague with his company in 1964 with great success.

HUNGARY

For most of the nineteenth century ballet in Hungary was dominated by foreigners. Most choreographers and teachers came from abroad (especially Vienna). The international stars of the Romantic era were very popular at both the Ofen Court Theater and the National Theater, including Fanny Elssler in 1846 and Augusta Maywood, who choreographed *Rendezvous at a Masked Ball* in 1847.

In the 1850s Emila Aranyvari became the first Hungarian ballerina, and work by several Hungarian choreographers – like Szöllösy, Farkas, Kaczer, Veszter and Kilanyi – began to appear. The major influence during this period was Italian. Resident ballet master Frederico Campilli produced most of the great Romantic ballets during his tenure (1847–85) and laid a firm foundation for the subsequent Hungarian Ballet company.

The opening of the Budapest Opera House and the founding of the Hungarian Ballet in 1884 marks the real beginning of Hungarian ballet. In 1899 and again in 1901 the Imperial Ballet from the Maryinsky appeared in the city and made a great impression. As a result of the increased interest, the iconoclastic Nicola Guerra was hired as ballet director. Guerra's stay in Budapest (1902–15) sparked the first flowering of ballet in Hungary. He brought new life to the company, choreographing 19 ballets, including *The Adventures of Love* (1902), *Carnival of Venice* (1903), *Hungarian Dance Suite* (1907), *Prometheus* (1913) and *The Games of Amor* (1913). He also was an excellent teacher, producing students like Emilia Nirschy, Anna Palley and Ferenc Nádasi.

From the 1920s to the mid-1930s Ede Brada (1879–1953) acted as ballet master. Some of his most popular ballets were *Princess Malve*, *Prince Arghyrus* and *Carnival in Pest*. He was succeeded by his son Rezsö in 1935.

The 1930s also saw the growing influence of the brilliant character dancer Gyula Harangozó, who added many ballets to the repertory. During the same period Nádasi emerged as Hungary's most important teacher, eventually becoming ballet master in 1937 and the first director of the Budapest State Choreographic Institute in 1946. Jan Cieplinski, the Polish choreographer, also was an important figure on the Hungarian ballet scene between the wars. Principal dancers of the period were Bella Bordy and Karola Szalay.

Since the war the Budapest State

Opera company has operated in a close and highly beneficial relationship with the Soviet ballet establishment, with many Russian ballet masters and guest choreographers like Vainonen, Messerer, Zakharov, Lavrovsky, Ansimova, Gusev

Ballet Sopianae was formed from a single but extremely talented class of the National Ballet's school. Eck remains choreographer today.

Imre Eck's ballet Cobweb an avant-garde work for the Pecs-based Ballet Sopianae, which he founded in 1960 to promote his modern ideas.

and Chaboukiani. However, the theater also regularly sends touring companies abroad and invites a western influence at home. Ashton staged his *La Fille Mal Gardée* in Budapest in 1971, Lander produced *La Sylphide* and *Etudes* in 1973 and in 1974 Béjart presented *Firebird*, *Webern Opus 5* and *Le Sacre du Printemps*. At present Hungary's chief choreographer is L Seregi, who has produced ballets to Khachaturian's *Spartacus* (1968), Bartok's *The Wooden Prince* and *The Miraculous Mandarin* (both 1970), Delibes's *Sylvia* (1972) and Hidas's *The Cedar* (1975).

Another important Hungarian troupe is Ballet Sopianae, a small group of young dancers organized in 1960 by Imre Eck to promote avant garde choreography in a chamber-ballet setting. Today the company is directed by Sandor Toth, while Eck serves as artistic director and chief choreographer; it has been very well received on its foreign tours.

POLAND

The first theater in Poland opened in the Royal Palace in Warsaw in 1643; some early productions included *Ballet de la Reine* (1654) and *Ballet à la Occasion du Sacre de Sa Majesté le Roi Jean III* (1676). The Opera House was built in 1724. The most notable event in its early history occurred in 1727, when the ballet *Perserpine* caused a great scandal with its alleged licentiousness.

The National Theater was founded in 1765, and for most of its first years Italian ballet masters ran the company. The first Polish ballet of note was not seen until 1788 when *Wanda, Queen of Polonia* was produced by students at the Warsaw ballet school, which had been founded by François Gabriel Le Doux (1755–1823) in Grodno and had moved to the capital in 1785.

In 1818 a resident company was established at the National Theater under the direction of Louis Thierry and with Julia Mierzyńska he choreographed *Marriage at Ojcow*, based on some folk tales from Crakow province. Mierzyńska also was the first important Polish ballet mistress (1801–31). The next director, Maurice Pion, did much to raise the company's technical standards. In 1833 the troupe moved to the new Wielki (Grand) Theater, and an associated school was established in 1834.

In 1843 Filippo Taglioni was engaged as director and during his tenure the first Polish choreographer, Roman Turczyno-wicz (1813–82), returned from his studies in Paris to stage the new Romantic ballets. Turczynowicz took over from Taglioni in 1853 and was succeeded in 1866 by Carlo Blasis, who presented *Faust* with Taglioni and Grisi as guest artists.

Poland was liberated and unified in 1918, and Piotr Zajlich (1884–1948) was put in charge of reorganizing the company at the Wielki Theater. He also added many modern works to the repertory, using soloists like Halina Szmol-cówna (1892–1939), Irena Szymańska (b 1899) and Zygmunt Dubrowski (1896–1973).

Prague saw the formation of an independent company in 1939. It was called Ballet Polska and Nijinska was its chief choreographer, mounting an all-Polish program at the Paris World Exhibition to the delight of her fans.

Warsaw, of course, was totally destroyed in World War II, and from 1945–65, while waiting for a new theater to be built, the company made do in the Roma Cinema. The time was not wasted, however. By the time the new Wielki Theater opened they had developed a balanced repertory of both classic and modern ballets with the help of many guest choreographers in addition to Poles like Stanislaw Miszszyk (b 1910), Eugeniusz Papliński (b 1908), Leon Woizikowsky and Witold Gruca (b 1927). Today the Wielki is directed by Maria Krzyszkowska

and in addition to its regular offerings it also encourages experimental choreography by new, young choreographers like Jerzy Makarowski, Marta Bochenek and Mariquita Compe.

In 1986 the Warsaw company brought a production of *The Sleeping Beauty* to the Edinburgh Festival. These performances showed the problems of isolationism that are imposed on Eastern-Bloc countries. Without the constant cross-fertilization so prevalent in the West, these dancers have become inbred and mannered. They are no longer up to the level of excellence seen in the major Western or Russian companies. Equally, the production designs seemed old-fashioned. Dancers need the challenge and excitement of new experiences and ideas if they are to continue to refine and expand their art. Any satisfaction with the status quo quickly leads to backsliding.

Ballet did not take hold in the provinces until after World War I, when ballet companies were formed at the Grand Theaters in Poznan and Lvov. Jan Cieplinski ran an independent company outside Warsaw from 1922–24.

Today there are 16 ballet companies in Poland, most closely tied to Moscow and Leningrad. The four state ballet schools – in Warsaw, Poznan, Bytom and Gdansk – offer nine-year courses. In addition, there is a special department for future teachers at the Warsaw High School of Music.

Noted Polish dancer and choreographer Witold Gruca partnered by Krystyna Mazurowna in his ballet The Red Inn.

FRANZ HILFERDING
1710–68

Franz Hilferding grew up in a family of actors and comedians, and by the time he was 25 was well established as one of the most popular dancers at the Viennese court. In 1749 he also was appointed court dancing master.

Hilferding was a pioneer of *ballet d'action*. Many of his ballets, which date from 1744 on, are mime/dance versions of classic tragedies – like Racine's *Britannicus* or Voltaire's *Azire*. Although he was a prolific choreographer (producing more than 30 ballets between 1752 and 1757 alone), none of his works survive today.

In 1857 he moved to Russia, leaving his former pupil, Gasparo Angiolini, in charge at the Kaertnerthor Theater. He worked in both Moscow and St Petersburg, doing a great deal to raise the standard of Russian ballet – and also instructing the young prince who would become Paul I.

Returning to Vienna in 1765, he and Angiolini traded places. When Noverre arrived in 1767 he and Hilferding became embroiled in a bitter argument over who was the real inventor of *ballet d'action* – a contest that Angiolini continued in his old teacher's behalf long after Hilferding's death.

ANNA HEINL
1753–1808

Anna Heinl was born in Bayreuth and by the time she was 14 was a good enough dancer to be hired by the Stuttgart Theater. She arrived there in 1767, only a few weeks after Noverre had departed for Vienna. The excellent company he had established remained, however, and Heinl took full advantage of both the training that was available and the exposure to some of the best dancers in Europe.

Heinl was an impressively large, if well-proportioned, woman. When she made her debut in Paris in 1768 the French found her size as impressive as her dancing, and she was immediately nicknamed 'La Belle Statue.' Her dancing style was strong, confident and precise, as befitted her majestic figure. She was famous for her pirouette *à la seconde*, which she is said to have invented, and also for her ability to revolve very slowly without losing her balance.

Though her appearance on the stage may have been noble and aloof, in private she wholeheartedly embraced the prevailing social mores of the Opéra. According to one of her rivals, she had 'such a chaotic mass of lovers that no-one can discover the truth.'

Within four years Heinl's popularity had grown so great that a contemporary critic called her 'the glory of Germany . . . the solace of France . . . and the foremost dancer in Europe.'

Predictably, Gaetano Vestris saw her success as a threat to his own and his son Auguste's positions, and began casting her in minor roles. After 20 years as the undisputed idol of Paris, Vestris had overestimated his own power and underestimated Heinl's popularity. The Parisians, realizing what was happening, began booing his appearances on stage and cheering hers.

Eventually the situation became so uncomfortable that Heinl requested a leave of absence. In 1771 she joined Noverre in London, where she appeared in the first ballet production at King's Theatre. Her name appeared on London programs for several seasons.

Noverre received his appointment as ballet master at the Opéra in 1776, and Heinl returned with him to Paris, where she was welcomed enthusiastically. Her first appearance was in Noverre's *Apelles et Campasne*, which she turned into a great success despite Maximilian Gardel's strenuous attempts to sabotage the production.

Once they were no longer in direct competition, she and Gaetano Vestris discovered that they had much in common, even though he was 24 years older than she. Soon they were living together, and in 1782 they decided to retire. The decision caused a great deal of distress among balletomanes in Paris, but the two dancers were very happy. Heinl must have fit well into the Vestris' tight family circle. In 1791 she gave birth to Vestris's son and the following year they were married. Despite the difference in their ages and their checkered pasts, they were a devoted couple, and Heinl died within a few months of her husband.

THERESE HEBERLE
1806–40

Therese Heberle began her career with Horschelt's notorious Kinderballett, joining the Italian Opera in London after the children's company disbanded in 1821.

After a few years, during which she became increasingly popular, she retired to marry a Neopolitan banker. It was an unfortunate alliance in that her husband soon lost all of her money, but Heberle returned to the stage and embarked on a new, even more spectacular career in Italy. She became so popular in Milan, in fact, that when Grisi appeared there she was called 'La Piccola Heberle.'

PAUL (PAULO) TAGLIONI
1808–84

Marie Taglioni's younger brother Paul was born in Vienna. He studied dance with Jean-Francois Coulon, one of the most famous teachers in Paris, as well as with his father. His debut was made with his sister, in a *pas de deux* in Stuttgart in 1824, and he danced as her partner for several years.

In 1829, shortly after the Taglionis finished their engagement in Stuttgart, Paul married the ballerina Anna Galster and the two settled in Berlin. For several decades, however, he continued to make guest appearances as a dancer and choreographer in the other European cities: he was a soloist in Vienna from 1826–29 and a regular guest choreographer there be-

Paul Taglioni, talented and prolific choreographer.

tween 1853 and 1874: he did some of his most exciting choreography in London in the 1840s and 1850s: served as ballet master in Naples from 1853–56: and filled the same position in Milan from 1861–62. In 1856 he was made ballet master in Berlin and held this post until 1883.

Taglioni's first ballets were seen in 1835. As a choreographer he combined a sound grasp of fundamentals with a love for new technical devices. *Electra* was the first ballet lit by electricity, and he used roller skates in *Les Plaisers de l'Hiver*. His other important ballets include *Undine, die Wassernymphe* (1836), revised as *Coralia* in London in 1847; *Don Quixote* (1839); *Thea oder die Blumenfee* (1847), produced in London the same year as *Thea ou la Fée aux Fleurs; Les Metamorphoses* (London, 1850), presented in Berlin as *Satanella oder Metamorphosen* in 1852; *Flick und Flock* (1858); *Sarandapal* (1865), revived for the opening of the Vienna Court Opera in 1869; *Fantasca* (1869); *Militaria* (1872); and his own version of *Coppélia* (1882). The music Taglioni commissioned from P Hertel for his 1864 Berlin production of *La Fille Mal Gardée* still is used in Russia. Most of his productions starred his daughter Marie until 1866.

FANNY ELSSLER
1810–84

Fanny Elssler, Marie Taglioni's stylistic counterpart and greatest rival, was born in Vienna, into a musical family. Her father had worked as copyist and valet to Haydn, but the composer died in 1808, and by the time Fanny was born the family was so poor that her mother was taking in washing to help feed her five children.

When Elssler was seven she and her older sister Thérèse were sent to the ballet school at the Kaertnerthor Theater where they studied first with Jean Aumer, then with Filippo Taglioni – showing such talent and poise that soon they were appearing in children's roles.

Domenico Barbaja, director of the theater, spotted Fanny's potential immediately, and took her with him to Naples in 1824. There she made great progress artistically – and also socially, becoming the mistress of Leopold, Prince of Salerno. Their son Franz was born in Vienna in 1827 but his birth was kept secret and he was placed in a foster home

so that his mother could continue her career.

In 1829 Fanny contracted an alliance with Friedrich von Gentz – one of the outstanding German intellectuals of his day, an advisor to Metternich, and an elegant, kind gentleman. Under his tutelage Fanny was inspired to polish her manners and learn to speak cultured German and French. Despite the fact that he was 65 when they met (she was 19), she was sincerely devoted and grateful to him, maintaining a vigil at his deathbed in 1832.

At that time she and Thérèse were appearing as leading dancers in Berlin, where Fanny had fallen in love with Anton Stuhlmüller. Soon she was pregnant again – but since their reputations had spread, it did not prevent the Elssler sisters accepting an engagement at Her Majesty's Theatre in London in February 1833. A few months later little Theresa was born. Until she was about nine she was raised by Harriet Grote, wife of the British Member of Parliament and historian George Grote.

In London Thérèse began developing her talents as a choreographer (*Le Fée et le Chevalier*, 1833, and *Armide* 1834), while Fanny continued working on the rapid, passionate dancing style that would make her famous. In May 1834 Dr Véron, director of the Paris Opéra, saw one of her performances and immediately recognized the opportunity to develop an exciting (and lucrative) rivalry between Ellsler and the reigning favorite, Marie Taglioni.

Elssler opened in Paris in September 1934 and was an instant success. Her lively, sensuous dancing was a novelty after Taglioni's chaste, ethereal, dreamy style. In addition, she was a very beautiful woman – something which could never be said for the round-shouldered, rather unattractive Taglioni. For the next six years Elssler danced happily in Paris, with off-season engagements in Bordeaux, Berlin, Vienna and London. Her popularity grew greater every year. In 1836 she introduced a Spanish dance, the 'cachucha,' in Coralli's *Le Diable Boiteux*; her audiences were shocked – and returned to see the scandalous dance again and again. Soon Taglioni gave up the contest and set out for Russia, leaving Elssler in sole possession of the Opéra stage where she achieved two more noteworthy successes – in *La Gypsy* and *La Tarantule* (both 1839).

In 1840 she set off to tour the United

Fanny Elssler in her famous Le Diable Boiteux.

States, accompanied by her cousin Kathi Prinsten, her partner and teacher James Sylvain (James Sullivan, 1808–56), a maid, her coachman Charles (who remained in the New World, setting up a livery stable with Elssler's backing) and Henry Wikoff, her American sponsor who was a combination of business manager, publicist and, eventually, her lover.

The story of Elssler's triumphal tour of America is well known: New York, Baltimore, Washington, Boston, Philadelphia, New Orleans, even Havana caught 'Ellslermania,' and the tour was extended several times over. In order to stay away, she had had to break her contract with the Opéra (where, in any case, Carlotta Grisi had taken her place). When she finally returned in 1842 it was to England, where she appeared in several successful productions, including *Un Bal sous Louis XIV* in 1843 and Perrot's *La Esmeralda* in 1847. She also toured extensively on the continent, appearing in Brussels during the 1843–44 season, dancing many times in Vienna, Berlin and Budapest, and making a three-year tour of Italy (where she appeared with Perrot in his productions of *Faust* and *Catarina* at La Scala).

Finally, early in 1848, she accepted an engagement in St Petersburg. She was 38, but any lessening of her technical ability was more than offset by her improved acting and her still-startling beauty. The emotional Russians gave her a tremendous reception in St Petersburg and her triumph was even greater in Moscow. When she gave her farewell performance in *La Esmeralda* after 103 appearances in two years, the entire audience was in tears; 300 bouquets were thrown onto the stage, and half the house followed her home, cheering. After two more seasons dancing in Germany and Austria, Elssler retired, making her last appearance in *Faust* in Vienna on 21 June 1851. She then settled down to live in quiet luxury, first in Hamburg, and then in Vienna near Thérèse. She died of cancer 33 years later.

Today a charming little museum at Eisenstadt, near Vienna, houses memorabilia of Hayden and the two Elssler sisters.

JOSEPH HASSREITER
1845–1940

Joseph Hassreiter was born in Vienna and devoted his entire life to the advancement of ballet in the city. He studied at the Vienna Court Opera Ballet School and joined the company as a soloist in 1870.

Between 1891 and 1920 he served the company in many capacities – as ballet master, director of the school and teacher for the soloists. He also gave private lessons to members of Austria's Imperial family.

His first ballet, *The Fairy Doll* (1888), was his most popular work and remains in the repertory to this day. However, he also choreographed 48 other works, including *Sonne und Erde*, *Rouge et Noir*, *Rund um Wien* and *Jahreszeiten der Liebe*.

HEINRICH KROLLER
1880–1930

Heinrich Kröller, who was to become one of the most influential figures in German ballet in the early part of this century, studied both in Munich at the Court Opera Ballet School and in Paris with Léo Staats and Carlotta Zambelli ('La Grande Mademoiselle').

Kröller was appointed soloist in Munich in 1901 and later worked in Dresden, as *premier danseur*. During the difficult years between the wars, when modern dance all but ousted classic ballet in Germany, he served as ballet master in Frankfurt and Munich (1917–19), at the Berlin State Opera (1919–22) and in Vienna (1922–28).

A prolific choreographer, his ballets include the first German production of Strauss's *Legend of Joseph* (1921), *Couperin Suite* (1923), *Schlagobers* (1924) and *Skyscrapers* (1929). Though he was certainly influenced strongly by the modernists, he never lost sight of the traditions upon which a ballet is based, and played an important role in keeping ballet alive in Germany.

FERENC NADASI
1893–1966

Ferenc Nádasi, one of the founders of ballet in modern Hungary, was born in Budapest and studied there with Jakob Holczer and Henrietta Spinzi. From 1909–12 he danced in Russia, then returned as soloist to the Budapest State Ballet.

In 1921 he left to tour abroad, also taking the opportunity to study further with Cecchetti and Guerra. Back in Budapest in 1936 he soon became ballet master, ballet director and, in 1946, director of the Budapest State Opera Ballet School.

In that position Nádasi proved that his greatest talent was for teaching; virtually all of the present generation of Hungarian dancers owe their training to

him. Following his resignation in 1962 he headed the committee that wrote *Method of Classic Dance* (1963), which has become one of the standard works on academic ballet training.

LEON WOIZIKOWSKY
1899–1975

Leon Woizikowsky (originally Wojcikowski) was born in Poland and trained by Cecchetti at the Warsaw Imperial Ballet School. In 1916 he joined Ballets Russes and became known as one of the outstanding character dancers of his generation. Some of his most famous roles were The Polovtsian chief in *Prince Igor*, Petrouchka, Niccolo in *Les Femmes des Bonne Humeur* and the Corregidor in *Le Tricorn*.

Woizikowsky remained with Diaghilev until the company disbanded in 1929; he then toured with Pavlova (1929–31) and danced with Ballet Russe de Monte Carlo (1932–34). After a short time (1935–36) touring with his own company, Les Ballets de Leon Woizikowsky, he spent the war years travelling with Ballet Russe de Colonel de Basil.

In 1945 he became ballet master at the New Theater in Warsaw and also opened a school there. In 1958 he moved to Lon-

Leon Woizikowsky, pioneer of Polish ballet.

don where he taught and worked for the London Festival Ballet, revising *Petrouchka* in 1958 and *Schéhérezade* in 1959. He also served as ballet master for both Massine's Ballets Européens de Nervi (1959) and the London Festival Ballet (1961).

From the early to the mid-1960s Woizikowsky taught at the Cologne Institute for Theatrical Dance, then at Bonn University. In 1974 he retired and returned to end his days in Warsaw.

JAN CIEPLINSKI
1900–1972

Jan Cieplinski received his ballet training in his hometown of Warsaw, and after graduation joined the company at the Wielki Theater.

After touring the United States and Canada with Pavlova's company in 1921, he returned to Poland, where he remained as ballet master and choreographer for several years. During this period he specialized in producing ballets to music by Polish composers, such as Stanislaw Moniuszko, Zygismund Moszkowski and Míeozyslaw Karlovicz.

In 1925 Cieplinski joined Diaghilev's Ballets Russes; from 1927 to 1931 he was ballet master and chief choreographer at the Royal Opera House in Stockholm,

then worked for the Budapest State Opera Ballet from 1932 to 1934. After a brief stay in Warsaw he was off to Argentina, where he worked at the Teatró Colon in Buenos Aires.

At the beginning of World War II, in 1936, Cieplinski returned to Warsaw to direct the ballet school; he then moved to Budapest in 1943. In 1948 he spent a season in London, choreographing for the Anglo-Polish Ballet. That was followed by another season in Buenos Aires in 1949, after which he opened his own studio in London.

In 1959 Cieplinski moved to New York where, as the last phase in his truly international ballet career, he ran a studio until his death.

KURT JOOSS
1901–79

Kurt Jooss, the first twentieth-century choreographer to attempt a synthesis of classic and modern dance, was born in Wesseralfingen, Germany. He studied in Stuttgart where in 1920 he met Rudolf von Laban. The following year he accompanied von Laban to Mannheim where he continued his study of modern dance and by 1922 he had become the master's assistant and principal dancer.

In 1924 Jooss was appointed ballet master at the Münster State Theater. He also formed the Neue Tanzbuhne (New Dance Group) with Sigurd Leeder and Aino Siimola (who he married in 1929). The group toured extensively in Germany between 1924 and 1926 – and in addition to his already full schedule, Jooss continued to study classical ballet in Vienna and Paris, along with beginning to do his first choreography.

In 1927 he was appointed director of the Essen Folkwang School of Music and in 1930 became ballet master at the Essen Opera House. During this time he created his most famous work, *The Green Table* (1932).

However, Jooss's political views did not endear him to the rapidly rising Nazi Party, and in 1933 he was forced to quit Germany for England. There, he and Leeder settled in Dartington and founded Ballets Jooss. The company toured the world during the war, exerting an influence on contemporary ballet that has not yet been fully appreciated. The usual lavish, expensive costumes and sets were replaced with practical, easily carried props, and Jooss even took his own lighting equipment along to save time and avoid unexpected deficiencies. Jooss's dancers were men and women, not boys and girls, and in his works he allowed them to break out of the usual elegant,

A scene from Kurt Jooss' famous work The Green Table.

Vaslav Orlikowsky staging Cranko's Prince of the Pagodas *for the Vienna Staatsoper.*

During her later career she expanded beyond the confines of modern dance, choreographing many standard and classic ballets in addition to her own original works. She was responsible for instituting an active, flourishing company in Hanover, and overall must be considered one of the most influential figures in modern European ballet.

RUDOLF KOLLING
1904–70

Rudolf Kölling was born in Hanover and studied classic and modern dance, the latter with Wigman and von Laban.

He began his career with the Berlin State Opera Ballet, and during World War II was ballet master at the German Opera House in Berlin (1939–44). Under his leadership the company became one of the most active and vital groups in Germany at the time.

After 1945 Kölling worked for a time in Weimar and East Berlin, then moved to West Germany and lived in Munich and Münster. In 1949 he choreographed the first German postwar production of Stravinsky's *Le Sacre du Printemps*.

ERIKA HANKA
1905–58

Erika Hanka was born in Vincovci, Croatia, to an old Austrian military family. She studied dance with Bodenwieser in Vienna and with Jooss in Essen.

In 1936 Hanka joined the Dusseldorf Ballet as a soloist, and within a short time was made ballet mistress as well. She remained with the company for three years, then worked in several other German cities including Cologne, Essen and Hamburg.

The Vienna State Opera invited Hanka to serve as guest choreographer in 1941, and her production of *Joan von Zarissa* to Werner Egk's music was so successful that in 1942 she was offered the post of ballet mistress. Later she was made director, a post she held until her death.

As a choreographer Hanka staged some 50 ballets – strong, dramatic works in a modern idiom. Her most popular production was *The Moor of Venice* (1955); other successes include *Titus Feuerfuchs* (1941), *Hollische G'schicht* (1949), *Homerische Sinfonie* (1950), *Hotel Sacher* (1957) and *Medusa* (1957).

pretty ballet mold and be heavy, ugly or strong if the dance warranted. At the same time he made full use of the classic vocabulary – and thus frequently found himself under fire from both sides.

In 1947, after the war, the company disbanded and Jooss spent some time in Santiago de Chile before returning to Essen in 1949. There he reestablished the Folkwang Ballet and School, running the organization until 1953.

With the exception of the period 1954–56 when he was ballet master in Dusseldorf and a season from 1963–64 when he formed another touring company, Jooss spent the remaining years until his retirement in 1968 as a freelance teacher and choreographer. Even after he retired, however, he continued to control revivals of *The Green Table*.

YVONNE GEORGI
1903–1975

Yvonne Georgi, who made a great contribution to the development of ballet and modern dance in both The Netherlands and Germany, was born in Leipzig and began studying dance there before going on to train further at the Dalcroze Institute in Hellerau and the Wigman School in Dresden.

She made her debut in 1923 and in 1924 joined Jooss's company in Münster. She was appointed ballet mistress at the Gera Opera House for the 1925–26 season, and filled the same position in Hanover from 1926–31. While in Hanover she also opened her own school, and toured extensively in Europe and the United States – both as a soloist and as partner to the modern dancer Harald Kreutzberg. Soon he was known as one of Germany's most prominent modern dance interpreters.

In 1932 Georgi married a Dutch journalist and moved to Amsterdam where she worked for the Amsterdam Opera, established a school and eventually formed a company (which, in 1939, became the first Dutch troupe to tour the United States). She continued to work in Holland throughout World War II.

The year 1951 found her back in Germany as ballet mistress and choreographer at the Dusseldorf Opera. Then, in 1954, she was appointed director of the Hanover State Theater – a post she held for 16 years before becoming head of the dance department at the Hanover Academy of Music (1970–73).

Her most outstanding qualities, however, were the energy and perseverance that enabled her to keep her company in operation under almost impossible conditions during the war years and the difficult time that followed. She also was an indefatigable fighter for ballet's proper place vis à vis opera at the theater itself.

SONIA GASKELL
1904–74

Sonia Gaskell, born Sonja Vilkaviškis in Lithuania, began her dancing career with Diaghilev's Ballets Russes in Paris. Later, from 1936 to 39, she also taught in the French capital. Moving to Amsterdam, she continued her teaching career, and by 1949 was able to begin her first company, Ballet Recital.

In 1954 she became director of the Netherlands Ballet in The Hague. Gaskell had an extraordinary talent for organization along with her dedication to ballet, and the Netherlands Ballet provided the foundation for the resurgence of classic dance in Holland.

The Netherlands Ballet merged with Mascha ter Weeme's Amsterdam Ballet in 1961, to form the Dutch National Ballet, and for a time the two women shared direction of the company. Soon, however, ter Weeme went on to other projects, leaving Gaskell to run the company until 1968.

Though she choreographed many ballets, it is through her work as a teacher and especially as an administrator that Gaskell is remembered today – as one of the most important pioneers of twentieth-century ballet in The Netherlands.

GYULA HARANGOZO
1908–74

Gyula Harangozó, a prominent Hungarian character dancer, choreographer and ballet master, studied at the Budapest State Opera Ballet School and joined the company in 1926.

Harangozó is most famous for his ballets set to Bartok's music: *The Wooden Prince* (first version, 1939), and *The Miraculous Mandarin* (first version, 1945). His other works cover a wide range of subjects and styles, from *Romeo and Juliet* (1936) to *Mattie the Gooseboy* (1960). In addition to his work for the State Opera Ballet he has choreographed many productions for film and television.

JOHN CRANKO
1927–73

John Cranko was born in South Africa and began studying dance at the Cape Town University Ballet School. He then transferred to the Sadler's Wells School in London and eventually joined the Sadler's Wells Theatre Ballet.

Early in his career he emerged as one of Britain's leading young choreographers, producing works for Sadler's Wells (later the Royal Ballet) and Ballet Rambert that included: *Tritsch-Tratsch* (1946); *Pineapple Poll* and *Harlequin in April* (both 1951); *The Shadow* (1953); *The Lady and the Fool* (1954); *The Prince of the Pagodas* (1957); and *Antigone* (1959).

In 1961 Cranko became director of the Württemburg Staatstheater in Stuttgart, and within a few years he had turned it into one of the most lively, exciting companies in the world. The group's large and varied repertory, its excellent dancers, and its extensive tours soon won it an honored place among international ballet centers, as well as establishing Cranko as a major influence in contemporary ballet. He also served as chief choreographer for the Bavarian State Opera from 1968–71.

Though he was adept at many styles, Cranko's special talent was for full-length, dramatic ballets. Some of his later productions were: *The Catalyst* (1961), *Daphnis and Chloë* (1962), *L'Estro Armonico* (1963), *Jeu de Cartes* (1956), *Eugene Onegin* (1965), *The Taming of the Shrew* (1969), *Brouillards* (1970), *Ebony Concerto* (1970), *Carmen* (1971) and *Traces* (1973).

His untimely death on a return flight from America was a great loss to ballet in our time.

A popular Cranko ballet is Taming of the Shrew, *which is performed by the Stuttgart and Royal Ballets.*

Rosella Hightower, the Oklahoma-born ballerina who had a brilliant European career, as Marie Taglioni in Pas de Quatre.

It is often assumed that the United States had had no real contact with ballet prior to 1840 and the arrival of Fanny Elssler. But Elssler was just one of a series of fine dancers, both European and American, who were seen regularly on the stages of New York, Philadelphia, Boston and other cities.

Beginning in the mid-eighteenth century, dancers from England and the Continent braved the long, terrifying voyage across the Atlantic to seek their fortunes in the New World. Some of the earliest visitors on record were the Placides, French dancers who came to New York in 1793 and never returned to Europe. Other visitors during the first four decades of the nineteenth century were Mlle Celeste, Mme Lecomte and Mlle Augusta (1806–1901) – a German dancer who became extremely popular in America. The Petipas also toured the country, as did Paul and Amalia Taglioni. M and Mme Paul Hazard, who had been trained in France and danced in Paris, Brussels and Germany, opened one of the first ballet schools in the country, in Philadelphia. Both were talented teachers, and by the 1830s they were producing a respectable number of competent students.

Nor were all the good dancers in America foreign imports. During the eighteenth century John Durang (1768–1822), son of a Revolutionary Army veteran and one of George Washington's favorite entertainers, was probably the first noteworthy American dancer. He was based in Philadelphia and was famous for his hornpipes and harlequinades. In the nineteenth century outstanding dancers included Julia Turnbull (1822–87), one of America's leading Romantic ballerinas, and George Washington Smith – a popular *danseur noble* who partnered Elssler during her stay. Mary Ann Lee (1823–99), a graduate of the Hazards' school, made her debut in 1837. She was very popular; after studying in Paris with Coralli she returned in 1844 to become America's first Giselle and also danced many of Taglioni's and Elssler's roles. Her contemporary, Augusta Maywood, who also was trained by the Hazards, was the first American to manage to establish a successful career in Europe.

Although the United States was no stranger to good ballet, nothing prepared the country for the descent of Fanny Elssler. The Austrian ballerina's beauty and her passionate sensual dancing – along with entrepreneur Henry Wykoff's able publicity campaign – soon had the major American cities in a turmoil. Nathaniel Hawthorne hung her picture on his wall between St Ignatius Loyola and St Francis Xavier. Emerson, when his companion at a performance described Elssler's dancing as poetry, replied, 'No, it is religion.'

In Washington, DC, the Senate recessed on the day of her first performance, and the exuberant Senators unhitched the horses from her carriage and hauled it through the streets themselves. In Havana, one admirer presented her a box of solid gold 'cigars.' All over the country clothing, soap, champagne and shoe polish were named after her. There had never been anything like it before, and it would be many years before cinema and the mass media could create another star who even began to approach her popularity.

At the beginning of the twentieth century the Italian ballerina and teacher Cia Fornaroli was ballet mistress at the Metropolitan Opera in New York (1909–13), and Adeline Genée made several successful tours of the country. For the most part, however, classic ballet in the United States – as in Europe – was considered a Russian phenomenon. Ballets Russes's appearances in New York in 1916 and 1917 reinforced this notion, as did Pavlova's very successful tours be-

Mikhail Mordkin, former Russian star, who taught in the USA and whose Mordkin Ballet became the foundation of American Ballet Theatre.

fore and after World War I.

After the war there was a great influx of dancers. Fokine settled in New York and began his own company. Adolf Bolm struck out further west: he staged several ballets for the Civic Opera in Chicago (including *Krazy Kat*, 1920); in San Francisco he organized the San Francisco Opera Ballet in 1932, making it the oldest professional company in America today. Massine also spent much of his time in America. In 1937 Mikhail Mordkin, formerly one of Pavlova's partners, established his own company, the Mordkin Ballet.

During the 1930s Americans began taking an active role in ballet as well. Ruth Page was emerging as an active, creative choreographer in Chicago. Catherine Littlefield (1905–51) organized the Littlefield Ballet, which became the Philadelphia Ballet in 1936. The troupe produced the first full-length *Sleeping Beauty* in America in 1937 and toured Paris, Brussels and London. On their return to America, Littlefield moved the entire group to Chicago, where they performed at the Civic Opera. In 1937 William Christensen took over the San Francisco Opera Ballet, beginning the association his family continues to enjoy with ballet in that city.

But the most important event in the decade occurred in 1933, when a young American ballet lover, Lincoln Kirstein, travelled to Europe to ask George Balanchine to return with him to New York. Kirstein and a friend, Edward Warburg, were convinced that with Balanchine they could 'further the tradition of classical theatrical dancing' and promote 'the growth of a new national art in America.'

At first Balanchine was a bit staggered by the enormity of their plans and under other circumstances might have refused the offer outright. But he had just terminated an uncomfortable engagement with Colonel de Basil's company, and Europe was firmly in the grip of the Great Depression. Besides, the more he thought about the idea, the more it appealed to him; soon he was very excited at the prospect of creating 'something new from something very basic.'

On 1 January 1934 the School of American Ballet opened in New York, in a studio formerly belonging to Isadora Duncan. After almost a year of hard work the company (the American Ballet) was ready to present its first season, but its offerings were not universally acclaimed. John Martin of the *New York*

Times (the first full-time dance critic in the United States) echoed popular opinion when he objected strenuously to the choreographer's 'Riviera esthetics.' At that time of intense nationalism and solidarity in the face of economic disaster, most intellectuals were inclined toward modern dance, a 'real' American art form, rather than ballet, which was considered an effete relic of an aristocratic and decadent Europe.

In this they did Balanchine an injustice. The Russian-born citizen of the world had an immediate, instinctive understanding and love for America's democratic spirit and zest for life. This affinity is shown most clearly in the choreography he developed for Broadway and later Hollywood – for though American Ballet struggled along until 1941, it never was wholly successful. His dances for musicals like *On Your Toes* (with its famous gangster ballet, 'Slaughter on Tenth Avenue'), *The Goldwyn Follies*, *The Boys from Syracuse*, *Cabin in the Sky* and *I Married an Angel* were enormously popular.

In choreographing his ballets, Balan-chine (despite Martin's comment), was abandoning the Diaghilev/Ballets Russes style and returning to the classical tradition of Petipa and Ivanov, but it was a clean, streamlined, very American classicism, stripped of the frills and furbelows that cluttered the original Russian choreography. One of his productions for American Ballet's first performance, *Serenade*, is still in the New York City

A scene from George Balanchine's modern classic Serenade *with Merle Park, Georgina Parkinson and David Adams of the Royal Ballet.*

Ballet's repertory. An abstract, lyric ballet to Tchaikovsky's *Serenade for Strings*, it replaces plot with a demonstration of pure style.

Though American Ballet was still struggling, Kirstein founded a second troupe in 1936. This small touring company, called Ballet Caravan, was established to provide work for more dancers, and especially to encourage younger choreographers. Its 1938 season, for example, featured two very American works that have become landmarks in the development of ballet. *Filling Station* by Lew Christensen, to music by Virgil Thomson, celebrates life on the American highway and Eugene Loring's *Billy the Kid* (music, Aaron Copeland) relates the life of the famous outlaw in the context of the settling of the West. Kirstein, who had a special fondness for American history and folklore, went to great lengths to encourage efforts like these.

American Ballet's greatest rival during the 1930s was Ballet Russe de Monte Carlo, the troupe organized by René Blum and Colonel de Basil. They had come to America in 1933 at the invitation of impresario Sol Hurok. Though their first engagement at the St James Theater in New York and their subsequent tour had not been financially successful, Hurok continued his support and eventually the group managed to put itself on a sound financial footing.

Ballet Russe de Monte Carlo had years of professional experience stretching back to the Imperial Schools of old Russia, as well as an accomplished group of dancers including Alexandra Danilova (who, with Fredrick Franklin, led the company for many years) and, of course, the 'baby ballerinas.' By 1941, when the United States entered World War II, its tours were an annual event, eagerly awaited throughout the country – especially in cities that had no other opportunity to see ballet. More than any other, this group was responsible for establishing a solid audience for ballet throughout the United States, outside the major cultural centers. Soon it was, in all but name, a completely American company – a transition marked by the production of Agnes de Mille's Wild West story *Rodeo* in 1942. It continued to be the main touring company in America until 1962.

In 1940 a small company called Ballet Theater, which had been founded the year before by former members of the Mordkin Ballet, changed its name to American Ballet Theater – one of

America's great ballet companies had been born. The previous organizations had concentrated on the traiditional Russian school, but ABT's first director, Richard Pleasant, was committed to presenting as many styles and periods as possible. In this he was fully supported by the company's patron, Lucia Chase, a former pupil of Mordkin's and an unfailing supporter of the group ever since. For their first season, ABT presented ballets by no less than 11 choreographers – including Bolm, de Mille, Dolin, Fokine, Andrée Howard, Loring, Nijinska and Tudor. Chase had established the new group on a grand scale; there were over 100 dancers, including Anton Dolin and Yurek Shabelevsky. Ballerinas Markova and Baronova joined the group the following year and later Alicia Alonzo, Nora Kaye and Janet Reed became important members of the company.

Pleasant served in the armed forces during World War II, and the company had several directors until 1945 when Chase and Oliver Smith took over joint control. In 1946 the spelling of the name was changed to American Ballet Theatre to commemorate a highly successful London tour.

The 1940s were splendid years for ABT. Fokine choreographed his last two ballets for the company before he died of pleurisy in 1942. A third, the comedy *Helen of Troy*, was completed by David Lichine. In 1942 Massine produced *Aleko* to music by Tchaikovsky, with costumes and sets

George Balanchine discusses a technical point during a break in rehearsal. His influence on contemporary choreography has been considerable.

Antony Tudor partnering Nora Kaye in his masterpiece Pillar of Fire *which he created for the American Ballet Theatre in 1942.*

by Chagall; the next year he offered *Mam'zelle Angot* – a lighthearted comedy starring himself as the barber and the great Nora Kaye (b 1920) as the Mademoiselle. Agnes de Mille produced the harrowing *Fall River Legend*, based on the story of Lizzie Borden, in 1948.

Jerome Robbins, who began as a dancer with the troupe, contributed several important ballets to the repertory. His best-known work from this period is *Fancy Free*, which premiered in 1944 and is still ABT's hallmark. The simple story of three sailors trying to pick up two girls in a New York bar is full of humor, vitality and fun – told in a skillful blend of ballet, show dancing and jazz.

Other choreographers who emerged from ABT include Michael Kidd (b 1919); Kaye's husband, Herbert Ross (b 1926); William Dollar; Glen Tetley – and later Eliot Feld (b 1943); Michael Smuin (b 1938); and Dennis Nahat (b 1946). But by far the most important choreographer to be introduced by ABT is Antony Tudor, whose intense psychological works like *Pillar of Fire* (1942) represent a new

dimension in narrative ballet.

Both Natalia Makarova and Mikhail Baryshnikov joined ABT after defecting from the USSR. Makarova (b 1940) left the Kirov in 1970. Her major roles with ABT were *Swan Lake* and *Giselle*. She staged 'The Kingdom of the Shades' from *La Bayadère* in 1974, and in 1980 mounted the only Western production of the full-length ballet.

Baryshnikov (b 1948) defected in 1974. He quickly became the undisputed 'star of stars' at ABT. His chief partner was Gelsey Kirkland (b 1953), who left New York City Ballet to dance with ABT in 1974. *Giselle* and *The Nutcracker* (in a new version by Baryshnikov) were their most impressive roles. In addition to *The Nutcracker* (1977), Baryshnikov staged *Don Quixote* (1978) and *Cinderella* (1983).

Above: Violette Verdy, the French-born dancer who has had a great career as ballerina, first with ABT but principally with New York City Ballet.

Above right: Suzanne Farrell in Balanchine's Union Jack, *NYCB's contribution for the bicentennial celebrations in 1976.*

Right: Square Dance *with Merrill Ashley and Sean Lavery, NYCB, is a typical Balanchine ballet to music by Vivaldi and Corelli.*

Top left: During a New York City Ballet appearance in London at the Royal Opera House, Balanchine rehearses the company in Union Jack.

Far left: Balanchine has taken his works all over the world with the New York City Ballet. This is a scene from the Edinburgh Festival.

Left: Suzanne Farrell, the supreme Balanchine dancer who has created many roles for him, demonstrates her fantastic leg extension.

Page 186. Top: Mikhail Baryshnikov appearing with American Ballet Theater, partnered by Gelsey Kirkland in their production of Giselle, Act I.

Page 186/7, Bottom: Act II of Giselle, ABT. The Wilis, commanded by their terrible Queen Myrthe, summon forth the spirit of the wronged Giselle.

Page 187, Top: The Joffrey City Center Ballet, founded by Robert Joffrey and based at the New York City Center since 1966.

In 1976 ABT had the biggest hit of the decade in the rambunctious and unorthodox *Push Comes to Shove*, which was created specifically for Baryshnikov by modernist Twyla Tharp. She has since devised several other works for ABT.

Baryshnikov was appointed artistic director in 1980. In 1985 Britain's Sir Kenneth MacMillan was appointed associate director. He mounted his *Romeo and Juliet* for the company in 1985. He choreographed Andrew Lloyd Webber's *Requiem* (1986) and a new version of *The Sleeping Beauty* (1987).

In 1946 Balanchine and Kirstein launched Ballet Society. Its primary objective was to present new ballets to a subscription audience but it also sponsored lectures, films and publications – including the periodical *Dance Index*. Though Ballet Society's list of choreographers included many young Americans like Todd Bolender (b 1914) and John Taras, the primary choreographer was always Balanchine.

Ballet Society owned an auditorium named the New York Center of Music and Drama and in 1948 a series of performances there so impressed Morton Baum, head of the finance committee for the New York City Center, that he asked Kirstein if he would like to re-form Ballet Society into a city-supported group. Kirstein replied, 'If you do that for us, in three years I will give you the finest ballet company in America.'

Between them he and Balanchine have kept that promise. Today the New York City ballet is America's best-known and most respected company internationally. Though it tours America infrequently, its fame has spread, thanks to film and television. Since 1964 it has operated out of the New York State Theater in Lin-

Below: Dance Theatre of Harlem performs a diverse repertory, from the great classics to modern works like Tetley's Voluntaries.

Right: Stephanie Baxter as Eve and Eddie Shellman as Adam in Manifestations for Dance Theatre of Harlem by Arthur Mitchell, its founder.

coln Center; its school has produced some of America's best dancers, including Maria Tallchief, Patricia Wilde, Allegra Kent, Melissa Hayden, Jacques d'Amboise, Edward Villella, Suzanne Farrell, Gelsey Kirkland, Kyra Nichols and Darci Kistler.

Balanchine's sleek ballets are almost universally regarded as among the major twentieth-century artworks. In 1975 the company celebrated the lengthy and fruitful collaboration between Balanchine and Stravinsky. This 'Stravinsky Festival' marks one of the high points in the history of NYCB. This was followed with a 'Ravel Festival' (1978) and a 'Tchaikovsky Festival' in 1981.

Throughout its history New York City Ballet has been dominated by Balanchine, that prolific and original choreographer whose distinctive neoclassical style is now the real star of the company. This unified image has been enhanced by Balanchine's continued distaste for the star system: his dancers are listed in alphabetical order, and soloists, or even members of the *corps de ballet*, are given the chance to dance leading roles. The dance itself is of paramount importance, and the performer makes his or her impact through the choreography.

Balanchine died in 1983. The management of the company has since been split between Jerome Robbins and former dancer Peter Martins (b 1946). One of the many Danish men who has joined NYCB, Martins danced with the company from 1969. He was the chief partner for that quintessential Balanchine ballerina, Suzanne Farrell. He began choreographing in 1978 with *Calcium Night Light*. The Balanchine repertory will always be the bedrock of NYCB, but Martins has turned into a prolific choreographer. Robbins, who has made works for NYCB since 1950, also continues to provide new ballets for America's largest (110 dancers) company.

One of the most important smaller companies in the United States is the Joffrey Ballet, formed in 1956 when Robert Joffrey and a few friends set out on tour in a rented station wagon. From this modest beginning the group soon acquired a devoted coterie of admirers and even its own choreographer, Gerald Arpino (b 1928). It had many financial struggles and several times during the 1960s seemed to be on the brink of extinction. In 1966, however, it was invited to fill the NYCB's place at the City Center. In 1982 the Joffrey began to move its base of operations to Los Angeles, but the company still continues to present an annual City Center season.

Arpino's works dominate the repertory. For more than a decade his youthful, free-spirited *Trinity* (1971) served as the company's signature piece. Opinions remain sharply divided about the merits of Arpino's flashy, purposefully lightweight works.

Much of the rest of the repertory is devoted to early twentieth-century classics. The Joffrey has a large number of Ashton ballets, including *Façade* and *A Wedding Bouquet*. Several of the Diaghilev works, notably *Parade,* can also be seen. Kurt Jooss's *The Green Table* is a regular in the repertory as well.

Joffrey himself rarely choreographs. His *Astarte* (1967) has been called the first mixed-media ballet. It used television, gigantic projections and rock music to create a new contemporary look.

Twyla Tharp choreographed her first major ballet, *Deuce Coupe,* to pop songs by the Beach Boys in 1973. Other figures from experimental dance, such as Laura Dean and the collective known as Pilobolus, have mounted works on the Joffrey. The company also performs Cranko's full-length *The Taming of the Shrew.*

Two other important ballet companies currently operating in New York are the Dance Theatre of Harlem and the Eliot Feld Ballet. Harlem is America's first all-black classical company. Founded in 1968 and still directed by Arthur Mitchell (b 1934), the company has a repertory of Balanchine ballets and modern works by Tetley, Taras and others. In 1984 Harlem staged Mitchell's version of *Giselle*. Pre-

Robert Joffrey's City Center Ballet rapidly grew in size after its foundation and has now become one of the most important of the small companies.

serving the traditional choreography, Mitchell transferred the locale to the American South. The result is a ballet that both suits the company and enhances the audience's understanding of a nineteenth-century classic.

Eliot Feld (b 1943) was a dancer with American Ballet Theatre when he began choreographing. *Harbinger* (1967) and *At Midnight* (1969) were immensely successful at ABT. He founded his own troupe in 1969 and continues to direct this small ensemble (about 24 dancers). Feld's group is the resident company of the Joyce Theater, NY, a medium-sized dance house that opened in the early 1980s.

Other major classical companies are spread out across the country. San Francisco Ballet is the oldest and one of the most vigorous. Its former director, Michael Smuin, gave the company a high profile with his elaborate productions of *Romeo and Juliet* (1976) and *The Tempest* (1980). His *A Song for Dead Warriors* (1977) was a highly theatricalized saga of the American Indian in modern society. Other major companies include the Pennsylvania Ballet, the Boston Ballet, Ballet West in Salt Lake City, Utah, and the Washington Ballet, a small troupe that has undergone dramatic changes thanks to popular resident choreographer Choo San Goh (b 1948). Like Feld, Goh is one of the most prolific and generally respected of the younger generation of choreographers.

Throughout the country there are literally hundreds of companies, ranging from solid, professional organizations to university groups and semiprofessional or even amateur civic ballets. Many of these companies are members of the National Association for Regional Ballet, which is dedicated to promoting dance at the local level.

GEORGE WASHINGTON SMITH
1820–99

George Washington Smith, who was born in Philadelphia and – like Durang – did most of his work there, began his theatrical career as a child clog dancer.

In 1840 he joined Fanny Elssler's touring company, eventually dancing in some productions as her partner, and also taking the opportunity to study further with her regular partner, James Sylvain. By the time Elssler left, Smith was the leading American male dancer of his time. In 1846 he became the first American Albrecht, in a performance of *Giselle* in Boston.

He was appointed principal dancer and ballet master at the New York Bowery Theater in 1847, and in 1850 moved to Brougham's Lyceum Theater where he staged (and appeared in) several Romantic ballets. Following his engagement at the Lyceum he toured the country with Lola Montez, then spent some years as a freelance choreographer with many companies (including the Ronzani Ballet, where he worked with Enrico Cecchetti). His last position was as ballet master at Fox's American Theater in Philadelphia, where he also opened a school.

Smith's son Joseph (1875–1932) later became one of America's best-known choreographers for musicals.

AUGUSTA MAYWOOD
1825–76

Augusta Maywood, the first American ever to challenge the best European dancers on their own ground, was the daughter of two English actors. Her mother and father (Henry August Williams) were divorced in 1828 and when Mrs Williams remarried another Englishman, Robert Maywood, her two daughters took their stepfather's name.

Robert Maywood was manager of the Chestnut Street Theater in Philadelphia, and from the beginning it was clear that the older child, Mary Elizabeth, would follow in the family's dramatic tradition. Augusta, however, was sent to the Hazards' ballet school when she was 10. She proved to be so talented that within two years she was pronounced ready to make her debut.

On 30 December 1837, 'La Petite Augusta' (a reference to Mlle Augusta, the popular German ballerina) appeared as Zelica, the leading role in *The Maid of Cashmere* – an adaptation of Filippo Taglioni's *Le Dieu et la Bayadère*. Appearing in the same production was another of the Hazard's pupils, Mary Ann Lee. The performance was a tremendous success, and the two girls were the talk of the city. A while later in New York Maywood again attracted enthusiastic attention with her appearances as Zelica, and as Dew Drop in *The Mountain Sylph* (an American version of *La Sylphide*).

On 1 May 1838 the 13-year-old Augusta set out for Paris – closely chaperoned by her mother, who was determined to guard her from the (very real) temptations of the Opéra. For a year she worked hard with Mazilier and Coralli. Her debut in 1839 – in a special *pas de deux* with Charles Mabille in *Le Diable Boiteux* – received excellent reviews. Her appearances in *La Tarentule*, *Nina*, *La Fille Mal Gardée* and *Le Diable Amoureux* were equally successful.

One day at the end of the summer of 1839 the young girl disappeared, and it was several days before her frantic mother discovered that she had eloped with Mabille. The couple had planned to sail to England, marry in Gretna Green and find work in London – but Augusta, being a minor, had no passport and they were escorted back to Paris in disgrace. A few weeks later, however, Mrs Maywood succumbed to her daughter's pleading and the two were married.

In May 1840 Maywood and Mabille left the Opéra and began an engagement in Marseille. Their daughter, Cécile Augusta, was born in January 1842. For the first half of 1843 they danced in Lyon, then accepted a long engagement at the São Carlos Opera in Lisbon. In 1845 Augusta left abruptly, without her husband or child. She was pregnant again, and both knew the child could not possibly be his. They obtained a legal separation, but remained on good terms, accepting a lucrative joint engagement at the Kaertnerthor Theater in Vienna without hesitation.

In Vienna Maywood got off to a rather slow start (her reviews in *Giselle* were not as good as Fanny Elssler's), but in the two years she remained in the city her popularity steadily increased. She also began teaching and had a third child – by yet a third man.

In 1847 she left Vienna for La Scala

in Milan, and the next 12 years, which she spent touring in Italy, represented the high point of her career. A program from La Scala for an 1853 production of *L'Arabia* lists her as *prima ballerina assoluta* – the highest rank possible – and her speed and spirited technique captured enthusiastic audiences all over Italy, in Venice, Trieste, Bologna, Rome, Padua, Ancona and Viterbo.

At last Maywood got tired of having to depend on the often unreliable managers of local theaters and became the first dancer ever to form her own touring company – complete with a *corps de ballet*, costumes, props and music.

In 1858 Mabille died and Maywood was free to marry her current lover, a charming, cultured Italian from Bologna named Carlo Gardini. In 1859 they settled in Vienna, Maywood's favorite city, and she retired from the stage to open a ballet school.

In June 1864 Maywood gave birth to a son, who died within a few hours. Shortly after, Gardini – who claimed the child had not been his – returned to Italy where he eventually opened his own school in Sasso-Marconi. In Vienna Maywood continued to operate her establishment very successfully; she also choreographed several pieces and worked as ballet mistress at local theaters.

When she fatally contracted smallpox at the age of 51, however, her death went unnoticed by her thousands of former admirers.

MIKHAIL MIKHAILOVICH MORDKIN
1880–1944

Mikhail Mordkin, one of the pioneers of American ballet, graduated from the ballet academy in Moscow in 1899. He joined the Bolshoi as a soloist and soon became the company's ballet master.

In 1909 he joined Diaghilev in Paris for his first season, then set out on tour with Pavlova. He also was a member of the All-Star Imperial Russian Ballet, a group (including Geltzer, Lopukova, Idzikowsky and Volinine) that toured the United States in 1911–12.

Following his engagement Mordkin returned to Moscow in 1912 and remained in Russia through the Revolution. He returned to the USA in 1923. By 1924 he was firmly established in New York. In 1926 he organized the Mordkin Ballet, but the company lasted only a short time and he turned to freelance choreography and teaching. His training and experience were greatly needed in the development of the young American ballet movement. In 1937 he was able to reestablish his company, which then became the basis for Ballet Theatre in 1939.

ADOLF BOLM
1884–1951

Adolf Bolm was born in St Petersburg and studied at the Imperial Ballet Academy there, with Karsavina and Legat. He joined the company at the Maryinsky after his graduation in 1903 and became a soloist in 1910.

In 1908–09 he organized Pavlova's first tours and accompanied her on her travels. His dancing in Ballets Russes's first performance in Paris, in the Cossak Dance from *Prince Igor*, was one of the highlights of the evening. In 1911 he officially resigned from the Maryinsky and travelled with Diaghilev's troupe around Europe, to South America, and even to the United States.

After Ballets Russes's second American tour in 1917, Bolm stayed behind and organized Adolf Bolm Ballet Intime – in addition to teaching, choreographing and producing new ballets, and arranging dances for productions at the Metropolitan Opera in New York.

Moving west in the early 1920s, Bolm became ballet master and *premier danseur* at the Chicago Civic Opera. In 1924 he founded Chicago Allied Arts, Inc; the company lasted three years, with Ruth Page as prima ballerina.

Following a brief stay in Buenos Aires at the Colón Opera in 1928, Bolm moved to Hollywood, where he choreographed ballets for several movies including *The Mad Genius, The Men in Her Life* and *The Life of Cellini*. In 1933 he joined the San Francisco Opera company, which he had helped organize, as guest choreographer and ballet master.

In 1939 Bolm returned to New York to help Ballet Theater prepare for its opening season; his version of *Peter and the Wolf* (1940) was very successful. He served as ballet master in 1942–43. The last work he choreographed for the group was *The Firebird* (1945), which starred Markova and Dolin.

He then retired to Hollywood, where he taught and worked on his memoirs. He is remembered today as one of the most influential figures in the early development of twentieth-century ballet in America.

MARQUIS GEORGE DE CUEVAS
1885–1961

The fascinating Marquis de Cuevas (whose original title was the Marquis de Piedrablanca de Guana de Cuevas) was a Chilean nobleman of Spanish descent. He lived his life in the grand manner of the nineteenth-century aristocrat, with flamboyant style, impeccable manners and even several (ultimately harmless) duels. His marriage to John D Rockefeller's granddaughter provided the means for indulging his grand passion – ballet – in suitable style: he owned his own private company.

In 1944 the International Ballet, the Marquis's first company, made its debut in New York. It lasted only one season, but in 1947 the Marquis decided to try again. This time he bought the Nouveau Ballet de Monte Carlo, changed its name to Le Grand Ballet du Marquis de Cuevas, added several works from International Ballet's repertory and took the troupe on the road.

Le Grand Ballet de Marquis de Cuevas was the first European company to include a strong contingent of American dancers and choreographers; Rosella Hightower, Maria Tallchief, Dollar and George Skibene are just a few of the famous dancers who appeared with the company. De Cuevas would have only the best and under his directorship the company flourished, appearing in most countries in the western world.

The Marquis died in 1961 after financing a spectacular production of *The Sleeping Beauty*. Like Ballets Russes, his company was too much his own creation to survive him for long.

THE CHRISTENSEN BROTHERS

Dedication to ballet often seems to run in families, including the Vestris family, the Prices, The Bournonvilles, the Sallés, the Elssler sisters and, of course, the Taglionis. In America the three Christensen brothers, William (b 1902), Harold (b 1904) and Lew (b 1909), have been instrumental in the development of ballet, especially in the West.

All three brothers were born in Brigham City, Utah, where their father was a violinist and conductor. They studied dance with their uncle (a ballet instructor in Salt Lake City), with Stefano Mascagno, and then with Luigi Albertieri – Cechetti's adopted son and one of his favorite pupils.

William began his career on the vaudeville circuit, dancing in a quartet that also included his brother Lew. In 1932 he stopped touring and moved to Portland, Oregon, where he opened a ballet school; the small company he was able to establish eventually grew into the Portland Ballet. William joined the San Francisco Opera Ballet as a soloist in 1937 and by the next year had become the company's ballet master and chief choreographer, a position he held for the next 20 years. In 1941 he founded the San Francisco Ballet – a group that has produced many excellent American dancers. Ten years later he was offered a position as professor at the University of Utah, in Salt Lake City, where he began – and for 20 years ran – their school of ballet and choreography. He also established the Utah Civic Ballet in 1952; by 1963 it had become a fully professional company, Ballet West, with William as its artistic director. A prolific choreographer, his long list of ballets for various companies includes: *Crown of Joy* (to Mendelssohn's 'Italian' Symphony); *Concerto* (to J S Bach's Violin Concerto in A Minor); *Caprice de Paris; Symphonia* (to Mozart's 'Hoffner' Symphony); and *La Fille Naive*. He also has produced many classic works like *Coppélia, Swan Lake* and *The Nutcracker*.

Harold, the middle brother, moved to New York and continued his studies at Balanchine's American Ballet School, eventually joining the company and also dancing for the Metropolitan Opera. Between 1936 and 1940 he was a member of Ballet Caravan, creating some important roles like the Motorist in Lew's landmark ballet, *Filling Station*. In 1941 he returned to San Francisco to join William's new company, the San Francisco Ballet, also dancing for the Opera Ballet there. In 1946 he retired from the stage to devote his time to teaching, as director of the San Francisco Ballet School.

Lew, the youngest, joined American

Ballet in 1935, and danced the title role in Balanchine's *Apollo*. As soloist, ballet master and choreographer for Ballet Caravan (1936–40) he created *Filling Station* (1938), which has become an American classic. During the 1941–42 season he was a soloist for Dance Players and the San Francisco Opera ballet. After serving in the army for the rest of World War II, he returned to New York. There he became a soloist and ballet master for Ballet Society (1946–48), remaining as ballet master when the troupe became the New York City Ballet. In 1952, when William accepted his new job in Utah, Lew took over as director and principal choreographer for the San Francisco Ballet. During his stage career many considered him to be the best *premier danseur* produced in America during the twentieth century. His ballets include *Pocahantas* (1936), *Jinx* (1942), *Con Amore* (1953) and many works for the San Francisco Ballet.

GEORGE BALANCHINE
b 1904–83

George Balanchine, the apparently ageless choreographer who has been a towering figure in American ballet for almost half a century, was christened Georgi Melitonovitch Balanchivadze. Both his father and mother were composers, and even as a child he was a skilled musician; it was his sister who wanted to become a dancer.

When his sister was scheduled for an audition at the Imperial Ballet Academy in St Petersburg, young George (who had just failed to be admitted to the Naval Academy) was sent to accompany her. There he was noticed by Olga Preobrajenska – who decided to admit him and not the girl. Becoming a dancer was the furthest thing from Balanchine's mind, and he immediately ran away from home. He was found, of course, and sent back to the academy, where he remained rebellious and supremely uninterested in dance until his first stage appearance – as Cupid in a production of *Sleeping Beauty*. That experience prompted an immediate about-face, and from then on he was devoted to his profession.

Balanchine studied both at the ballet academy and at the Conservatory of Music during the difficult years of World War I and then the Revolution, graduat-

George Balanchine rehearses Marjorie Tallchief.

ing with honors in 1921. By 1923 he already had developed an interest in choreographing pure dance (as opposed to 'story' ballets), and was dissatisfied with what he considered the stifling creative atmosphere in Leningrad. In 1924 he and several other dancers – including his first wife Tamara Gevergeva, Alexandra Danilova and Nicholas Efimov – were made part of a small touring group called the Soviet State Dancers. As soon as they reached Western Europe the four left the company and joined Diaghilev.

Soon Balanchine had become, with Massine, one of Ballets Russes's chief choreographers; his first production for the company, *Le Chant du Rossignol* (*The Nightingale*, 1946), marked the debut of the English ballerina Alicia Markova. Some of his other important ballets from this period include the rowdy *Barabou* (1925), *The Triumph of Neptune* (1926), and *Jack in the Box* and *Pastorale* (both 1927). His ballet *Apollo* (1928) was the beginning of a long, productive collaboration with Stravinsky. The last years with Diaghilev also produced: *The Gods Go A' Begging* (1928), to music by Handel arranged by Sir Thomas Beecham; *Le Bal* (1929), designed by the Italian painter de Chirico; and the powerful *Le Fils Prodigue*, to music by Prokofiev and starring Serge Lifar.

After Ballets Russes dissolved, Balanchine spent six months in Copenhagen (August 1929–January 1930). He did not

effect the immediate revolution in the Royal Danish Ballet that management had hoped for, but he was a great inspiration to many members of the company, including Harald Lander.

In 1932 he helped organize Ballets Russes de Monte Carlo, producing ballets like *Cotillion* (1932), and *Mozartiana*, *Errante* and *Seven Deadly Sins* (all 1933). But by the time Kirstein approached him in 1933 concerning beginning a company in America, he had begun to have serious differences of opinion with the management. He accepted the offer, and soon his initial skepticism had given way to enthusiasm.

The American Ballet, which was formally opened on New Year's Day 1934, did not have a smooth path to follow. Until the end of World War II, Balanchine picked up all the extra work he could find: at the Metropolitan Opera (until some more conservative members of the audience objected to his sophisticated offerings); and – with greater success – on Broadway and in Hollywood. Still, those first, difficult years saw the production of several important ballets, including *Serenade* (1934), the crisp *Concerto Barocco* and the opulent *Ballet Imperial* (both 1941). When Ballet Society moved to New York City Center in 1948 it was the end of many years of instability and the beginning of Balanchine's long tenure as America's premier choreographer. His ballets may sometimes be uneven, but they are always original – and his best works, like *Agon*, *Bugaku* and *Liebslieder Waltzer*, are extraordinary.

Margot Fonteyn and John Gilpin in Night Shadow.

Balanchine is primarily associated with 'abstract' ballets which celebrate dance alone, depicting moods and relationships rather than telling stories. ('Why should we do Shakespeare?' he demands. 'Shakespeare has already done Shakespeare.') Nevertheless, he has produced some dramatic ballets with great success – including *Le Baiser de la Fée* and *Don Quixote, La Somnambula (Night Shadow), A Midsummer Night's Dream* and *Coppélia*.

In addition to his aversion to the star system, which he feels subverts dance in favor of the performer, Balanchine is known for his predisposition toward women. It is a trait he readily admits: 'In my ballets, woman is first. . . . Ballet, for me, is a feminine form.'

In his choreography, which he describes as a skill, not a mysterious artistic process, he has taken the classic Russian technique – itself a combination of the French, Italian and Danish schools – and transformed it into something uniquely American – long-legged, athletic, brilliant and democratic. His work has already ensured him a place among the most important figures in the long history of ballet. He died in 1983.

RUTH PAGE
b 1905

Ruth Page, whose name is synonymous with 'ballet' in Chicago, was born in Indianapolis, Indiana, and began studying dance professionally in 1917 when she was 12 years old. By 1918 she was touring in South America with Pavlova's company, and in 1919 created the title role in Bolm's *Birthday of the Infanta*.

From the 1920s to the early 1950s she danced all over the world, and her tours made her one of the best-known American ballerinas. She began choreographing while she was ballet mistress and prima ballerina for the Chicago Summer Opera (1929–33). One of her most famous works, *Frankie and Johnny*, was first performed at the Chicago Federal Theater in 1938. Later she became known for her adaptations of operas. These include: *Susanna and the Barber* (Rossini's *Barber of Seville*, 1955); *Camille* (Verdi's *La Traviata*, 1957); *Carmen* (1959); *Die Fledermaus* (1960); *Pygmalion* (Suppe's *Die Schöne Galathée*, 1961); *Bullets or Bon Bons* (Oscar Strauss's *The Chocolate Soldier*, 1965); and *Mephistophela* (*Faust*, 1966).

For over half a century she has been the leading figure in ballet in Chicago, from her appearances in the Chicago Allied Arts Performances (1924–26) and with the Ravinia Opera Company (1926–31) to her long association with the Chicago Lyric Opera and her own ballet companies. In addition she can be credited with introducing the first jazz ballet, the first black ballet, the first ballet by Aaron Copeland and for arranging Rudolf Nureyev's first appearance in America.

LUCIA CHASE
b 1907–86

Lucia Chase studied ballet with many of the top teachers of her time, including Mordkin, Fokine, Tudor, Vilzak and Nijinska. She was a ballerina with the Mordkin Ballet in 1938-39.

Possessed of a great love for the dance, she never hesitated to use her large private fortune in the service of the art. But more than this, it was her enormous zest, energy and clear-sightedness that has made the American Ballet Theatre (which she and Oliver Smith founded in 1940) one of the two top companies in America today – and have given her the well-deserved title, 'First Lady' of American ballet.

WILLIAM DOLLAR
b 1907–86

William Dollar, who emerged as another of America's best-known male dancers in the 1930s and 1940s, was born in St Louis,

Lucia Chase, Agnes de Mille and Annabelle Lyon in de Mille's Three Virgins and a Devil.

Missouri. He received his training from Fokine, Mordkin, Balanchine, Pierre Vladimirov and Volinine.

From leading dancer at the Philadelphia Opera Ballet he went on to work with American Ballet (1936–37), Ballet Theater (1940), Ballet Caravan (1941) and The New Opera Company (1942). He also danced with the International Ballet, Ballet Society, Grand Ballet de Monte Carlo and Grand Ballet du Marquis de Cuevas.

Dollar has made significant contributions to ballet abroad as well. For example, he helped establish a state ballet school in Teheran, Iran; worked as guest choreographer and ballet master at Teatro Municipal in Rio de Janeiro, Brazil; and also was connected with the Paris-based touring company, Le Theatre d'Art du Ballet. Two of his best-known ballets are *Constanzia* (1944) and *Le Combat* (1949).

LINCOLN KIRSTEIN
b 1907

Lincoln Kirstein, one of the most influential figures on both the American and international ballet scenes, was the Harvard-educated son of a wealthy family.

As a young man he was responsible for persuading George Balanchine to emigrate to America in 1933 and for founding the American Ballet. Since then he has remained in the forefront of ballet activity in the United States – as director of American Ballet and now the New York City Ballet, as founder of Ballet Caravan and Ballet Society, and as founder of the periodical *Dance Index* (which he edited, 1946–48).

Kirstein also is the author of several important books on the art and history of ballet, including *Dance* (1935), *Ballet Alphabet* (1939), *The Classic Ballet* (1952), *Movement and Metaphor* (1969) and *Nijinsky Dancing* (1975).

AGNES DE MILLE
b 1909

Agnes de Mille is the daughter of writer-director William C de Mille and her uncle was the famous movie magnate Cecil B de Mille.

De Mille toured extensively as a recital dancer between 1928 and 1942, but it is

Agnes de Mille in Stage Fright.

as a choreographer that she is best known. She was one of the first to introduce 'Americanisms' into the academic ballet vocabulary and her *Rodeo* (1942) and *Fall River Legend* (1948) are now ranked among the best American ballets. Some of her other works are *Obeah Black Ritual* (1940), *Drums Sound in Hackensack* (1941), *Tally Ho* (1944), *The Harvest According* (1952), *The Bitter Wierd* (1962), *The Wind in the Mountains* (1965) and *A Rose for Miss Emily* (1970).

She also has choreographed many popular musicals, including *Oklahoma* (1943, film version 1955), *One Touch of Venus* (1943), *Bloomer Girl* (1944), *Carousel* (1945), *Brigadoon* (1947), *Gentlemen Prefer Blondes* (1949) and *Paint Your Wagon* (1951).

She is the author of six books (the latest is *Dance in America*, 1980) and many articles. These, plus her many television appearances and lecture/demonstrations, have made her one of the leading spokeswomen for dance in America today.

ANTONY TUDOR
b 1908

Antony Tudor, a native Londoner whose original name was William Cook, did not begin studying ballet until he was 19,

when he began training with Marie Rambert. A clerk in Smithfield Market (London's huge meat market), he had seen performances by Pavlova and Ballets Russes and had determined to become a dancer himself.

By 1930 he had joined Rambert's company as both a dancer and as her assistant, and the next few years saw a rapid shift of interest from dancing to choreography. Some of his most important works date from his association with Rambert: *Cross-Gater'd* (1931); *The Planets* (1934); *The Descent of Hebe* (1935); and two acknowledged masterpieces, *Jardin aux Lilas* (*Lilac Garden*, 1936) and *Dark Elegies* (1937).

In 1938 Tudor and Hugh Laing formed the short-lived London Ballet, which soon merged with Ballet Rambert; in 1940 the two moved to New York where, for the next 10 years, Tudor worked for Ballet Theater. *Pillar of Fire* (1942), *Romeo and Juliet* and *Dim Lustre* (both 1943), *Undertow* (1945) and *Shadow of the Wind* (1948) were the major ballets he composed for the company.

During the 1950s and early 1960s Tudor worked for the Royal Swedish Ballet (1940–50 and 1963–64), as director of the Metropolitan Opera Ballet School, and as a member of the faculty of the Julliard School of Music – a position he has continued to hold since 1952.

Antony Tudor's The Leaves are Fading, *ABT*.

Since the mid-1960s he has travelled extensively all over the world, restaging old ballets and creating new ones like *Shadowplay* (1967), *Knight Errant* (1968), *The Divine Horseman* (1969), and *Fandango* and *Cereus* (both 1972). In 1974 he became Associate Director of American Ballet Theatre.

Tudor has been called 'the choreographer of sorrow.' Unlike Balanchine, who explores movement for its own sake, Tudor uses movement to reveal innermost feelings and thoughts. The combination of psychology and social comment in *Lilac Garden*, the portrayal of grief in *Dark Elegies*, and the study of desire and jealousy in *Pillar of Fire* have added hitherto undiscovered dimensions to ballet. His powerful, introspective works have had an especially profound influence on American ballet, but they also have been milestones in the development of narrative ballet as a whole.

JEROME ROBBINS
b 1918

In addition to ballet, Jerome Robbins studied modern, Spanish and Oriental dance, and he has combined these elements with other forms like show dancing, jazz and tap to arrive at a style that is intensely personal and very American.

In 1940 he joined Ballet Theater and his first piece for that company, the lighthearted *Fancy Free* (1944), was an immediate hit. Since then he has worked with many other companies (from American Ballet Theatre and New York City Ballet to the Royal Danish Ballet and Ballet Russe de Monte Carlo). His ballets range from bouncy combinations of classic and popular dance like *Interplay* (1945); psychology in *Age of Anxiety* (1950); the narcissism of dancers themselves in *Afternoon of a Faun* (1953); and the morbid side of man's mind in *The Cage* (1951). *Moves* (1959) was a striking ballet – performed without music.

Robbins also has worked extensively on Broadway and in Hollywood, and has a long list of successful productions to his credit. These include *On the Town* (1945), *The King and I* (1951), *West Side Story* (1957), *Gypsy* (1959) and *Fiddler on the Roof* (1964).

His work has had – and continues to have – a great influence on American dance, not only in the academic ballet setting, but in the popular realm as well. Robbins returned to New York City Bal-

let in 1969. Since Balanchine's death in 1983, Robbins has shared the running of the company with Peter Martins. Among the many works from this second NYCB period are the monumental *Dances at a Gathering* (1969), Bach's *Goldberg Variations* (1971), Ravel's *In G Major* (1975) and Prokofiev's *Opus 19/The Dreamer*, choreographed in 1979 for Baryshnikov. In *Glass Pieces* (1984), Robbins used music by avant-garde composer Philip Glass. In *Brahms/Haydn* (1985), he and modern choreographer Twyla Tharp collaborated jointly.

JOHN TARAS
b 1919

John Taras began his dancing career at the age of nine when he appeared with a Ukranian folk-dance ensemble, and choreographed his first piece when he was 13. He began studying ballet seriously in 1936, working with Rokine, Vilzak and Schollar, and at the American Ballet School. In 1940 he danced with Ballet Caravan; when that company folded in 1941 he worked for a time with the Littlefield Ballet in Philadelphia.

Jerome Robbins's popular comic ballet The Concert. *first performed by NYCB in 1956.*

From 1946–48 he was associated with Ballet Theater, for which he also choreographed *Graziana*. He then appeared with various companies, including Ballet Society and Original Ballet Russe, until 1948 when he joined the Grand Ballet du

Robbins's beautiful version of Afternoon of a Faun.

Rosella Hightower at her school in Cannes.

Young students prepare for class at Hightower's school.

Marquis de Cuevas. Since 1959 he has been ballet master of the New York City Ballet; he also has had guest engagements with many of the world's best companies and has staged a number of Balanchine's ballets abroad.

In 1985 Taras returned to American Ballet Theatre as an associate director.

ROSELLA HIGHTOWER
b 1920

Rosella Hightower, born in Ardmore, Oklahoma, followed in Augusta Maywood's footsteps as a major American dancer who spent the best years of her career dancing in Europe.

Following an engagement with Ballet Russe de Monte Carlo (1938–41), Hightower spent the war years in America, with Ballet Theatre (1941–45).

In 1947 she joined Nouveau Ballet de Monte Carlo, remaining with the company through its transformation into Grand Ballet du Marquis de Cuevas. When the Marquis died and the company disbanded in 1961 she retired, and has since made only occasional guest appearances. She continues to teach regularly abroad, however – especially for Ballet of the Twentieth Century, of which her daughter Dominique Robier is a member.

She was artistic director of the Paris Opéra Ballet from 1981 to 1983. Her productions there included new stagings of *The Sleeping Beauty* and *The Nutcracker*. After leaving Paris, Hightower returned to her highly respected school in Cannes.

GEORGE SKIBINE
1920–81

George Skibine's father, Boris, was a member of Diaghilev's *corps de ballet*, and thus the young man had easy access to the best teachers during his formative years – including Preograjenska, Lifar and Fokine.

After engagements with Ballets Russe de Monte Carlo (1938–39), Colonel de Basil's Ballet Russe (1939–41), and Ballet Theater (1941–42), Skibine joined the US Army. For the rest of World War II (1942–45) he worked in Combat Intelligence, where he made top sergeant and was awarded the Bronze Star, five campaign medals and two Bronze Arrowheads.

Above: Tallchief and Skibine in Daphnis and Chloë.   Right: Marjorie Tallchief as Ariadne, Harkness.

When the war was over Skibene decided not to return to ballet, and in 1946 Sol Hurok found him working as interpreter and secretary to a New York art dealer. He was soon convinced to start dancing again – this time for the Markova-Dolin company.

In 1947 Skibene married the talented ballerina Marjorie Tallchief, who was noted for the expressiveness and elasticity of her dancing, and the two appeared with Ruth Page's Chicago Ballet. In 1957 they were made *danseurs étoiles* at the Paris Opéra, and from 1958—62 Skibine directed the company. From 1964–66 he was artistic director for the Harkness Ballet. Since 1969 he has been artistic director of the Dallas Civic Ballet, while his wife teaches in the city.

Skibine's elegance and handsome, romantic appearance, combined with considerable technical ability, made him a popular dancer during his stage career. In addition he has choreographed many ballets, including *Tragédie à Verone* (1950), *Annabel Lee* and *The Prisoner of the Caucasus* (both 1951), *Idylle* (1954), *Romeo and Juliet* (1955), *Daphnis and Chloë* (1959), *Les Noces* (1962), *Bacchus and Ariadne* (1964), *The Firebird* (1967), *Les Banderlog* (1969) and *Carmina Burana* (1970).

Maria Tallchief, sister to Marjorie, was New York City Ballet's leading ballerina.

MARIA TALLCHIEF
b 1925

Maria Tallchief was born in Fairfax, Oklahoma; with her sister Marjorie, she was one of the first native Americans to win international recognition in ballet. She studied with Ernest Belcher, Nijinska, Lichine and at the American Ballet Theatre school.

At first Tallchief had a difficult time deciding whether to become a ballerina or a concert pianist, but an appearance in the Hollywood Bowl when she was 15 (in Nijinska's *Chopin Concerto*) swung the balance in favor of dance.

During World War II she toured with Ballet Russe de Monte Carlo, and in the summer of 1947 she accompanied Balanchine to the Paris Opéra (they were married from 1946–52). Later in 1947 Tallchief joined Ballet Society, and then became the New York City Ballet's leading ballerina, appearing in almost all of Balanchine's ballets. She left in 1965, however, remarking that while she did not object to being listed alphabetically in the program, she was very tired of getting her roles assigned that way. Since 1966 she has lived in Chicago. In the late 1970s she began a company which is now known as Chicago City Ballet. The repertory is composed mainly of Balanchine classics and works by resident choreographer Paul Mejia (husband of New York City Ballet star Suzanne Farrell). Before her retirement in 1987, Farrell was a frequent guest star with the company.

In her prime Tallchief was considered the best technician America ever produced. The Capezio Dance Award which she received in 1965 reads, 'Her artistry which encompasses superb technical discipline, command of style and arresting individuality, is admired, respected and applauded around the world. Thus, as an American ballerina, she has brought luster to American ballet itself, and has contributed immeasurably in placing it on an equal footing with the ballet standard of those European cultures which first nurtured the art of ballet.'

GLEN TETLEY
b 1926

Glen Tetley fully intended becoming a doctor. He studied premedicine at Franklin and Marshall College in Lancaster, Pennsylvania, and was enrolled in Col-

Glen Tetley rehearsing his ballet The Tempest *for Ballet Rambert.*

umbia Medical School when he started studying modern dance with Hanya Holm.

From 1946–51 he danced with Holm's company, and also served as her assistant for several Broadway productions – in the meantime obtaining a Bachelor of Science degree from New York University (1948). Beginning in 1949 he also studied classic dance with Margaret Craske and Antony Tudor.

An outstanding performer in both genres, Tetley danced with the New York City Opera (1952–54), the John Butler Company (1955), the Joffrey Ballet (1956–

57), Martha Graham's company (1958) and American Ballet Theatre (1960). In 1962 he moved to Europe and joined the Netherland Dance Theater. Eventually he became artistic codirector of the troupe (with van Manen) – a position he held until 1970.

As John Cranko's successor at the Stuttgart Ballet (1974–76), Tetley was able to maintain the momentum that Cranko had established. His ballets – cool, enigmatic and aloof – had previously been strictly in the modern idiom, but since the mid-1970s he has begun to allow elements of classicism to creep in.

MODER

DANCE

Glen Tetley's avant-garde ballet Mutations parts of which are performed in the nude, danced by the Netherlands Dance Theater.

Alwin Nikolais' avant-garde ballet Imago, *which demonstrates his love of striking shapes in costumes and scenery.*

THE PIONEERS

The history of ballet is the story of organizations, movements, and traditions, of companies, theaters and trends, as well as individuals. Modern dance, on the other hand, is almost entirely the story of personalities, of dancers, who devise their own philosophies and set their own, unique styles, passing them on to their students who then break away to create something new and just as personal. Thus, studying the history of modern dance is rather like tracing the story of an extended family through several generations.

Modern dance began in America early in the twentieth century when the precursors of the artists we know today began their own rebellions against both the formality and artifice of ballet and the banality of popular show dancing of the period. Their techniques and styles were very different; what they had in common was a dissatisfaction with the options then available to dancers and the ultimate goal of conveying to their audiences a sense of inner and outer reality – an aim that still inspires modern dancers today.

LOIE FULLER (1862–1928) had no formal dance training, but developed her distinctive style by herself. Her dance technique was only minimal; instead she manipulated clouds of swirling gauze or tulle under colored lights to achieve kinetic sculptural effects. She never told a story in her pieces, preferring to create moods or depict natural phenomena like flowers, insects, or fire, in six- to seven-minute dance segments.

Following a modestly successful engagement in Chicago, Fuller saved enough money to sail for Europe, appearing first in Germany and then in a 45-minute program at the Folies Bergère in Paris. There she was an immediate hit; she soon became known as the 'intellectuals' dancer' because of her many admirers like Anatole France and William Butler Yeats. In 1900 a special theater was constructed for her at the Paris World's Fair.

Fuller's two most famous dances were her first, *The Serpentine Dance*, composed in 1891, and *Ballet of Light*. Her last work, *L'Escalier Monumental*, was produced just before her retirement in 1925.

Though she left no technique and established no school, Fuller set a lasting example in the use of stagecraft. Her use of lighting was revolutionary; she mixed her own colors; experimented with phosphorescent salts, and used avant garde techniques like indirect lighting from beneath the stage. According to Isadora Duncan, who worked with her in Paris for a time, she had many imitators, but no equals. The stage effects she created were not matched in the annals of modern dance until the arrival of Alwin Nikolais in the 1950s.

ISADORA DUNCAN (1878–1927) still has a great appeal today – so much so that the reality of Duncan the dancer and the legend of Isadora the free spirit have become hopelessly entangled. Her admirers present a picture of a sensitive, spiritual woman who made her entire life a tribute to love and art; her detractors depict an overweight nymphomaniac with dyed hair who drank too much. Neither view is important for our purposes; more to the point is Duncan's stature as one of the spiritual founders of modern dance, whose motivation – if not her technique – is still an important part of the genre today.

Duncan was born in San Francisco, where her mother raised her to recognize and appreciate good music. We know little about her early training. She herself declared that she first danced in her mother's womb; on a more mundane level, it is probable that she had at least a few ballet lessons. When she was in her teens she began making appearances as a showdancer in Chicago under the auspices of theatrical manager Augustin Daly. But while she was dancing on music hall stages and later at society parties in New York, she already saw herself as 'the spiritual daughter of Walt Whitman,'

Isadora Duncan's free style of dancing was a radical departure from anything previously seen.

Isadora Duncan had a great love of ancient Greece.

and the rediscoverer of dance itself.

By 1900 Duncan had saved enough money to get herself and her family to Europe on a cattle boat. In London she met with some success, spending her free time at the British Museum, absorbing Greek culture. In Paris she joined a touring group organized by Loie Fuller. She gave her first recital – and took her first lover – in Budapest. Once begun her career swung steadily upward, and she became increasingly popular. In 1904 she and her sister Elizaneth opened a school in Berlin. In 1905 she toured Russia, making a great impression on young Michael Fokine; she had great sympathy with the plight of the Russian serfs and after the Revolution returned frequently to the Soviet Union, opening another school there in 1921. In Paris she was surrounded by admirers – painters, sculptors and poets who showered praises upon her.

Despite her following in Europe, however, her return visits to America (in 1909, 1911, 1917 and 1922) were not very successful. However, this was more a reaction to her moral and political views than an aversion to her dancing.

Duncan's private life might even be considered unconventional by today's standards – and in a society just beginning to emerge from the Victorian Age it was a source of constant scandal. She was generous to a fault, with her money and her love as well as her art, and almost totally impractial; the magnificent home she decided to build in Greece for her family was almost complete before anyone realized that it was miles from the nearest water supply.

Her open espousal of free love and the right of a woman to bear children whenever and by whom she pleased caused the most gossip. Her three children (one of whom died in infancy) were the products of her open (indeed, well-publicized) affairs with E G Craig and the American millionaire Paris Singer. When she finally did marry in 1922 it was to Serge Essenin – a Russian poet 20 years her junior (who committed suicide in Paris a year later).

Duncan's dancing was so personal that it is almost impossible to reproduce today; her recitals were series of improvisations that were never systematized and seldom repeated. Simplicity was the keynote of her performances: she used a bare stage with only her famous blue curtains as a backdrop; her costumes were plain, often daring 'Greek' tunics or robes; her feet were bare (which was shocking in itself); and she used basic, everyday movements rather than high kicks, leaps and turns. But her music (by the likes of Wagner, Gluck, Beethoven and Tchaikovsky) had tremendous strength, and her art lay in her ability to emotionally visualize that music, as well as in her dynamic stage presence that could almost hypnotize an audience.

Her love of ancient Greece is shown in works like *Bacchus and Ariadne* (1901), *Orpheus* (1904), *Iphigenia in Aulis* (1905), *Oedipus* (1915) and *Iphigenia in Tauris* (1916). Her identification with the underdog who challenges the status quo is typified by one of her most stirring and successful pieces, *Marseillaise* (1915), and in *Marche Slav* (1917) – a powerful tribute to the Russian peasants' struggle for freedom.

Duncan believed that she was cursed by machines, and ironically, she and her children died in accidents involving automobiles. Dierdre and Patrick were waiting for her in a parked car in Paris when the brakes slipped and the car rolled over an embankment into the Seine; both were drowned. Duncan met her own death in an equally bizarre accident in Nice. She set out to go for a ride in an open car, saying gaily to her friends, 'Adieu, mes amis. Je vais à la gloire.' The car began to move, her long, floating scarf – which had caught in the spokes of the wheel – tightened, and her neck was broken instantly.

RUTH ST DENIS (1880–1968) and her husband/partner **TED SHAWN** (1891–1972) are the two great pioneers of modern dance who had the most direct influence on its future development in the United States.

St Denis began her career as a teenager, struggling along with minor parts in Broadway musicals and with small touring companies. One day in a drug store, in Buffalo, New York, she caught sight of an advertising poster for Egyptian Dieties cigarettes which showed a most unauthentic goddess sitting on a throne. Somehow that poster crystalized her own yearning for something more than the banal dancing she was doing, and inspired her to create her own, new kind of dancing. With the energy and single-mindedness that were to characterize all her interests for the rest of her life, she buried herself in research on ancient Egypt.

But before she could get the money together to produce *Egypta* she was – again, typically – sidetracked by a model of an East Indian village at Coney Island, which set her off on a new track. The result of this next obsession was *Radha*, the work that she always considered her greatest masterpiece. It was first performed at the New York Theater to music by Delibes in 1906.

Almost immediately St Denis left on a tour of Europe, which lasted three years and brought her great popularity in London, Paris and Berlin. Rather than staying to enjoy her triumph, like Fuller and Duncan, she returned to America in 1909, finally finished *Egypta*, and set out on her first big American tour.

Her 'Oriental' dance programs may not have been any more authentic than the cigarette poster had been, but audiences loved their combination of exotic mysticism and sensuality. St Denis herself had a slim figure, which she enhanced with seductive costumes, and a pretty face that could at times appear strikingly beautiful. Her hair, which turned snow white by the time she was 30, only added to her charm. She was an extraordinarily graceful dancer, with a back and arms so supple that a group of German doctors once asked to examine her – to see if her arms had bones like everyone else's. She was skilled at manipulating veils and scarves so that they seemed to be floating extension of her body. Despite her quite genuine interest in Eastern philosophy and metaphysics, she never let mysticism overshadow the realities of show business. As Murray Louis, who danced with her company when she was in her 60s put it, 'Half her life was spent with the gods, and the other half seemed to have been spent touring.'

Ted (Edwin Meyers) Shawn was in his third year as a theological student at the University of Denver when he contracted diptheria. His doctors cured the disease, but their treatment left him paralyzed from the waist down. The young man recovered the use of his limbs through sheer will power, and as soon as he could walk began taking dancing lessons to further strengthen his leg muscles. He first saw St Denis in 1911; by 1914 he was her pupil and rapidly became her partner, then her husband.

As a team, the two were unbeatable. Shawn was a good choreographer and dancer, whose sturdy, robust, clean-cut style provided an excellent counterpoint to St Denis's graceful, sinuous dancing. His love of spectacle and elaborate costumes matched her own. However, it was his organizational ability, tremendous capacity for work, and his determination to overcome every obstacle that really ensured their success and their place in history as major influences in the development of modern dance.

In 1915 the two opened their first Denishawn school in Los Angeles as Shawn had decided that they needed a base, as well as a supply of dancers – and a steady income. Denishawn existed from 1915–32 in one form or another, with frequent interruptions and even changes in name as one or the other partner went on tour, or left temporarily after a disagreement. Other Denishawn schools were franchised all over the country.

In many ways, Denishawn was as much a way of life as a school; there were many pet animals around, a tennis court and swimming pool for exercise, and as much time as possible was spent outdoors. The courses ran the gamut from classic ballet techniques to Oriental, Indian, native American and Spanish dancing. Shawn, convinced that well-educated dancers must be familiar with every form of the art, even imported Japanese sword dancers and Hawaiian hula

dancers. The school was the scene of constant experimentation, with dances set to poetry, percussion scores or nothing at all. Through all this activity Shawn functioned as the administrator and primary teacher. 'Miss Ruth,' as she became universally known, was a muse much more than an instructor and inspired a whole generation of dancers as if by magic. As a result of their efforts, the Denishawn company became the most popular and highest paid troupe in the United States.

In 1932 St Denis and Shawn finally parted company for good. St Denis went on tour with an all-female group, concentrating more and more on religious themes. She continued to be an active performer, teacher and lecturer until she was well into her 80s.

One of Shawn's principal concerns throughout his career was to dispel the

Ted Shawn performing his Eagle Dance.

notion that dancing was effeminate, and in 1933 he established an all-male troupe that toured the United States for seven years, attempting to prove his point. His farm, 'Jacobs Pillow,' in the Berkshire mountains of Massachusetts became the company's home base. Its weekly performances there began drawing full houses, and soon the Jacob's Pillow Summer School and Dance Festival – one of the most influential American modern dance centers – was born.

Shawn never stopped working, teaching and writing; his many books include *Ruth St Denis: Pioneer and Prophet, Gods Who Dance, Every Little Movement* and an autobiography, *One Thousand and One Night Stands*. He also was responsible for introducing many foreign companies and artists to America, including the National Ballet of Scotland, the Celtic Ballet of Scotland and Ballet Rambert. He was made a Knight of the Order of Danneborg for his work on behalf of the Royal Danish Ballet in the United States.

MAUDE ALLAN (1883–1956) was born in Toronto, where her parents both practiced medicine. However, since she spent most of her childhood in San Francisco, she always thought of herself as an American.

As a child she was trained as a musician. Later she became interested in Greek art, and dancing seemed a logical way to combine the two. One of her goals was to revive Greek classic dance – an interest she shared with Isadora Duncan, who had great influence on her work.

Allan made her debut in Vienna in 1903 with *The Vision of Salome* which remained her most popular presentation for the rest of her career. She was an overnight sensation in London (1907), Moscow and St Petersburg (1909), and the United States (1910). During the next 18 years she travelled all over the world, including South Africa, Asia, the Antipodes, South America, Egypt, Gibraltar and Malta.

Her speciality was 'free dancing,' performed to the light classics (like Grieg or Mendelssohn). Though she was entirely self-taught, her beauty, her graceful style, and the consistently high quality of her productions did much to attract enthusiastic audiences for modern dance.

In 1928 Allan settled in London and opened a school. She remained there for the rest of her life, even volunteering as an ambulance driver during the Battle of Britain – when she was almost 60.

THE FIRST GENERATION

Martha Graham's The Owl and the Pussycat *with Liza Minelli as the Narrator, Yuriko Kimura as the Pussycat and Tim Wengerd as the Owl.*

During the 1920s a passion for interpretive dancing swept America. Delsarte's studies of expressive gesture (well publicized by lecturer Genevieve Stebbins) and Dalcroze's Eurythmics (theories of movement and music) had school children, college students and society matrons all over the country performing a sort of simplified ballet in bare feet and flowing robes. Isadora Duncan's fame and Denishawn's tours had introduced audiences and dancers alike to the concept of a new form of serious theatrical dancing. The ground work had been laid for the first generation of modern dancers, who began developing the art as we know it today.

MARTHA GRAHAM (b 1894) was – and remains today – probably the single most influential figure in the history of modern dance. Her name has become synonymous with modern dance, and is recognized even by those who have never seen a performance. In addition, her work has been carried on and expanded by the extraordinary number of talented dancers and choreographers produced by her teaching methods – including Merce Cunningham, Erich Hawkins, Anna Sokolow and Paul Taylor.

Graham was born in Allegheny, Pennsylvania, and was raised in the Presbyterian faith and the Puritan tradition. Her strict upbringing is reflected in her work. The conflict between responsibility and personal desire appears in many of her pieces; she has bitterly attacked the sort of repression associated with Puritanism and, perhaps most important, she has always tried to tell the truth in her work – just as her father insisted she do as a child.

In 1914 the Graham family moved to Santa Barbara, California, and it was here that Graham, who was then in high school, first saw Ruth St Denis dance. She always had been interested in dancing, and now was determined to make it her career. Still, she had to wait until her father had died before she dared enroll in Denishawn in 1916. There Shawn, who describes her than as 'plain, awkwar, and abnormally shy,' told her that she had no talent for dance.

At Denishawn she was intrigued by 'Miss Ruth's' mysticism, but did most of her work with Shawn, who soon changed his mind about her talent. By 1919 she had begun teaching as well (counting among her pupils the then-unknown Bette Davis), and she toured England

The incredibly influential Martha Graham only retired from the stage in 1969, at the age of 75.

with the company in 1922. As time went on, however, Graham became increasingly disenchanted with the Denishawn organization. Like many others, she felt that the exposure to so many different sorts of dances left little time to explore any of them in depth, and that often commercialism triumphed over idealism.

In 1923 Graham left California for New York, where she danced with John Murray Anderson's Greenwich Village Follies for two seasons. In 1925 she became an instructor at the Eastman School for Dance and Dramatic Action in Rochester, New York. Her first appearance as a concert dancer (with a tiny company that totalled only four people) was at the 48th Street Theater in New York in 1926.

The Martha Graham School of Contemporary Dance, which was to become the leading school of its kind in the world, opened its doors in 1927, and by 1929 the company – now expanded to 16 dancers – was ready to present an entire season in New York. Her first major work was produced for this season; called *Heretic*, it depicts the attempts of a progressive individual to wrestle with the massive forces of intolerance. Her most important production during these early years was *Primitive Mysteries* (1931), based on certain Southwest American Indian religious ceremonies. It was a tour de force that placed her in a central position

among the early modern dance choreographers.

Graham's major purpose always has been to make visible innermost feelings – grief, joy, hatred, love, jealousy and passion. Her techniques, like those of most other modern dancers, have been invented as she went along. For Graham, breathing is the primary source of dance and the basis of movement. In the beginning her concentration on the opposing forces of contraction and release made her dances jerky; their intensity and the feeling of strain that they engendered were quite foreign to audiences used to watching ballet, which tries to appear smooth and effortless.

In 1934 Graham joined the teaching staff at the Bennington College School of Dance, and the support she received from that institution during the next eight years made many of her productions possible. She also received a Guggenheim Fellowship in 1935 – the first dancer to be so honored.

During this period she began looking at the forces that shaped America. *Heretic* was expanded into *American Provincials* (1934), a work loosely based on Hawthorne's *The Scarlet Letter*. *Frontier* (1935) presented a portrait of a young pioneer woman, bravely and confidently squaring up to a new life on the limitless plains. This production also marked the beginning of Graham's long, productive

collaboration with the designer Noguchi.

Letter to the World (1940) was inspired by the life and work of Emily Dickinson, though the poet appears only in fragments of her verse. The rest is an exploration of dual personality: One Who Speaks (the outwardly quiet, well-behaved Emily) and One Who Dances (the emotional, passionate, inner Emily). It was one of the first successful attempts to link dance with spoken verse.

In 1944 *Appalachian Spring* culminated Graham's Americana phase. This spacious, optimistic story of a young couple taking possession of their new home became her best-known and most loved work. Her powers as a choreographer were at their peak; Noguchi's spare, elegant set established the mood perfectly; and Aaron Copeland's outstanding score has become a classic in its own right.

Dark Meadow (1944) is an affirmation of faith in the cycle of birth, death and rebirth. It is the bridge between Graham's earlier works and her movement toward themes taken from Greek mythology, history and the Old Testament, as illustrations of universal psychological traits. *Cave of the Heart* (first seen as *The Serpent*, 1946), based on the legend of Jason and Medea, was billed as 'a dance of possessive and destroying love.' *Errand into the Maze* (1947) was suggested by Theseus and the Minotaur, but really concerns a secret fears. *Night Journey* (1947) examines the Oedipus story. The high point of the production was Jocasta's duet with Oedipus (originally danced by Erich Hawkins), in which Graham contrasted marital love and maternal affection.

Graham, a name synonymous with modern dance.

A scene from Graham's Seraphic Dialogue.

In 1954–55 Graham's company toured the world, including the Far East and the Middle East. *Seraphic Dialogue* (1955) pictured Joan of Arc reflecting on her life as maid, warrior and martyr. The same device was used in 1958 in *Clytemnestra*. Graham departed from her usual format to produce a full-length work in which the tragic queen, in Hades, watches scenes from her life pass in review. This powerful drama, with its conflict of passion and duty, is generally considered to be one of Graham's greatest compositions.

Graham retired from the stage in 1969 at the age of 75, after a career spanning more than 50 years, but she still continued to choreograph new dances, teach and direct her company. When Rudolf Nureyev expressed an interest in working with her, Graham choreographed two works for him: *Lucifer* (1975), which he danced with Margot Fonteyn, and *The Scarlet Letter* (1977). Both works garnered a lot of publicity, but neither has remained in the active repertory. In the 1980s Graham's company bridged the decades-old gap between modern dance and

ballet by presenting seasons at both the Metropolitan Opera House and the New York State Theater. In 1984, Graham's company became the first outside troupe ever to dance at the Paris Opéra.

Over time her technique has become softer and more lyrical, but she has never compromised her principles or lessened the demands she makes on both dancers and audience. Nor has she ever diluted the fundamental passion that has motivated her work from the earliest days. Her School of Contemporary Dance is still the leading institution in the world, with two others (the Batsheva Dance Company in Tel Aviv, founded in 1964, and the London Contemporary Dance Theatre, founded in 1966) closely connected to it.

DORIS HUMPHREY (1895–1958) and **CHARLES WEIDMAN** (1901–75) have not achieved Graham's measure of fame, but their company played a major role in the development of modern dance.

Humphrey grew up near Chicago in a musical family, where her love of dancing was encouraged; she studied many forms of dance as a child, including ballet –

giving her a classical foundation that set her apart from most early modern dancers. In 1917 she joined Denishawn and by 1919 was on the school's faculty.

Weidman arrived at Denishawn in 1920 from his home town of Lincoln, Nebraska. He was shy, serious and naive – but had an underlying comic streak which Shawn was at pains to encourage.

Like Graham, Humphrey and Weidman gradually became uncomfortable with the Denishawn philosophy, as well as with the personality cult that had grown up around its two founders; in 1927 they left the group, following a conversation with Shawn in which he referred to himself as 'the Jesus Christ of the dance.' Together with a fellow rebel, Pauline Lawrence (1900–71), they set out for the East Coast.

Humphrey, who was small and rather severe but according to Shawn 'a lovely, lyrical dancer,' was the intellectual, the theoretician. With Weidman she developed her theory of 'fall and recovery,' which places all dance movements somewhere between the motionlessness of perfect balance and complete surrender to the law of gravity. During the early years of the company she was mainly interested in working out the mechanics of her theory, producing intelligent but very simple dances like *Water Study* (1928), which took place in silence, with gongs to cue the dancers.

Though her theories sound difficult and esoteric, Humphrey's main concern was for people and their problems, not with dance technique. *The Shakers* (1931) was an early study of human conflict, hinting at sexual repression beneath the religious frenzy of the nineteenth-century sect.

Her most ambitious project was the heroic *New Dance* trilogy (1935–36), which examines man's relation to man. The first part, *Theatre Piece*, is a satire on the hectic, competitive quality of life; the second, *With My Red Fires*, studies the destructiveness of possessive love; part three, *New Dance*, is a joyful picture of a utopia where the individual and the group can coexist in harmony. In 1938 she choreographed *Passacaglia and Fugue in C Minor*, to music by J S Bach; it was an excellent demonstration of her skill in arranging group dances, and today is considered the best of her abstract works.

Together she and Weidman complemented each other perfectly, as partners and as choreographers. His comedy dances offset her more intellectual pieces in their programs, and he lightened her often terribly serious view of dance. He was famous for his talent as a mime, but his works often had a serious purpose beneath the hilarious action. *Quest* recorded an artist's progress in the face of various obstacles (critics, trial by trivia, and so on); beneath its nonsense, *Opus 51* was an experiment in 'kinetic pantomime' but it was also a reaction against the solemnity that often threatened to overcome the Bennington College dance programs. *On My Mother's Side* and *And Daddy Was a Fireman* were friendly, funny, warm sketches of himself and his family.

The Humphrey-Weidman company had a deep and lasting influence on the development of modern dance. In addition to inspiring many students (the most famous of whom was José Limón), it was the first to present full evening-long works and the first to include both men and women from the very beginning. Pauline Lawrence, the mainstay of the group through most of its existence, is often overlooked – primarily because she always took care to keep out of the limelight. But behind the scenes the tiny, dark, reserved woman functioned as pianist, costume designer, lighting specialist, publicist and business manager – in short, she was the rock upon which the whole enterprise was founded.

In 1945 an arithritic hip forced Humphrey to retire from the stage, but she continued to participate actively in the modern-dance world. As artistic director of Limón's company, she choreographed many more important productions, including *Lament for Ignacio Sanches Mejias* (1946) and *Day on Earth* (1947). She played an important part in establishing the Julliard School's dance department, and also taught at the Connecticut College School of Dance. Her success as a teacher can be seen by the number of excellent dancers who emerged from the two companies – including William Bales, Ruth Currier, Louis Falco, Eleanor King, Katherine Litz, Jennifer Muller and Sybil Shearer.

Weidman, meanwhile, formed his own company and toured with it extensively during the 1940s and 1950s His later conpositions included *A House Divided* (1945), a serious work about the Civil War and a sensitive tribute to Abraham Lincoln, and *Fables For Our Time* (1947) – witty illustrations of some of James Thurber's stories. After he stopped dancing in public he devoted himself to teach-

Carmen de Lavallade and Jack Dodds in Lester Horton's Dedication to Jose Clemente Orozco.

ing and choreography. One of his later pieces is *Brahm's Waltzes, Opus 39* (1967), a clean, abstract work of pure dance, dedicated to Humphrey.

HANYA HOLM (b 1898) came to the United States in 1931 from Germany. There she had studied with Dalcroze in Hellerau before joining Mary Wigman's company as dancer and teacher in 1921.

Her original purpose in coming to New York was to open a branch of the Wigman School there; the school flourished, and by 1934 Holm was one of the 'Big Four' at Bennington (along with Graham, Humphrey and Weidman). But she became convinced that Wigman's style and techniques were too intrinsically European to be successfully transplanted into American terms. In 1936 the two amiably parted company, and the school became known as the Hanya Holm Studio. She became an American citizen in 1939, and her son served with the US armed forces during World War II.

Holm's contributions were as a teacher and choreographer rather than as a dancer. She combined elements of her German training – discipline, a scientific approach and the concept of space as an integral part of movement – with the new rhythms and sense of freedom she discovered in America. By stressing basic principles rather than specific techniques, she was able to stimulate an extraordinary creativity in her students.

Holm was an excellent technician and her choreography was original and exciting. Her most famous work is *Trend* (1937), which pictures society eventually rising triumphant from a morass of injustice, dictatorship, money worship and the futility of war. Her concert pieces continued to contain this strong element of social comment throughout the 1930s and 1940s, from *Tragic Exodus* (1939) and *They Too are Exiles* (1940) to *Insect Comedy* (1948).

In the late 1940s Holm introduced an element of theatricality into her work

which enhanced the technical excellence of the choreography, and went on to exploit the new combination in a number of highly successful Broadway musicals like *Kiss Me Kate* (1948), *My Fair Lady* (1956) and *Camelot* (1960), as well as composing dances for opera and film. The Hanya Holm Studio remained one of the most important modern dance schools in New York until it closed in 1967.

HELEN TAMARIS (1905–53), another of the founders of modern dance in America, was born Helen Becker and grew up on New York's Lower East Side. She changed her name after reading a line in a poem: 'Thou art Tamaris, the ruthless queen who banishes all obstacles.'

Her family first sent her to dancing classes when she was eight, and as soon as she finished high school she entered the *corps de ballet* at the Metropolitan Opera, studying further with Rosina Galli. She remained with the company for three seasons, but objected to ballet's subordinate position and left to strike out on her own.

For some time she supported herself by performing in nightclubs and revues. Finally, in 1927, she was able to produce her first solo recital in New York's Little Theater. One of the items in that program, *1927*, was performed to excerpts from Gershwin's *Rhapsody in Blue*; it was one of the first serious uses of jazz in modern dance.

In 1928 Tamaris was invited to dance at the Salzburg Festival. She was the first American to appear there since Isadora Duncan, and her performance aroused great enthusiasm. The rest of her European tour was equally successful and she enjoyed meeting artists like Picasso and Mary Wigman, but she was happy to get home again. Throughout her career, she got most of her inspiration from the ex-exploration of American sources and rhythms.

Tamaris was one of the first artists to take black culture seriously, and she is most famous today for her *Negro Spirituals* (which evolved from 1928–42). Her other most famous pieces include *Walt Whitman Suite* (1934), a vigorous, enthusiastic tribute to his poetry, and *Cycle of Unrest* (1935) and *Momentum* (1936), strong commentaries on American society.

Since she had had no contact with Denishawn, she felt no need to react against 'show biz' tactics, and was never afraid to say her piece prettily. Nor was she inclined to develop intellectual theories about technique and movement; she had had enough of that in ballet. As a result, her dances were healthy, unpretentious and, above all, entertaining expressions of feelings. They were often criticized as shallow and theatrical by more 'serious' modern dancers.

In 1929 she opened her School of American Dance, and almost immediately approached Graham, Humphrey and Weidman with the idea for Dance Repertory Theater. Her notion was to create a single audience for modern dance rather than a collection of audiences devoted to various personalities. Despite support from others, like Agnes de Mille, the group fell apart after only a few seasons as each dancer was afraid of becoming submerged by the others. The school, however, continued to function until 1945.

During the Depression Tamaris began a productive association with Lee Strasburg's famous acting school, teaching the actors fundamental body movements and in turn learning much about acting. She toured the Midwest in 1936, and was active in helping organize both the First National Dance Congress and the American Dance Association. As first president of the ADA, she was responsible for ensuring that dance was adequately represented in the WPA-sponsored Federal Theater project.

The Federal Theater in New York closed in 1939 and by 1942 Tamaris was dancing at the famous Rainbow Room; she had virtually left the concert stage for good. Her wartime activities included productions like 'Porterhouse Lucy the Black Market Steak,' which was included in a play sponsored by the US Department of Agriculture titled *It's Up To You* (directed by Elia Kazan).

When the war was over she embarked on an entirely new career as a choreographer for Broadway and Hollywood. Her Broadway credits include *Up In Central Park* (1945), *Showboat* (1946), *Annie Get Your Gun* (1946) and the revue *Inside USA* (1948).

Tamaris would be celebrated for her devotion to American themes in any case, but she also did much to show both the dance community and audiences that good dance could also be fun.

LESTER HORTON (1906–53), the only major figure in the early days to work primarily on the West Coast, began his dance training in his home town of Indianapolis. He also studied classic dance with Adolf Bolm in Chicago.

As a boy he had developed a consuming interest in native American legends, artifacts and ceremonies, and when he first moved to Los Angeles in 1928 he made his living directing Indian dance festivals. He soon became known as an authority on the subject and in 1932 formed a small group to present Indian pageants – which were generally more popular for their exotic costumes than for the dancing. In 1934 he produced the first version of his most famous work, *Salome*.

In 1943 Horton opened his own school and continued to operate it even after a neck injury forced him to retire in 1944. The company worked mainly on the West Coast, only appearing in the East three times: in New York in 1943 and 1953, and at Jacobs Pillow in 1953. It was the first racially integrated troupe in the country; blacks, whites, Mexican-Americans, Japanese – anyone who had talent was welcomed, at a time when few others dared do the same.

Horton's enthusiasm was not always based on practicality; scholarships were given to anyone who needed them, and his grandiose projects often fell flat for lack of funds. His school continually teetered on the edge of bankruptcy, but the legacy of his teaching lives on today in his students – like Alvin Ailey, Bella Lewitzky, Janet Collins, Carmen de Lavallade, Joyce Trisler and James Truitte.

THE SECOND GENERATION

By the end of World War II the original founders of modern dance had produced a crop of talented students who, as children often do, dispensed with their 'parent's' well-worn theories and shibboleths and set out to create their own kind of dance. The great battle for position and respectability had been fought and partly won; it was not always necessary for the second generation to take themselves or their art with the same deadly seriousness that had so often characterized their predecessors.

ERICK HAWKINS (b 1909) graduated from Harvard (with a major in Greek) before beginning his dancing career at the School of American Ballet, and later with Harald Kreutzberg. He danced with American Ballet from 1935–37 and also with Ballet Caravan from 1936–39.

In 1938 he met Martha Graham at Bennington and joined her company as a guest artist. He remained to become her regular partner and eventually (in 1948) her husband. Two of the many roles he created were The Husbandman in *Appalachian Spring* and He Who Beckons in *Dark Meadow*.

Hawkins and Graham were divorced in 1950 and the next year he left the company to form his own group with composer Lucia Dlugoszewski and sculptor Ralph Dorazio. His dances are soft, serene and impressionistic, usually featuring Dorazio's elaborate sets and costumes.

He considers the 'quality of movement' the most important factor in his work. Some of his better-known pieces are: the somewhat oriental *Here and Now With Watchers* (1957); the inventive *8 Clear Places* (1960); *Naked Leopard* (1965); *Angels of the Inmost Heaven* (1971); *Classic Kite Tales* (1972); and *Greek Dreams with Flute* (1973), a graceful tribute to classical antiquity.

MERCE CUNNINGHAM (b 1919) was one of the first to break away from the theories of the first generation. Born in Centralia, Washington, he first studied on the West Coast, then in 1939 became the second man to join Martha Graham. He created roles like the Revivalist in *Appalachian Spring*, finally leaving to start his own company in 1945.

Cunningham has made a conscious effort to free himself of any of the accepted modern dance traditions and techniques. As a result, he has been considered highly controversial for some 25 years – an unusual achievement. He is basically concerned with movement for itself alone, without any dramatic or emotional connotations, and the movements in his dances are ordered by chance (the throw of a die or the whim of the dancers). Action takes place all over the stage, not in one isolated area after another, so that the work can be viewed from many angles.

His theory on composition is that the various elements of a dance – music, choreography, design – are independent and only happen to occupy the same space and time. This novel approach to production has attracted many avant garde musicians and artists, from composers like his long-time friend John Cage, David Tudor and Gordon Mumma to designers like Andy Warhol, Jasper Johns and Robert Rauschenberg.

Some of his best known works are: the intellectual *Suite for Five in Space and Time* (1956); the funny *Antic Meet* (1958); and the dark, oppressive *Winterbranch* (1960). In direct contrast is *Summerspace* (1958). This bright, fast-paced work, filled with its flurries of shooting leaps, entered the repertory of New York City Ballet in 1966. Both here and with the Boston and Cullberg ballet companies, *Summerspace* was performed in *pointe* shoes. *Rainforest* (1968) is a sensual, almost erotic dance embued with animal imagery. The quiet, sometimes cautious and seemingly instinctual movement is augmented by Warhol's décors of hovering helium-filled silver pillows.

Throughout his lengthy career, Cunningham has remained in the vanguard. He was one of the first choreographers to explore the relationship between dance and video. In the 1970s he and cameraman Charles Atlas devised a series of dances created specifically for video viewing. In 1981 Cunningham reversed the usual creative process and turned his video project *Channels/Inserts* into a stagework.

An infamous presentation format, known as *Events*, began on a European tour in 1964. Confronted with a non-theater performance space in a Vienna museum, Cunningham decided that a normal program of dances would not be a success. To solve the problem, he strung together bits and pieces of the repertory into one long non-stop event lasting approximately 90 minutes. In the ensuing years, the company has now done more

Rand Howard as the Coyote in Erick Hawkins's 1979 ballet, Plains Daybreak.

Merce Cunningham at rehearsal.

Elizabeth Walton and Dan Wagoner in Taylor's Scudorama.

among the first and second generations of modern-dance choreographers.

Carolyn Brown, a tall dancer of startling intensity, was Cunningham's first and major partner (1952–72). His former company members who have gone on to establish choreographic careers of their own include Viola Farber, Douglas Dunn, Remy Charlip, Steve Paxton, Charles Moulton, and Karole Armitage.

Now approaching 70, Cunningham still continues to perform. In recent works, such as *Pictures* (1985), he brings to the stage an awesome sense of power and a self-contained, even meditative, sense of truth.

PAUL TAYLOR (b 1930) is almost impossible to classify. He is usually described as a Graham-Cunningham veteran, and in fact has danced with both companies – with Cunningham in 1953 and with Graham from the mid-1950s to 1960. But he also has studied with Pearl Lang, Limón, Humphrey and Antony Tudor, and has appeared with classic as well as modern companies (Balanchine composed

a special variation for him in a New York City Ballet production of *Episodes*).

Whatever his pigeonhole, Taylor's art stands alone. Creativity and imagination are not uncommon attributes among modern dancers; a real sense of humor appears even less often. His dances are energetic, graceful and witty, with an innate musicality which sets Taylor apart

than 200 of these. Each one is different from the other.

As the years have passed Cunningham's techniques have come to look more and more like those of contemporary ballet. The speed with which his dancers move, coupled with his insistence on clean, clear lines and precision, have given his company a pristine edginess that is unique

Merce Cunningham and his company in his work Variations V, *premiered in 1965.*

Previous page: Center, Erick Hawkins Dance Company, Agathlon; *Top left, The Merce Cunningham company rehearse; Top right, Paul Taylor and Bettie de Jong in* Public Domain.

from many of his colleagues. This last trait, along with his highly developed sense of form, takes him close to ballet. His most popular early work, *Aureole* (1962) – a simple, bounding buoyant quintet to Handel – was taken into the repertory of the Royal Danish Ballet in 1968. Since that time it has been added to the roster of many classical companies around the world. *Airs* (1978) is a series of lush partnerings to baroque music. It has entered the repertory of American Ballet Theatre. The Joffrey Ballet staged *Arden Court* in 1986. Originally devised for his own company in 1981, it is danced to Renaissance music from English composer William Boyce. This brilliant display piece of virtuoso dancing makes a particularly fine showcase for the strongly athletic male dancers whom Taylor favors.

Among Taylor's vast output of works are *3 Epitaphs* (1960), set to authentic New Orleans funeral music (dirge-like but unmistakably jazz), and a two-act evocation of the seasons, *Orbs* (1966), danced to Beethoven string quartets.

When Taylor himself stopped performing in 1974, his choreographic talents moved on to an even higher plane. His first piece after retirement was *Esplanade* (1975). This joyous, high-speed evocation of music by Bach ranks as one of the top masterpieces of contemporary choreography. Limiting his dancers to running, skipping, hopping, jumping, walking and even crawling, Taylor created a bubbling cornucopia of movement that transformed the everyday into the sublime. *Polaris* (1979) proved an intriguing experiment. The same choreography is performed twice in a row. The second time through there are different dancers, changes of costume, lighting and music, the idea being that all the secondary elements of a dance influence and color how an audience actually sees the steps.

In 1980 Taylor became perhaps the first choreographer to come successfully to grips with Stravinsky's *Le Sacre du Printemps*. Discarding the scenario which Nijinsky used in 1913, Taylor devised a knock-about comedy plot concerning a mob of gangsters trying to kidnap a baby. The hero is a Clark Kent type who travels into a mysterious Chinatown in an attempt to rescue the babe for its mom. Funny, and often macabre, it reveals

Taylor's dark and frequently even morbid sense of humor to the full.

Many future choreographers have been among Taylor's dancers. Notable alumni include Twyla Tharp, Laura Dean, Dan Wagoner and David Parsons.

ANNA SOKOLOW (b 1912) studied with Margaret Curtis at the Metropolitan Opera Ballet School and at the School of American Ballet, as well as with Graham. Thus, though she danced in Graham's company from 1930–39, she was not a typical protegée; in addition to her classical training, she was motivated much more by sociological and political concerns than by emotional issues.

In 1939 she was invited to give a series of concerts in Mexico City – and ended up living in Mexico half-time for the next 10 years. It was a profitable period for both sides, which resulted in the establishment of Mexico's first modern dance company and some of Sokolow's most important dances – like *Lament for a Dead Bullfighter* and the six-part *Lyric Suite*.

Rooms (1955) remains her best-known and most powerful work. Uncompromisingly dark, it is set in a bleak and impersonal urban world where lost and lonely individuals are battered by the cacophony of progressive jazz and their own failed dreams. An indictment of modern society, *Rooms* is a powerful comment on man's

inhumanity to man. It has entered the repertory of the Netherlands Dance Theater, the Joffrey Ballet and the Alvin Ailey Dance Theater. Switching to the little and helpless people who were trapped in the Holocaust, Sokolow created the horrific *Dreams*, in 1961. Her work is never easy to watch, but it is based on a bedrock of integrity. She is a stern commentator on modern society and its injustices. Sokolow has taught for many years in the dance department of the Juilliard School of Music in New York.

JEAN ERDMAN danced with Graham's company from 1938–43, when she formed her own touring group.

In the late 1940s Erdman became interested in choreographing experimental ballet-play productions. She produced Sartre's *Les Mouches* (*The Flies*) in 1947; in 1954 a text by William Saroyan provided the basis for *Otherman, or the Birth of a New Nation*. In 1963 she wrote, choreographed and directed *The Coach with the Six Insides*, based on James Joyce's *Finnegan's Wake*.

In 1972, after a period as director of the New York University School of Arts, Erdman established The Open Eye, which she described as 'a base for total theater.' One of the group's most ambitious productions was *Moon Mysteries* – a series of three poetic plays by Yeats.

Betty Jones and José Limón in his Moor's Pavane.

José Limón in Chaconne *to music by Bach.*

JOSE LIMON (1908–72) was Doris Humphrey's most famous student. Born in Mexico and raised in Arizona, he attended the University of California in Los Angeles, planning to become a painter. He changed his mind abruptly after seeing a Humphrey-Weidman performance in New York in 1928, and for the next 12 years was associated with their company.

Limón was not by any means a natural dancer: he had little sense of balance and a poor sense of direction, his large, somewhat clumsy body was strong but not supple and he was a slow learner. But he was a tremendous worker and had an infallible sense of the dramatic which, with his romantic appearance, made him a stage presence to be reckoned with. He is unusual among modern dancers in that he was just as happy dancing in other choreographers' works as in his own. Those who knew him agree that he was a splendid person – invariably warm, cheerful and generous.

In 1940 he left the Humphrey-Weidman group (with their blessing) to set out on a concert career; he and Pauline Lawrence were married in 1942. The next year he was drafted into the army, and spent the rest of the war in Special Services, directing and appearing in army camp shows.

In 1947 he organized the José Limón American Dance Company. With Humphrey as artistic director and dancers like Ruth Currier, Betty Jones, Pauline Koner and Lucas Hoving, it established itself almost immediately as one of the country's outstanding modern dance troupes. It was the first company to be sent abroad on a goodwill tour by the State Department. Unlike most similar groups, his company survived him. Its dancers still have a reputation for being some of the best-trained in the business, and Limón is still regarded as one of the most distinguished personalities in the history of modern dance.

Limón's dances are usually very dramatic; his characters may be saints, fools or sinners – but they are never ciphers. His most famous work is *The Moor's Pavane* (1949). Set to music by Purcell, it retells Shakespeare's *Othello* in the context of an old court dance; anger and jealousy simmer beneath the surface politeness and gallantry of the four dancers, finally exploding into murder at the climax. His other important pieces include *La Malinche* (1949), *The Exiles* (1950), *Emperor Jones* (1956) and *I, Odysseus* (1962).

ANN HALPRIN (b 1920) began her dancing career with Humphrey and Weidman in 1945. In 1948, however, she moved to the West Coast, opening her own studio in San Francisco. In 1955 she founded Dancers' Workshop, which was organized to establish a means of collaboration between dancers, painters, architects and musicians; her Summer Workshops were begun in 1959.

From 1963 she began to attract increasing attention at various European festivals; her debut in New York in 1967 was raided by the police because it contained a nude scene. Halprin is recognized today as one of the earliest and most active pioneers of dance 'happenings'; her works include *BO'ULU BO'ICI BO'EE*, *Animal Ritual*, *Initiations* and *Transformations*.

SYBIL SHEARER (b c.1918) is another important graduate of the Humphrey-Weidman company. She also studied ballet, and danced with Agnes de Mille in 1941. In 1942 she moved to Chicago, where she began her long association with designer/lighting specialist Helen Morrison. In 1959 she and Morrison were able to establish the Sybil Shearer Company in Winnetka, where they converted the Community Theater into a dance theater. In 1962 she was appointed artist in residence at the National College of Education in Evanston, where she still works and teaches.

Even in the eclectic world of modern dance, Shearer has always been an outsider – though as a dancer she had incredible control over her body and was one of the outstanding technicians of her time. She sees dance in cycles, each dance linked to its predecessor and successor. At first the cycles were fairly short, but they tended to become longer and longer; in 1949 one cycle was taking an entire afternoon to perform. One of her best known works is *Once Upon a Time* (1951), a suite of 11 solos.

Shearer sometimes tries the patience of even her most devoted admirers with what appears to be self-indulgent, rather pointless choreography in some of her dances. Nevertheless, she remains one of the most important figures – and greatest individualists – in American modern dance.

ALWIN NIKOLAIS (b 1912) has been called 'the magician of the theater.' He studied with virtually all of the masters of modern dance, but was most influenced by Hanya Holm. He also acknowledges a great debt to the Bau-

The great stagemaster, Alwin Nikolais.

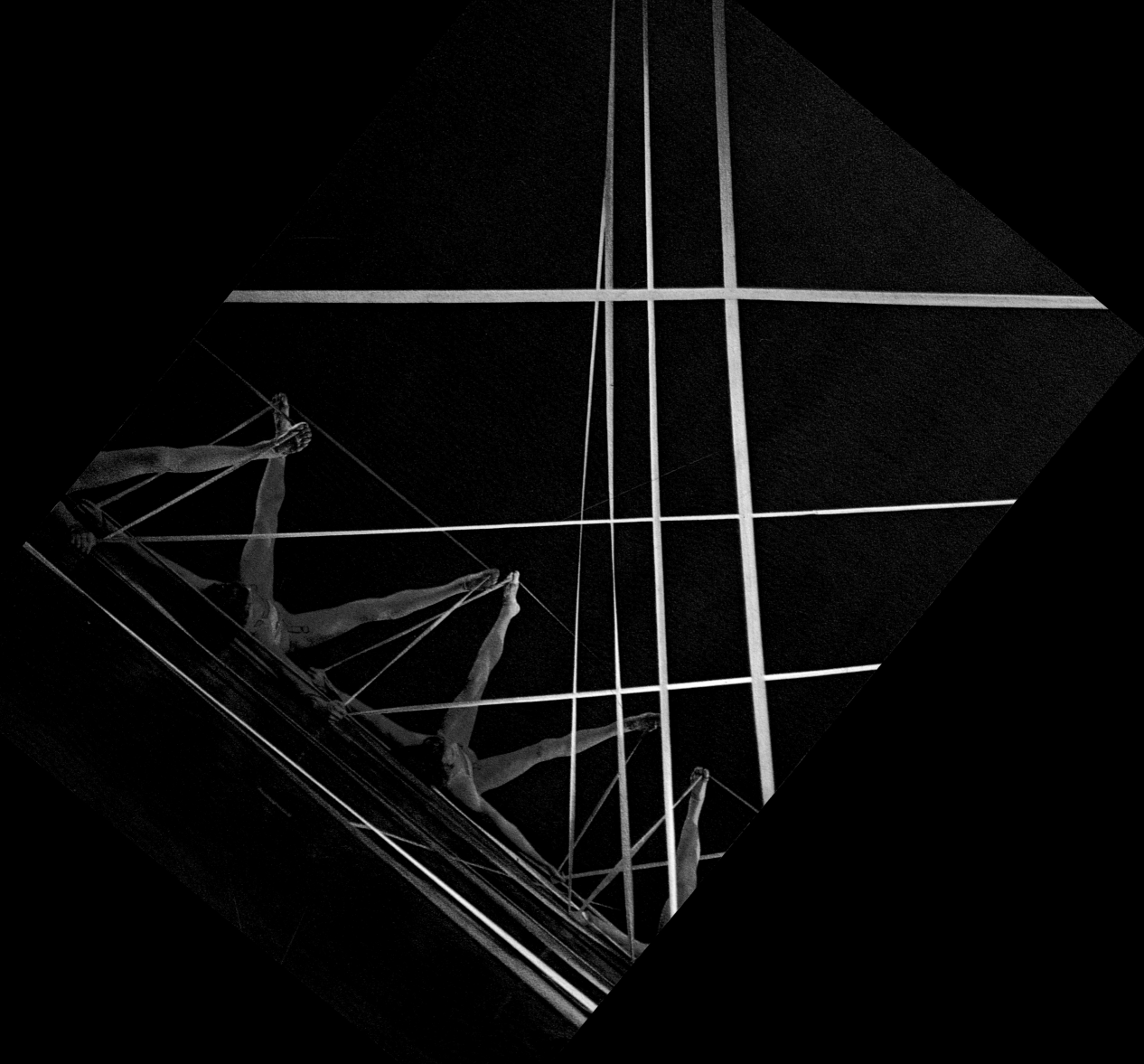

Previous page: In Tensile Involvement *as with* Imago *(above) Nikolais demonstrates his love of blending dancer and scenery.*

haus school of art and architecture (founded in Germany by Walter Gropius in 1919).

Nikolais was born in Southington, Connecticut, and even as a child was fascinated by the theater. He got his start in show business as a piano player for silent films, and later worked as a puppet master. After World War II (when he served in the Signal Corps) he took over the Henry Street Playhouse in New York and immediately began working to implement his own vision of what dance theater should be like: a total experience in which dancers supply the kinetic energy in ever-changing patterns of light, sound and movement.

His first productions, like *Lobster Quadrille* (1949) were for children; his most famous work is the brilliant *Imago, or The City Curious* (1936). Other pieces include *Kaleidoscope* (1956), *Illusion* (1961), the poignant *Sanctum* (1964), *Tower* (1965) and the chilling *Tent* (1968).

Nikolais considers every aspect of a production equally important. He calls himself an 'artistic polygamist' and takes a hand in everything – choreographing the dances, composing the (usually electronic) music, planning the lighting and designing the daring stage sets and frequently fantastic costumes (which as often as not are sculptures with dances inside them). His whole purpose is to dazzle the audience with these polished, complex, mixed-media experiences or 'sound and vision pieces,' and to blur the distinction between reality and illusion.

His view of dance as theater has had a great influence, and he is considered a pioneer in the use of lighting and materials. He also is an excellent teacher and has written many books and articles.

GLEN TETLEY, who is discussed more fully in the preceding chapter, was another of Holm's students. Most of his career has been spent in the area between ballet and modern dance, and he is one of the most influential links between the two forms today.

ALVIN AILEY (b 1931) is probably the best known of all the excellent dancers produced by Lester Horton's school in Los Angeles. He made his debut with Horton's Dance Theater in 1950 and directed the company from Horton's death in 1953 until it disbanded the following year.

In 1954 Ailey moved to New York, where he studied modern dance with Graham, Weidman and Holm, ballet with Karel Shook, and acting with Stella Adler. He supported himself by acting in off-Broadway plays, dancing in Broadway musicals and choreographing productions for the Metropolitan Opera.

By 1958 he was ready to organize his own company, the Alvin Ailey American Dance Theater, which toured extensively in the United States and, after 1964, overseas as well (it was the first modern-dance troupe to tour Russia). For several years the company was based at the Brooklyn Academy of Music; since 1972 it has been the resident modern-dance company at the New York City Center.

Ailey is a prolific choreographer who puts his experience in the theater to good use in productions that combine elements from jazz, primitive, modern and classic dance. His two most famous works are *Blues Suite* (1958), which is about a night at an old Southern 'sporting house,' and *Revelations* (1960), the universally acclaimed tribute to the triumph of courage and determination over adversity that has become the company's signature piece. *Quintet* (1968) looks at the private troubles behind the glittering masks in the popular music field, while *Maskela Language* (1969) presents a grim picture of the plight of blacks in South Africa. *Cry* (1971) is a tribute to black women, and Judith Jamison (b 1944) has turned it into one of the most exciting experiences in all of dance. Other works are set to music that ranges from Benjamin Britten (*Sea Change*, 1972) and Vaughan Williams (*The Lark Ascending*, 1972) to Duke Ellington (*Reflections in D*, 1962) and, perhaps unexpectedly, Pink Floyd and Janis Joplin (*Flowers*, 1971).

Though Ailey has retired from the stage he remains active both as a teacher and as a choreographer trying to find the middle ground between ballet and modern dance (Jamison, for example, was trained as a ballerina in Philadelphia). He also is interested in keeping the modern-dance classics alive, and periodically revives works by people like Ted Shawn, Katherine Dunham and Pearl Primus. The Alvin Ailey City Center Dance Theater is probably the best-known black dance company in America today – and is certainly one of the most exciting that can be seen anywhere.

The Alvin Ailey City Center Dance Theater's universally acclaimed ballet Revelations.

Based on the surging power of the Negro spiritual, Revelations *is a tribute to the triumph of courage and determination over adversity.*

KATHERINE DUNHAM (b 1912) and **PEARL PRIMUS** (b 1919) are both academics as well as theatrical people, and have both made great contributions in the area of black dance – from an anthropological as well as an entertainment standpoint.

Dunham, who usually is credited with 'putting black dance on the map,' wrote her Masters thesis at the University of Chicago on the dances of Haiti, and has continued to do extensive research in the field ever since, concentrating on black dance on the West Indies.

In 1938 Dunham was appointed dance director for the Negro Unit of the Federal Theater project, Chicago branch and in 1939 she was dance director of the New York Labor Stage Project (which produced the famous musical *Pins and Needles*). It was not until 1940, when she put together a company to present her own *Tropics and Le Jazz Hot – From Haiti to Harlem*, that she really began her career as one of the most sought-after choreographers for Afro-American dances. Soon, in addition to concert work, she was choreographing for musicals (like *Cabin in the Sky*, 1940) and films (like *Stormy Weather*, 1943).

Between 1945 and 1955 the Dunham School of Dance in New York became the focus for black dance in America, and Dunham's company toured extensively; they were especially popular in Europe. In 1963 she choreographed a new production of *Aïda* for the Metropolitan Opera, and in 1965–66 was cultural advisor to the President and Minister of Cultural Affairs in Dakar, Senegal. She currently directs the Performing Arts Training Center at Southern Illinois University, East St Louis branch.

Some of Dunham's best loved works, which were enhanced by the striking designs of her husband, John Pratt, include: *Shango, Bahiana, L'Ag'ya, Rites de Passage, Nostalgia, Blues, Flaming Youth* and *Ragtime*.

Primus began her college career in medicine, but eventually obtained her PhD in anthropology from Columbia. While she was in school she also studied with the New Dance Group, making her stage debut in 1941 and giving her first solo recital in 1943.

In 1944 she formed her own company, which soon became well known for its presentations of West Indian, African and primitive dances, choreographed both authentically and in the idiom. With her husband, Percival Borde,

Primus did extensive research, both in the West Indies and in Africa. In 1959 she was a delegate to the Second World Congress of African Artists and Writers in Rome, and that same year spent six months in Liberia, as an advisor to the government in planning a new performing arts center. In 1962 Rebekah Harkness sponsored her company's tour of Africa. Today Primus still is active as a teacher and choreographer.

ANGNA (ANITA) ENTERS (b 1907) never formally studied serious dance, but developed her own, unique form of dance/pantomime. From her debut in 1922 until the outbreak of World War II she toured extensively in the United States and Europe, presenting her speciality – character vignettes – to appreciative audiences. One of her most famous roles was as the Queen of Heaven in the work entitled *Moyen Age* (1926) in which she enacted the story of a woman's reaction to the Crucifixion in the spirit and style of a medieval painting. Her other characters cover a wide range, from Boy Cardinal – a Renaissance figure – to the dancer in *American Ballet – 1914–1916*, a parody of social dancing. In 1938 she gave the first theatrical performance in New York's Museum of Modern Art, playing 13 different characters in her original pantomime, *Pagan Greece*.

After her retirement from the stage Enters settled in Los Angeles where she became a script writer for MGM. But even while she was performing she wrote several books and exhibited her own paintings. She also has taught at various American universities and colleges.

EDWIN STRAWBRIDGE (?–1957) was another dancer who went his own way, outside the mainstream of modern dance. He first became interested in the stage while studying law at Lafayette College in Pennsylvania.

Strawbridge began his career as a dancer with Bolms's Ballet Intime, the Littlefield Ballet, and eventually Ruth Page's Ravinia Opera company. In the mid-1930s he established his own company, called Junior Programs, to present theater and his own version of dance/mime in productions for children. Over the next 20 years Junior Programs toured the United States, and Strawbridge became so involved with their productions that he finally stopped performing altogether. One of his best pieces was *The Eagle* (1929), in which his forceful per-

sonality and striking appearance brought the solitary, proud bird to life on the stage.

JAMES WARING (1922–75), whom Jack Anderson has called 'the most paradoxical of all American choreographers,' was born in Almeda, California, and began studying dance at the San Francisco Ballet School. Following World War II, which he spent in the armed forces, he resumed his studies in New York, listing among his teachers Vilzak, Tudor, Merce Cunningham, Halprin and Louis Horst (musical director for Graham's company from 1926–48).

For most of his career (1949–66) he ran his own company; he was then artistic director of the Ballet Stage Company and, until his death, artistic director of The New England Dinosaur, a Boston-based modern dance troupe. He was a prolific choreographer, producing many ballets and solos for companies like the Manhattan Festival Ballet, the New England Dance Theater, the Netherlands Dance Theater and the Pennsylvania Ballet.

Waring, who was routinely mixing classic, modern and nondance gestures long before anyone else, had an extraordinarily facile mind; with seeming ease he produced pieces that combined refinement and vulgarity, wit and sensitivity, order and the distortion of order. As an artist, he tended to see things in graphic as much as in choreographic terms. He was a brilliant costume designer, but strangely, he never showed an interest in design, lighting or decor.

It is impossible to categorize Waring's works. At one end of the spectrum, *At the Cafe Fleurette* (1968) is a nostalgic, friendly, and only gently teasing piece set to music from Victor Herbert's operettas and dedicated to Vernon and Irene Castle. Then there is *Poets Vaudeville* (1963), a fantastic happening in dance, song and mime, or *Spookride II* (1970), which requires dancers to first demonstrate classic ballet technique, then abandon it for mime or ordinary movement.

Waring's choreography has already made its mark in the area where ballet and modern dance touch each other. He will live even longer through his pupils, for he was an excellent teacher. He is remembered best by those who knew him, however, for his modesty, innate kindness and his never-failing readiness to help his friends and colleagues.

THE POST-MODERN GENERATION

The dance revolution begun in the 1960s with a new generation of young American choreographers has been given the all-encompassing rubric of 'post-modern.' This convenient lable covers such a broad base of divergent creativity that its only true value is chronological.

Just as the creators of modern dance had seen themselves as revolutionaries storming the sacred temple of ballet, so the new dancemakers saw themselves as rebels against the strictures of Graham, new breed of dancer in all sorts of unexpected places. Parks, gymnasiums, rooftops and artists' lofts all became alternatives for theaters.

Humphrey, Limón and their followers. In place of the high drama and theatricality of Graham, the post-modern choreographers went in search of a way of dancing that would be pertinent to their own daily lives. The goals and achievements of the post-moderns are all concerned with the whys, hows and wherefores of dance. The

Twyla Tharp's brash Push Comes to Shove *(1976) featured Mikhail Baryshnikov's joyous debut in American choreography.*

generation of the 1960s dealt with the here and the now. They questioned the validity of all accepted rules and devised new ways of movement, performed by a

Two exemplary precursors of this movement worked in the 1950s. Each is an apt illustration of how the post-moderns would approach choreography. John Cage, Cunningham's musical collaborator, composed a 1952 piano solo called *4' 33"*. It consisted of a pianist sitting at the keyboard for four minutes and thirty-three seconds. Not a single note of music was ever played. In 1957, Paul Taylor, still a fledgling choreographer, presented a now notorious concert which included *Duet*. During this piece, Taylor and his partner held a single unmoving pose (she sat in a chair; he stood beside her) while the telephone's talking clock counted off three minutes of time. This, in turn, led to the most infamous of all dance reviews. It began with Taylor's name, was followed by four inches of absolutely blank space and ended with the critic's name at the bottom.

Both of these works encompass a questioning attitude towards art which was to sweep through the dance world of the 1960s. Even today, many of the results of that questioning remain highly controversial.

The post-modern movement had its first home at the Judson Church in New York's Greenwich Village. Here, beginning in 1962, a series of group concerts brought the new choreographic ideas into focus. Yvonne Rainer (b 1934) wrote a manifesto which stripped dance of its pretentions, glamorous excess and virtuosity. In their place, Rainer proposed a new way of dancing open to one and all, rather than just to those who had refined their technique through years of classroom study. According to Rainer, anyone should be able to dance and any pedestrian movement was worthy of being part of a dancework.

Steve Paxton (b 1939) used these principles to create a new form of dance, called contact improvisation. This mode of performance uses the natural weight of the body and involves the performers in a give-and-take dependency upon one another and upon the pull of gravity. Rather than resisting the natural flow of the body's own energy, the performer surrenders to it. Virtuosity is replaced by each individual dancer's innate movement capabilities.

Meredith Monk (b 1943) and Trisha Brown (b 1936) led the way in exploring alternative performance spaces. Monk,

who is also her own composer, devised large group events in unorthodox settings ranging from abandoned parking lots to the nave of a cathedral. (Unlike many of her fellows, Monk never abandoned an essential love of theater. Her work has always maintained an element of mysterious ritualism.) Brown, on the other hand, abandoned both theatricality and music. She devised 'task' dances and 'equipment' pieces with rules that drew inspiration from sports and games. A famous series of Brown's pieces hooked her dancers into a harness-and-tackle device which allowed them to cantilever themselves out from a wall with their bodies parallel to the floor below. The *Walking on the Walls* dances found performers walking down the façades of buildings, spiralling down treetrunks and, most memorably, walking around the gallery walls of New York's Whitney Museum.

Minimalism, so prominent in all art forms of the late 1960s and 1970s, reached a post-modern apogee with Lucinda Childs (b 1940) and Laura Dean (b 1945). Both women choreographed group works using series of repetitive movements that slowly built up gradually evolving patterns of dancing. Childs uses highly rhythmic cantering, running, skipping steps which swing and arc in geometric patterns. Dean bases her patterns on spinning – both in place like a top, and in bigger circling configurations.

Twyla Tharp (b 1942) began as one of the most rigorous of the post-moderns. She never favored the pedestrian gestures used by so many choreographers of her generation. Instead she devised fiendishly complex displays of human mathematics, such as *The Fugue* (1971). In silence, a trio of dancers use a basic movement phrase which they slow down, do backwards, in counterpoint, perform sideways and in all sorts of other inventive permutations. The effect is akin to a human calculator.

In 1971 Tharp broke new ground with *Eight Jelly Rolls* (performed to the ragtime jazz of pianist Jelly Roll Morton). It is here that Tharp began to evolve a style of dancing which would eventually bridge the gap between the generations and bring post-modern choreographers to pre-eminence. Tharp found a way to be entertaining without having to abandon the intellectual questioning which is at the heart of post-modern choreography. From *Eight Jelly Rolls* onward, Tharp has created a style of movement that mixes skill with a rubbery, loose-limbed nonchalance that

is both giddily funny and visually adroit.

In 1973 Robert Joffrey took the revolutionary step of inviting Tharp to create a piece for his ballet company. The result was *Deuce Coupe*, a comedy of contemporary manners danced to hit tunes by those Californian crooners, the Beach Boys. It mixed all forms of dance, including classical ballet, into a snowstorm of activity which broke down the barriers between different dance styles by simply ignoring them. *Deuce Coupe* proved to be one of the most resounding successes of the 1970s and led to the even more complex *Push Comes to Shove* (1976) for American Ballet Theatre. Tharp is now recognized as the major choreographer of her generation. Her own company has evolved into a group of highly disciplined dancers who are as at home with ballet techniques as they are with any modern-dance format.

Tharp, Childs, Dean, Brown and other post-moderns have all found new ways of expressing their ideas about dance. As time begins to give us a perspective on their accomplishments, we can see that the major post-moderns are more akin to Balanchine and his formal questionings of time and space than to the mythological theatricality of Graham. The post-moderns have come a long way since 1962, but they still believe that dance should be about dancing and dancers, not about heroes and storybook characters.

New choreographers continue the process. Stephen Petronio (b 1956), a former member of Brown's company, uses the slippery style she developed in the 1970s, but adds a speed and intensity all his own. Molissa Fenley (b 1954) creates dances which use Childs's ideas of patterned repetition, but she performs them with a ferocious velocity that is unlike the loping elegance of Child's finest creations. Many other young artists are continuing the search for a personal means of expressing movement.

The major artists of the post-modern generation, such as Tharp, Childs and Dean, now regularly choreograph for the biggest American companies as well as continuing to work with their own ensembles. The revolution begun in 1962 has become a fundamental aspect of dance in the 1980s. Already, there are those who are challenging this aesthetic. Dance is, after all, constantly in flux, continually changing and evolving. The essence of dance is its immediacy and its creative drive. The focus is inevitably on the future and, of course, the future is always intriguingly unpredictable.

EUROPE

Robert North's popular Colour Moves for Ballet Rambert has a rainbow series of backdrops designed by painter Bridget Riley.

The roots of modern dance in Europe and America are inextricably entangled. For example, the theories of the Frenchman Delsarte and the Swiss Dalcroze had a great impact on both American dancers and audiences; dancers like Wigman and Kreutzberg were welcomed in the United States, and of course Hanya Holm played a major role in the development of American modern dance. For its part, America sent dancers like Fuller, Duncan, St Denis, and later Graham, Cunningham and Taylor to Europe, with a new vision of what dance could be like.

Despite the many points they have in common, however, modern dance on the two continents is radically different in many respects – in large part the result of the vast differences between them in outlook and experience. For example, as Martha Graham has pointed out, the word 'frontier' connotes a challenge and a feeling of excitement to an American, to a European it signifies a barrier. This kind of difference in perspective is bound to have an effect, especially on an art form as responsive to inner feelings as modern dance.

There also has been much more 'intermarriage' between ballet and modern dance in Europe, especially during the period between the two world wars. While the early American dancers were fighting to establish themselves outside the ballet tradition, many of their counterparts in Europe (particularly Germany and the Netherlands) were confidently working in municipal theaters as ballet masters and mistresses – but producing works much more in the modern than the classic idiom. Thus the distinctions between the two forms rapidly became blurred.

The great forerunner of modern dance in both Europe and America was François Delsarte (1811–71). His life did not begin auspiciously; both his parents and his older brother died when he was very young, leaving him a destitute orphan, wandering the streets of Paris, until he was adopted by a kindly cleric, Père Bambini.

As a youth Delsarte trained as both an actor and a singer, and in 1830 embarked on a promising career at the Opéra Comique. However, because of the inadequate training he had received, his voice failed four years later. The experience left him determined to discover a better way to train singers and actors.

He also was unhappy with the highly stylized, artificial acting techniques current in Paris at the time. With the meticulousness of a scientist and the enthusiasm of an artist, he set out to study gesture – especially gesture under stress – in real life. He hid behind park benches to watch children playing in the park, and not only noted their movements, but also documented how the movements of nurses who liked children differed from those who did not. He even visited the site of a disastrous mine explosion to record expressions of worry and grief at first hand.

Delsarte's fame during his lifetime was based on his reputation as a professor of singing and recitation. During his most active period (1839–59) he was respected throughout Europe; the King of Bavaria sent all his leading singers to Paris to study with the great teacher, and the top-ranked actors and opera singers (like Jenny Lind) sought him out for private lessons. It is his study of gesture, however, that ultimately has proved to have the most profound influence.

The complex system that Delsarte finally arrived at divided the body into three major zones: the head (intellectual), truck (emotional) and limbs (physical). Each division was subdivided three time and then divided again. Gesture was restricted by time, motion and space. This system, which is explained in detail by Ted Shawn in *Every Little Movement*, was adapted by one of Delsarte's pupils, Steele Mackaye, into a program of exercises called 'Harmonic Gymnastics.' Meanwhile, another devotee, Gertrude

Irreverent and theatrically inventive, Michael Clark epitomizes the British new wave.

Above: Lucy Burge in Frederick Ashton's homage to an American pioneer, Five Brahms Waltzes in the Manner of Isadora Duncan.

Stebbins, toured the United States, lecturing on the Delsarte theories.

Delsarte died in 1871, after some 10 years of ill-health and increasing poverty, before Mackaye could arrange for him to come to the United States. The popularity of his system grew by leaps and bounds; by the 1890s Americans could buy Delsarte corsets, cosmetics, gowns, even a Delsarte wooden leg. However, in the process his original ideas became completely distorted; eventually his name became a joke, conjuring up visions of stout matrons in 'Greek tunics' solemnly devising 'statue poses' in gardens and drawing rooms. Though many American dancers – including Duncan, St Denis, and Shawn – were exposed to Delsarte's principles, it was a long time before the true extent of his influence was realized.

It was in Germany and Austria that modern dance found its most devoted adherents during the first half of the twentieth century. Part of the reason may have been that, despite its long, illustrious history, ballet never had captured the imagination of the people in the same way it had in, say, France or Denmark. Perhaps, too, the introspective, philosophical bent of early modern dance, with its concern for inner states of being, appealed to something in the German character.

The foundation of German (and European) modern dance was laid by Emile Jaques-Dalcroze (1865–1950). Dalcroze was born in Vienna and received his musical training at the Conservatory in Geneva, with Leo Delibes in Paris, and with Anton Bruckner in Vienna. His wide-ranging interests encompassed all the arts; he directed a theater in Algiers when he was only 20.

Dalcroze's system of harmonious bodily movement, called eurythmics, was developed while he was teaching at the Geneva Conservatory (1892–1909), as a way to help his students develop a sense of rhythm. His aim was to bring the body under control of the mind by translating sounds into physical movements. Students began by learning an unconscious technique of bodily response to music, and eventually were able to improvise interpretations, using gesture, into entire compositions.

In 1905 Dalcroze demonstrated his technique in the United States, and in 1910 he resigned from the conservatory to establish the Jaques-Dalcroze School at Hellerau, near Dresden. The school, originally dedicated to advanced musical education, flourished and expanded to include all forms of modern theater experimentation. It soon became one of the most stimulating artistic centers in Europe. In 1913 Diaghilev visited the school and was so impressed by the demonstration he saw that he hired one of Dalcroze's students, Miriam Rambam, to teach members of his own company. Most of the Ballets Russes dancers saw no reason to augment the training they already had received in the Imperial Russian schools, but Miss Rambam (who was, of course, the young Marie Rambert) had a definite effect on Nijinsky's choreography – especially in *Afternoon of a Faun*. Kurt Jooss, Mary Wigman and Hanya Holm all worked at Hellerau at one time or another.

Dalcroze returned to Geneva in 1915 and founded the Institut Jaques-Dalcroze there; the same year, the first Jaques-Dalcroze Institute was opened in the United States. The Hellerau school moved to Austria, near Vienna, in 1920; it was renamed the Hellerau-Laxenburg School and was directed by Ernst Ferand and Christine Baer-Frissell. Between 1920 and 1938, when the Nazi invasion forced its closing, it graduated some 3000 pupils.

Though Delsarte and Dalcroze are important influences, it is Rudolf von Laban (1879–1958) who is generally acknowledged as the 'father of modern dance' in Europe. Von Laban was born in Hungary and studied ballet as a boy. He did not take much to it, but while he was taking a world tour with his father he became greatly attracted to Asian dance. When they returned to Europe he began studying with one of Delsarte's pupils in Paris.

In 1910, after a dancing career that took him to most major German cities and to Vienna (1907–10), he opened a school in Munich (where Mary Wigman was one of his pupils). He spent the years during World War I in Zurich, then returned to Germany in 1919, working in Nuremburg, Stuttgart (where he first encountered Kurt Jooss) and Mannheim. In 1936 he organized the dances for the Olympic Games in Berlin; he could not long tolerate the Nazi regime, however, and two year later he emigrated to England, joining Jooss and Sigurd Leeder at Dartington. He remained in England, founding the Art of Movement Studio in Manchester in 1946, with Lisa Ullman.

Von Laban's most important contribution to dance was as a theoretician rather than as a choreographer or dancer. With a Germanic passion for analyzing and ordering principles into a consistent philosophy, von Laban formulated a systematic approach to dance. He used ballet, Delsarte, folk dancing, mathematics, geometry and anatomy to 'dissect out' the basic elements that create and control movements. He even experimented with a crystal icosahedron (20-sided geometric figure) as big as a man to develop an exhaustive chart of all possible types and directions of movement – a system he called eukinetics. He also investigated the relation of the body to the space around it (choreutics) and explored the connection between psychology and movement.

His system of dance notation (called Schrifttanz or Labanotation), which was published in 1928, is his most lasting monument. It is a highly accurate, de-

Below: The Martha Graham-style London Contemporary Dance Theatre in Consolation of the Rising Moon *by its director Robert Cohan.*

Bridge the Distance, *a Siobhan Davies work for London Contemporary Dance Theatre, has a core of modern lyricism.*

Requiem, *for the Stuttgart Ballet which Cranko had directed, starred Marcia Haydee. She succeeded Cranko as artistic director.*

tailed system. Written from the point of view of the dancer, it includes symbols for each joint or surface of the body, and all possible movements (leaping, turning, touching, and so on) and can record the patterns made by a large group or the position of an individual dancer's thumbs. While he was in England he also adapted his systems to study movement and movement notation for industry.

Germany's most famous dancer, Mary Wigman (1886–1973), began her career during the period between the wars, when interest in expressionistic dance was at its height. She had begun her studies before World War I at Hellerau (where her classmates laughed at her awkwardness), and during the war had worked with von Laban in Switzerland. After 1919, however, she set out on her own to develop her personal approach to dance. Her

Below: The dynamic energies of a performance by London Contemporary Dance Theatre are based on a vivid sense of ensemble unity.

Right: 3 Epitaphs, *a ballet by Paul Taylor premiered in 1956 and revived for LCDT in 1970. Rauschenburg's costumes depersonalize the dancers.*

Below: Choreographer Richard Alston set his elegant Voices and Light Footsteps *to a selection of Monteverdi madrigals.*

school in Dresden, which she opened in 1920, soon became a major focal point for German modern dance – with pupils that included Yvonne Georgi, Hanya Holm, Harald Kreutzberg and Gret Palucca.

Wigman added emotion to von Laban's rather cold, scientific approach; in her view, dance had to consist of both ecstacy and form. Her pieces, however, were emotional, but certainly not ecstatic. On the contrary, they were generally dark, gloomy and often macabre, more concerned with fate than with hope or action. Much of her work was a reflection of her time; somber dances that hinted at the primordial forces beneath the veneer of civilization.

Another hallmark of Wigman's technique was her awareness of space – not in an intellectual sense, like von Laban's, but emotionally. She saw space as a tangible medium with which the dancer interacts, the way a swimmer interacts with water. The relation between dance and music also interested her, and many of her early dances were performed with little or very simple music, in an attempt to free them from the dominance of any musical form.

By 1926 Wigman had formed her own company and opened several more schools. She made her London debut in 1928 and in 1930 appeared for the first time in America. There the quiet, composed dancer with the stocky, muscular body, gray-green eyes, and low, pleasant voice was received with enthusiasm. She returned several times during the early 1930s, presenting dances like the mysterious *Face of the Night, Pastoral, Summer Dance, Storm Moods, Monotony Whirl,* and the swirling *Gypsy Moods.*

She continued to work in Hitler's Germany for the first few years, but she was not popular with the Nazis and after her appearance at the 1936 Olympics her schools were closed and she virtually dropped out of sight. In 1946 she began slowly picking up the pieces, working in Leipzig, where friends had gotten her an appointment at the Music Academy. In 1949 she moved to West Berlin, and the Wigman school again played an important role in German modern dance, until it closed in the mid-1960s.

Jochen Ulrich's ballet for the Tanz Forum der Oper der Stadt Köln, Out of Doors.

Kurt Jooss, Wigman's colleague in the growth of expressive dance in Germany, is discussed at greater length in the chapter on German ballet. It is interesting to note that in America Jooss's works are considered ballets, while in countries like England or France, where the ballet tradition is stronger and more pervasive, he is looked upon as a modern dancer.

One of Wigman's best-known pupils, Yvonne Georgi, was instrumental in the development of dance in both Germany and the Netherlands. Another, Harald Kreutzberg (1902–68), became internationally known as Germany's leading male modern dancer. Kreutzberg, whose superb craftsmanship was the outer manifestation of an inner exuberance and virtual obsession with dancing, began touring extensively with Georgi in the late 1920s and early 1930s. After the war he revisited the United States (in 1947, 1948 and 1953) and continued his concert career in Europe. In 1955 he moved to Bern, Switzerland and opened a school; though he formally retired from the stage in 1959, he continued to teach and occasionally choreograph until his death.

With the emergence of Pina Bausch in the late 1970s, modern dance once again became a major force in West Germany. Born in 1940, Bausch studied in Essen and worked with Jooss before going to New York to study with Tudor at the Juilliard School and perform with the Metropolitan Opera Ballet. She returned to West Germany, where she was appointed director of the Wuppertal Dance Theatre in 1973. She staged highly original productions of Gluck's operas *Orpheus and Eurydice* and *Iphigenia in Tarus* in 1974 and 1975, as well as *Le Sacre du Printemps* and the Brecht-Weill *The Seven Deadly Sins*.

However, it is with her entirely original works, such as *Café Mueller, Bluebeard, 1980, Waltzer* and *Nelken* (Carnation) that Baush has made her strongest statements. With these pieces she has earned a reputation as the most influential choreographer of the generation (countless artists in America, England, Australia and all over the European continent have been affected by her work.

Her works are often exceptionally long – some last nearly four hours. Each of them uses dance, everyday movement and, above all, multilingual dialogue to create a total theatrical experience. Much of the text is drawn directly from the real lives of

Above: London Contemporary Dance Theatre shows the strong influences of Martha Graham in works such as Robert Cohan's Agora.

her company. The result is presented in a shifting, fractured and at times surrealist montage. The highly personal context is somewhat diffused and distanced by the costumes (usually evening wear of the 1930s and 1940s).

Bausch's eternal theme is the relation between the sexes and man's individual place in our depersonalized society. She seems to hold out little hope for mankind, yet makes the viewer feel great compassion and a certain admiration for her performers.

The dancing itself is often based on repetitive gesture. She also incorporates social dances into her works, along with tongue-in-cheek chorus lines that have a scruffy charm in their ineptitude. Bausch was one of the first major choreographers to exploit fully the sexual disease of modern times: both with humor (her men often don frilly party dresses) and with horror (*Bluebeard* is one long relentless struggle of failed couplings).

Each of these pieces is somehow directly connected to the natural word as well:

Nelken covers the stage floor with 10,000 pink and white carnations, the stage for *Bluebeard* is strewn with autumn leaves. Other pieces use water and grass as their starting points.

Bausch's impact is based on a belief that dance can deal with real issues of life and living and can do so in a way that is both imaginative and at the same time accessible to the average theater-goer.

In France, where the Bausch company regularly plays to overflowing houses of cheering audiences, modern dance has become a prolific and creative art form. The current trend began when American dancer Carolyn Carlson (b 1943) was given the unprecedented position of *danseuse étoile choregraphique* at the Paris Opéra (1974–80). A former member of the Nikolais Dance Theater, Carlson set up a choreographic workshop in the basement of the Opéra, taught open classes there and created pieces which were performed in special modern evenings in the theater. Gradually, she too evolved a highly personalized, essentially theatrical style; but, unlike Bausch, Carlson's works have a fluid ease and even a modern romanticism to them.

She and another American (and ex-Nikolais dancer) living in Paris, Susan Buirge (b 1940), helped train a whole new generation of French dancers who, in the 1980s, came into their own with a radical new style of dance theater that mixes alienation and glamour. Cunningham has been another great influence in France and his clear, sharp techniques of movement are often visible underneath all the theatrical trappings.

Carlson left the Opéra in 1980. She then spent three seasons running her own troupe at the Teatro Fenice in Venice. In 1984 she returned to Paris, where she worked as a soloist and teacher for a season before again forming a new company in 1985.

The Paris Opéra Ballet has since established a special modern wing for the company. Known as the GRCOP (Groupe de Recherche Choregraphic de l'Opéra de Paris), it is discussed in more detail in the French Ballet chapter.

The Centre National de Danse Contemporaine is based in Angers. Its purpose is to train professional dancers of the highest caliber. Guest teachers and choreographers of international importance work

Maurice Béjart's imaginative choreography and spectacular productions have filled whole stadiums in Europe with eager audiences.

Above: The nude scenes in Glen Tetley's ballet for the Nederlands Dans Theater in 1970 caused a sensation.

Overleaf: Ballet Rambert, always eager to break fresh ground, holds experimental ballet workshops in which young choreographers can show their work.

there on a regular basis. Nikolais was director from 1977 to 1981. Viola Farber spent a fruitful three years in residence (1981–83).

There are now state-supported companies in *maisons de culture* all across France. Perhaps the most important of these is run by Maguy Marin in Creteil. She, too, favors large group spectacles performed as evening-length pieces.

Modern dance was the first kind of dance to become really popular in The Netherlands, beginning in the 1920s when Gertrude Leistikow founded schools in Amsterdam, The Hague, Rotterdam and Utrecht. The first native Dutch dancers included Jacoba van der Pas, Else Dankmeyer and Angela Sydow. Tours by the Jooss Ballet, the Swiss dancer Trudi Schoop and Kreutzberg all helped promote the cause of modern dance, as did the work of people like Georgi and Florrie Rodrigo.

Two distinct new voices from Belgium are Jan Fabre (b 1958) and Anne Térésa de Keersmaeker (b 1961). Fabre is a creator of spectacle to rival Bausch in both length and symbolic evocation. *The Power of Theatrical Madness* is a five-hour epic that engulfs the audience in a series of emotionally charged scenes which range from the violent and actually dangerous to the comedic and the absurd. Gargantuan in scale and spilling over with pungent imagery, Fabre's works are avant-garde operas for the alienated. Simultaneously

assaulting and deadening the viewers' senses, his works are a mix of experiment, endurance and gladiatorial stamina. Next to Bausch, Fabre is Europe's most controversial new-wave artist. De Keersmaeker is much more closely linked with the American post-moderns, notably Lucinda Childs. She creates tightly organized patterns of repetitive movement like the Americans, but she Europeanizes her work with an emotional atmosphere. In *Rosas danst Rosas*, the four women performers seem victims of their own making, victims of society. They dance with an emotional vulnerability which transforms formalism into an unspecified, but undeniable, atmosphere of sexual exploitation.

Another important Dutch modern dancer is Lucas Hoving, who studied with Rodrigo and Georgi in Holland, then with Jooss in England. In the mid-1940s, after some time with the Jooss Ballet, he emigrated to the United States, where he became a citizen and began a long association with José Limón. Since his retirement he has divided his time between America and Holland. His most popular work is *Icarus*, a retelling of the classic myth.

Modern dance has been popular in Scandinavia, especially Sweden, since Isadora Duncan toured there in the early 1900s. During the first half of the century, while ballet was in decline, modern dancers like Wigman, Jooss and Kreutzberg still could attract large audiences.

Modern and classic dance have been closely allied in Sweden since the 1940s when Birgit Cullberg and Ivo Cramér formed the Swedish Dance Theater (1946–47) to present avant-garde ballets. Sweden's best-known contemporary choreographer, Birgit Åkesson, has choreographed several productions for the Royal Swedish Ballet, including *Sisyphus*, *Minotaur* and *Rites*, to scores composed by musicians like Karl-Birger Blomdahl and Ingvar Lidholm. Cullberg's sons, Niklas and Mats Ek, have both become dancers. Mats Ek (b 1945) has also choreographed several works for the Cullberg Ballet. In 1976 he used bop and folk music for a colorful *St George and the Dragon*. His dramatic works include *The House of Bernarda Alba* (1978).

The American pioneers of modern dance – Allan, Duncan and Fuller – all appeared in London, and Martha Graham first danced there in the early 1950s. Modern dance did not really begin to catch on, however, until her appearances in London and Edinburgh in 1963, closely followed by visits from Merce Cunningham and Paul Taylor. It was traumatic for some dance-goers and critics, but the

exposure led to increasing experimentation and a refusal on the part of many British dancers to accept old patterns.

Shortly thereafter the London School of Contemporary Dance was founded – the only school in Europe authorized to teach Graham's techniques and approach – and modern dance was finally established. In 1969 the organization moved to The Place in northwest London, where the London Contemporary Dance Theatre had its premier performance on 2 September.

Robert Cohan (b 1925) has been the director of the company since its beginning. An American who danced with Graham before arriving in London, Cohan is a choreographer firmly committed to the Graham ideal. His dramatic dances teem with an intense emotionalism.

Siobhan Davies (b 1950) is the foremost British choreographer to work with LCDT on a regular basis. A product of the company's school, her own style is decidedly less dramatic than Cohan's. She blends the Graham aesthetic with the principles of Merce Cunningham. The result is more movement-oriented (in an abstract sense) than Cohan's choreography, and definitely less concerned with narrative than most dancemakers who create in the Graham mold. Many of her dances, such as *Bridge the Distance* (1985), evoke atmospheres and personal relationships between the dancers, but rarely resort to direct storytelling. Quiet, even subdued, Davies's dances have a fluid and lyrical appeal.

In 1966, when Ballet Rambert elected to abandon classical ballet for modernism, thd company took the first step towards a distinctively British contemporary dance form. However, the first steps were taken with a strong influx of American aid. Glen Tetley staged several of his works for Rambert, and created many others specifically for the company. The peak of his influence came in 1979 when he staged his first full-length piece of choreography, *The Tempest*. Rambert took on extra dancers for the project, which virtually monopolized all creative energies at Rambert for an entire season.

Norman Morrice (b 1931) began dancing with Rambert in 1952. He was one of the major architects of the 1966 policy changes. He choreographed several works before he left Rambert in 1974, but his lasting influence was in planning and administration.

Christopher Bruce (b 1945) began with Rambert in 1963. He starred in many Tetley productions and began making his own dances in 1969. Among his most distinctive creations is *Cruel Garden* (1977). Inspired by the life and poems of Federico Garcia Lorca, Bruce collaborated on the work with Lindsay Kemp, that magician of radical theater. *Cruel Garden* proved one of Rambert's most enduring popular hits. In *Ghost Dances* (1981), Bruce used the folk music of South America to depict the deaths of the 'little people' who are the pawns of political struggle and revolution. *Sergeant Early's Dream* (1984) also utilized folk music and movement motifs – in this case sea songs of the Irish coast. Bruce's use of international folk steps owes a debt to Juří Kylián, with whom he has worked in Holland. Bruce was appointed resident choreographer for London Festival Ballet in 1985. He has also worked in the musical theater and done original choreography for television.

Robert North (b 1945) is an American who first came to England to study with London Contemporary Dance School in 1967. He danced with LCDT and then in the USA with Graham before returning to Britain. He joined Rambert as an associate choreographer in 1975. He served as the company's artistic director (1981–85) and now works as a freelance choreographer. His most popular work is an all-male, mock-macho comedy, *Troy Game* (1974). His *Death and the Maiden* (1984) shows his dramatic links with the Graham tradition.

Richard Alston (b 1948) is developing into Britain's most innovative and important young choreographer. He studied with London Contemporary Dance School before forming his own small group, Strider (1972-75). He then went to New York to study with Merce Cunningham. He returned to London in 1978, was appointed Rambert's resident choreographer in 1980 and became its artistic director in 1986. As Morrice had in 1966, Alston swept away the accumulations of years in an effort to begin afresh. He immediately invited several young British choreographers to create new works for the company's diamond jubilee season at the Sadler's Wells Theatre in June 1986. The result was hugely popular with audiences and won several prestigious awards. New works by Alston and Bruce shared the stage with creations by Royal Ballet dancer Ashley Page, Ian Spink (who had formed a Strider offshoot called Second Stride) and Michael Clark; all of them added vitality to the latest Rambert incarnation.

Alston's own works, such as *Wild Life* (1984) and *Zansa* (1986) and even the sly Tharp-like comedy *Java* (1985), show a speed and intricate deftness more akin to Cunningham than any other European choreographer. In 1983, Alston created *Midsummer*, his only work to date for a classical ballet company, in this case the Royal Ballet.

Alston was a formative influence on Michael Clark (b 1962). Born in Scotland, Clark joined the Royal Ballet school at 13 and became a Rambert dancer four years later. He figured prominently in Alston's choreography. *Soda Lake* (1981) was a solo in silence tailored to Clark's exceptional dance talents.

Clark, too, went to Cunningham's studio in New York before founding his own radical London-based company in 1984. Clark has caught the imagination of the British public, with a special corner on the youth market. He creates joke-filled, gender-bending dances alive with anarchy, cartoonish clowning and streetwise savvy. It's all performed to the latest in rock music, played at deafening volume, and dolled up in camp avant-garde costumes. Clark's total theater is filled with a flamboyance and assurance which some find liberating, while others view it as self-indulgent.

Whichever opinion turns out to be correct in the long run, there is no question that Clark is bringing a new vitality to British dance. It is a vitality that can only add to the general sense of creativity currently infusing the English dance world.

Other centers of contemporary dance active in England today include Laverne Meyer's Northern Dance Theatre in Manchester, the Western Theatre Ballet and, of course, Ballet Rambert.

Though it has taken much longer, modern dance has been finding increasing acceptance even in France in recent years. In 1973 Merce Cunningham was invited to the Opéra as guest choreographer (producing *Un Jour ou Deux*). Carolyn Carlson was appointed *danseuse étoile choréographique* at that august institution in 1974; her works there include *Densité, 21.5, L'Or des Fous, Les Fous d'Or, Sablier Prison, Il y a Juste un Instant* and *Wind, Water, Sand*.

Overall, while modern dance in Europe never again has reached the heights it attained in Germany and Holland between the wars, it is still alive and vital. The most interesting trend is toward its interaction with classic dance, an area in which Europe equals, if not leads, the United States.

CHRONOLOGY OF BALLET 1400-1982

	1400s	1500s	1600s	
Italy	1462: Domenico di Piacenza writes first known treatise on dance 1489: Bergonzio di Botta presents his dinner ballet at Tortona **1494: Charles II of France invades Italy**	1581: Fabrizio Caroso publishes *Il Ballarino* 1584: Teatro d'Olympico, with proscenium arch stage, opens in Verona	1604: Cesare Negri publishes *Nuovi Inventioni di Balli*	
France		**1533: Catherine de Medici marries Henry II of France** 1581: Belgiojoso stages *Le Ballet Comique de la Reine* 1588: Arbeau publishes *Orchesographie*, the first French treatise on dance	1651: Louis XIV makes first appearance in public as dancer 1653: Louis XIV portrays the Rising Sun in *Le Ballet Royale de la Nuit* 1669: Louis XIV founds Academie Royale de la Musique (Paris	Opera); ballet performances move from palace ballroom to proscenium arch theater 1681: first professional female dancers appear on a French stage, in *Le Triomphe de l'Amour*
Russia			**1689: accession of Peter the Great**	
United Kingdom			1605: Jonson begins writing masques (in collaboration with Inigo Jones) 1634: Milton writes *Comus* 1640: last masque, *Salmacida Spolia*, produced at Whitehall for Charles I **1642: Civil War begins** **1660: restoration of monarchy**	1661: theater at Lincoln's Inn Fields opens 1663: theater in Drury Lane opens 1682: Thomas Betterton, manager of Drury Lane, begins importing French dancers
Scandinavia			1634: von Kuckelsom stages first Danish *ballet de cour* 1638: de Beaulieu stages first Swedish *ballet de cour*	
Low Countries			1638: first theater opens in Amsterdam 1658: first female dancers appear on stage in Amsterdam c. 1669: first Dutch *ballets de cour* produced for William of Orange	
Central Europe			1600: *The Liberation of Peace* performed in Darmstadt 1609: first court ballets in Stuttgart 1643: first theater in Poland opens in Royal Palace, Warsaw	
United States			**1620: Pilgrims land at Plymouth, Massachusetts**	

	1700s	*10s*	*20s*	*30s*	*40s*
Italy				1737: Teatro San Carlo opens in Naples	
France		1713: ballet school attached to Opera 1714: Duchess of Maine presents mime version of *Les Horaces* at her château	1727: Salle makes debut at Opera	1735: opera-ballet reaches peak with Rameau's *Les Indes Galantes* 1739: La Barbarina astounds Paris with *entrechat huit*	
Russia				1738: Lande founds Imperial Ballet School in St Petersburg	
United Kingdom	1705: Haymarket Theatre opens	1716: Marie Salle and her brother make debuts at Lincoln's Inn Fields under John Rich 1717: John Weaver presents *The Loves of Mars and Venus* at Drury Lane		1733: Salle's production of *Pygmalion* causes a sensation at Lincoln's Inn Fields	
Scandinavia			1726: Lande takes charge of dancing at theater in Copenhagen's Lille Grønnegade		1748: first Royal Theater opens on Kongens Nytorv in Copenhagen
Low Countries	1705: small ballet company established at Theatre sur la Monnai in Brussels				
Central Europe		1717: Taubert writes first German treatise on dance	1724: first theater opens in Prague; Opera House opens in Warsaw		1742: Frederick the Great establishes Royal Opera House in Berlin 1744: Hilferding begins to choreograph *ballets d'action* in Vienna; La Barbarina triumphs in Berlin
United States					
Others					

50s	60s	70s	80s	90s
		1778: La Scala opens in Milan	1783: first mention of ballet in Rome	
1758: Noverre produces early *ballet d'action, Caprices de Galatee*, in Lyons		1772: Maximilien Gardel discards his mask at the Opera 1776: Noverre appointed ballet master at Opera	1789: Dauberval produces *La Fille Mal Gardée* in Bordeaux **1789: French Revolution begins**	
1758: Hilferding becomes ballet master in St Petersburg	**1762: Catherine the Great** 1766: Directorate of Imperial Theaters established to administer ballet, opera, and drama; Angiolini succeeds Hilferding	1774: Beccari founds ballet school at Moscow Orphanage		1794: Valberkh directs St Petersburg school; in Moscow, Petrovsky theater and school brought into Imperial system
1755: Garrick invites Noverre to produce *Les Fetes Chinoises* at Drury Lane			1781: Noverre appointed ballet master at King's Theatre	1796: Didelot produces *Flore et Zephyre*
		c.1770: Court Theater built at Christianborg Castle 1773: Royal Opera House opens in Stockholm 1775: Galeotti arrives in Copenhagen	1781: Antoine Bournonville joins Royal Swedish Ballet 1786: premiere of Galeotti's *The Whims of Cupid and the Ballet Master*	
1759: Noverre arrives in Stuttgart 1761: Angiolini presents *Don Juan* 1765: National Theater founded in Warsaw 1767: Noverre arrives in Vienna				1792: ballet school founded in Munich 1793: Vigano begins first engagement at Kaertnerthor Theater in Vienna
		1776: Declaration of Independence	1780s: John Durang's dancing popular in Philadelphia and other major cities	1793: Placide arrives in New York

	1800s	10s	20s	30s	40s
Italy		1813: Imperiale Regio Accademia di Danze established at La Scala; Vigano begins staging his 'choreodrammi' in Milan		1837: Blasis appointed director of La Scala academy	
France	**1804: Napoleon declared Emperor of France**	**1815: Napoleon defeated at Waterloo**	1828: Marie Taglioni makes debut at Opéra	1832: Taglioni's *La Sylphide* officially opens Romantic era in ballet 1834: Elssler makes debut at Opéra; marks appearance of the 'pagan' Romantic ballerina	1841: *Giselle*, starring Grisi, marks high point of Romantic ballet
Russia	1801: Didelot arrives in St Petersburg to direct Bolshoi Theater 1805: Petrovsky Theater destroyed by fire		1825: Moscow Bolshoi Theater opens	1837: Marie Taglioni arrives in St Petersburg for first time 1839: Delsarte begins most active period as teacher of singing and recitation	1842: Christian Johansson accompanies Taglioni to St Petersburg; Andreianova becomes first Russian Giselle 1848: Elssler takes Russia by storm; Perrot begins work in St Petersburg
United Kingdom			1826: Blasis appointed choreographer and soloist at King's Theatre	1830: Blasis publishes *The Code of Terpsichore* 1833: Elssler sisters appear at King's Theatre **1837: Queen Victoria ascends throne** 1837: King's Theatre becomes Her Majesty's Theatre	1841: Lumley hires Perrot for Her Majesty's Theatre 1844: Perrot presents *La Esmeralda*; Clara Webster dies in fire on stage at Drury Lane 1845: premier of Perrot's *Pas de Quatre*
Scandinavia	1803: Filippo Taglioni engaged as soloist in Stockholm	1813: August Bournonville dances in public for first time	1829: Bournonville appointed ballet master at Royal Theater in Copenhagen	1839: Grahn leaves Denmark for international career	1841: Marie Taglioni tours Sweden 1842: premiere of Bournonville's *Napoli* 1846: premiere of Selinder's *People of Vaarmland*, in Stockholm
Low Countries		1819: Jean-Antoine Petipa made first ballet master in Brussels			
Central Europe	1801: Vigano presents *The Creatures of Prometheus* in Vienna	**1815: Congress of Vienna** 1815: Horschelt's Children's Ballet becomes popular 1818: National Theater opens in Munich	1821: Filippo Taglioni and Barbaja in charge at Kaertnerthor Theater 1824: Taglioni family arrives in Stuttgart		1843: Filippo Taglioni directs National Theater in Warsaw
United States				1837: Maywood and Lee make debuts in Philadelphia	1840: Elssler begins triumphal American tour
Others					

50s	*60s*	*70s*	*80s*	*90s*
1859–70: Unification of Italy			1881: Manzotti stages *Excelsior*, one of his earlier 'colossal' ballets	
		1870: Saint-Leon completes choreography for *Coppélia*		1890s: Fuller a sensation at Folies Bergère
		1870: Franco-Prussian war; Siege of Paris		
1858: Saint-Leon replaces Perrot	1861: Petipa produces *The Pharaoh's Daughter*	1870: Petipa officially named ballet master in St Petersburg	1885: Zucchi first dances in Russia	1890: Cecchetti arrives to dance in *Sleeping Beauty* 1892: Premiere of *The Nutcracker* 1894: Stepanov's book on dance notation published 1895: Legnani introduces 32 *fouettés* in *Swan Lake*
1850: Grisi makes last appearance in Western Europe, in Paul Taglioni's *Les Metamorphoses*			1887: Lanner appointed ballet mistress of Empire Theatre	1897: Genee makes London debut **1899–1902: Boer War**
		1877: Bournonville retires 1879: Beck makes debut with Royal Danish Ballet; first state theater opens in Helsinki		1894: Beck made director of Royal Danish Ballet
		1871: first performance of *Coppélia* outside France, in Brussels 1872: Lucien Petipa made ballet master in Brussels		
1856: Paul Taglioni becomes ballet master in Berlin	**1866–71: Unification of Germany** 1869: Opera House opens on Ringstrasse in Vienna		1884: Hungarian Ballet founded; Budapest Opera House opens	
	1861: Civil War begins			

	1900s	10s	20s	30s	40s
Italy		1916: Diaghilev and Massine winter in Rome; prepare *Parade* and present *Les Femmes des Bonne Humeur*	**1922: Mussolini in power** 1925: Cecchetti returns to Italy, to become director at La Scala 1929: Diaghilev dies in Venice		
France	1909: Diaghilev presents Ballets Russes in first Paris season; Fokine stages *Les Sylphides*, one of first abstract ballets	1912: Nijinsky shocks Paris with *Afternoon of a Faun* 1919: Ballets Russes presents Massine's *Le Tricorne*	1924: Balanchine joins Ballets Russes	1930: Lifar becomes director at Opera 1932: Blum and de Basil form Ballets Russes de Monte Carlo; Kurt Jooss's antiwar ballet *The Green Table* wins international competition in Paris	1945: Les Ballets de Champs Elysees founded 1947 Marquis de Cuevas takes over Nouveau Ballet de Monte Carlo, calling it International Ballet 1948: Ballets de Paris founded by Petit
Russia	1900: Gorsky begins work in Moscow 1903: Petipa resigns 1904: Duncan first visits Russia 1905: Fokine arranges the *Dying Swan* for Pavlova	**1917: Russian Revolution**	1923: Balanchine appears in Lopukhov's abstract *Dance Symphony*, at Gatob in St Petersburg 1927: Premiere of Tikhomirov's *The Red Poppy* in Moscow	1932: Premiere of Vainonen's *The Flames of Paris*	1940: Ulanova stars in Lavrovsky's *Romeo and Juliet* at the Kirov, in St Petersburg 1944: Ulanova and Lavrovsky transferred to Moscow
United Kingdom		1910: Pavlova arrives in England 1916: Astafieva opens school in London	1920: Rambert opens school in Notting Hill Gate; Association of Operatic Dancing (now Royal Academy of Dancing) founded 1922: Cecchetti Society founded 1926: de Valois arrives in London; Ashton presents first work at Lyric Theatre 1928: Wigman makes London debut	1930: Camargo Society founded 1931: de Valois becomes director of new Vic-Wells Ballet; Rambert begins Ballet Club performances 1933: Ashton choreographs *Les Rendezvous*; Jooss and Leeder establish Ballets Jooss 1935: Vic-Wells becomes Sadler's Wells Ballet; Markova-Dolin Ballet formed 1936: Tudor choreographs *Jardin aux Lilas* at Mercury 1939: Ballet Club becomes Ballet Rambert	1941: Ballet Rambert presents Gore's *Confessional* 1946: Sadler's Wells Ballet moves to Covent Garden; Ashton premieres *Symphonic Variations*
Scandinavia	1906: Duncan tours Scandinavia 1908: Pavlova makes first appearance outside Russia, in Stockholm 1909: premiere of Beck's *The Little Mermaid*	1915: Beck retires	1920: de Mare forms Les Ballets Suedois 1921: Gue appointed ballet master in Helsinki	1930: Lander appointed director of Royal Danish Ballet	1948: premiere of Lander's *Etude*
Low Countries		1914: Gertrude Leistikow begins to introduce modern dance to Holland		1933: Schwezoff establishes ballet school in The Hague 1936: Georgi Ballet founded	1941: Georgi Ballet becomes Amsterdam Opera Ballet 1945: Snoek founds Scapino Ballet 1947: ter Weeme founds Ballet der Lage Landen 1949: Collins reorganizes Opera Ballet
Central Europe	1902: Cecchetti ballet master at National Theater, Warsaw 1903: Allen makes debut in Vienna	1910: Dalcroze establishes school at Hellerau; von Laban opens school in Munich	1920: Wigman opens school in Dresden	**1933: Hitler in Power in Germany** **1939: Germany invades Poland**	1941: Hanka takes over as ballet mistress at Vienna Opera House **1945: Germany surrenders**
United States	1906: premiere of St Denis's *Radha* 1907: Genée makes first American tour 1909: Fornaroli becomes ballet mistress at Metropolitan Opera in New York 1909: Duncan returns to US for first tour	1915: first Denishawn school opens in Los Angeles 1916: Ballets Russes makes first appearance in New York **1917: US enters WWI**	1920: Bolm becomes ballet master at Chicago Civic Opera 1926: University of Wisconsin offers first degree program in dance 1927: Graham opens School of Contemporary Dance	1932: Ted Shawn Male Dancers organized; premieres of *Primitive Mysteries* and *The Shakers* 1933: Ballet Russe de Monte Carlo begins touring US; Bolm helps found San Francisco Opera Ballet 1934: Balanchine and Kirstein open School of American Ballet 1935: premiere of Balanchine's *Serenade* 1936: Kirstein founds Ballet Caravan; Hanya Holm Studio opens in New York 1938: Ballet Caravan presents *Filling Station* and *Billy the Kid* 1939: Ballet Theater founded by Chase and Pleasant; Georgi Ballet tours United States	1941: Shawn founds Jacob's Pillow Dance Festival **1941: US enters WWII** 1942: premiere of de Mille's *Rodeo* 1943: Horton opens school in Los Angeles 1944: American Ballet Theatre presents Robbins's *Fancy Free* 1944: premiere of Graham's *Appalachian Spring* 1945: Merce Cunningham founds own company 1946: Balanchine and Kirstein found Ballet Society 1948: Ballet Society becomes New York City Ballet 1948: Halprin opens studio 1949: Limon first presents *The Moor's Pavane* 1949: Sadler's Wells visits NY
Others		1913: Genée tours Australia and New Zealand	1926: Pavlova tours Australia	1938: Original Ballet Russe tours South America; Winnipeg Ballet Club founded in Canada	

50s	60s	70s	80s	90s
1950: Susannah Negri establishes small company at Teatro Regio in Turin	1960: Carla Fracci forms touring company		1980-83: Carolyn Carlson's modern company in residence at Teatro Fenice, Venice	
1951: Lander joins Opera	1963: Festival International de Danse begins in Paris	1973: Merce Cunningham engaged as guest choreographer at Opéra	1984: Nureyev appointed director of the Paris Opéra Ballet	
1956: Bolshoi's first foreign tour to Western Europe 1957: premiere of Grigorovitch's *The Stone Flower* in St Petersburg 1959: Bolshoi makes first appearance in New York	1968: Bolshoi's *Spartacus*		1986: Bolshoi Ballet tours United Kingdom	
1950: Markova and Dolin form Festival Ballet 1956: Sadler's Wells becomes Royal Ballet; Fonteyn made DBE; West forms Western Theatre Ballet in Bristol	1962: Nureyev joins Royal Ballet, begins partnership with Fonteyn 1963: Graham appears in London and Edinburgh 1965: Ballet Rambert reorganized into smaller group for experimental ballet 1966: London Contemporary Dance Theatre founded 1969: Western Theatre Ballet becomes Scottish Theatre Ballet, based in Glasgow	1976: Norman Morrice succeeds MacMillan as director of the Royal Ballet	1984: Peter Schaufuss appointed director of London Festival Ballet 1986: Anthony Dowell becomes director of the Royal Ballet 1986: Richard Alston appointed director of Ballet Rambert in conjunction with company's Diamond Jubilee season	
1950: Lander leaves Copenhagen; Volkova arrives and annual Ballet Festival begins; Tudor hired as director of Royal Swedish Ballet; first production of Cullberg's *Miss Julie* 1953: Skeaping directs Royal Swedish; Den Norske established	1965: Flindt takes over Royal Danish Ballet 1966: Royal Danish Ballet tours United States	1974: Den Norske Ballet makes first American tour 1979: Royal Danish Ballet's Bournonville Festival	1981: Norwegian Ballet performs Tetley's *The Tempest*	
1954: Netherlands Ballet established in The Hague 1959: Amsterdam Ballet formed from Opera Ballet and Ballet der Lage Landen; Harkavy forms Netherlands Dance Theater in The Hague	1960: Béjart forms Ballet of the 20th Century in Brussels 1961: National Ballet formed from Amsterdam Ballet and Netherlands Ballet	1971: Béjart presents *Nijinsky* 1976: Jiří Kylián becomes director of Netherlands Dance Theatre	1985: Béjart's 25th anniversary with Ballet of the Twentieth Century	
	1960: Cranko appointed director of Stuttgart Ballet	1973: Pina Bausch appointed director of Wuppertal Dance Theatre 1973: John Neumeier becomes director for Hamburg State Opera Ballet 1974-76: Glen Tetley artistic director for Stuttgart Ballet	1983: Basel Ballet pays first visit to the USA	
1956: Joffrey Ballet established 1958: Alvin Ailey American Dance Theater founded		1971: Dance Theatre of Harlem founded 1972: New York City Ballet's Stravinsky Festival 1973: Tharp choreographs *Deuce Coupe* for Joffrey Ballet	1980: Baryshnikov appointed director of American Ballet Theatre 1983: Jerome Robbins and Peter Martins succeed Balanchine as the co-directors of New York City Ballet 1985: Kenneth MacMillan joins the staff of American Ballet Theatre	
1951: National Ballet of Canada founded in Toronto 1953: Winnipeg Ballet Club becomes Royal Winnipeg Ballet	1962: Australian Ballet established		1987: Glen Tetley named artistic advisor to the National Ballet of Canada	

GLOSSARY OF BALLET TERMS

Sissone, *a soft leap from fifth position.*

A list of all the important ballet terms would fill an entire book – and it is possible to enjoy ballet without knowing any of them. But in order to read about ballet and understand it, one needs to know something about the vocabulary – which is, for the most part, in French. Only the most essential terms are given here; there are many excellent dictionaries for those who want to study the technical language further.

Adagio As in music, a slow execution. Generally the controlled, flowing movements are more difficult to perform than the quicker *allegro* steps. The *adagio* is usually the highlight of the *pas de deux* in a classical ballet.

Air, en l' In the air.

Allegro As in music, a quick, lively execution. *Allegro* work consists of fast turns, jumps and beats.

Arabesque A pose executed by balancing the body on one leg and extending the other to the rear; the head and arms are held in an harmonious position to achieve a continuous line from fingertip to toe. There are many variations of the *arabesque*.

Arrière, en To the rear.

Assemblé A jump in which the dancer brings the feet together in the air, landing in a *demi-plié* in fifth position. There are many variations of this jump.

Demi-plié (*in fifth*) *aids jumping and landing.*

Attitude A pose in which one leg is raised to the back, with the knee bent at a 90-degree angle and kept higher than the foot; it was devised by Carlo Blasis, based on Giambologna's statue of Mercury. There are many different types of *attitude*. In the *attitude en avant* the bent leg is raised in front of the body.

Avant, en To the front.

Ballabile Dance numbers (usually in waltz time) performed by the *corps de ballet* in classic productions. 'The Waltz of the Flowers' in *The Nutcracker* is a good example.

Ballerina In modern usage, a principal female soloist in a ballet company. In Russia it is an official title awarded only after a long apprenticeship.

Ballet d'action A ballet that tells a story, such as *Swan Lake*.

Ballon Lightness, elasticity and bounciness; the ability of a dancer to land lightly after a jump.

Barre A wooden or metal rail attached to a studio or classroom wall, held lightly for support during warm-up exercises. For adults the *barre* is usually set at 42 inches.

Battement A beating step with several variations (*battement battu, fondu, frappe, tendu,* etc). A *grand battement* is a high kick in any direction; a *petite battement* is a light tapping by the working foot against the supporting leg.

Battement frappe en avant (*to the front*).

Batterie A term that encompasses the entire collection of beats – *brisés, cabrioles, entrechats* and *royales*.

Arabesque en efface, demi-pointe.

Beat A kind of movement which involves tapping one leg or foot against the other during a step or jump.
Box The hard portion at the tip of a *pointe* shoe, made from seven layers of cloth that have been stiffened with a special glue.
Brisé A broken (or beaten) step; there are more than 20 variations.

Cabriole A jump in which the legs are fully extended and beaten before landing. Usually performed by male dancers.
Cambré A movement in which the body is arched from the waist.
Caractère A type of dancing that emphasizes character development rather than pure classical form. *Caractère* roles often involve light comedy; the *caractère* dancer frequently must exhibit more technical virtuosity and speed than the *danseur noble* and tends to be shorter physically.
Chassé A travelling step in which one foot slides after (literally chases) the other.
Classical ballet A full-length (five- or six-act) ballet, divided into sequences of pantomime and pure dance; developed in Russia by Marius Petipa during the late nineteenth century.
Corps de ballet The members of a ballet company who have not yet attained the rank of soloist.
Coryphée Originally, a dancer who

performed with small groups. Today it is often applied to a fifth-year member of the *corps de ballet* and represents a rank directly below that of soloist.
Croisé Crossed. One of the basic positions in *épaulement*.

Danse d'école Classic dance, based on the five positions. The vocabulary of ballet.
Danseur A male dancer. Leading male dancers in a company are referred to as *premiers danseurs*.
Danseuse A female dancer. Leading female dancers are referred to as *premières danseuses*.
Danseuse en travesti A female dancer in a male role.
Déboulés Turns in which the dancer steps rapidly from one foot to the other while rotating.
Dedans, en Inward; a movement that leads toward the dancer's body.
Dégagé A step in which the working foot is disengaged in preparation for the next step.
Dehors, en Outward; a movement that leads away from the dancer's body.
Demi-caractère The type of dancer or dancing that combines elements of both *caractère* and pure classical dancing.
Developpé A step in which the leg is slowly unfolded from the hip and extended in the air in any direction. Ideally, the raised foot is at or near shoulder level.

Diagonale, en Diagonally.

Ecart, grand The splits (as in acrobatics).
Echappé A jump in which the dancer moves from an odd- to an even-numbered position (for example, from fifth to second) and back again; can be performed on *pointe* or *demi-pointe*.
Effacé Shaded. One of the two basic positions of *épaulement*, in which the torso and body are placed obliquely to the audience.
Elancer To dart.
Elevation The ability to attain height and lightness in jumping. Steps of elevation are those done in the air as opposed to on the ground.
Enchainement A series of linking steps.
Entrechat A jump during which the feet cross each other three or more times before landing. There are various ways of counting *entrechats*, depending on the school or method.
Epaulement Refers to a special way of tilting the head and shoulders instead of holding the hips, shoulders, and head square. A relatively recent invention.

Relève efface devant, *demonstrating* épaulement.

Attitude en croise, *devised by Carlo Blasis.*

Developpé en avant, *foot level to shoulder.*

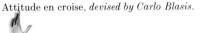

Etendre To stretch.
Extension The ability to raise the straightened leg from the hip and hold it as high as possible, while still maintaining correct body position.

Face, de Forward.
Fish Dive One of the most spectacular lifts in *adagio* work.

In fouettés *the leg is extended while turning.*

Fouetté A whipping movement. There are many types of *fouettés*; the most common is the *fouetté rond de jambe en tournant* in which the working legs whip outward in a circular movement, causing the body to turn like a top. Usually done in a series, like the 32 *fouettés* performed by the Black Swan in Act III of *Swan Lake*.

Glissade A gliding *terre à terre* step; one of the most important travelling steps.
Glisser To slide.

Grande jeté en arabesque effacé.

Glissade, *a sliding step which begins* and ends *in fifth.*

Jeté A jump or leap, with many variations.

Leg warmers Long wool stockings (minus the foot) worn over tights to keep the leg muscles warm and supple.

Leotard A tight, one-piece practice garment, said to have originated with Jules Leotard, a nineteenth-century French trapeze artist.
Libretto The story told by a ballet.

Maître de ballet Ballet master; he runs the daily classes and rehearsals of a ballet company. Until recently, he was responsible for choreography as well. The feminine form is *maîtresse de ballet*.
Manège, en In a circle.
Movements There are seven basic movements in classical ballet: *élancer, étendre, glisser, plier, relever, sauter,* and *tourner*.

Neoclassical A ballet style developed by George Balanchine, based on the classical ballets devised by Petipa in Russia.
Noble A type of dancing that represents pure classical style; often used to describe male dancers (as in *danseur noble*).

Pas A step. Also used to describe the number of people taking part in a dance (*pas seul*, a solo; *pas de deux*, a duet, etc) or to indicate which person or group is to dance a particular sequence.
Pas de bourrée A series of small, rapid steps performed on *pointe* or *demi pointe*. There are at least 23 variations of this step.

Pas de bourrée, *a series of small rapid steps.*

Pas de deux A dance arranged for two people, usually a man and a woman. It was the highlight of the classical ballets of Petipa and other nineteenth-century choreographers.

Passé A transitional step; the dancer's toe is pointed and passed behind the knee of the supporting leg.

Passé, one leg is moved from front to back.

Demi-plié à la seconde, *heels remain on floor.*

Penché Leaning.

Piqué Stepping directly on the pointed toe of the supporting foot in any position; *piqué* turns in a circle are often seen in classical ballet and are sometimes substituted for *fouettés*.

Pirouette A full turn on one foot executed on *pointe* or *demi-pointe*. There are many types of *pirouettes*.

Plié A movement that involves bending the knees while the feet are on the ground. In a *demi-plié* the heels remain on the ground; in a deeper (*grand*) *plié* they are slightly raised.

Plier To bend.

Pointe The toe. *En pointe* or *full pointe* refers to dancing on the tip of the toe with the help of blocked *pointe* shoes; only women dance *sur la pointe*. *Demi-pointe* refers to dancing on the ball of the foot, as high as possible without being *en pointe*; both men and women dance *sur la demi-pointe*.

Pointe shoes Toe shoes, usually made of soft leather covered with satin, and with a reinforced toe (*see* box).

Bourrée *on* pointe.

Porté Lifting.

Position The five basic positions, which are performed with both feet on the ground, form the basis for all steps in classical ballet.

Poussé Literally means pushed; a term used to describe positions in support work.

Profil, de In profile.

Raked stage A stage that slopes upward, away from the audience; often found in European opera houses. Can cause great difficulties for performers used to dancing only on level stages.

Régisseur A stage manager; he supervises the physical aspects of the productions and is responsible for the stage during performances.

Relève A movement which involves rising, on one or both feet, to *pointe* or *demi-pointe*.

Relever To raise.

Révérence A curtsey or bow.

Romantic ballet A style that developed

Relève en arabesque effacé sur pointe.

Soubresaut, *a forward jump from fifth position.*

in Europe as part of the Romantic movement in all the arts; it is commonly dated from 1832, when Marie Taglioni appeared in *La Sylphide*. Two notable occurrences during the Romantic period were the introduction of toe dancing and the relegation of male dancers to a secondary role.

Rond de jambe A circular movement in which the working foot describes a semicircle on the floor (a *rond de jambe de terre*) or in the air (a *rond de jambe en l'air*).

Sauter To jump.
Shank The inner sole of a *pointe* shoe; made of thick leather.
Sickle A movement in which the dancer rolls his or her weight to the outside of the foot rather than concentrating it on the ball of the foot.
Sissonne A jump that basically involves springing into the air with both feet, from fifth positions, and landing on one foot; there are many variations.

Rond de jambe à terre.

Soubresaut A forward jump; the dancer straightens both legs directly under the body and lands in a *demi-plié*.
Soloist In the hierarchy of a dance company, the rank between the *corps de ballet* and the *ballerina/danseur*.
Spotting A technique used when turning, to minimize dizziness; the dancer picks a fixed point in the distance and keeps his/her eyes on it throughout the turn.

Terre à terre Steps performed on the ground; the feet never leave the floor at the same time.
Tights Thin, colored leg-coverings worn by dancers; the forerunners of pantyhose.
Tour en l'air A turn in the air, usually performed by male dancers, following a jump from fifth position. Double turns are often seen but triples are rarer.
Tourner To turn.
Turnout The pose in which the legs and feet are at a 180-degree angle to the body; one of the foundations of classical ballet.
Tutu The costume worn by female dancers in classical ballets; features a tight bodice and a short skirt made of many layers of net. The *tutu* is almost never used in modern ballets.

Vamp The front of the box on a *pointe* shoe.
Variation A solo.

INDEX

ACKNOWLEDGMENTS

The author would like to thank Jesse Davis of Mike Davis Studios for writing the captions, selecting the photographs and for supplying all the photographs except for those listed below:

Royal Academy of Dancing pp 18, 26–27, 48 (top), 50 (top left), 62 (top), 63 (top), 64 (both), 65, 68 (left), 70 (both), 71 (left), 75 (bottom), 78 (bottom), 91, 92 (bottom), 125 (top right), 150 (both), 174, 176, 181, 183 (top), 194, 195, 205, 210, 216, 217 (top)
Victoria and Albert Museum pp 9, 17, 24, 25, 28, 30, 31 (both), 32, 33, 36, 38 (left), 39 (top left), 42 (top), 43 (top), 47 (top two), 48 (bottom), 59, 60, 61, 62 (bottom), 63 (bottom), 66, 67, 68 (right), 69, 73, 74 (top left and right), 93 (bottom), 101 (top), 102 (top and left), 124, 151, 165, 175, 203, 204, 240
Dutch National Ballet p 163
Den Norske Ballet (photo by Karsten Bundgaard) p 148 (both)
Polish Cultural Institute p 173

The author would also like to thank Susan Garratt and Pamela Todd for reading the text
Jane Laslett, the editor
Laurence Bradbury, the designer
Penny Murphy for preparing the index